AGING
Biology and Behavior

AGING

James G. March, Editor in Chief
Graduate School of Business
Stanford University
Stanford, California

Aging: Biology and Behavior, edited by James L. McGaugh and
Sara B. Kiesler

Aging: Social Change, edited by Sara B. Kiesler, James N. Morgan,
and Valerie Kincade Oppenheimer

Aging: Stability and Change in the Family, edited by Robert W. Fogel,
Elaine Hatfield, Sara B. Kiesler, and Ethel Shanas

AGING
Biology and Behavior

Edited by

JAMES L. McGAUGH
Department of Psychobiology
University of California, Irvine
Irvine, California

SARA B. KIESLER
Department of Social Science
Carnegie-Mellon University
Pittsburgh, Pennsylvania

ACADEMIC PRESS
A Subsidiary of Harcourt Brace Jovanovich, Publishers
New York   London   Toronto   Sydney   San Francisco

This project was supported by Grant No. NOl-AG-8-2111, awarded by the National Institute on Aging.

ACADEMIC PRESS, INC.
111 Fifth Avenue, New York, New York 10003

United Kingdom Edition published by
ACADEMIC PRESS, INC. (LONDON) LTD.
24/28 Oval Road, London NWI 7DX

Library of Congress Cataloging in Publication Data
Main entry under title:

Aging--biology and behavior.

Papers originally presented at a symposium held at
Woods Hole, Mass., June 22-24, 1979.
Includes bibliographies and index.
1. Geriatric--Congresses. 2. Aging--Congresses.
3. Gerontology--Congresses. I. McGaugh, James L.
II. Kiesler, Sara B., Date. III. March, James G.
IV. National Research Council (U.S.). Committee on
Aging. V. National Institute on Aging.
RC952.A1A34   618.97   81-10915
ISBN 0-12-040001-4   AACR2
ISBN 0-12-040021-9 (pbk.)

PRINTED IN THE UNITED STATES OF AMERICA

81 82 83 84   9 8 7 6 5 4 3 2 1

COMMITTEE ON AGING

Contents

II

AGING BRAIN AND BEHAVIOR

III

COGNITIVE AND SOCIAL FUNCTIONING

List of Contributors

Numbers in parentheses indicate the pages on which the authors' contributions begin.

LISA F. BERKMAN (345), Department of Epidemiology, Yale Medical School, New Haven, Connecticut 06520

DAN G. BLAZER (329), Center for the Study of Aging and Human Development, Duke University Medical School, Durham, North Carolina 27706

WILLIAM BONDAREFF (141), Ethel Percy Andrus Gerontology Center and Department of Psychiatry, University of Southern California, Los Angeles, California 90007

ROBERT N. BUTLER (1), National Institute on Aging, 9000 Rockville Pike, Bethesda, Maryland 20205

RICHARD G. CUTLER (31), Gerontology Research Center, National Institute on Aging, Baltimore City Hospital, Baltimore, Maryland 21224

GEORGE M. FOSTER (115), Department of Anthropology, University of California, Berkeley, Berkeley, California 94720

SARA GERLING* (201), Department of Psychobiology, University of California, Irvine, Irvine, California 92717

* Present address: Department of Biology, Skidmore College, Saratoga Springs, New York 12866.

GLORIA Y. GOLDEN (283), Human Development and Aging Program, University of California, San Francisco, San Francisco, California 94143

EDWARD J. GREEN (159), Department of Psychology, University of Illinois, Champaign, Illinois 61820

WILLIAM T. GREENOUGH (159), Department of Psychology, University of Illinois, Champaign, Illinois 61820

LISSY F. JARVIK (231), Psychogenetics Unit, Brentwood VA Medical Center, Los Angeles, California 90073 and Department of Psychiatry and Biobehavioral Sciences, University of California, Los Angeles, Los Angeles, California 90024

STANISLAV V. KASL (345), Department of Epidemiology and Public Health, Yale University, New Haven, Connecticut 06510

LAURENCE J. KOTLIKOFF (97), Department of Economics, Yale University, New Haven, Connecticut 06520

ELLEN J. LANGER (255), Department of Psychology and Social Relations, Harvard University, Cambridge, Massachusetts 02138

RICHARD S. LAZARUS (283), Department of Psychology, University of California, Berkeley, Berkeley, California 94720

GARY LYNCH (201), Department of Psychobiology, University of California, Irvine, Irvine, California 92717

WILLIAM A. SATARIANO† (311), Division of Epidemiology, School of Public Health, University of California, Berkeley, Berkeley, California 94720

JOANNE STEUER (231), Department of Psychiatry and Biobehavioral Sciences, University of California, Los Angeles, Los Angeles, California 90024 and Psychogenetics Unit, Brentwood VA Medical Center, Los Angeles, California 90073

MERVYN SUSSER (77), Sergievsky Center and Division of Epidemiology, Columbia University, New York, New York 10032

S. LEONARD SYME (311), Division of Epidemiology, School of Public Health, University of California, Berkeley, Berkeley, California 94720

SHERWOOD L. WASHBURN (11), Department of Anthropology, University of California, Berkeley, Berkeley, California 94720

† Present address: Cancer Registry, Department of Social Oncology, Michigan Cancer Foundation, Detroit, Michigan 48201.

Foreword

This book is one of three volumes examining some possible social and behavioral science research perspectives on aging. The others are: *Aging: Stability and Change in the Family*, edited by Robert W. Fogel, Elaine Hatfield, Sara B. Kiesler, and Ethel Shanas; and *Aging: Social Change*, edited by Sara B. Kiesler, James N. Morgan, and Valerie Kincade Oppenheimer. The papers were solicited by the Committee on Aging of the National Research Council in response to a request from the National Institute on Aging.

The reason for the request was uncomplicated. As the phenomena of aging become more salient to private lives, effective research on aging becomes more critical to public policy and personal understanding. Most analyses suggest that there will be more money for research on aging over the coming years and that shifts in research funding will be incentives for shifts in research attention. Past experience warns, however, that although financial resources are necessary for an outstanding research program, they are rarely sufficient. In order for a public agency to influence the direction of important research, it must entice the community of scholars not only with money but also with a sense of the challenges and opportunities that the field provides. It must influence the individual professional enthusiasms that collectively determine the allocation of significant research creativity. In such a spirit, the National Institute on Aging asked the National Research Council's Committee on Aging to organize a series of workshops at which experienced gerontologists and other social and behavioral scientists might discuss research ideas of possible relevance to future work on aging.

Organizing and implementing the workshops and the resulting volumes have involved many members of the research community. The 14 members of the Committee on Aging, the 65 contributors to the volumes, the 63 other participants in the workshops, and the 80 colleagues who reviewed the papers submitted for the volumes all contributed their time and expertise. In many cases, this represented a considerable personal commitment. On behalf of the committee, I want to thank this large band of generous colleagues, and particularly the editorial group of Robert W. Fogel, Elaine Hatfield, Sara B. Kiesler, James L. McGaugh, James N. Morgan, Valerie Kincade Oppenheimer, and Ethel Shanas. With no personal gain and little glory, they did the job. At the usual risk of promoting ordinary behavior into heroics, I calculate the professional fees foregone as being on the order of $1,000,000 and happily record the amount as a grant from the research community to the Academy and the Institute.

For most of the scientists who participated in this effort, however, the activity has had little connection to eleemosynary instincts. What more could a reasonable person ask from life than that it provide a few opportunities to exchange ideas with people who have some? The willingness of important research scientists to write papers for these volumes attests to the intellectual stimulation they found in fundamental research questions about aging. On behalf of my research colleagues, therefore, I want to thank the National Institute on Aging and the National Academy of Sciences for their parts in creating some occasions for such pleasures.

In particular, we owe a debt to some Washington colleagues. The original request to the Academy came from Robert N. Butler, Director of the National Institute of Aging, to David A. Goslin, Executive Director of the National Research Council's Assembly of Behavioral and Social Sciences. Both of them, as well as Betty H. Pickett, former Associate Director of the extramural collaborative research program of NIA, Matilda White Riley, Associate Director of NIA for social and behavioral research, and Shirley P. Bagley, health scientist administrator at NIA, contributed considerably to the climate of support that sustained the effort.

In addition, there was a small, tolerant staff in Washington. Elaine McGarraugh of the Committee on Aging and Christine L. McShane of the Assembly of Behavioral and Social Sciences managed the many details of bringing the papers together for the books. They cajoled an unlikely crew of widely scattered contributors with patient humor and peristaltic persistence and edited the volumes for the Academy with the sweet and sour sense and firmness that distinguish good editors. The one indispensable person, however, was Sara B. Kiesler. Before she left to return to academe, she served as study director for the project. Without her exceptional professional breadth and imagination, as well as her high style of dealing with ideas and people, the committee would have been unable to function. She deserves primary credit for having brought it all together.

As usual, it is necessary to exonerate all of these people, as well as the United States government, the National Academy of Sciences, the Assembly of Behavioral and Social Sciences, the National Institute on Aging, and innumerable universities from responsibility for what the individual authors say. The sensible things they have written are doubtless attributable to their colleagues, and to the Committee on Aging. But the foolish things are their own.

JAMES G. MARCH, CHAIR
Committee on Aging

Preface

We human beings share with the other animals a common fate: We develop, we live for a time, and we die. The life-span of some animals is measured in only hours or days. We human beings have years, but for most of us, they remain the biblical threescore and ten. The time we have to live—whether short or long—is marked by continuing change. Some facts of behavioral and biological development are obvious, such as physical growth and the maturation of thinking. Some facts of aging are equally obvious. But while growth and development of the young have been studied extensively, biological and behavioral changes with aging have received much less attention. Consequently, many interesting and important questions about age-related changes in biological processes and behavior remain unasked or incompletely answered.

This volume addresses behavioral changes in aging related to biological processes. As we age, our behavior continues to change. We accumulate knowledge, skills, and, we hope, wisdom. The mechanisms underlying our behavior also change throughout life, along with our nervous systems, muscles, and endocrine systems. Further, with age we accumulate injuries and diseases and become susceptible to new injuries and diseases. As a consequence of biological changes—whether due to endogenous processes of aging or to injury or disease—our ability to act and to

change our behavior may be altered. The social and economic consequences of behavioral disabilities in the elderly are enormous, notwith-
standing the benefits of maturity.

The chapters in this volume attest to the fact that we are beginning
to understand some aspects of aging, including the nature of changes in
brain plasticity with aging, factors influencing life-span, and environmental and social influences on health in the elderly. Such information
is needed, along with that provided by developmental studies, if we are
to understand biological and behavioral changes over the life-span. Beyond that, knowledge of the processes and mechanisms of aging may
provide important insights into basic biological and behavioral processes.
Finally, as we increase our understanding of aging, we should increase
our ability to provide ways of coping with the problems and potential
of the elderly.

The planning of this volume began when the National Research Council's Assembly of Behavioral and Social Sciences appointed a Committee
on Aging, with James G. March as its chair. A subcommittee, whose
members were James S. Jackson, James L. McGaugh, and Roy L. Walford, worked with James March and Sara B. Kiesler to select topics for
a workshop on Biology, Behavior, and Aging, which was held in Woods
Hole, Massachusetts, in June 1979. The committee is grateful to all those
who participated in the workshop (their names appear in Appendix A)
and to those who reviewed the chapters in this volume (listed in Appendix
B). We thank Elaine McGarraugh for her assistance with all of the details
of the workshop and for assisting Christine L. McShane in the editing
of the manuscripts. We also thank James March for his many contributions to the planning of the workshop and volume and for his sustained
interest and support throughout the project.

AGING
Biology and Behavior

chapter 1

Overview on Aging: Some Biomedical, Social, and Behavioral Perspectives

ROBERT N. BUTLER

In the twentieth century, life expectancy of the average American has increased by more than 50%. Basic improvements in sanitation, immunization, and medical care have resulted in a decrease in the number of deaths during infancy, childhood, and, for women, the childbearing years. Only 20% of all newborns in 1776 lived into their sixties, compared with over 80% in 1980. Life expectancy at birth for the total population has jumped from 48.2 years at the turn of the century to 73.2 years in 1978.

This triumphant increase in survivorship prompted the federal government to create the National Institute on Aging (NIA) in 1974, as part of the National Institutes of Health. The NIA's mission is to support, conduct, and promote social and behavioral—as well as biomedical—research on aging. That the United States Congress judiciously gave the institute such a broad mandate reflects the complex nature of the aging process. Its various manifestations and underlying mechanisms must be addressed by the best fundamental, scientific, and scholarly concepts and methods.

The National Institute on Aging was pleased to support the Committee on Aging, chaired by James G. March of Stanford University and directed by Sara B. Kiesler of Carnegie-Mellon University, under the auspices of the National Research Council's Assembly of Behavioral and Social

1

AGING
Biology and Behavior

Sciences. It has been a privilege, too, to be involved in its major workshops on stability and change in the family, the elderly of the future, and the relationship of biology and behavior in aging, the results of which are offered in this volume.

STABILITY AND CHANGE IN THE FAMILY

Changes in the demographic profile of the U.S. population—particularly the increase of three-generational and multigenerational families—have given rise to much speculation about the role of the family. Those caught up in a romanticized portrayal of years past sometimes create the impression that something quite destructive has happened to the family. It is argued that the elderly were venerated in ancient and not-so-ancient societies, and they still are in "primitive" and oriental cultures. The extended family is cited as a powerful umbrella of warmth and support.

In reality, historians, sociologists, and others know that the extended families of the past were in large part the result of high fertility. These families were characterized by many siblings, uncles, and aunts but not necessarily many generations. There simply were not a great many survivors. One indication of this fact is that in the 50 years from 1920 to 1970, the likelihood for a 10-year-old youngster to have two living grandparents has risen from 40 to 75%.

The extended multigenerational family of this century offers a new kind of opportunity for care and support. In some parts of the United States, we are already witnessing a formalized network of family support as families band together to help relatives no longer able to care for themselves because of the devastating and destructive course of organic brain diseases. Senile dementia of the Alzheimer's type, the most common form of irreversible organic brain disease and perhaps the fourth or fifth leading cause of death in the United States, is marked in its extreme form by disorientation, confusion, severe mental impairment, destruction of the personality, urinary and fecal incontinence, and the high likelihood of a need for institutionalization. Because the patient may remain physically robust while intellectually devastated, it may become very difficult for the family to provide proper care at home. We are beginning to see the growth of various organizations in the United States and in Canada to assist and offer information to relatives of Alzheimer's disease victims and to sponsor research that might lead to new knowledge to prevent and treat that disorder.

The family as an activist organization has also resulted in formal networks wherein friends, relatives, and older people themselves become effective advocates for the rights of the elderly, in some cases monitoring nursing homes and other health and social service programs that serve elderly clientele. Oregon and Detroit have developed models for such family organizations.

There are, of course—and there always have been—problems in families and problem families in which there are conflicts, feelings of guilt, and even brutality. On the basis of a study of victimization and the elderly conducted in Washington, D.C., in the late 1960s by the Washington School of Psychiatry, the "battered old person syndrome" is described (Brostoff *et al.* 1972), in which the domestic life of some older people is marked by physical brutality, without respect to social or economic class.

In addition to raising a number of questions on the role of the family, increased survivorship demands that we take a closer look at the older woman, who throughout most of her adult life is typically the major caregiver in the family support system. Peter Uhlenberg (1979) has noted the changing character of the life of the American woman. In 1870, only 44% of all women in the United States who survived past 15 years of age ever experienced what we now think of as the normal course of the life-cycle; that is, growing up, marrying and having children, watching their children grow up and leave home, growing older, becoming widowed, aging, and dying. Today, American women have a life expectancy at birth of 77.1 years and generally outlive men by 8 years. Therefore, this is not only a century of old age, but also a century of older women.

Because of the different life expectancies of the sexes, many of the problems as well as the opportunities of old age pertain to older women. Women constitute some 75% of the residents of nursing homes, for example, largely because they outlive those who might have cared for them in their old age. The elderly women in these last few decades of the twentieth century suffer an additional handicap. The cohort born from 1905 to 1910—those who had their main childbearing years at the height of the severe American economic depression of the 1930s—has been called a low fertility cohort. Of this cohort 22% had no children, 20% had only one, and still another 20% had two children.

Social and behavioral research studies such as those supported by the National Institute on Aging can do much to enhance our understanding of the ways in which families of various racial, ethnic, and cultural groups function. Such studies might also help in the development of the data bases that will rid us of misconceived notions of old age and allow us to promote effective public policy. We hear a good deal now about the "graying of America"; I have used that phrase myself in an effort to sensitize the American public to the striking changes in the age composition of our society. We must be careful, however, about the negative attitudes attached to phrases like the "graying of the health budget." While the Medicare and Medicaid programs have had an impact on skyrocketing national health expenses, the fact that health costs are now accumulated in later life is due in large part to the postponement of illness and related health costs from earlier years. Demographic research might alleviate misunderstandings about the costs associated with old age as well as fears that liberalization of Medicare home care benefits might lead to increased drains on the federal treasury, as those families that currently provide for elderly relatives request federal support. I know of no evidence to support this fear. In fact, this has not been the experience in those European countries that have provided more generously for home health care.

THE ELDERLY OF THE FUTURE

When we talk about the elderly of the future, we obviously cannot do so in a vacuum. The control of childhood diseases as well as improvements in the treatment of infectious diseases, cardiopulmonary diseases, and cancer demand that we take the time to reevaluate old age as a normal, natural stage of the life-cycle. While to this point I have emphasized the needs of an aged population, we might do better to consider the needs of an *aging* population. Although by the year 2030 as much as 20% of the United States' population will be 65 years of age or older, the majority will be under 65; the overall median age will be 37.6 years. Clearly, we must look to the implications of a changing age structure on problems in the areas of labor, housing, and health care.

Paralleling the social needs of a population with a changing age structure is an increased interest in gerontology and geriatrics. In order to enhance the quality of life of older people, we must also develop the knowledge to treat and prevent the diseases that currently interfere with normal, healthy aging. Gerontology or research on aging offers a new approach to diseases in an effort to retain or restore those physiologic and behavioral functions altered with the passage of time. We have already found that the immune system weakens with age, thus making the body more susceptible to viruses, bacteria, and noxious environmental agents. A close look at normal aging may help us isolate age-related changes in the immune system and the central nervous system as well as hormonal and regulatory capacities. Research in these areas might ultimately delay the onset or mitigate the severity of a variety of diseases and disabilities that become more frequent with age.

Geriatrics is the branch of medicine that deals with the complexities of old age, namely, multiple diseases, changes in the expression of illness, and alterations in such functions as pain reaction and temperature response. Geriatric medicine refers not only to this body of knowledge, but also to a needed change in the negative attitudes and the lack of information that prejudice many doctors, nurses, and other health providers who work with elderly patients. It is not enough to have financing mechanisms like Medicare to meet the medical needs of older people when formal training programs do not include material on basic aging and clinical geriatrics. Incorporating this information into medical school curricula will guarantee that the health care system will respond more effectively to older people of the future.

Studies by research gerontologists of healthy volunteers living in the community—ranging from youth to old age—provide a practical means for understanding normal aging and gaining a glimpse of the elderly of the future. The National Institute of Mental Health's human aging studies (1955–1966), the Duke University studies (1955 through the present), and the Baltimore longitudinal study of aging (1958 through the present) are among those that have examined aging by identifying types and rates of change in the same individuals over time.[1] Many misconceptions regarding age have disappeared as a result—including the misguided notions that all intellectual functions automatically decline with age and that cerebral blood flow and oxygen consumption show decrements in relationship to age alone. It may also be possible for gerontologists to capitalize on any of the 40 longitudinal studies conducted in the United States, particularly since the 1920s, many of which are still active. Some, such as the famous Framingham study in Massachusetts, began as community studies of risk factors. Others, such as the Terman "gifted child" study and the Oakland-Berkeley studies, began as developmental studies of children in the 1920s.[2]

While we cannot precisely predict social changes of the future, we must not restrain our imaginations. The idea that prosthetic devices might

---

[1] For the NIMH human aging studies see Birren *et al.* (1971), Granick and Patterson (1971); for the Duke University studies see Palmore (1970, 1974); for the Baltimore longitudinal study of aging see Butler (1977).

[2] For the Terman "gifted child" study see Terman *et al.* (1925), Burks *et al.* (1930), Terman and Oden (1947), Terman (1959); for the Oakland-Berkeley studies see Block and Hann (1971), Elder (1974).

compensate for lost physical functions in the elderly is just one example of the potential of technology. As Paul Valery wrote, ''The responsibility of the educated is to prepare man for what has never been.''

BIOLOGY AND BEHAVIOR OF THE ELDERLY

The interrelationship of biology and behavior is no less crucial in old age than at any other time. The need for multidisciplinary research is apparent as we make plans for studies on nutrition and aging, drugs and aging, and sleep problems of the aged, to name only a few. Perhaps most exciting, however, is the interaction of biomedical and psychosocial factors in the debate on the possibilities of life-span extension. In this area, in particular, issues of feasibility are closely linked with those of the desirability and the necessity for socioeconomic reconstruction that would follow.

One might wonder which is more restrictive—our limited intellects or our finite lives. Our understanding of the human brain has begun to increase at a rapid pace with the explosion of new research findings in the area of neuroscience. Not long ago, senility was thought to be an inevitable untreatable manifestation of cerebral arteriosclerosis. We now know that this is not so; in fact, preliminary findings suggest that an enzyme replacement therapy somewhat analogous to the use of L-dopa in the treatment of Parkinson's disease might one day be used to arrest the symptoms of Alzheimer's disease. It was also once thought that the functions of damaged brain cells were irretrievably lost; yet research supported by NIA indicates that undamaged brain cells can compensate for damaged ones in transmitting nerve signals. In much the same way, our understanding of the mechanisms of longevity and senescence is contingent on far-reaching advances in molecular biology, genetics, and biochemistry.

Although advances in the basic sciences have the potential for providing a robust extended life-span, we must also look at the other influences that act on mental and physical health. What, for example, is the effect of environmental stress on health and disease? What is the impact of boredom and adventure on the quality of life? How does physiology relate to sexual behavior?

Aging research in the areas of biology, medicine, and the social and behavioral sciences is likely to offer rich rewards in the next several decades. The need for such research is compelling, considering the extraordinary demographic changes in the United States' population and the staggering health costs that public policymakers associate with old age. The likelihood of some success is reflected in the fascinating and scholarly scientific questions that are being formulated, including increased attention to well-defined epidemiological studies of disease in old age. The 1981 White House Conference on Aging, the 1982 United Nations World Assembly on Aging, and the Resolution on Aging of the World Health Organization will all include a major emphasis on the broad range of research disciplines needed to develop an understanding of normal human aging. We expect the social and behavioral sciences to play a major role in all of these initiatives. Solving the problems of old age requires the concurrent application of the latest and best information available from the biological sciences, clinical medicine, and studies of personal and social behavior.

REFERENCES

Birren, J. E., Butler, R. N., Greenhouse, S. W., *et al.*, eds. (1971) *Human Aging I: A Biological and Behavioral Study*. National Institute of Mental Health, ADAMHA, Publication No. (ADM) 77–122. Washington, D.C.: U.S. Department of Health, Education, and Welfare.

Block, J., in collaboration with Hann, N. (1971) *Lives Through Time*. Berkeley, Calif.: Bancroft Books.

Brostoff, P. M., Brown, R. B., and Butler, R. N. (1972) "Beating up" on the elderly: Police, social work, and crime. Public Interest Report No. 6. *International Journal of Aging and Human Development* 3:319–322.

Burks, B. S., Jensen, D. W., and Terman, L. M. (1930) *Genetic Studies of Genius, Volume 3. The Promise of Youth: Followup Studies of a Thousand Gifted Children*. Stanford, Calif.: Stanford University Press.

Butler, R. N. (1977) Research programs of the National Institute on Aging. U.S. Department of Health, Education, and Welfare *Public Health Reports,* 92(1):3–8.

Elder, G. H., Jr. (1974) *Children of the Great Depression*. Chicago: University of Chicago Press.

Granick, S., and Patterson, R. D., eds. (1971) *Human Aging II: An Eleven-Year Followup Biomedical and Behavioral Study*. National Institute of Mental Health, ADAMHA, Publication No. (ADM) 77–122. Washington, D.C.: U.S. Department of Health, Education, and Welfare.

Palmore, E. B., ed. (1970) *Normal Aging: Reports from the Duke Longitudinal Studies, 1955–1969*. Durham, N.C.: Duke University Press.

Palmore, E. B., ed. (1974) *Normal Aging II: Reports from the Duke Longitudinal Studies, 1970–1973*. Durham, N.C.: Duke University Press.

Terman, L. M. (1959) *Genetic Studies of Genius, Volume 5. The Gifted Group at Mid-Life*. Stanford, Calif.: Stanford University Press.

Terman, L. M., assisted by Baldwin, B. T., Bronson, E., Devoss, J. C. *et al.* (1925) *Genetic Studies of Genius, Volume 1. Mental and Physical Traits of a Thousand Gifted Children*. Stanford, Calif.: Stanford University Press.

Terman, L. M., and Oden, M. H. (1947) *Genetic Studies of Genius, Volume 4. The Gifted Child Grows Up*. Stanford, Calif.: Stanford University Press.

Uhlenberg, P. (1979) Demographic change and problems of the aged. Pp. 153–166 in M. W. Riley, ed., *Aging from Birth to Death: Interdisciplinary Perspectives*. Boulder, Col.: Westview Press.

PART I

LONGEVITY, AGING, AND MORTALITY

chapter 2

Longevity in Primates

SHERWOOD L. WASHBURN

In the last 100 years, the expectation of length of life for human beings has increased dramatically. With the origin of agriculture some 10,000 years ago, both the number of human beings and the usual length of life increased, but the age of the oldest people changed very little. The average length of life is affected by many environmental factors that have changed in recent time, especially in the last few years. Maximum life-span has changed far less, and the genetically determined maximum life-span potential has probably not changed at all (Cutler 1976). The result is a situation that is entirely new from the point of view of evolution—a very large number of human beings living to ages far beyond those that were normal for the species.

There never was selection for healthy old people, and the ability to live to old age is a by-product of selection for evolutionary success at much younger ages. Table 2.1 shows the estimated age at death for Neanderthal and Upper Paleolithic human beings. Approximately half were dead by age twenty, and even in the combined series only three individuals lived more than 50 years. Among recent hunter-gatherers a few people lived longer, but Birdsell (1975, p. 377) estimates that less than 5% of precontact Australian aborigines lived past 50.

Among early agricultural peoples, the number of people was much

11

AGING
Biology and Behavior

TABLE 2.1
Ages at Death of Fossil Humans[a]

Series	Percentage of Neanderthal	Percentage of Upper Paleolithic
SUBADULT Number	39	76
Age in years		
0–11	38.5 ⎫ 48.8	38.2 ⎫ 54.0
12–20	10.3 ⎭	15.8 ⎭
ADULT 21–30	15.4 ⎫	19.7 ⎫
31–40	25.6 ⎪ 51.2	14.5 ⎪ 46.0
41–50	7.7 ⎪	9.2 ⎪
51–60	2.5 ⎭	2.6 ⎭
Totals	100.0	100.00

[a] Adapted from Vallois 1961, p. 223 in *Social Life of Early Man*, edited by Sherwood L. Washburn, Viking Fund Publications in Anthropology, No. 31. Copyrighted 1961 by the Wenner-Gren Foundation for Anthropological Research, Incorporated, New York.

greater, but the expectation of life was not very different (see Table 2.2). I will return to the problem of expectation of life among earlier peoples. The problem is raised here to give the background for the comparison of human life-span with that of other primates. From the evolutionary point of view, there are three related questions. First, how long is the period of immaturity or preparation? How long does it take for the species to become mature? Second, how long are the adults biologically

TABLE 2.2
Age and Sex Distribution of Skeletons from an American Indian (Larson) Cemetery[a,b]

Age interval	Male	Female	Total
0–1	—	—	254
1–4	—	—	94
5–9	6	9	48
10–14	4	6	14
15–19	10	21	31
20–24	10	15	25
25–29	12	10	22
30–34	25	10	35
35–39	21	18	39
40–49	20	14	34
50–59	10	15	25
Sample total	118	118	621

[a] From Owsley and Bass 1979, p. 148.
[b] Less than 5% live past age 50.

adapted to the problems of living effectively? Third, how long may some individuals live under optimal environmental conditions? It should be stressed that the first period is a cost; for selection to favor long infant and juvenile periods, those periods must result in the greater reproductive success of adults. Reproductive success in the second period determines the evolutionary success of the species, and the third period is a by-product.

The three phases of the life-span may be called: preparation, adaptation, and decline. In contemporary human beings, each phase is much longer than in any other primate, as shown in the highly simplified and abridged Table 2.3.

For comparative purposes, the period of preparation may be described by numerous criteria and ends with full maturity, usually some years after sexual maturity. The delay is especially great in males. Maturity may be defined by: the eruption of the third molar tooth, the completed eruption of the canine tooth in males, or the union of the proximal epiphysis of the humerus. Sexual maturity is usually close to the time of eruption of the second molar tooth but may be earlier (in macaques) or later (after the eruption of the third molar in *Presbytis rubicundus*). There is a great deal of individual variation in all these criteria, but the comparative trends are clear.

The period of adaptation is, very approximately, twice the length of preparation. Theoretically, the period of decline may be long, but under preagricultural conditions it was not. The chimpanzees of the Gombe Reserve are the only population of free-ranging chimpanzees that have been studied long enough and in enough detail to make estimates of age at death possible. Despite the fact that predators had been eliminated, only one individual is estimated to have lived more than 35 years (Teleki *et al.* 1976), and survival to 30 was rare. In Japanese macaques, only 1 of 61 females lived more than 24 years, and nearly half the mature

TABLE 2.3
Length of Phases of Primate Life-Span in Years[a]

| | (Immaturity) Preparation | | | (Maturity) Adaptation | Decline (decreasing effectiveness) |
| | Eruption of molars: | | | | |
	First	Second	Third		
Human	6	12	18	18–45	45–75
Chimpanzee	3	6	10	10–30	30–50
Macaque	2	4	6	6–20	20–35

[a] From Moore and Lavelle 1974, p. 180, Nass 1977, p. 311.

animals died between 15 and 21 years of age (Sugiyama 1976, p. 280). According to Bramblett (1969), few baboons survive more than 20 years in East Africa. This estimate is particularly important because, in contrast to the situations in the Gombe Reserve and in Japan, the baboons were not fed and there were numerous carnivores. Obviously more information is needed on expectation of life under natural conditions, but the data suggest that few animals survive beyond the end of the period of adaptation.

The period of decline is something new and depends on the protection of the animals so that they may continue to live in spite of decreased strength, slower reactions, and accumulating deficits in vision, hearing, and taste. The estimates of life-span given in Table 2.4 are the products of human protection, not of the natural situation.

It must be remembered that the order of Table 2.4 is not an evolutionary order. It is an order of contemporary primates grouped by the times their ancestors became separated from the forms that ultimately led to human beings. For example, there never was a New World monkey

TABLE 2.4
Length of Life in Contemporary Primates Based Primarily on Records from Zoos (in Years)[a]

Great apes	50	Orangutans, Chimpanzees, Gorillas
Small apes	35	Gibbons
Old World monkeys	35–40	Macaques, baboons
	30	Vervets (*Cercopithecus*), Mangabeys
	25	Colobines
New World monkeys	45–50	Cebus monkeys
	35	Spider monkeys
	15	Marmosets (*Callithricidae*)
Prosimians	35–40	Large lemurs
	15–20	Small prosimians, mouse lemurs, lorises, galagoes
Tarsier	13	
Tree shrew	12	

[a] Thanks to Richard G. Cutler for calling my attention to the chart prepared by Marvin L. Jones for a meeting on aging in Santa Barbara, January 1979. Marvin L. Jones kindly sent me an updated version of the poster on aging in mammals. The data are summarized in "Aging Research on Nonhuman Primates," edited by D.M. Bowden (Bowden and Jones 1979, pp. 1–13). Data on length of life are summarized in the chart on p. 2. Thanks are particularly due to Marvin L. Jones for his continuing efforts to gather accurate information on aging in mammals.

in human ancestry. New World and Old World monkeys separated some 35 million years ago, and since then 70 million years of evolution have passed: 35 in the New World, and 35 in the Old World. There has been parallel evolution in both kinds of monkeys. For example, brains have become larger independently in many different lines, and the length of life in Cebus monkeys may be just as new as their long prehensile tail. Because the fossils are small with small brains, it might be guessed that monkeys had a life-span of 15 years at the time of separation of the New World and Old World forms, but that is only an informed guess, not fact or science in the sense that we usually use these terms. In contrast to the uncertainty of the evolutionary picture, the great evolutionary increase in life-span between marmosets and cebids is a fact, and if the short spans are regarded as primitive, the adaptive reasons for the increase are well worth study and understanding. The contemporary forms do not represent stages in primate evolution, but study of the living primates as well as the fossils gives a much fuller appreciation of the nature of primate adaptation and evolution.

It is the confusion of comparison and evolution that led Hodos and Campbell (1969) to discuss the *scala naturae* and why there is no theory in comparative psychology (also Hodos 1970). Evolutionary theory requires the use of both fossils and information from contemporary animals. Error comes from confusing these two sources of information and acting as if the contemporary forms could be treated as ancestors. This problem is carefully discussed relative to learning by Ehrlich *et al.* (1976).

LENGTH OF LIFE IN PRIMATES

Early estimates of the length of life in primates underestimated life-span. For example, Zuckerman (1933, p. 27) gave 26 years as the maximum life of chimpanzees in captivity—approximately half the present estimate of life-span. Other estimates were similarly off, and only baboons and macaques were estimated correctly. Figure 2.1 gives estimates of primate life-spans that were reasonable a few years ago. It should be noted that not only have the estimates of the life-spans increased, but also the apparent evolutionary order is not as simple as it seemed. Gibbons do not live longer than Old World monkeys, and, as shown in Table 2.4, some New World monkeys live longer than any Old World monkeys.

It is evident that much more is known about animal care than even a few years ago, and as a result estimates of life-span are often 100% greater than those found in the literature. Estimates will surely increase

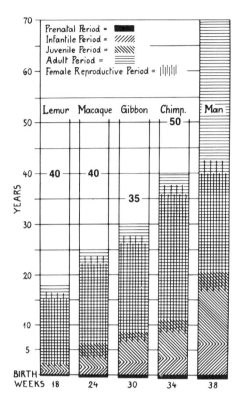

70 —
Prenatal Period = ▰▰▰
Infantile Period = ///////
Juvenile Period = ＼＼＼＼＼
Adult Period = ≡≡≡
60 —
Female Reproductive Period = ‖‖‖‖‖

Lemur Macaque Gibbon Chimp. ＝Man＝
50 —   50

40 — 40   40
                        35
30 —

20 —

10 —

5 —
BIRTH
WEEKS 18   24   30   34   38

YEARS

Figure 2.1. Life-spans corrected with data not available to Schultz. (From Schultz 1969, p. 149.)

even more because of improvements in animal care, and animals that are "old" today probably lived under less than desirable conditions for the early part of their lives.

In reducing the very large number of species for which there are known life-spans in captivity to the small number of estimates given in Table 2.4, I have followed two rules. First, since interest is in maximum longevity, if life-span has been recorded for closely related species, I have taken the longest. Second, since we are reasonably sure that the recorded life-spans are too short, I have rounded estimates upward. For example, in one case a member of the genus *Lemur* is 35 years old and still living; another was 39 at the time of death. In Table 2.4, the life-span of *Lemur* is 40 years, a very small correction if one looks at the history of changing estimates of life-span. Furthermore, in the case of prosimians, the very large forms are all extinct. *Megaladapis,* which became extinct only a few thousand years ago, was as large as a small donkey, and it is hard to believe that such an animal did not live longer than the lemurs mentioned above. In most cases, length of life (as shown in Table 2.4) is close to the longest record from captivity, but Table 2.5 shows a series of comparisons in which the corrections are very large. For example, the longest recorded life-span for a Bornean orangutan is 30 years, but it is 50 years for a Sumatran orangutan. My guess is that this difference is due to the fact that many more Sumatran orangutans have been kept in captivity for much longer periods of time, not to genetic differences between the populations of orangs. Similarly, 19 years for siamang gibbons is surely much too short; because of larger body size, siamangs might be expected to live longer than the small gibbons, possibly 40 years.

The revisions of estimates of length of life given in Table 2.5 may seem large, but several may still be too low. For example, recorded length of life for the New World spider monkey changed from 24 to 35 years between the time Cutler gathered the information for his 1976 paper and the time of Jones's 1979 survey of mammalian longevity. There may be no reason to suppose that 35 years is a useful estimate of life-span for spider monkeys; it would not be surprising if the large New World monkeys (spider, howler, Cebus) all had life-spans of 40-plus years, and the currently recorded life-spans reflect primarily the ease with which these animals adapt to the problems of life in zoos.

Since all this information concerns captive animals, it is very important to remember that some primates adjust to captive conditions much better than others. It is no accident that estimates of life-span for macaques

TABLE 2.5
Estimate of Life-Span in Primates

Primates	Current estimates	Revised estimates
Great apes		
Bornean orangutan	30	50
Pygmy chimpanzee	25	50
Small apes		
Siamang gibbon	19	40
Old World monkeys		
Proboscis monkey	13	35
Colobus, Presbytis	25	35
Gelada baboon	19	40
New World monkeys	12	35
Howler	15	30
Sakis		
Prosimians		
Sifaka (Propithecus)	18	35
Tree shrew	5	15

and baboons have been consistently high compared with those for other Old World monkeys. These animals are hardy, surviving in heat or cold and on a wide variety of diets; many individuals have been kept in zoos, laboratories, and primate centers.

One kind of primate that has been particularly difficult to keep in captivity are the Colobinae (Napier and Napier 1967). Napier and Napier (p. 283) state that in the period 1959–1963 only 21 births were recorded in the zoos of the world. In a colony of 34 *Presbytis entellus* kept by Phyllis Dolhinow at the University of California, Berkeley, there have been births of 39 animals that survived more than 3 months since 1972. The adult females give birth regularly and there is no problem in raising colobines in captivity, but it will be many years before reliable estimates of life-span will come from such a colony.

The colobines have very large stomachs and finely chewed leaves are fermented in the stomach. Other primates that eat large quantities of leaves and have viscera adapted to this diet (howler monkeys in the New World and sifakas among the prosimians) are also difficult to maintain in zoos and therefore have very short recorded life-spans. The order of the probable correction is suggested in Table 2.5.

There is no evidence that structures like a greatly elongated caecum (sifakas, Indriidae), intestines (howlers, *Alouatta*), or a greatly enlarged and specialized stomach (colobines) were present in ancestral primates. From the point of view of evolution, these are recent specializations, and the very structures that give adaptive success in nature make them difficult to care for in zoos.

The case of the gelada baboon is quite different. Geladas are closely related to other baboons, and life-span should be at least twice what is recorded at present.

Tree shrews (Tupaia) provide an interesting case. As recently as 1976, length of life was estimated at 5.5 years, and this figure has been used to estimate the situation in early primates. New records shown life-spans of more than 12 years, and they might easily live 15 years, judging from what has happened to other estimates of life-span.

Maximum Life-Span Potential

The figures in Table 2.4 refer to life-span, the length of life actually recorded for captive animals with small corrections. A comparable figure for human beings might be 75, rather than the 110 suggested as the maximum life-span potential. The problem may be seen in the records of longevity of members of the family Lorisidae. Eight records give life-spans of from 12 to 16 years (14 average), but one potto lived 22 years and 7 months. (Jones assures me that this is an accurate record.) This is 8 years or 50% more than the average—suggesting that most recorded life-spans for small prosimians are very low and that maximum life-span potential might easily be twice the longevity recorded in zoos. One galago survived 25 years. My belief is that there are so many uncertainties in estimates of life-span that added guesses on maximum life-span potential have little meaning.

Reconstructions of Life-Span

It would be very useful if life-span could be estimated from other traits that are more easily available. For example, in a very general way longevity is correlated with size. Among the land mammals, the largest are all long-lived; one hippopotamus is still alive at 55; a rhinoceros is still alive at 45; an elephant that is known to be at least 57 is estimated to be well over 60 (Jones 1979). But the correlation is only very general. Human beings do not fit this pattern, and a life-span of some 50 years might be expected on the basis of size. One Cebus monkey lived 47 years, and two others aged 42 and 45 are still alive. Life-span of a small New World monkey is close to that of gorillas. This is particularly remarkable when one considers the care given the great apes—surely far more than is given the Cebus. The increase in currently known length of life in small prosimians (25) is not more than double in gorillas.

The age of maturation has also been used to estimate possible life-spans. The problem is much the same as for body size. Hippos and rhinos are sexually mature at 5 years (Asdell 1964), as are some monkeys but not gibbons. Even within one species the time of maturation is greatly affected by the environment, probably mostly by diet. For example, Cutler (1976) uses 17–19 years as normal for human beings and multiplies by 5 to get a possible maximum life-span potential of some 90-plus years. But the age of menarche in Europe has declined from more than 17 to less than 12 in the last 200 years. Consider what happens to estimates of life-span potential if different times of maturation are used: $19 \times 5 = 95$ years; $15 \times 5 = 75$ years; $12 \times 5 = 60$ years. It is my belief that the late maturation and small body size of Europeans of many years ago was the result of inadequate diet and that maturation at 14–15 years was usual for human beings. At present the slowest-maturing apes and the fastest-maturing human beings actually may mature at the same age, yet there is no suggestion that the life-spans are similar.

The ratio of brain size to body size has also been correlated with life-span. Neither size is simple from a biological point of view. The complexity of brain size has been stressed by Holloway (1966), but body size is also complex. Jerison (1973) estimates biological intelligence (EQ) as low in howler monkeys (*Alouatta*) and leaf monkeys (*Presbytis*). But the brain of *P. entellus* is larger than that of a gibbon, and the difference is in the viscera and associated proportions of the trunk. It is the same monkeys that proved hard to keep in captivity because of specialized diet and viscera that have high body weights and so are rated low in biological intelligence. The need for considering the biological components of body size is shown by the comparison of human males and females. Males have larger brains relative to body size and so a longer predicted length of life and higher biological intelligence. I cannot resist remarking that, if the comparison had come out the other way, the males making these studies might have looked for the reason—which is, obviously, that females are on the average fatter. Quantity of fat is not related to brain size, so if the body weights are corrected for the amount of fat, sex differences disappear.

Clearly the human brain has been reorganized in addition to becoming larger. For example, compared to a chimpanzee, human arms are much smaller and legs larger. But the part of the cortex controlling hand skills has become much larger in human beings. The ability to learn speech is added, which requires a great deal of brain, usually on the dominant side. It is my belief that the greatly increased length of the preparation phase in human development is directly related to functions that are new, that require reorganization of the brain, and that are, at best, dimly reflected in the gross size of the brain.

Comparisons and Evolution

There is a wealth of biological information on contemporary primates, and much of it is useful in providing a background for human conditions and making possible experimental approaches using animals that are much more closely related to us than mice or rats. No one doubts the importance of comparative biological information on contemporary primates, but it is no accident that in Bowden's *Aging in Nonhuman Primates* (1979) evolution is considered only in the introduction. Likewise, in the 22 chapters of Bourne's *Nonhuman Primates and Medical Research* (1973) only one chapter is devoted to evolution. That does not mean that evolution is unimportant. As the late Dobzhansky has stated, "Nothing in biology makes sense except in the light of evolution" [Dobzhansky *et al.* 1977]. It does mean that the practical use of primates in biomedical research proceeds with little regard to evolutionary theory. The choice of a particular kind of primate is based on extensive past experience, not on theoretical evolutionary grounds. Comparative studies

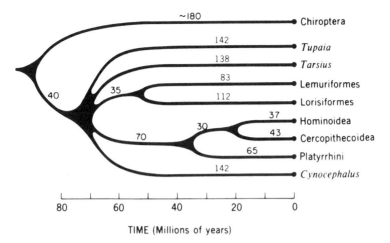

Figure 2.2. Albumin plus transferrin immunological phylogeny of the primates. The numbers refer to immunological distance units. (From Sarich and Cronin 1976, p. 149.)

provide information to the person interested in evolution far more than the study of evolution helps in the choice of laboratory animals.

The problems in studying primate evolution arise from the paucity of fossils, the nature of the evolutionary process, and great differences in personal opinions. Figures 2.2 and 2.3 give a view of the primates based on the immunological studies of Sarich and Cronin (1976, p. 149). According to Sarich and Cronin, human beings have been separated from

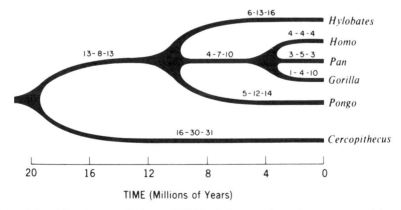

Figure 2.3. Albumin, transferrin, and DNA phylogeny of monkeys, apes, and human beings. The numbers refer to immunological distance of albumin, transferrin, and DNA in that order. (From Sarich and Cronin 1976, p. 151.)

the African apes for a relatively short period of time (still some millions of years!). Paleontologists put the separation at 20–40 million years. Fossils are too few and fragmentary to settle the issue.

Since the life-span is approximately the same in the orangutan and the African apes, it is possible that the common ancestor of human beings and apes had a comparable longevity. But, if the common ancestor was much smaller, a shorter life-span might be expected. My guess is that, according to one's opinions on the length of time that human beings have had a separate evolutionary history and depending on one's guesses on what the ancestral form was like, life-span might be reasonably estimated at 30–50 years. The uncertainty comes from the lack of well-preserved fossils and from parallel evolution. All contemporary primates have larger brains than their ancestors of long ago, and comparisons of contemporary forms give no direct clues to the conditions in the ancestral forms.

HUMAN EVOLUTION: THE LAST FOUR MILLION YEARS

In contrast to the earlier phases of primate evolution, there are substantial data for the events of the last 4 million years, especially for the last 3 million years. In briefest summary, the footsteps found at Laetoli by Mary Leakey and her co-workers show that human beings were fully bipedal by some 3.6 million years ago (Leakey 1979, Johanson and White 1979). Associated teeth and jaws are similar to those from Afar. By 3 million years, finds in Ethiopia, East Africa, and South Africa show that *Australopithecus* had a cranial capacity no larger than that of contemporary apes; most, possibly all, of the capacities are in the 400–500 cc range. By 2 million years, a large form of *Australopithecus* had appeared, and there were simple stone tools in South Africa, East Africa, and Ethiopia. Over the period 2 to 1 million years, the small form evolved into *Homo erectus*, and complex stone tools (Acheulian) appeared in the latter part of this time. *Homo erectus* was also in Java (Djetis) at this time.

Between approximately 2 million and 1.5 million years, the brain doubled in size, possibly from 500 to 1000 cc. After that, the increase was less than 50%. Although there are problems in understanding the fossil record, a possible interpretation is that our ancestors were small-brained bipeds for a long period of time, at least 2 million years, since the Laetolil footprints are clearly not the beginning of bipedalism. During this period, they probably made far more use of objects than do contemporary chimpanzees.

Stone tool manufacture marks the beginning of a new and more effective way of life. Hunting was present, and the large kind of *Australopithecus* became extinct. Given a history at least somewhat along these lines, how should the evolution be interpreted? The increase in cranial capacity is clear from well-preserved and well-dated specimens, but estimates of body weight are very uncertain. It is possible to make the case that the small *Australopithecus* was small, more or less the size of contemporary chimpanzees, and that there had already been some increase in brain size–body size. It is also possible to place the large form of *Australopithecus* well within the range of contemporary human beings and to think that there has been little or no important increase in body size over the last 2 million years.

Body size has proved to be exceedingly difficult to estimate, and even the weights of contemporary apes are given very differently. The problem is in part that unless very complete skeletons are found, estimates based on the contemporary forms may be misleading. For example, in one australopithecine (only one of hundreds) both humerus and femur are known. The humerus was large, but estimates of weight have relied primarily on leg bones, and so are probably all too low.

If the evolution from early biped to *Homo sapiens* is viewed as an increase of three times in brain size, the interpretation may be approached in two quite different ways. One is to stress that the difference is mainly size, disregard the archeological record, assume body weights, and calculate life-spans. The other is to try to see how the unique features of the human brain may correlate with the record (i.e., the factors that led to selection for larger brains).

On life-span, there is some direct evidence from bones. Mann (1975) has shown that in human beings the eruption of the permanent teeth has slowed, the second molar does not show in an X-ray at the time the first molar has erupted. The same is the case for the second and third molars. The delay in eruption time is clearly reflected in maturation. In apes, the tooth that is about to erupt next is calcified by the time the preceding tooth has erupted. The australopithecines were like human beings. There is strong direct evidence for the slowing of development. This method can surely be improved, but as matters stand maturation in the australopithecines should probably be regarded as primarily human, rather than apelike, despite their small brains.

Holloway's (1966) position that the human brain has undergone extensive reorganization is strongly supported by recent studies. Compared to ape or monkey, the areas of the human brain related to hand skills are very large. From the point of view of evolution, it can be speculated that all this new structure is the result of the evolutionary success of tool-making. The first stone tools appear in the record as the brains became larger, rapidly increasing beyond the range of the apes. Complex tools, tools really difficult to make, appear with *Homo erectus*. Myers (1978) has shown that the control of sounds in monkeys is in the limbic system, contrasting with the cortical control in human beings. Whenever this new system of communication appeared, it is now the basis for all human societies, and surely the split brain cases should have ended any remaining doubts on the localization of language. The greatly increased social functions of the human brain are hard to localize but are made clear by the way deaf children strive to communicate, learning 1200 to 1300 signs with minimal effort (in contrast to a chimpanzee learning some 200 signs as a result of great human effort). As Holloway (1966) noted, the cells in the human cortex are larger than those of apes, have more processes, and are spaced farther apart. The increase in the size of the brain between ape and human being is far more than a matter of just size. If further data are needed showing the importance of organization rather than size alone, Gazzaniga and LeDoux (1978) cite cases in which one entire hemisphere was removed without affecting language or IQ.

The difference between the brains of apes and human beings cannot be understood if only brain size and body weight are analyzed. That may be the least important part of the problem. The technical skills, social effectiveness, and linguistic abilities made possible by the brain are evolutionarily new. There is every reason to believe that the evolutionary rates that correlate with the new functions were also new and not mere continuations of rates that had persisted from the long-distant past.

The long period of preparation and 40-plus years of adaptation are the result of the evolutionary success of the new human way of life. A by-product of this evolutionary success is the possibility of a long period of old age, if the environment is optimal.

Neanderthals

The most numerous and by far the best-known of the fossil humans are the Neanderthals (Trinkhaus and Howells 1979). They existed in Europe and adjacent areas from some 100,000 to 35,000 years ago. As emphasized by Vallois (Table 2.1) and even more by Wolpoff (1979), length of life was short. Trinkaus (1978) describes the life of the Neanderthals as "rigorous" and states that all the older skeletons show signs of traumatic injuries. The Neanderthal skeleton is massive and Trinkaus believes that this correlates with the dangerous way of life.

Homo sapiens sapiens and Length of Life

Beginning about 40,000 to 35,000 years ago, the large browridge an-cient forms of human beings were replaced by anatomically modern human beings, people like ourselves. There were major changes in the way of life. Technology became far more complicated. People crossed water to Australia, invaded the Arctic, and entered the New World. The social and technical revolution is usefully outlined by Lenski and Lenski (1974, p. 131). What appears to have been the greatest behavioral change in human evolution was accompanied by no change in the size of the brain. Describing human evolution in terms of brain size–body size lumps the last 100,000 years together and places ancient human beings, whose way of life changed exceedingly slowly, with anatomically modern human beings with their rapidly changing customs.

Lovejoy *et al.* (1977) give the information on age at death for a pre-contact American Indian population from the Libben site. There were many burials (1289); great efforts were made to find traces of infants. Numerous criteria were used in estimating age. This study is probably the most reliable of any available at the present time. As shown in Table 2.6, few individuals lived past 45. Survivorship is shown in Figure 2.4. The oldest individual was estimated to have been 55 years old. The survivorship shown in Figure 2.4 seems to have been representative of our species until long after agriculture. Death rates were very high in the first 4 years, then low until the middle twenties, then slowly increas-ing, until there are few survivors after 45.

There were local exceptions to the general situation. For example, Laughlin (1972, p. 386) gives a life table for Aleuts (Table 2.7). He further

TABLE 2.6
Length of Life in Precontact American Indians: Libben Site[a]

Years	Skeletons	Percentages
0–5	513	40
6–15	186	14
16–25	141	11
26–35	269	21
36–45	147	11
46–	33	3
Totals	1289	100%

[a] From C.O. Lovejoy *et al.*, Paleodemography of the Libben Site, Ottawa County, Ohio, *Science* 198: 291–293. Copyright 1977 by the American Association for the Advancement of Science.

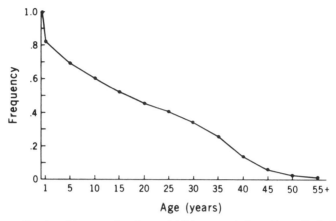

Figure 2.4. Survivorship curve for the total Libben population. (From C. O. Lovejoy *et al.*, Paleodemography of the Libben Site, Ottawa County, Ohio, *Science* 198: 291–293. Copyright 1977 by the American Association for the Advancement of Science.)

comments (p. 387) that he found no Eskimo over 55 in a large archeological series and that the Aleuts appear to have lived in an environment that allowed the old to be economically useful even in advanced age.

A different kind of evidence, which strongly supports the theory that our ancestors were fully adapted to live only to 45 or 50 or a few more years, is given by the nature of the aging process itself. Work rate starts to decrease in the 30s. Hand strength, vital capacity, and kidney function all decline. Oxygen uptake during exercise declines. Fertility declines, and the frequency of fetal abnormalities increases rapidly after 35 (Figure 2.5). If the physical capabilities of adult human beings are regarded as

TABLE 2.7
Age at Death in the Aleuts of the Aleutian Islands and the Eskimos of Labrador[a]

	Aleut		Eskimo	
	N	Percentage	N	Percentage
1–15	150	30.55	38	34.55
15–25	41	8.35	10	9.09
25–45	103	20.98	29	26.36
45–65	117	23.83	20	18.18
65–80	58	11.81	13	11.81
80–100	22	4.48	0	0.00

[a] From Laughlin 1972, p. 386. Copyright © Oxford University Press.

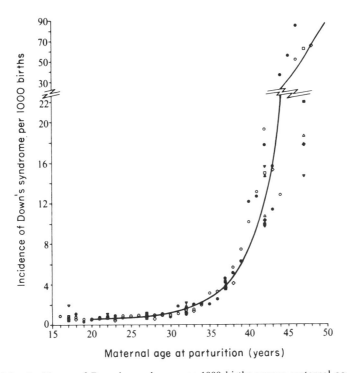

Figure 2.5. Incidence of Down's syndrome per 1000 births versus maternal age at parturition. (From Crowley *et al.* 1979, p. 418.)

adaptations to the ancestral way of life, the adaptation was to the period 20–45 years.

Viewing old age as a by-product of adaptation at younger ages helps to explain why the rates of aging may be so different in different individuals. As Lapin *et al.* (1979, p. 35) have stated, "There is often no correlation between the manifestations of aging in different systems." Evolution shows why this is the case. High correlations are the result of selection, and there never was selection for healthy old people. The old were already dead before their genes could affect the course of human evolution.

The attainment of maximum life-span potential is partially the result of the new environment of modern technology and medicine, and it is partially luck. If none of the aging systems reaches a fatal level, then great age may be achieved. But for most, great age will be associated with handicaps, impairments severe enough to have caused death in our ancestors.

ACKNOWLEDGMENTS

My thanks to Alice Davis for editorial assistance in preparing the manuscript, and to the Alfred P. Sloan Foundation for contributing to the completion of this work.

REFERENCES

Asdell, S. A. (1964) *Patterns of Mammalian Reproduction*, 2nd ed. Ithaca, N.Y.: Cornell University Press.

Birdsell, J. B. (1975) *Human Evolution: An Introduction to the New Physical Anthropology*, 2nd ed. Chicago: Rand McNally College Publishing Company.

Bourne, G. H. (1973) *Nonhuman Primates and Medical Research*. New York: Academic Press.

Bowden, D. M. (1979) *Aging in Nonhuman Primates*. New York: Van Nostrand Reinhold Co.

Bowden, D. M., and Jones, M. L. (1979) Aging research in nonhuman primates. Pp. 1–13 in D. M. Bowden, ed., *Aging in Nonhuman Primates*. New York: Van Nostrand Reinhold Co.

Bramblett, C. A. (1969) Non-metric skeletal age changes in the Darajani baboon. *American Journal of Physical Anthropology* 30:161–172.

Crowley, P. H., Gulati, D. K., Hayden, T. L., Lopez, P., and Dyer, R. (1979) A chiasma-hormonal hypothesis relating Down's syndrome and maternal age. *Nature* 280:417–418.

Cutler, R. G. (1976) Evolution of longevity in primates. *Journal of Human Evolution* 5:169–202.

Dobzhansky, T., Ayala, F. J., Stebbins, G. L., and Valentine, J. W. (1977) *Evolution*. San Francisco: W. H. Freeman and Co.

Ehrlich, A., Fobes, J. L., and King, J. E. (1976) Prosimian learning capacities. *Journal of Human Evolution* 5:599–618.

Gazzaniga, M. S., and LeDoux, J. E. (1978) *The Integrated Mind*. New York: Plenum Press.

Hodos, W. (1970) Evolutionary interpretation of neural and behavioral studies of living vertebrates. Pp. 26–39 in G. O. Schmitt, ed., *The Neurosciences*. New York: Rockefeller University Press.

Hodos, W., and Campbell, C. B. G. (1969) Scala naturae: Why there is no theory in comparative psychology. *Psychology Review* 76:337–350.

Holloway, R. L. (1966) Cranial capacity, neural reorganization, and hominid evolution: A search for more suitable parameters. *American Anthropologist* 68:103–121.

Jerison, H. J. (1973) *Evolution of the Brain and Intelligence*. New York: Academic Press.

Johanson, D., and White, T. D. (1979) A systematic assessment of early African hominids. *Science* 202:321–330.

Jones, M. L. (1979) Life Span in Mammals. Chart for meeting on aging, Santa Barbara, Calif.

Lapin, B. A., Krilova, R. I., Cherkovich, G. M., and Asanov, N. S. (1979) Observations from Sukhumi. Pp. 14–37 in D. M. Bowden, ed., *Aging in Nonhuman Primates*. New York: Van Nostrand Reinhold Co.

Laughlin, W. S. (1972) Ecology and population structure in the Arctic. In G. A. Harrison and A. J. Boyce, eds., *The Structure of Human Populations*. Oxford: Clarendon Press.

Leakey, M. D. (1979) Footprints in the ashes of time. *National Geographic* 155:446–457.

Lenski, G., and Lenski, J. (1974) *Human Societies: An Introduction to Macrosociology.* New York: McGraw-Hill.

Lovejoy, C. O., Meindl, R. S., Pryzbeck, T. R., Barton, T. S., Heiple, K. G., and Kotting, D. (1977) Paleodemography of the Libben Site, Ottawa County, Ohio. *Science* 198:291–293.

Mann, A. E. (1975) *Paleodemographic Aspects of the South African Australopithecines.* Philadelphia: University of Pennsylvania Publications in Anthropology, No. 1.

Moore, W. J., and Lavelle, C. L. B. (1974) *Growth of the Facial Skeleton in the Hominoidea.* New York: Academic Press.

Myers, R. E. (1978) Comparative neurology of vocalization and speech: Proof of a dichotomy. Pp. 59–73 in S. L. Washburn and E. R. McCown, eds., *Human Evolution-Biosocial Perspectives.* Menlo Park, Calif.: Benjamin/Cummings Publishing Co.

Napier, J. R., and Napier, P. H. (1967) *A Handbook of Living Primates.* New York: Academic Press.

Nass, G. G. (1977) Intra-group variations in the dental eruption sequence of *Macaca fuscata fuscata. Folia Primatologica* 28:306–314.

Owsley, D. W., and Bass, W. M. (1979) A demographic analysis of skeletons from the Larson Site, (39WW2) Walworth County, South Dakota: Vital statistics. *American Journal of Physical Anthropology* 51:145–154.

Sarich, V. M., and Cronin, J. E. (1976) Molecular systematics of the primates. In M. Goodman and R. E. Tashian, eds., *Molecular Anthropology.* New York: Plenum Press.

Schultz, A. H. (1969) *The Life of Primates.* London: Weidenfeld and Nicolson.

Sugiyama, Y. (1976) Life history of male Japanese monkeys. In J. S. Rosenblatt *et al.,* eds., *Advances in the Study of Behavior.* New York: Academic Press.

Teleki, G., Hunt, E. E., and Pfifferling, J. H. (1976) Demographic observations (1963–1973) on the chimpanzees of Gombe National Park, Tanzania. *Journal of Human Evolution* 5:559–598.

Trinkaus, E. (1978) Hard times among the Neanderthals. *Natural History* 87:58–63.

Trinkaus, E., and Howells, W. W. (1979) The Neanderthals. *Scientific American* 241:118–133.

Vallois, H. V. (1961) The social life of early man: The evidence of skeletons. In S. L. Washburn, ed., *Social Life of Early Man.* Chicago: Aldine Publishing Company.

Wolpoff, M. H. (1979) The Krapina dental remains. *American Journal of Physical Anthropology* 50:67–114.

Zuckerman, S. (1933) *Functional Affinities of Man, Monkeys, and Apes.* New York: Harcourt, Brace and Company.

chapter 3

Life-Span Extension

RICHARD G. CUTLER

The subject of life-span extension is usually associated with a specialized field of study on developing means to lengthen the life-span beyond what might be considered normal. This objective contrasts with that of most other fields of the health-related sciences, in which the objective is the development of means so that more people can enjoy a normal life-span in better health. Both objectives, however, involve the maintenance or improvement of human health, the basic difference being that extension of the normal period of health is usually involved in efforts to reduce the more global effects of the aging process. More specifically, life-span extension research is aimed toward a more uniform extension or maintenance of good health and vigor, whereas other approaches not normally regarded as life-span extension research are aimed toward the cure or prevention of specific, more localized types of diseases or dysfunctions.

The aim of life-span extension research is not simply to enable persons to live older longer but to learn how general good health can be maintained for a longer-than-normal period of time. An individual may not necessarily have a longer-than-normal life-span as a consequence of having a more uniform and healthy life, but it is generally believed that a longer life-span would frequently be the outcome of a prolonged period

31

AGING
Biology and Behavior

of good health. Whether a longer-than-normal life-span would be a desirable outcome despite the fact that people do live longer in better health is currently a subject of serious debate.

Efforts to extend life-span or to uniformly prolong or maintain health have had a long and complex history (Gruman 1966, Medvedev 1975, Comfort 1979). Although successes have been found in the cure and prevention of many diseases, the prospect of uniform health prolongation or life-span extension has appeared hopeless. Only over the past few years, because of the remarkable progress being made in the biological and medical sciences and the increasing fraction of older persons in our population who are in declining health, does the possibility of prolongation of health appear to need reevaluation. In this chapter, I shall review some of the major ideas and experimental data bearing on the possibility of uniform health and life-span extension. Although an attempt has been made to cover all relevant work, this review should not be considered exhaustive and in many cases probably reflects the personal and biased viewpoint of the author.

DEFINING LIFE-SPAN

Life-span can have several meanings. In terms of an individual, the meaning is quite clear: life-span is simply how long an individual lives from birth to death. In dealing with populations, however, the terms *mean life-span* and *maximum life-span potential* are commonly used. Starting at birth with a given number of individuals (say, 100,000), the mean life-span is the age at which 50% of these individuals have died. It has been found that the mean life-span of a population is determined by environmental hazards and nutritional and medical health care as well as genetic factors. Following this population until the last individual dies defines the age stated as maximum life-span potential. This value is much more difficult to determine experimentally because of the large initial population required. Consequently, maximum life-span potential is known reasonably accurately for only a few laboratory animals (mouse and rat) and for human beings. Instead of maximum life-span potential, which represents the age at which death of 100% of the population occurs, life-span has also been defined as the tenth decile of survivorship, the age at which 90% of the population has died. This value is sometimes used because of the smaller number of individuals required for its determination (Smith and Walford 1977).

Although mean life-span is subject to many environmental variables, maximum life-span potential and, to a slightly lesser extent, the tenth decile of survivorship are relatively independent of these variables and thus appear to reflect more accurately the innate biological potential of a species for maintaining life. For example, as environmental hazards have steadily decreased over the past several thousand years and nutrition and medical care have improved, there has been a steady increase in mean life-span of human beings from about 30–40 years to its present value of about 70 years. However, maximum life-span potential has remained constant at about 100 years (Cutler 1978b, 1980b). Similar results are found for other species, particularly primates and laboratory animals. Thus, maximum life-span potential appears to reflect a unique biological characteristic of a species.

It has also been found that the general rate of aging, as measured by the rate of loss of maximum performance capacity to carry out physiological functions, is roughly inversely proportional to a species' maximum life-span potential (Cutler 1978b, 1980b). These data strongly support the concept that a species with greater maximum life-span potential is indeed capable of maintaining health for a longer period of time and thus ages less rapidly. Thus, maximum life-span potential of a species could be said to reflect the characteristic aging rate of that species.

The difficulty of using maximum life-span potential in practice is the apparent impossibility of determining an absolute, constant value for a given species. This is because it always seems possible to further decrease the environmental hazards and to improve nutritional and medical care, which would be expected to increase maximum life-span potential further. Maximum life-span potential (or the tenth decile of survivorship) is therefore only of practical value as a relative figure used for comparative purposes in estimating an animal's innate aging rate.

Maximum life-span potential has been estimated for a large number of mammalian species and was found to range from 2 to 3 years for voles and other small rodents to about 100 years for human beings, the longest-lived of all mammals (Flower 1931, Napier and Napier 1967, Jones 1968). Although these data are constantly being modified, there now appears to be reasonable evidence supporting the existence of a wide range of aging rates or innate capacities of different species to maintain general health and resistance to disease as a function of time.

DISTRIBUTION OF AGING

It is obviously important in understanding the biological nature of aging to determine whether there exist any organisms that do not age and are therefore potentially immortal. Although in the past it appeared as if animals showing apparently unlimited growth might be free of aging, this does not now appear to be true (Comfort 1979). At least all multi-cellular forms of life appear to undergo an aging-like process if death from other causes can be eliminated (Cutler 1972, Comfort 1979).

In looking for immortal forms of life, it has always been confusing how to define the continuously dividing unicellular organism such as bacteria or transformed tissue culture cells. For example, a culture of bacterial cells never dies if allowed to grow indefinitely, and so bacteria are frequently said to be immortal. However, it appears unlikely that organelles such as mitochondria, cellular structure, and chromatin have indefinite life-spans. For example, we have obtained preliminary evidence that the *E. coli* genome undergoes replication for only a fixed number of cycles (Cutler 1972). Also, in conditions under which they do not or cannot divide, unicellular organisms appear to have finite life-spans (Cutler 1972).

Senescent animals are rarely found in their natural environmental niche (Cutler 1976b, 1978b, 1980a). A senescent individual is defined here as an animal that is now at the age at which it has considerably less than optimum health, vigor, and resistance to disease. Clearly, within this definition there can be different degrees of senescence. The prob-ability of death for an animal living in its natural environmental niche appears to be a constant throughout life, regardless of the chronological age of the individual, a situation that results in an exponentially declining survival curve (Cutler 1978b, 1980b). However, if we take the same species and place it in captivity, a sigmoid-type of survival curve is found. The animals now live much longer, show senescence, and most will die of dysfunctions related to aging (Cutler 1976b, 1978b, 1980b).

Also, the probability of death for many animals in the wild, which is usually caused by accident or predators, appears to be inversely pro-portional to the species' maximum life-span potential or aging rate in captivity. Species with longer maximum life-span potentials, as deter-mined in captivity, have in proportion a higher probability of living longer in the wild before they are killed. Thus, animals with innate longer capacities to maintain health on the average utilize most of the capacity but seldom go beyond it while living in their natural ecological niche. There appears to be no excess or deficiency in innate longevity potential that might serve as a disadvantage to the animal's evolutionary success. This observation implies that there is a biological price to pay for lon-gevity, and that longevity is only extended when evolutionary advantages for a longer period of good health outweigh the cost (Cutler 1976b, 1978b, 1980b).

More comparative studies are needed of animals having different in-nate potentials to maintain uniform health and vigor in captivity and in the wild (particularly for the primates) to determine the generality of these preliminary observations. As it now stands, these results strongly suggest that senescence is rarely found in animals living under natural conditions and is therefore likely to be undesirable and not to have been positively selected for during evolution. Instead, increased general health maintenance and resistance to disease leading to greater longevity appear to be selected factors, rather than processes causing further aging.

Different maximum life-span potentials of mammalian species, ranging from 2 to 100 years, do not appear to be a result of some innate biological-limiting characteristic of each species, but reflect the evolutionary se-lective advantages of having a certain time-dependent capacity of main-taining health. It should be strongly emphasized at this point that this idea of the evolution of longevity as a positive selective factor has far-reaching implications in our scientific approach to studying the biological nature of health maintenance processes in the human being and the loss of health due to aging (Sacher 1975, Cutler 1975).

Is senescence for the human being, then, as we find it in our population today, unnatural and an artifact of our civilization? The mean survival for human beings a few hundred years ago was about 30–40 years and probably was about 20–30 years a few thousand years ago (Deevey 1960, Acsádi and Nemeskéri 1970). Death was usually due to warfare, acci-dents, disease, predators, or malnutrition. The rather recent increase in the mean life-span over the past 200 years has been largely the result of improved sanitary conditions, better year-round nutrition, and a sub-stantial reduction in the death of children. The probability of becoming chronologically old enough to show significant decline in health or se-nescence was therefore rare in what might be called the human being's more natural ecological niche, as it is for other animals.

It is also important to realize that the human being's age-dependent decline in health and physiological performance and increased suscep-tibility to disease does not become serious until past the age of 30–40 years (Shock 1952, 1961, 1970, Kohn 1978). This statement implies that the fairly recent increase in the human mean life-span has resulted in increasing the fraction of persons having less than optimal health and vigor and being more susceptible to disease and many age-related dys-functions—rather than the reverse, as is often thought.

There are now indications that the mean life-span of human beings will not increase much beyond the 75-year range it has today (Upton 1977, Comfort 1979). This is a result of life-span being increased from

30 to 75 years by keeping persons older physiologically for a longer period of time. And with the aging process always continuing at the same rate, there is clearly a limit of just how old physiologically a person can or would want to be, regardless of the intensity and quality of medical care available. In fact, if all of the major killers of human beings today, such as cancer and cardiovascular disease, were completely eliminated, only about 20 additional years of mean life-span for the population overall would be gained; and these additional years would be years deeper into physiological old age (Kohn 1978).

The aging rate determines the period of good health as well as the period of declining health and has remained constant for human beings over the past 40,000 years or so (Cutler 1975, 1976a). Thus, an increase in maximum life-span potential appears to be possible only by decreasing the overall aging rate, which in turn would result in a correspondingly uniform prolongation of health. In this context, it is of interest to speculate what might happen to today's population structure in terms of age distribution if maximum life-span potential instead of mean life-span were to increase, as has happened in the past (Cutler 1978a, 1980a).

Take a limiting case of a population in which the aging process has been completely eliminated, living under the existing environmental hazards we have today in the United States, in which the mean health status is that of a 30-year-old male. For this population, the mean life-span is calculated to be about 350 years. Clearly, there would be no senescent individuals, death always being from causes other than aging, but life-span would still be finite. Proceeding from no aging to a situation in which some aging occurs would give a smaller mean life-span potential and a slight increase in the fraction of population in the senescent category at very old age. Thus, a reduction in the aging rate tends to decrease the fraction of senescent individuals in the population—not increase it, as is sometimes thought. Also, by decreasing the aging rate, a more natural balance between innate health maintenance capacity and intensity of environmental hazards would once again be approached as it existed in the past, when the decline of health due to aging was extremely rare (Cutler 1978b, 1980a, 1980b).

BIOLOGY OF GENERAL HEALTH MAINTENANCE: A UNIQUE ROLE FOR BIOLOGICAL GERONTOLOGY

The aging process probably affects every physiological and mental function of an organism, and the complexity of aging is likely to equal the complexity of the developmental processes that initially created the organism. It is therefore becoming evident that even the complete elimination of the major causes of death today, which is the major aim of medical science, would have little impact on prolonging uniform health or even the mean life-span (Goldschmidt and Jillson 1975, Medical World News 1977, Gerjouy 1979). This is simply because of the global effects of aging on the organism. Elimination or cure of a few specific diseases or organ dysfunctions will have little effect on a person suffering from many more problems. Instead, a more uniform decrease in aging rate throughout the entire body is required to provide a true prolongation of health.

In view of the complexity of the aging process, the success in achieving such a uniform decrease in aging rate lies with the possible existence of primary aging processes and/or health maintenance processes that would underlie, as causative agents, the many different age-related dysfunctions (Cutler 1972, 1976a, 1976b, 1978b, 1980a, 1980b). A search for such primary aging processes and how they might be controlled would also represent a unique approach that should be characteristic of the field of biological gerontology. Gerontological research in the biomedical sciences would then have a more clearly defined role.

BIOLOGICAL NATURE OF AGING

Most work in gerontology today is still of the descriptive type, and much more is needed. Nevertheless, there is now a sufficient data base to develop a few rational working hypotheses on possible aging mechanisms and perhaps, most important, on how aging rate might be governed.

The oldest and still most popular category of hypotheses on the mechanism of aging considers aging as a pleiotropic phenomenon, that is, a harmful by-product of otherwise necessary biochemical, physiological, and developmental processes (Cutler 1972, Lamb 1977, Strehler 1977, Kohn 1978, Comfort 1979). These hypotheses are generally classified as the "passive" type. Examples are: (a) wear-and-tear hypothesis: accumulation of damage at the cellular or intracellular levels, leading to cell loss and general dysfunction (Kohn 1978); (b) running out of a genetic program of differentiation and development: lack of stable, nondestructive type of growth control, development, and neuroendocrine regulatory systems (Finch 1976); and (c) dedifferentiation: harmful by-products of metabolism and development altering the proper differentiated state of cells, resulting in improper cellular function (Ono and Cutler 1978).

A second category of hypotheses is generally classified as the "active" type and appears to be less popular. These hypotheses generally state that aging is not a result of something going wrong with the organism because it is simply alive, but rather aging is the result of an active genetic program that evolved for the long-term benefit of the species. In this category, we have the genetic-programmed hypothesis of aging, where genetic-programmed senescence is the normal and last stage of the genetic program of development (Kanungo 1975, Denckla 1975).

Each of these categories of hypotheses suggests at least some general guidelines of how life-span extension might be implemented. Still very little is known about the biological nature of aging or which hypothesis might be more correct, and so there is presently a general lack of good solid guidelines on how aging might be controlled. Instead, most life-span extension experiments have been based on educated guesses. For example, certain toxic by-products of metabolism, such as free radicals, have been proposed to cause damage leading to aging. This is certainly theoretically possible from what we know now about aging, but there is little experimental support that free radicals are sufficiently plentiful to indeed be dangerous to an organism. Nevertheless, free radical scavengers or antioxidants have been tested for possible antiaging effects (Harman 1978). Another approach has been to investigate key physiological or regulatory processes, such as the neuroendocrine or immune systems, in the hope that, because these major physiological systems are clearly critical to the general health of the animal, they might also have an important role in aging. Thus, experiments are undertaken to enhance or stabilize such critical systems and to determine what effects these procedures might have on the aging process.

Methods and Results of Some Life-Span Extension Experiments

A major problem in life-span enhancement experiments is that of measuring the resultant effect on life-span and general health of the animals (Comfort 1979). The most frequently used method is to determine how long a given population of animals lives in terms of either a mean life-span value, a tenth decile survivorship value, or a maximum life-span potential value. But if one obtains an increase in the mean life-span value and not in maximum life-span potential, what does it mean? Has the aging rate been decreased, the general vigor of the animal increased, or simply have the environmental hazards somehow been decreased? The answers to these questions are still troublesome, but most investigators, recognizing the high dependence of mean life-span on a great number of environmental factors, would prefer to obtain increased maximum life-span potential because of its more clear implication that aging rate has truly been decreased.

There is also a question of whether it is theoretically possible to extract biological aging data from actuarial data, particularly from the cross-sectional life-span tables (Maynard-Smith 1966, Lamb 1977). The problem is that of distinguishing the influence of environmental factors and other random components of survival in a population of many animals from the influence of the aging process determining the age-dependent probability of death of an individual animal.

One of the most serious attempts to explain actuarial survival data in terms of biological parameters of the individual animal has been by Sacher. He suggested that the Gompertz equation can be divided into a vulnerability and an aging rate component (Sacher 1977). The advantage of this method in efforts to study the effect of life extension methods would be in determining whether the vulnerability or the aging rate component is being affected. On investigating a number of different life extension methods, Sacher suggested that most methods affect the vulnerability component and not the aging rate. He has claimed that only nutritional restriction and lower body temperature so far have been shown to affect the aging rate (Sacher 1977). From this type of analysis, Sacher has suggested that it might be possible to increase duration of health (by decreasing the vulnerability component) without decreasing the aging rate or maximum life-span potential (Sacher 1977, Havighurst and Sacher 1977).

The possibility of two major classes of biological components determining life-span of the individual rather than one (the aging rate) is still controversial. Could it be that the different durations of health and maximum life-span potential seen in different species are dependent on these two components? More specifically, is the immune or neuroendocrine system of a human being at its peak of health less vulnerable and therefore more resistant to disease and degeneration than the chimpanzee at its peak of health? Or do both human being and chimpanzee have the same vulnerability at their peak of health but have different innate differences in their individual aging rates? Are the components determining vulnerability different from the components determining the aging rate and, if so, how might vulnerability and the aging rate be related? Perhaps the vulnerability and aging rate components postulated by Sacher are related to the continuously acting and developmentally linked aging processes that have been proposed by Cutler (1978a). For reasons mainly noted by Maynard-Smith (1966) and Lamb (1977), I seriously question whether we can determine from actuarial data whether there really exist two separate biological components determining health duration. It appears improbable that biological aging rate information of an individual through-out the life-span can be obtained from time-dependent cross-sectional frequencies of deaths in a population. But, if true, these two components would certainly be important to consider in any life extension experiment.

Clearly, the parameters most meaningful in measuring health main-tenance potential concern the duration of health and resistance to disease of individuals, and not actuarial death rates of a population. To obtain this information, a number of different physiological factors need to be measured, such as immune, heart, kidney, and lung functions; structural and morphological factors should also be measured, such as collagen solubility, bone density, and the amount of age pigment present in cells (Kohn 1978, Comfort 1979). The basic problem, however, is that these measurements are frequently complex and expensive. Some investigators have therefore compromised and have used both a tenth decile survi-vorship value and a few simple biological measurements, such as adapt-ability to changing temperature or collagen solubility (Walford 1975, 1979).

RESTRICTION OF NUTRITION

Over 45 years ago, it was discovered (but not as a prediction of some aging hypothesis) that chronic restriction of nutrition could nearly double (from 3.5 to 5 years) the life-span of male rats (McCay et al. 1935, 1939, 1962, see Young 1979 for recent review). The restricted diet could be one of reduced calories, a change in the ratio of protein-to-fat-to-car-bohydrate, or a combination of these (Berg 1960, Berg and Simms 1960, 1961, Ross 1976, Young 1978). Overall, it appears that restricted calories in an otherwise balanced diet with vitamins and minerals is most effec-tive. Calorie restrictions of 50% and 25% result in increased life-spans of almost double and about 32%, respectively.

The effects of diet restriction on the general health status of rats are mixed and depend on the type of diet and degree of restriction (Ross 1961, Young 1978, 1979). Some diseases are decreased in frequency by as much as 50–90%, such as glomerulonephritis, myocardial fibrosis, peribronchial lymphocytosis, prostatitis, and endocrine hyperplasias. The effects on tumor incidence are variable. Some types are decreased in frequency, such as epithelium and endocrine tumors. Others, such as urinary bladder and thyroid, are unaffected, and still others, such as all carcinomas and reticulum cell sarcomas of lymphoid organs, actually increase in frequency. There is also a general increase in infant mortality (restriction being started after weaning), a stunting of growth, and im-pairment in structural, functional, and behavioral development (Ross 1976). In addition, diet-restricted animals have a greater susceptibility to bacterial and parasitic infections. The intensity of these side effects are roughly proportional to the degree of restriction.

Restricted nutrition has successfully lengthened life-span in a number of species, including rats, mice, guinea pig, fish, *Daphnia, Drosophila,* and the rotifers (Barrows 1972). Unfortunately, few long-lived mammalian species such as the dog have been studied, so it is not clear whether this method would work for the human being. Considering the general health problems and other unknowns associated with restricted-nutrition life extension, it is not surprising that this method has not become popular for human beings.

In addition to continuous restriction of calories, limited life-span extension can be obtained by *ad libitum* feeding of lower percentage protein diets and by varying the time during the life-span at which restricted nutrition is started (Stucklíková *et al.* 1975, Leto *et al.* 1976a, 1976b). In general, when nutrition restriction is delayed (after the age of weaning), there is less life-span extension (Ross 1961, 1976, Young 1978).

A rough correlation has also been found showing that the slower the rate of development obtained by restricted nutrition, the longer the animal lives. Important exceptions to this rule are known: for example, intermittent fasting (fasting and *ad libitum* feeding every other day) increases life-span without substantially slowing down rate of development (Carlson and Hoelzel 1946, Gerbase-DeLima *et al.* 1975). However, diets that promote a rapid rate of growth and an early maturational age do not generally lead to a longer and more healthy life-span, as is sometimes thought (Goodrick 1980).

The mechanism of prolonging life-span by restricted nutrition is far from clear, and perhaps a number of different mechanisms are involved, depending on the type of restriction being used (Barrows 1972, Barrows and Kokkonen 1978, Comfort 1979, Weindruch *et al.* 1979). Some of the mechanisms being considered are a lowering of body temperature, a lowering of specific metabolic rate, a slowing of developmental rate, and a repression of the immune system against autoimmune disease.

Most important, there is the serious possibility that restricted nutrition might not actually extend maximum life-span potential beyond that which is normal for the animal in the wild (Wulf and Cutler 1975). For example, it appears unnatural for animals to eat *ad libitum* (to have all they want to eat all the time) as they do in the laboratory. A more natural feeding situation is feast and famine. It is therefore possible that *ad libitum* feeding produces a complex spectrum of diseases and dysfunctions that restricted nutrition and periodic fasting–feeding programs eliminate. What we may be studying here is not the effect of restricted nutrition on extending life-span but instead the effect of overeating on shortening life-span. This is a fundamental question, for diet restriction is often cited as being perhaps the most effective means to lengthen normal life-span, which could be completely incorrect.

Of course, it is of interest to learn how overeating might shorten life-span and give rise to diseases that are in many aspects similar to normal aging. In addition, it would be of interest to determine if restricted diet or periodic fasting stimulates some natural antiaging processes, such as selective protein degradation (Wulf and Cutler 1975). Also, because human beings now essentially eat *ad libitum*, studies on diet restriction effects on health maintenance processes are clearly of importance (Tannenbaum and Silverstone 1953).

The degree of life-span extension by restricted nutrition is impressive and is still the only method that has clearly extended maximum life-span potential in mammals. Even if the restricted nutrition diet does not reduce the normal aging rate but rather reduces the onset frequency of disease and returns an animal in captivity to a wild-type health status, these results are no less important.

HYPOTHERMIA

Theoretically, one might expect that, if aging is the result of by-products of metabolism, a reduction in the rate of metabolism should decrease aging rate. This idea came from Rubner's data, which showed that most animals consume a constant amount of calories per gram body weight over their life-span regardless of their maximum life-span potential or specific metabolic rate (Rubner 1908, Pearl 1928). From mouse to dog to elephant, the amount of energy expended has been found to be about 200–300 kcal/g. Considering the great range found in maximum life-span potentials and specific metabolic rates of different species, this finding is impressive and is likely to have some fundamental meaning related to aging (Cutler 1972). It also appears that one way life-span may have evolved was simply to decrease specific metabolic rate.

A number of mammals and birds appear to be exceptions to Rubner's rule by living too long for their high specific metabolic rate. However, these animals have been found to have diurnal and/or seasonal variations in body temperature and consequently in specific metabolic rate. For example, the *Peromyscus* deer mouse would be predicted to have a mean specific metabolic rate according to body size about 35% higher than is actually found, but these animals frequently enter a torpor condition nightly, which substantially reduces their daily metabolic rate. Hummingbirds and bats have a very high specific metabolic rate when flying, but their body temperatures decrease about 13–17°C and 3–6°C, respectively, when they are resting or sleeping. When the lower specific metabolic rates are taken into consideration, these animals are not much different from most other animals in total life-span calorie consumption. However, there are important exceptions to the constant total life-span expenditure of energy, some being lower and a few much higher. Human beings are the most exceptional, with an unusually high value of about 800 kc/g. Because of the potential importance of life-span calorie consumption to aging, it has been a useful indicator of innate longevity potential, along with maximum life-span potential (Sacher 1959, 1975, Cutler 1975, 1976a).

Experimentally lowering body temperature to extend life-span has met with some success (Liu and Walford 1972). Poikilotherms are obviously easier to work with. Lowering the temperature of *Drosophila* from 26°C to 20°C throughout the life-span almost doubles its maximum life-span potential (Pearl 1928, Miquel *et al.* 1976). Experimental variation of body temperature at different stages of the life-span in *Drosophila* shows that in early life temperature effects were minimal but became more important afterward (Maynard-Smith 1962). Liu and Walford (1975) found a similar result for fish. A decrease of 5–6°C for the South American annual fish of the Genus *Cynolebias* increased maximum life-span potential by 75-100%. Moreover, retardation of the aging process is indicated by a decrease in the rate of collagen insolubility. It is also of interest that these annual fish, when kept in the first half of their life-span at 20°C and then transferred to 15°C, lived much longer than those kept always at 15°C, those kept at 15°C than transferred to 20°C, or those kept always at 20°C for their life-spans. Thus, lower temperature during the later phase of life appears more beneficial to lengthen life-span.

It is much more difficult to lower body temperature for long periods of time in mammals without some type of harmful side effect, and as yet no life-span studies have been made using this method. However, animals can be found whose body temperature naturally decreases, such as those animals undergoing torpor or hibernation, as already noted. These animals live unusually long in relation to their specific metabolic rate when active, but total calories consumed over their life-span remains similar to most other species. Also, hibernating animals prevented from hibernating have reduced life-spans compared with animals allowed to hibernate (Kayser 1961). Hypothermia in mammals can be induced for short periods of time by drugs, and experiments with rodents have indicated an increased resistance to infection, parasites, and irradiation at lower than normal body temperature (Liu and Walford 1972, Kent 1978). Unfortunately, it appears that long-term life-span studies are hampered by the animal's becoming tolerant to the hypothermic effects of the drugs currently being used (Liu and Walford 1972).

When homeothermal animals such as rats are placed in a low-temperature environment (such as 9°C), their body temperatures still remain fairly constant, but specific metabolic rate increases substantially (Kibler *et al.* 1963). Under these conditions, the animals have a much shorter life-span, and a number of age-dependent diseases in the animals are accelerated in onset frequency, including some types of cancer. Much of the calorie consumption of small animals goes into production of body heat, not into energy of movement. Could it be that by-products of heat generation are more harmful than other forms of energy generation? These results strongly support the idea that at least some metabolic components of energy consumption are involved in determining life-span.

Another interesting effect of lowered body temperature is that it appears to act as a potent suppressive regime for both humoral and cellular immune processes in poikilotherms (Liu and Walford 1972). Thus, if autoimmunity is an important component of aging, suppression of the immune system (particularly in the later phases of life) may be beneficial, as was shown for the South American annual fish. In this respect, it should be kept in mind that the effect of lower body temperature on increasing life-span is not necessarily one of lowering specific metabolic rate (Liu and Walford 1972). The metabolic rate is not always decreased on lowering body temperature and may actually be increased in certain cases.

But whatever the mechanism(s) of temperature effects might be, it is clear that small changes on the order of 1–5°C can substantially influence the fundamental aging rate of an organism. A nightly lowering of the body temperature of a person during sleep by only 1–2°C may be relatively simple to do and yet may have significant effect on increasing life-span (Comfort 1979).

NEUROENDOCRINE SYSTEM

When hormones were discovered, there was great hope that they might be used successfully in reducing the aging rate and perhaps even in rejuvenating sexual function in human beings. Unfortunately, apart from the age-dependent decrease in a number of 17-ketosteroids, no single hormonal change has been found to correlate with senescence, no single endocrine organ that can be removed without fatal results has produced a decreased aging rate, and no hormones are known to produce more than limited or apparently secondary reversal of senile changes (Andres and Tobin 1977, Eskin 1978, Comfort 1979).

An important exception to this might be the effect dehydroepiandrosterone (DHEA) has. DHEA is known to decrease significantly with age in human beings and laboratory animals, and its replacement in rats results in an increased resistance to a number of carcinogens and in a less aged appearance (Schwartz 1975b, Schwartz and Perantoni 1975). It has been suggested that DHEA may act as an antipromotor of cancer, whose loss might make cells more prone to transformation and dedifferentiation (Schwartz, personal communication).

If aging is not due to a lack of some type of hormone, then it might be due to its presence. A. V. Everitt and others have presented an impressive argument that most hormones of the anterior pituitary, thyroid, adrenal cortex, and gonads either accelerate physiological aging or increase the incidence of age-related pathology in the kidney and cardiovascular system (Everitt and Burgess 1976). Some of the major support for this hypothesis is from experiments showing that hypophysectomy reduces the secretion of these hormones and retards aging.

V. M. Dilman (1971, 1976, 1979) proposed that intrinsic age-dependent changes occur in the hypothalamus, which slowly increases its threshold to hormonal feedback suppression. He has suggested that it is this time-dependent graded elevation of threshold sensitivity to feedback suppression that leads to the timing of the program of normal growth and development. However, continual elevation of the threshold throughout life (an overrunning of the genetic program of development) causes alteration in reproduction and adaptive homeostasis. A normal functional condition can be maintained for a short period of time by compensatory oversecretion of hormones, but finally this leads to "diseases of compensation." Examples of these are obesity, prediabetes, adult-onset diabetes mellitus, atherosclerosis and hypertension, lower resistance to infection, and some forms of cancer. Like Everitt, Dilman is proposing that the continuation of the neuroendocrine program of development beyond sexual maturation leads to oversecretion of hormones and to many of the age-related diseases. And why would this program continue, when such continuation would result in decreased health for the animal? An answer may be that the animal in the wild would normally be killed by natural causes much before these endogenous effects are evident.

Experiments are now being carried out to extend life-span according to the above hypothesis by developing drugs to reduce the compensatory reactions (Dilman 1976). Although no significant extension with such drugs has yet been reported, nutritional restriction (which is a form of dietary hypophysectomy) and removal of the pituitary are known to extend the maximum life-span potential of rats.

There is also some evidence suggesting that hormones associated with development and maturation may be of a harmful pleiotropic nature. Five species of Pacific salmon are known to die shortly after spawning (Robertson 1961, Robertson and Wexler 1960). The cause of death is related to the very high levels of adrenal corticosteroids resulting from adrenal cortical hypertrophy. Senescence of the salmon can be prevented by castration before maturation. These castrated fish then go on living more than twice the normal life-span. A similar effect is found for the European eel if it is prevented from returning to the sea (Lekholm 1939). Also, removal of the optic gland of the octopus has been found to increase its life-span substantially (Wodinsky 1977).

C. Finch has also proposed that age-related changes after sexual maturation occur result from an extension of the neural and endocrine mechanisms that control earlier development (Finch 1976). He has organized an impressive argument suggesting that time-dependent changes in neural, endocrine, and target-tissue interactions can lead to senescence by creating an imbalance of proper neuroendocrine control processes. In effect this would create a so-called regulatory cascade of hormonal imbalance, much in the same manner as suggested by Dilman and Everitt. The major criticism I find with Finch's hypothesis is that he has failed to describe a specific mechanism that could lead initially to the regulatory cascade and also why different species have different maximum life-span potentials.

If aging is due to an increasingly imbalanced neuroendocrine system, then how might one restore this balance and thus increase life-span? One of the most striking findings in the aging mouse is the progressive imbalance between dopaminergic and colinergic tones (Finch 1977). These observations closely resemble those seen in Parkinson's disease, which has often been called an accelerated aging phenomenon (Horita 1977). Dopaminergic drugs such as levodopa have been used to treat Parkinson's disease. It has been found that high concentrations of levodopa, when given to mice in their diet, extended fertility and prolonged the mean life-span by about 50% (Cotzias et al. 1974, 1977). However, in these experiments, unusually short-lived mice were used, which is a common problem in many life-span extension experiments. Levodopa has also prolonged the lives of patients with Parkinson's disease in comparison to persons with the disease prior to the advent of levodopa (Cotzias et al. 1977).

Rats placed on a tryptophan-deficient diet (an essential amino acid) early in their life were retarded in growth rate and the time required to reach the age of sexual maturation (Segall and Timiras 1975, 1976). After 17–28 months of age, the rats were returned to a tryptophan-present diet, where they gained weight and grew to normal size. These rats were then fertile and had superior thermoregulatory response compared with the control animals of the same chronological age. Noting that the neurotransmitter serotonin is synthesized with tryptophan as a precursor, these experiments suggest that a decrease in the rate of the neuroen-docrine program of development could perhaps result in life-span ex-tension (Timiras 1978).

D. Denckla and co-workers have perhaps found the most impressive means to rejuvenate and extend health in old animals (Denckla 1975). It is well known that specific metabolic rate gradually decreases with age in mammals. However, when specific metabolic rate is measured in animals of different ages with body temperature maintained at a constant level, a very dramatic drop with age becomes apparent. This means of measuring specific metabolic rate is called the *minimum oxygen con-sumption rate* and was developed by Denckla (1974). Denckla recognized that with increasing age, specific metabolic rate becomes more difficult to increase by injecting an animal with thyroxine hormone. Thus, it appeared as if old animals were slowly becoming resistant to thyroxine hormone. It is interesting in this respect that many aspects of aging do appear like a hypothyroid condition. It is also important that induction of a number of enzymes by thyroxine decreases markedly with age (Schwartz *et al.* 1979). The remarkable discovery that Denckla made was that by removing the pituitary in old rats (30 months of age) and supplementing their diet with thyroxine, a return to the normal young level (6 months of age) was seen both in minimum oxygen consumption rate and in the animals response to thyroxine. Moreover, there also appeared to be a rejuvenation of a number of physiological functions in the older animals to a level similar to young, such as the ability to reject xenografts, clear carbon from the blood, vascular relaxation, immune response, rate of hair growth, and the level of RNA synthesis (Bilder and Denckla 1977, Parker *et al.* 1978, Bolla and Denckla 1979, Scott *et al.* 1979, Miller *et al.* 1980).

Denckla has suggested that the pituitary may secrete a hormone-like factor that slowly reduces the sensitivity of cells to thyroid hormone. Aging is therefore a hypothyroid-like condition. Hypophysectomy re-moves the secretion of this thyroxine-inhibiting factor and thus rejuven-ation occurs. It is still not clear if the hypophysectomized animals have a longer life-span, but so far results at least indicate life-span is not reduced (Denckla, personal communication). Lower specific metabolic rate and retardation of development and growth cannot be used to explain the rejuvenation seen in these animals. Also, a remarkable aspect of these studies is the indication that some aspects of aging can not only be slowed down but actually are reversed to a juvenile level.

Overall, these data support the concept that, although hormones are necessary for life, they may also have long-term adverse effects. The problem now appears to be the identification of the most harmful effects of these hormones and to determine whether a decrease in these levels is both desirable and possible. Hypophysectomy and castration are, of course, very crude means to effect such a decrease, but perhaps more direct types of chemical control will be found.

Although the neuroendocrine system appears to be importantly involved in the aging process, how would the involvement of this system explain the evolution of longevity, considering that most mammals have a common spectrum of hormones? Do longer-lived species have some type of protective factor against the long-term adverse effects of these hormones? It may be so, but there is also another possibility. As noted before, longevity appears to be closely related to duration of growth and development. Thus, one way of effectively eliminating the harmful side effect of a hormone at age 7, for example, when sexual maturation may occur, is to postpone maturation until 14 years of age. Support for a decrease in overall rate of development as a natural means of life-span extension is found in the good correlation found in the primate species between length of development time and maximum life-span potential (Cutler 1978b). It could be that there is no easily available protection against the pleiotropic harmful effects of development other than its simple postponement. In this respect, it is also of interest to note that the continuous growth rate of astrocytes throughout life may have long-term detrimental effects on proper brain function (see Lynch and Gerline, this volume). Accordingly, the rate of growth of the central nervous system also appears to be proportionally slowed down in animal species having slower rates of aging and thus longer maximum life-span potentials. This would serve as another good example of a developmental process necessary for early life but detrimental in later life, whose harmful effects were postponed by a decrease in rate of development of the entire organism, including the development of the nervous system.

Reversibility of Aging

As we have seen, a popular concept of aging is that it is a result of some type of age-dependent accumulation of damage caused by toxic by-products of metabolism or development. For example, metabolic by-products (such as the hydroxyl radical) could act to destroy membranes, chromatin, and other critical cellular components, leading to serious cellular impairment and/or cell death. The implication of such a hypothesis is that the aging process is probably irreversible, since the type of damage being accumulated would be considered to be of the irreparable type, otherwise it would not have been able to accumulate. On the other hand, we could postulate that the damage is reparable if only the cells had sufficient repair levels. Here, the net accumulation of damage would be viewed as a result of overwhelming the protective and repair systems of a cell. As yet, there is still no good evidence that cells do accumulate damage with age of a sufficient magnitude to account for the aging of the organism. Another difficulty is distinguishing what is genuine cell damage and what might be changes due to dedifferentiation or epigenetic mechanisms, which may be of either benefit or harm to the organism.

The most well-known altered components of a cell that have been said to accumulate with age are the abnormal proteins described by Gershon and his co-workers (Gershon *et al.* 1976). An age-dependent increase in the amount of such abnormal proteins having less specific activity has been reported to occur in mouse and nematodes. These altered proteins are suggested to be the result of a post-translational modification process consisting of an oxidation of the methionine residues forming methionine sulfoxide. The age-dependent increase in the amount of these altered proteins has been suggested to be the result of an age-dependent decrease in a specific protein repair system, such as methionize sulfoxide reductase (Gershon *et al.* 1976, Reiss and Gershon 1978, Reiss 1979). Certainly, if a great number of proteins were undergoing such structural modification, this would contribute to general cellular dysfunction. However, it appears that most enzymes do not appear to decrease in specific activity with age (Finch 1972). Moreover, the existence of abnormal proteins in older animals has not yet been confirmed by other laboratories, and in fact a number of recent reports have failed to confirm Gershon's findings (Weber *et al.* 1976, Petell and Lebherz 1979). Their existence must await further experimental work.

As already noted, Finch has presented a good argument that much of the aging of an organism may be due to small regional changes in the neuroendocrine control centers of the brain. He emphasizes that most of the other areas of the body (nonendocrine tissues) are either not aged endogenously or are aged due to extracellular neuroendocrine factors (Finch 1976). Important to his argument is the return of fertility in old mice and rats, such as the demonstration that progesterone can reactivate ovulatory cycles (Eskin 1978). Also, the experiments of Denckla and co-workers (Denckla 1975) have shown that hypophysectomized old animals return to a young level in terms of a number of physiological and cellular factors, indicating that some type of rejuvenation may be taking place. Some aspects of these rejuvenation experiments have recently been repeated in C57BL/6J mice by D. Harrison (personal communication). In addition, old hypophysectomized animals have shown a remarkable level of return to the condition of a young animal in terms of a number of morphological and cellular factors (Johnson and Cutler 1980). Thus, we should not be too confident that aging is the result of an accumulation of irreversible damage or that at least some aspects of aging are not reversible.

The possible epigenetic or dedifferentiated nature of aging has not received much attention as yet. Briefly, this hypothesis states that the state of differentiation arrived at after the last stages of development are complete in the young animal is inherently unstable (Cutler 1978b, 1979, Tolmasoff *et al.* 1980). Instead, a positive effort or biological cost has been postulated to be required for the maintenance of the differentiated state of cells. For human beings, selective pressure would act to maintain this positive effort to preserve the differentiated state of cells up to about 30–40 years of age. After this, age-selective pressure would decrease and a slow random-like dedifferentiation of cells would be predicted to occur, giving rise to the aging process. It is suggested that the rate of dedifferentiation would be determined by the mean level of mutational and/or epigenetic-like alterations of the cell's genetic apparatus. This is illustrated in the following diagram.

| (Net rate of damage input) $\longrightarrow$ | Mean mutational and/or epigenetic load in genetic apparatus | (Net rate of damage removed) $\longrightarrow$ |

The initial rate of damage input would be determined by the organism's overall specific metabolic rate and the stage of development. (The stage of development is important in view of possible hormonal effects on genetic susceptibility to perturbations.) The net rate of damage input is determined by the initial rate of damage input minus the many possible protective and scavenging processes that exist in cells and act to lower the damage input. Examples of such processes are superoxide dismutase, glutathione peroxidase, and catalase (Tolmasoff *et al.* 1980). The net rate of damage removed would be determined by the kind and extent of genetic repair processes present and level of damage that exists at a given instant of time in the genetic apparatus.

In this model, all genetic damage is assumed to be reparable and an equilibrium state is assumed to exist. At equilibrium, damage input equals damage output, and there is a net mutational/epigenetic alterational load in the genetic apparatus that is constantly turning over, but whose average magnitude remains constant over the life-span of the animal. The probability that critical dedifferentiated events occur is then postulated to be proportional to this turnover rate. These dedifferentiated events are not likely to be reversible because, although they were initially created by genetic alterations that are reparable, they are maintained after the genetic damage has been removed. For example, different states of dedifferentiation of mammalian tissue culture cells can be induced by mutagenic agents. These new differentiated states are stable in following cell generations, but frequently no mutations in the DNA can be found. It is predicted from this model that longer-lived species carry a small net mutational/epigenetic alterational load in their cells as a result of higher levels of repair and protective processes and/or a lower specific metabolic rate and a slower overall rate of differentiation and development. These cells would then have an overall lower time-dependent probability to dedifferentiate, and thus a longer life-span would result.

Experimental support for this hypothesis has been found in the age-dependent relaxation of gene repression. For example, an age-dependent derepression of globin genes is found in the mouse and the human brain and for a c-type endogenous virus (MuLV) in mice (Ono and Cutler 1978, Florine et al. 1980). Also, indirect support is found in the dedifferentiated nature of many types of cancer (an age-related disease), in autoimmune diseases, and in a number of age-related slow virus diseases (Pitot and Heidelberger 1963, Manes 1979). Further support for this hypothesis is found in that longer-lived species appear to have higher levels of DNA repair (Hart and Setlow 1974) and more effective means to detoxify mutagenic agents (Schwartz 1975a, Schwartz and Moore 1977), and recently we have found an excellent correlation between the endogenous level of superoxide dismutase activity per specific metabolic rate and maximum life-span potential of primate species (Tolmasoff et al. 1980).

One of the main implications of this hypothesis is that, simply because brain cells are known to change their morphology with age (such as losing dendrites)(Bondareff 1979) and liver cells to have a decrease in the number of hormone receptors with age (Roth 1979), it does not necessarily mean this is the result of some type of intracellular accumulation of damage or impairment. Instead it could be a result of dedifferentiation. Thus, the cells from old animals may have no accumulated damage and may be completely normal in terms of basic vital cellular function. In terms of reversal of aging in this model, the problem appears much more difficult. Here, emphasis would be placed on prevention rather than on reversal methods.

Reduction of Toxic By-Products of Metabolism

The relatively constant amount of total calories consumed over the life-span by different mammalian species has strongly suggested that the aging rate is somehow related to metabolic rate (Rubner 1908, Pearl 1928, Sacher 1959, Cutler 1978b, Totter 1980). Extension of the life-span by lowering metabolic rate, decreasing body temperature, or undergoing periodic states of torpor and hibernation support this concept. An obvious question then is, what are the harmful by-products of metabolism or heat generation that could be responsible for aging?

By-products of oxygen metabolism have been intensely studied. There is now much evidence that a substantial number of free radicals are produced *in vivo* and that these agents can produce damage (Pryor 1976, Fridovich 1978, Totter 1980). However, most evidence is indirect. One of the most studied reactions that may be initiated by free radicals is lipid peroxidation (Tappel 1978). Many cellular components such as mitochondria and microsomal membranes contain relatively large amounts of polyunsaturated fatty acids that are subject to lipid peroxidation destruction. Lipid peroxidation may also lead to the formation of fluorescent, ceroid, and lipofuscin pigments, which are known to accumulate with age in the tissues of a number of animals. In addition to membrane peroxidation, a number of other normal reactions found in cells are known to produce hydrogen peroxide and the superoxide radical, which can then lead to the *in vivo* formation of the hydroxyl radical (Fridovich 1978). This radical is well known for its general toxicity to cells.

Only recently has it been recognized that cells have a number of repair and protective processes that appear to exist specifically to counteract by-products of metabolically produced toxic agents (Cutler 1972, Pryor 1976, Fridovich 1978, Leibovitz and Siegel 1980). For example, some protective enzymes against the superoxide radical and hydrogen peroxide are catalase, glutathione peroxidase, and superoxide dismutase as well as possibly vitamins C and E. In addition, there is a number of DNA repair systems that may not only be important in protecting cells from external radiation injury but also perhaps are even more important in repairing damage produced by endogenously generated damaging agents (Cutler 1972, Hart and Trosko 1976, Trosko and Chang 1978, Totter 1980).

Considering the large number of complex biochemical reactions present within a typical cell, it would be surprising indeed if there were not side-reactions that are of a harmful pleiotropic nature; that is, they have both an advantageous role and also a long-term, low-level detrimental effect. Perhaps the production of free radicals through oxygen metabolism is only a small fraction of the harmful agents that are constantly being generated within a cell. We are also becoming aware that much of the natural food as well as the processed food we eat is not entirely free of some type of low-level toxic action. Thus, it is not surprising to learn that animals have evolved specialized detoxification systems to handle the particular assortment of food a certain species eats (Conney 1967, Boyland and Chasseaud 1969).

Much of the human diet today is different from that of 10,000–20,000 years ago, and so perhaps we do not have the proper detoxification systems to handle some of these foods. Moreover, we have recently introduced insecticides and other potentially harmful chemicals and radiation hazards into our environment that may have long-term detrimental effects on both human and other forms of life. Many of these unnatural compounds may not be detoxified and, in fact, some are even known to be made more toxic, as evidenced by the metabolic activation of a number of precarcinogenic agénts (Hathway 1966, Sims and Grover 1974, Miller 1978). If aging is normally caused in part by incomplete detoxification of metabolic products, then it is possible that, due to the above mentioned changes in our diet and environment, our innate aging rate has increased slightly.

It is becoming clear that an essential aspect of life maintenance is the damage and/or epigenetic changes produced by the presence of toxic agents normally generated *in vivo* as by-products of essential metabolic reactions. The extent this type of changes occurs and the role repair and protective systems may play in governing the onset frequency of specific diseases such as cancer are now being investigated in a number of laboratories (Apffel 1976, Dix and Cohen 1980, Totter 1980). A relatively new question raised, concerning the topic of this chapter, is what relevance do these toxic by-products and the constitutive levels of related repair and protective processes have to general health maintenance and life-span, not just to specific diseases? Could it be that the extent of good health an animal species has is largely a matter of the degree to which repair and protective processes have evolved to protect an organism against its own endogenous production of toxic by-products?

Evidence for the possible relation between *in vivo* free radical levels and health would be the effect of antioxidants on life-span. Experimental results have been mixed and often confusing because of insufficient controls (Tappel 1968, Sacher 1977, Clemens and Fuller 1978). The antioxidants showing the most impressive effects are 2-mercaptoethylamine (2-MEA), a radioprotective agent; butylated hydroxytoluene (BHT), a food preservative; and ethoxyquin, a liver detoxifying agent (Harman 1978). These agents were added to the food of mice and were found to produce an increase in the mean life-span of about 20–30%. Greater life-span extension was found in shorter-lived species having high tumor incidence, as AKR and C3H mouse strains, but life-span extension was also found for the long-lived mouse strain, LAF_1. Antioxidants were also effective in increasing the life-span of *Drosophila* by about 20%, and vitamin E increased the life-span of the nematode by about 30%. For the *Drosophila* and nematode, an increase in both mean and maximum life-span was found (Harman 1978).

It is also of interest that antioxidants in the diet of mice or rats appear to have a significant effect in reducing cancer onset frequency and/or reducing the effects of a carcinogenic agent (Shamberger 1970, Wattenberg et al. 1977, Harman 1978). For example, butylated hydroxyanisol (BHA) and ethoxyquin inhibited the carcinogenicity of benz(a)propane (BP) and 7,12-dimethylbenz(a)-anthracene (DMBA) of the forestomach of mice.

These results are not free of controversy. Massie et al. (1976) report that ascorbic acid (vitamin C, and presumably an important antioxidant), at 0.001 M concentration in the drinking water of Drosophila, decreased life-span. Tappel et al. (1973) studied the effects of vitamins C and E, BHT, selenium, and methionine on the life-span of CD-1 mice. Although the rate of accumulation of fluorescent products (age pigments) was reduced, no increase in life-span was found. Kohn (1971) found that, when BHT and 2-MEA were given to the long-lived mouse strain C57BL/6J, the aging rate of the mice was unaffected. It was noted that antioxidants in the diet appear more important when survival of the animal was less than optimum. Further complicating the interpretation of life-span extension by antioxidant diets is the fact that the animals do not eat as well, are smaller, and have a slower rate of growth. Thus, some of the life-span extension found could be largely a restricted nutritional effect.

A very interesting model system used to study the effect of antioxidants has been the recessive mutant of Neurospora crassa called "natural death" (Munkres and Colvin 1976, Munkres and Minssen 1976, Munkres 1976a, 1976b). This mutant slowly undergoes a decreasing clonal growth potential under all nutritional conditions and eventually stops growing and dies. The primary molecular defect is not known, but much evidence suggests that this strain is deficient in a protective process against lipid auto-oxidation reactions. Evidence supporting this suggestion is that the life-span of the clone can be increased up to 80% by addition of dietary antioxidants or selenite. The senescing clones also accumulate a green fluorescent pigment in situ, and dietary antioxidant nordihydroguaiaretic acid prevents this accumulation. This green pigment has the spectral properties of lipofuscin, an end product of lipid auto-oxidation. It was also found that the mutant has higher than wild-type levels of superoxide dismutase, glutathione peroxidase, and glutathione reductase, indicating that perhaps these enzymes have been induced to higher levels in a attempt to correct the defect. This conclusion is supported by adding cumene hydroperoxide at sublethal concentrations to the wild-type Neurospora. After a period of time, the wild-type Neurospora was found to have unusually high levels of superoxide dismutase, glutathione peroxidase, and glutathione reductase. Moreover, the antioxidant nordi-hydroguaiaretic acid protects unadapted cells from this induction.

These data suggest that, similar to the DNA repair mutants found in bacteria and mammalian cells, there also exist mutants defective in protection against endogenously produced free radicals. Also, as with DNA repair mutants, a defect in this protective system can lead to accelerated aging and death of an organism. These data support both the existence of significant levels of free radicals *in vivo* and the essential role free radical protective processes may have in minimizing their harmful effects.

The age-dependent accumulation of age pigments is well known in many animals, particularly in heart and brain tissues. These pigments are called ceroid, chromalipoid, wear-and-tear pigment, yellow pigment, and, most commonly, lipofuscin (Strehler 1977). Lipofuscin is detected usually by its fluorescent properties, and good evidence has been presented that it is a product of lipid auto-oxidation (Tappel 1968, 1973, 1978). The rate of accumulation of lipofuscin appears to vary in proportion to the general aging rate of an animal, although few of these types of comparative studies have been undertaken. In a human being, with a maximum life-span potential of about 100 years, the rate of accumulation is about three times slower in the cerebellum, as with Rhesus, with a maximum life-span potential of about 35 years (Ordy and Brizzee 1975). It is not clear if lipofuscin pigment interferes with proper cell function, but much evidence suggests that it may at least be a good indicator of the degree of lipid peroxidation taking place within a cell, which in turn is related to cellular aging rate.

The housefly has an unusually high specific metabolic rate and would be expected to be highly dependent on protective processes against harmful oxygen metabolic by-products. Fluorescent age pigments are found to increase with age in the fly, as in other animals (Strehler 1977). However, when the flies are restrained in flight activity (by being placed in small containers), it was found that oxygen consumption and the rate of accumulation of pigment decreased proportionally (Sohal and Donato 1978). Moreover, the flies were found to live about twice as long in terms of maximum life-span potential. Also, the amount of age pigment reached at the end of the life-span for the longer-lived flies was equal to that of the shorter-lived flies; only the rate of accumulation of pigment was different.

These data further support the concept that the aging rate is directly related to the rate of oxygen consumption (specific metabolic rate) and the innate level of protection an organism may have against the harmful by-products of oxygen metabolism. For the housefly, if the rate of metabolism is decreased by restraining flight activity, then for a given level of protection (assumed to be unchanged and independent of flight activity), life-span is correspondingly longer.

Centrophenoxine is a drug that has been used in human beings to help presenile and senile confused states. This drug has been found to decrease brain lipofuscin pigmentation in guinea pigs and rats, but the mechanism of action is unknown. There are also reports that this drug does prolong the mean life-span of *Drosophila* (Sun and Samorojski 1973) and mice (Sun and Samorojski 1975, Sun and Seaman 1977).

There is evidence that a human disease may be caused by an inherited defect in protection against free radicals and lipid peroxidation. Patients with the Batten–Spielmeyer–Vogt (BSV) syndrome show losses of up to 50% of normal brain weight and substantial increase in lipofuscin pigment (Zeman 1974). The accumulation of pigment is related to the intensity of the disease. Persons with BSV syndrome have shown some improvement when given a combination of antioxidants, including vitamins C and E, butylated hydroxytoluene, ethoxyquin, and D-methionine.

Lipid peroxidation has the potential to disrupt many organelles, such as liposomes and perioxisomes (Tappel 1978). Addition of protective agents that would stabilize membranes against the lipid peroxidants would be another avenue of protection (Bender *et al.* 1970, Kormendy and Bender 1971a, 1971b, Hochschild 1973). A number of membrane-stabilizing agents were given in the diet of *Drosophila* and were found to increase mean life-span. Further studies with the long-lived mouse strain C57BL/6J, however, showed less effect. The membrane stabilizer dimethylaminoethyl *p*-chlorophenoxyacetate was the most effective for both flies and mice, increasing mean life-span about 30%. These experiments were complicated by the apparently toxic side-effects of these agents, and so much of the potential antiaging effect might have been masked.

If, indeed, there are toxic metabolic by-products of metabolism that are important in determining the innate life-span and aging rate of an animal, then longer-lived species should have higher levels of protection and repair processes against these by-products (Cutler 1972, 1976b, 1980b). This prediction has been confirmed in a few specific cases. The first support for this prediction was the correlation found between the extent of DNA excision repair and the maximum life-span potential of mammalian species (Hart and Setlow 1974 and J. Regan, personal communication). Later, it was found that a good inverse correlation exists between the level of activation of polycyclic hydrocarbons, precarcinogenic agents such as dimethylbenz(a)anthracene (DMBA), and maximum life-span potential of mammalian species (Schwartz 1975a, Schwartz and Moore 1977, Moore and Schwartz 1978). Thus, longer-lived species appear to activate potential carcinogens (and perhaps many other mutagenic agents) less readily than short-lived species. Recently, in our own laboratory, we found a good linear correlation between the ratio of superoxide dismutase specific activity per specific metabolic rate and maximum life-span potential in the liver, brain, and heart tissues of 2 rodent and 12 primate species (Tolmasoff *et al.* 1980). This latter correlation implies that the level of protective enzymes against oxygen toxicity is directly proportional to the total calorie consumption of a species over its life-span. Human beings, having the highest total life-span calorie consumption of 800 kc/g, compared with chimpanzees, having 400 kc/g, have in direct proportion a higher level of superoxide dismutase activity in the tissues per unit specific metabolic rate.

An age-dependent increase of collagen cross-linkage and insolubility has been found in many tissues (Kohn 1978, Comfort 1979). The early physico-chemical changes in the properties of collagen are likely to be a result of development, but later life changes could be a result of various metabolic by-products having cross-linkage properties (Bjorksten 1977). The biological effect of increased collagen cross-linkage in tissues might be an inhibition in the rate of diffusion of nutrients from capillary blood vessels to the cell. To examine this hypothesis, cross-linkage inhibitors were given to mice. These inhibitors are called lathyrogens, and some that have been used are b-aminopropionitrile (BAPN) and D-penicillimine. Kohn and Leash (1967) gave BAPN to rats but failed to observe any life-span extension. However, La Bella and Vivian (1978) gave BAPN to LAF/J mice for up to 18 months and found an increase in mean survival of about 2 months over the 33-month survival for the controls. Little change was noted in rate of growth or body weight.

Taken together, the general concept that aging rate is somehow related to metabolic rate appears to be gaining support. We are learning that there are many *in vivo*-produced toxic agents and corresponding counteracting protective and repair processes. Some of the more important toxic agents are related to oxygen metabolism and are involved in the production of oxidative radicals, which can produce a broad range of damage, including lipid peroxidation. Antioxidants and membrane-stabilizing agents have had only limited success in extending life-span, but clearly some experiments are impressive.

Most impressive, however, is the relatively new concept that the aging rate of mammalian species might be governed to a substantial degree by the constitutive level of protective and repair processes. If true, this concept could open up an entirely new field of medical research concerned with understanding the general biological nature of health maintenance and the determination of aging rate.

Immunological System

The immune system is essential for maintenance of health by minimizing foreign constituents in the body and is therefore a protective process of life functions. There are two major means by which age-related dysfunctions of the immune system are known to occur (Walford 1969, 1974, Yunis and Greenberg 1974, Makinodan 1979). One is an age-related decrease in the efficiency of humoral and cellular immune response capacities; the other is an increase in the autoimmune response. It is not yet clear whether these two types of dysfunctions are related to the same causative mechanism or if one might give rise to the other. It is interesting that the age-related dysfunction of the immune system appears to represent a harmful pleiotropic side effect of an essential life support system similar to the postulated long-term harmful pleiotropic side effects of metabolism and development.

Many of the major diseases associated with aging can be accounted for by the two mentioned dysfunctions of the immune system (Walford 1969, Yunis and Greenberg 1974). In particular, the types of dysfunctions associated with a low-grade graft–host reaction (autoimmune disease) are remarkably similar to many normally occurring age-related diseases in human beings. In addition, it is clear that the immune system plays a major role in our defense against cancer (Jose and Good 1973a). Thus, the age-related decrease in the functional capacity of the immune system and the associated increase in onset frequency of many diseases, including cancer, strongly suggest a causative role.

It is yet to be determined just how primary the age-related dysfunctions of the immune system are to aging. If it were possible to eliminate completely the age-related dysfunctions of the immune system, it would be important to know what changes in health maintenance and longevity would be found. Would the aging rate be substantially slowed down or would the onset frequency of a selected spectrum of diseases just be decreased slightly? There is evidence that athymic mice (with essentially no immune function) have a normal life-span when living in a germ-free environment. If prolongation of the functional life-span of the immune system leads to prolongation of general health and life-span, then this evidence would strongly imply an important role for the immune system in aging.

It is also important to determine what role the immune system may play in governing the different maximum life-span potentials we find for the mammalian species. Is the immune system in human beings, for example, somehow superior in qualitative features and by this mechanism does it provide better protection for human beings than, say, for the chimpanzee? And why is it that the rate of dysfunctions of the immune system appears to be correlated with the rate of aging of the different mammalian species (Makinodan 1977)? Could it be that the life maintenance processes operating in human beings ensuring longer functional life-span for the organs such as liver, brain, and heart are also the same life maintenance processes providing a longer period of functional life-span for the immune system? Or is the aging of the immune system not directly related to the aging of other organs but instead is an independent primary pacesetter of aging?

Although the immune system is extremely complex, much progress has been made in understanding its basic operation. From this knowledge, several lines of experiments have been developed to extend the functional life-span of the immune system. Restricted nutrition studies of rats and mice have now clearly shown that increased immune function can be extended toward the later years of life (Cooper and Good 1971, Jose and Good 1973b, Jose et al. 1973, Gerbase-DeLima et al. 1975, Walford 1975, Fernandes et al. 1978). For example, in experiments done by Walford and co-workers (Gerbase-DeLima et al. 1975, Weindruch et al. 1979), mice kept on an intermittent fasting diet underwent a delayed maturation of immune response, but the immune system then stayed "young" longer into later age. Such restricted nutrition also leads to longer maximum life-span potential. Here, the restricted nutritional diet was mild, for the animals were only slightly underweight, and life-span extension was about 20%. Similar restricted nutrition studies by Good and co-workers (Cooper and Good 1971, Jose and Good 1973b, Jose et al. 1973, Fernandes et al. 1978) have shown a substantial increase in the older animal's resistance to cancer. This may be a result of the diet-restricted animal's not developing a serum-blocking antibody that may inhibit cell-mediated immune destruction of a tumor.

Lowering body temperature of fish may extend life-span by reducing the autoimmune reaction of later life (Liu and Walford 1975, Walford et al. 1969). Thus, life extension effects of restricted nutrition and of lowered body temperature appear to have their optimum effects at opposite extremes of the life-span. Restricted nutrition is most effective during early life, and lower body temperature during later life. Perhaps one delays the immunodeficiency of normal aging, and the other prolongs the development of autoimmunity (Liu and Walford 1975).

Another means used to restore the immune system has been cell grafts (Good and Bach 1974, Kay and Makinodan 1976, Makinodan 1977, 1979, Walford et al. 1977). Here, immunocompetent cells are grafted from young to old individuals. Thymus, spleen, lymphoids, and bone marrow grafts have been used as well as different combinations. The life-spans of unusually short-lived mice, such as the hypophysectomized dwarf mouse and the NZB mouse, have been considerably extended. For longer-lived mice, the results were not encouraging. However, it has been found that the combined grafts of thymus and stem cells can restore a number of immunological functions of old mice to levels equal to or even exceeding those of young mice (Hirokawa *et al.* 1976, D. Harrison personal communication).

Splenectomy of longer-lived BC3F1 mice at 2 years of age can increase the mean life-span of this strain almost twofold (Makinodan 1977). However, this operation appears to prevent onset of reticular cell sarcoma, which the strain usually dies of, and is not a decrease in the aging rate.

Immunosuppressant drugs to reduce the onset of autoimmune disease have not been too effective (Peter *et al.* 1975). Imuran and cyclophosphomide have been used to reduce autoimmune reaction and to extend foreign graft survival, but these agents had only marginal life extension effects on long-lived mice. This may be in part due to the toxic side effects of these drugs. Mercaptoethanol has been reported to increase the sheep red blood cell response of long-lived old mice to the level of young adult mice (Kay and Makinodan 1976). This drug may act by influencing cyclic nucleotide metabolism of the T and/or B-type cells. Other immunostimulating agents that might prove effective in older animals are polynucleotides. Braun *et al.* (1970) have reported that double-stranded poly(A:U) increased response to sheep red blood cells in middle-aged mice.

A number of hormones have recently been discovered that appear to be required for normal production, maturation, and differentiation of T cells (Kent 1977a). At least seven different hormones or hormone-like factors have been isolated, including thymosin, thymopoietin I and II, thymic humoral factor (THF), thymus activity serum, lymphocyte-stimulating hormone, homeostasis thymus hormone, and thymic hypocalcemic factor (T^1 and T^2). The most studied of these factors is thymosin (Goldstein *et al.* 1974). This factor has been shown to prevent or substantially improve many dysfunctions associated with the immune system. So far, this factor has been most effective in animals and human beings in which thymosin is known to be deficient. There is, however, evidence that thymosin decreases with normal aging. To date, there are no reports of life-span extension in normally long-lived experimental animals that have been given any of the thymus hormones.

From these studies, it is clear that (*a*) the dysfunctions of the immune system are importantly involved in the disease-associated aging process and (*b*) that both reduction of disease frequency and prolongation of life-span can be obtained in the range of 10–30% by methods that operate to prolong the functional life-span of the immune system. In particular, bone marrow–thymus transplants and the administration of thymus factors appear promising. Thus, life-span extension by way of cellular engineering to correct for primary immunodeficiency, whether related to aging or to specific inherited disease, is highly probable in the future (Good and Bach 1974, Walford *et al.* 1977, Makinodan 1979).

Miscellaneous Drugs and Treatments

A relatively new area in the neurophysiology of aging is beginning to emerge, which might be called "geriatric neuropharmacology." Many so-called psychotropic drugs are presently being used to treat neuropsychiatric disorders in the elderly, particularly those patients with symptoms of "organic brain syndrome." The present approach has been mainly a matter of an educated guess of what drug or drug derivative might prove beneficial. Much emphasis has been placed on neurotransmitters such as acetylcholine, norepinephrine, dopamine, 5-hydroxytryptomine, λ-aminobutyric acid, and glycine (Horita 1977). Of these, acetylcholine and the biogenic amines such as dopamine and norepinephrine show the most promise for an important role in organic brain syndrome treatments. As this field develops, it will be of considerable interest to learn what effects these treatments will have on life-span extension. We have already seen that life-span extension can be obtained by L-dopa administration, and perhaps further efforts along these lines to reestablish a more youthful balance between the various neuroendocrine factors in the brain will make it possible to extend life-span significantly (Finch 1976).

A substantial amount of papers and publicity has been associated with the drug Gerovital, which is a special formulation of procaine (Kent 1976). This drug is claimed to have a very wide range of therapeutic values, ranging from a general antidepressant to increasing life-span for experimental animals (Ostfeld *et al.* 1977, Clemens and Fuller 1978). The validity of these claims is controversial, and the mechanism of its possible action is not clear. It has been suggested that Gerovital acts as an inhibitor of monoamine oxidase, but even this has been challenged (Clemens and Fuller 1978).

Ergoline derivatives have been used with more success in geriatric medicine. One of the more popular drugs is Hydergine, which is made up of a number of ergot alkaloids and is used to treat mental disturbance in the elderly (Hughes *et al.* 1976). In a number of well-designed tests with this drug, patients having symptoms associated with dementia have shown improvement, although the magnitude was not great. The mechanism of action of Hydergine is not known, but it has been suggested to improve blood flow to the brain and to reduce hypertension by its alpha-blocking properties. Another possible mechanism is that many ergoline derivatives are known to stimulate dopamine receptors, so perhaps Hydergine works in this manner (Corrodi *et al.* 1973).

Drugs that improve memory even in young adults have been used in the treatment of memory loss in the elderly. Piracetam (2-pyrrolidone-acetamide) has shown an enhancement of alertness, asthenia, and psychomotor agitation (Stegink 1972). Physotigmine, an acetylcholenesterase inhibitor, has shown an enhancement of both storage and retrieval of information in normal male subjects 19 years of age (Davis *et al.* 1978). Its effects on the elderly are not yet known.

Because of the large market for drugs that can be used in geriatric medicine, we will probably see a rapid increase in the number of these drugs becoming available for treatment of mental disorders of the elderly. Although Gerovital treatment has little beneficial value, drugs like Hydergine, Piracetam, and Physotigmine may be on the right track if they correct neurotransmitter imbalance, which is thought to underlie many basic aging processes. Thus, development along these lines may lead to extended maximum life-span potential, although this was not the reason why these drugs were developed.

More radical treatments that have been used for reducing the disabilities of old age are hyperbaric oxygen treatment (Martin 1974) and cell therapy (Kent 1977b). There is little if any good evidence that these treatments are beneficial. There are also a number of special diets that include antioxidants and large doses of vitamins, periodic fasting, reduced levels of protein, and even the advocacy of high levels of nucleic acids (Frank 1976), all of which claim to increase the general health of the aged. Such diets may have some merit, however others may actually be harmful.

Radical surgical operations have been proposed for life extension, such as comprehensive organ transplants. Even the transplantation of a complete head of an older person to a young recipient may become technically possible in the future, although it may not be advisable.

There is no drug or other treatment that I am aware of today that clearly and significantly prolongs health of life-span beyond its normal duration for humans. Yet, today there is much interest and experimentation to maintain general health. Unfortunately, many of the ideas and experimentation are overly optimistic and fail to consider the difficulties involved.

Enhancement of Endogenous Anti-Aging Processes

There is some evidence that low levels of stress or radiation increase life-span in insects (Ducoff 1972) and rodents (Sacher and Hart 1978). One explanation of these effects is that they might act to stimulate naturally occurring or constitutive anti-aging processes such as DNA repair systems or antioxidants to higher, more effective levels (Cutler 1978, Smith-Sonneborn 1979).

Also, stimulation of the organism's natural detoxification and repair systems, such as the mixed function oxidase system, have been reported for a number of nontoxic agents. This results in enhanced resistance to toxic and carcinogenic chemicals (Wattenberg et al. 1977, Benson et al. 1978, Montesano et al. 1979). Thus, enhancement of such natural defense and repair processes may act to lengthen life-span. This idea is supported by Smith-Sonneborn's results (1979) that life-span in *Paramecium* can be increased from about 180 to 240 fissions by treatment with UV irradiation, quickly followed by radiation with photoactivating light. Although the mechanism of how this works is not understood, the proposed hypothesis is that the UV irradiation induces a broad spectrum of repair and protective processes to remove the UV-induced damage. The cells are therefore left with little damage to repair but a higher than normal level of repair and protective processes, which presumably go on to reduce to a greater than normal extent the age-dependent accumulated damage in the cell. Similar induction of a cell's own protective and repair processes to higher than normal levels might also be the mechanism behind the alleged rejuvenation effects of hyperbaric oxygen therapy (Martin 1974), cell therapy (Kent 1977b), and nucleic acid therapy (Kent 1977c).

Other data previously noted in this review also support the hypothesis that the aging rate may be governed in part by constitutive levels of cellular repair and protective processes. These were (a) the correlation of DNA excision repair level with maximum life-span potential for a large number of mammalian species, (b) longer-lived mammals appear to activate precarcinogens at a lower rate than shorter-lived species, and (c) in primate species, there exists a good correlation between the ratio of superoxide dismutase specific activity per specific metabolic rate and life-span.

Considering how closely related genetically and biochemically the mammalian species are to one another, these data now more strongly support the hypothesis that longevity may have evolved in part by simply increasing the levels of genetic repair and protective processes. If this is true, it implies that the basic genetic information for increased health maintenance might already be within our cells, and that means only need be developed to induce its expression to even higher levels. Such enhancement of one's own genetic repair and protective processes might lead not only to an improved general maintenance of health and a longer maximum life-span potential but also to an increased resistance to many of the chemical and radiation hazards recently introduced into our environment.

In addition, when toxicity data derived from short-lived species such as rats are used to determine safe levels of environmental toxins for human beings, it appears that innate differences between the constitutive levels of genetic repair and protective processes in different species (which might be much higher in human beings than in rats) need to be taken into account.

GENETIC COMPLEXITY OF GENERAL HEALTH MAINTENANCE

As stated in the introduction of this chapter, the research being reviewed here is not aimed toward learning how to increase life-span so as to enable a person to be older longer but, instead, toward learning how a person's general health can be maintained for a longer period of time. The primary interest then is to learn of the biological nature of health maintenance, and toward this objective the aging process is studied simply because it is the major factor in general health loss. Toward this objective, the basic question being asked is, what are the key processes underlying general health maintenance and health loss? We know, for example, that a properly functioning immune system is required to preserve health, but then what preserves the immune system?

Insight into the problem of general health maintenance might be obtained through a comparative analysis of closely related mammalian species (particularly the primates) having substantial differences in maximum life-span potentials (Sacher 1959, Cutler 1972, Finch 1976, Cutler 1976a, 1978a, Sacher and Hart 1978). We find that a great range appears to exist in species' innate capacities to maintain health for a given period of time, in spite of their remarkable similarities in physiology and basic biology. For example, the human being is the longest-lived of all mammals and accordingly is able to maintain optimum performance of body functions for a greater period of time. Why is this so and how is the human being different from the chimpanzee, in view of the chimpanzee's having a maximum life-span of about one-half of the human being's and probably aging uniformly twice as fast in all physiological and mental functions. Few comparative studies have been done to answer these questions, and it is hoped that this important area of research will receive more attention in the future.

Estimations for the rate of evolution of longevity for human beings have indicated that only a few genetic changes (less than 0.6% of the genome) are likely to have been involved to uniformly prolong health (Sacher 1975, Cutler 1975a, 1975b). These genetic changes may be of a regulatory nature, acting simply to increase levels of expression of a common set of genes involved in key life maintenance processes found in all primate species (Cutler 1979, Martin 1979). In addition, Walford has presented an argument suggesting that the major histocompatibility complex (MHC) may be one of the principal genetic systems involved in controlling life-span (Smith and Walford 1977, Walford 1979, Meredith and Walford 1979, Walford and Bergmann 1979).

It is possible that the structural and regulatory genes concerned with many protective and repair processes are linked together under a few common regulatory genes in something like a ''superoperon.'' If this is true, it would be easier to understand how quickly life-span evolved in a uniform manner if a large number of enzyme levels needed to be changed. Support for this concept comes from the exciting work of Walford, who has found that mice with long life-spans have superior MHC systems and higher levels of DNA repair, and mice strains with shorter life-spans have a less effective MHC system with correspondingly less DNA repair (Walford 1979). Thus, it could be that the small segment of the chromosome making up the MHC system is where the ''super-operon'' governing aging rate resides. It would then be possible, perhaps, to find only a few key master regulatory genes within this region that need modification to extend life-span.

In this respect, it is also interesting to note that guanylate cyclase is activated by the presence of the hydroxyl free radical and may therefore be the detector of a control process that governs the proper levels of free radical antioxidants and repair processes (Mittal and Murad 1977). Support for this comes from our work showing an inverse correlation of guanylate cyclase activity with maximum life-span potential of primates. Also, Walford's group has found a significant age-dependent decrease in the ratio of cAMP/cGMP with age in mouse splenic lymphoid cells and a corresponding change in the related adenylate and guanylate cyclases (Tam and Walford 1978, Tam et al. 1979). Similar changes were found in Down's syndrome (Barnett et al. 1979). Thus, the level of the cAMP/cGMP ratio within a cell may be central to the control of a large number of different repair and protection processes. It is also known that the MHC loci is involved in governing the tissue levels of superoxide dismutase, catalase, and cAMP. We have observed that higher levels of superoxide dismutase, catalase, and cAMP correlate with longer life-span in congenic mouse strains (Cutler 1980c).

This evidence supports a limited gene involvement in health maintenance. Only a small amount of data currently support this hypothesis that a few regulatory genes may be involved in determining the aging rate. However, if this were true, then clearly prolongation of health and extended life-span may not be nearly so complex as previously thought.

SUMMARY AND CONCLUSIONS

The uniform nature of the age-dependent deteriorations that occur in human beings dictates that any significant prolongation of life-span in the future will require a uniform prolongation of general health maintenance. A unique role for gerontological research would be an inquiry into the biological nature of general health maintenance and the genetic/biochemical control of aging rate.

In view of the biological complexity of age-related loss of health, it is important to learn what, if any, success there has been in past experiments designed to increase life-span. Experimental evidence reviewed here indicates that life-span (or the aging rate) of many species, including mammals, can indeed be either shortened or extended. Most successful of these methods have been the nutritional restriction diet and the lowering of body temperature, although the antioxidant and membrane stabilization methods also seem promising. In addition, rejuvenation of the immune system by transplantation techniques and the re-establishment of possible neuroendocrine hormone balance (such as by hypophysectomy or drug therapy) indicate that many aspects of the aging process can be slowed down or even reversed.

There also appears to be no evolutionary advantage for senescence, as evidenced by the absence of senescent individuals in the population of most species living in their natural ecological niche. Thus, differences in maximum life-span potential among the mammals probably do not reflect innate biological limitations, but rather an optimum characteristic necessary for survival. Whether there is a biological limit on how long a mammal can live with its present design and constituents that make it up is not known. Thus, there appears to be no scientific basis to argue against the possibility of extending maximum life-span potential beyond its normal value.

A moderate degree of life extension in the future is likely to come first to a relatively few informed groups who will seek to optimize their nutrition, diets, and exercise. Drug therapy and methods used to lower body temperature, although indicating that life-span can be extended, will probably remain in the experimental stages for some time. The inherent problem with these methods is not only in finding out what works but also in determining what long-term side effects there might be.

The recent idea to enhance the expression of life maintenance processes that we may already have in our cells appears to hold much promise and may prove not only simpler to achieve but also much safer. The problem here is to first determine if such life maintenance processes do indeed exist, and then to learn how to enhance their expression.

It is too early to make any meaningful predictions on significant life-span extension for human beings in the near or distant future. However, if achievements found with laboratory animals are indications of what might be possible in the future, then reducing the mean aging rate of human beings to half its present value may not be too unrealistic. In spite of the aging process being extremely complex, it may very well be possible to sidestep this complexity by studying the processes governing the aging rate. These processes may be much less complex than the aging process *per se* and thus simpler to both understand and control.

In the past, it was thought that significant life-span extension was either biologically impossible or would occur only in the distant future (Neugarten and Havighurst 1977a, 1977b). This prediction is no longer tenable. In view of the life-span extension that has already been shown possible to achieve and the potential of more effective means to be developed in the future, it appears essential now to consider seriously the advisability of human life-span extension and how and to what extent such research activities should be encouraged and supported (Goldschmidt and Jillson 1975, Cutler *et al.* 1977, Cutler 1980b).

REFERENCES

Acsádi, G., and Nemeskéri, J. (1970) *History of Human Life Span and Mortality*. Budapest: Akademiai Kiado.

Andres, R., and Tobin, J. D. (1977) Endocrine system. Pp. 357–378 in C. E. Finch and L. Hayflick, eds., *Handbook of the Biology of Aging*. New York: Van Nostrand Reinhold Co.

Apffel, C. A. (1976) Nonimmunological host defenses: A review. *Cancer Research* 36:1527–1537.

Barnett, E. V., Chia, D., Fahey, J. L., Gatti, R. A., Gossett, T. C., Grossman, H., Hibrawi, H., Medici, M. A., Motola, M., Naeim, F., Sparkes, R. S., Spina, C., Tam, C. F., Van Lancker, J. L., and Walford, R. L. (1979) Immunological and biochemical studies of Down's syndrome as a model of accelerated aging. In D. Segre and L. Smith, eds., *Immunological Aspects of Aging.* New York: M. Dekker, Inc., in press.

Barrows, C. (1972) Nutrition, aging and genetic program. *American Journal of Clinical Nutrition* 25:829–833.

Barrows, C. H., and Kokkonen, G. C. (1978) Diet and life extension in animal model systems. *Age* 1:131–142.

Bender, A., Kormendy, C., and Powell, R. (1970) Pharmacological control of aging. *Experimental Gerontology* 5:97–129.

Benson, A. M., Batzinger, R. B., Ou, S. -Y. L., Bueding, E., Cha, Y. -N., and Talalay, P. (1978) Elevation of hepatic glutathione S-transferase activities and protection against mutagenic metabolites of benzo(a)pyrene by dietary antioxidants. *Cancer Research* 38:4486–4495.

Berg, B. N., and Simms, H. (1961) Nutrition and longevity in the rat. I. Food intake in relation to size, health and fertility. *Journal of Nutrition* 71:242–254.

Berg, B. N., and Simms, H. (1960) Nutrition and longevity in the rat. II. Longevity and onset of disease with different levels of food intake. *Nutrition* 71:255–263.

Berg, B. N., and Simms, H. (1961) Nutrition and longevity in the rat. III. Food restriction beyond 800 days. *Nutrition* 74:23–32.

Bilder, G. E., and Denckla, W. D. (1977) Restoration of ability to reject xenografts and clear carbon after hypophysectomy of adult rats. *Mechanisms of Ageing and Development* 6:153–163.

Bjorksten, J. (1977) Pathways to the decisive extension of the human specific life-span. *Journal of the American Geriatric Society* 25:396–399.

Bolla, R., and Denckla, W. D. (1979) Effect of hypophysectomy on liver nuclear RNA synthesis in aging rats. *Biochemistry Journal* 189:669–674.

Bondareff, W. (1979) Synaptic atrophy in the senescent hippocampus. *Mechanisms of Ageing and Development* 9:163–172.

Boyland, E., and Chasseaud, L. F. (1969) The role of glutathione and glutathione S-transferases in mercapturic acid biosynthesis. *Advances in Enzymology* 32:173–219.

Braun, W., Yajima, Y., and Ishizaka, M. (1970) Synthetic polynucleotides as restorers of normal antibody-forming capacities in aged mice. *Journal of the Reticuloendothelial Society* 7:418–424.

Carlson, A., and Hoelzel, F. (1946) Apparent prolongation of the life-span of rats by intermittent fasting. *Journal of Nutrition* 31:363–375.

Clemens, J. A., and Fuller, R. W. (1978) Chemical manipulation of some aspects of aging. Pp. 187-206 in J. Roberts, R. C. Adelman, and V. J. Christofalo, eds., *Pharmacological Intervention in the Aging Process.* New York: Plenum Press.

Comfort, A. (1979) *Aging: The Biology of Senescence.* New York: Elsevier.

Conney, A. H. (1967) Pharmacological implications of microsomal enzyme induction. *Pharmacological Reviews* 19:317–366.

Cooper, W. C., and Good, R. A. (1971) Effects of protein depletion on cell-mediated immunity. *Federation Proceedings* 30:351a.

Corrodi, H., Fuxe, K., Hokfelt, T., Lidbrink, P., and Ungerstedt, U. (1973) Effect of ergot drugs on central catecholamine neurons: Evidence for a stimulation of central dopamine neurons. *Journal of Pharmacy and Pharmacology* 25:409–412.

Cotzias, G. C., Miller, S. T., Nicholson, A. R., Maston, W. H., and Tang, L. C. (1974) Prolongation of the life-span in mice adapted to large amounts of L-dopa. *Proceedings of the National Academy of Sciences, USA* 71:2466–2470.

Cotzias, G. C., Miller, S. T., Tang, L. C., and Papavasiliou, P. S. (1977) Levodopa, fertility, and longevity. *Science* 196:549–551.

Cutler, R. G. (1972) Transcription of reiterated DNA sequence classes throughout the life-span of the mouse. Pp. 219–312 in B. L. Strehler, ed., *Advances in Gerontological Research*, Vol. 4. New York: Academic Press.

Cutler, R. G. (1975) Evolution of human longevity and the genetic complexity governing aging rate. *Proceedings of the National Academy of Sciences, USA* 72:4664–4668.

Cutler, R. G. (1976a) Evolution of longevity in primates. *Journal of Human Evolution* 5:169–204.

Cutler, R. G. (1976b) Nature of aging and life maintenance processes. Pp. 83–133 in R. G. Cutler, ed., *Interdisciplinary Topics in Gerontology* Vol. 9. Basel: S. Karger.

Cutler, R. G. (1978a) Alterations with age in the informational storage and flow systems of the mammalian cell. Pp. 464–498 in D. Bergsma, D. E. Harrison, and N. W. Paul, eds., *Genetic Effects on Aging*. New York: Alan R. Liss.

Cutler, R. G. (1978b) Evolutionary biology of senescence. Pp. 311–360 in J. A. Behnke, C. E. Finch, and G. B. Moment, eds., *The Biology of Aging*. New York: Plenum Press.

Cutler, R. G. (1979) Evolution of human longevity: A critical review. *Mechanisms of Aging and Development* 9:337–354.

Cutler, R. G. (1980a) Evolution and genetics of human longevity. In A. Viidik, ed., *Lectures on Gerontology*. London: Academic Press, in press.

Cutler, R. G. (1980b) Evolution of human longevity. Pp. 43–79 in C. Borek, C. M. Fenoglio, and D. W. King, eds., *Aging, Cancer and Cell Membranes. Advances in Pathobiology*, Vol. 7. New York: Thieme-Stratton Inc.

Cutler, R. G. (1980c) Stabilization of the Differentiated State of Cells: Possible Role of the Major Histocompatibility Complex Loci. *The Gerontologist* 20:88.

Cutler, R. G., Kalish, R. A., Gerjuoy, H., and Jonsen, A. R. (1977) Symposium: Prolongation of mental and physical health: Its possibility and advisability. *The Gerontologist* 17:141–142.

Davis, K. L., Mohs, R. C., Tinklenberg, J. R., Pfefferbaum, A., Hollister, and Kopell, B. S. (1978) Physostigmine: Improvements of long-term memory processes in normal humans. *Science* 201:272–274.

Deevey, E. S. (1960) The human population. *Scientific American* 203:195–204.

Denckla, W. D. (1975) A time to die. *Life Sciences* 16:31–44.

Dilman, V. M. (1971) Age-associated elevation of hypothalamic threshold to feedback control and its role in development, aging and disease. *Lancet* June 12:1211–1219.

Dilman, V. M. (1976) The hypothalamic control of aging and age associated pathology: The elevation mechanism of aging. Pp. 634–667 in A. V. Everitt and J. A. Burgess, eds., *Hypothalamus, Pituitary and Aging*. Springfield, Ill.: C. C. Thomas.

Dilman, V. M. (1979) Hypothalamic mechanisms of aging and of specific age pathology-V. A model for the mechanism of human specific age pathology and natural death. *Experimental Gerontology* 14:287–300.

Dix, D., and Cohen, P. (1980) On the role of aging in cancer incidence. *Journal of Theoretical Biology* 83:163–173.

Ducoff, H. S. (1972) Causes of death in irradiated adult insects. *Biological Review* 47:211–240.

Eskin, B. A. (1978) Sex hormones and aging. Pp. 207–224 in J. Roberts, R. C. Adelman, and V. J. Cristofalo, eds., *Pharmacological Intervention in the Aging Process*. New York: Plenum Press.

Everitt, A. V., and Burgess, J. A., eds. (1976) *Hypothalamus, Pituitary and Aging*. Springfield, Ill.: C. C. Thomas.

Fernandes, G., Good, R. A., Friend, P., and Yunis, E. J. (1978) Influence of dietary restriction of immunologic function and renal disease in (NZB X NZW) F_1 mice. *Proceedings of the National Academy of Sciences, USA* 75:1500–1504.

Frank, B. S. (1976) *Dr. Frank's No Aging Diet*. New York: Dial Press.

Finch, C. E. (1972) Enzyme activities, gene function and ageing in mammals: A review. *Experimental Gerontology* 7:53–67.

Finch, C. E. (1976) The regulation of physiological changes during mammalian aging. *Quarterly Review of Biology* 51:49–83.

Finch, C. E. (1977) Neuroendocrinology and autonomic aspects of aging. Pp. 62–280 in C. E. Finch and L. Hayflick, eds., *Handbook of the Biology of Aging*. New York: Van Nostrand Reinhold Co.

Florine, D. L., Ono, T., Cutler, R. G., and Getz, M. J. (1980) Regulation of endogenous murine leukemia virus-related nuclear and cytoplasmic RNA complexity in C57BL/6J mice of increasing age. *Cancer Research* 40:519–523.

Flower, S. (1931) Contributions to our knowledge of the duration of life in vertebrate animals. *Proceedings Zoological Society* 10:145–234.

Fridovich, I. (1978) The biology of oxygen radicals. *Science* 201:875–880.

Gerbase-DeLima, M., Liu, R. K., Cheney, K. E., Mickey, R., and Walford, R. L. (1975) Immune function and survival in a long-lived mouse strain subjected to undernutrition. *Gerontologia* 21:184–202.

Gerjuoy, H. (1979) A technology assessment of life extending technologies. In R. M. Lassman, ed., *Frontiers in Aging: Life Extension. International Journal on Aging and Human Development*, in press.

Gershon, D., Gershon, H., Jacobus, S., Reiss, U., and Reznick, A. (1976) The accumulation of faulty enzyme molecules in aging cells. Pp. 227–232 in S. Shaltiel, ed., *Metabolic Interconversion of Enzymes*. Berlin: Springer-Verlag.

Goldschmidt, P. G., and Jillson, I. H. (1975) A comprehensive study of the ethical, legal and social implications of advances in biomedical and behavioral research and technology. Baltimore, Md.: Policy Research Inc.

Goldstein, A. L., Hooper, J. A., Schulof, R. S., Cohen, G. H., Thurman, G. B., McDaniel, M. C., White, A., and Dardenne, M. (1974) Thymosin and the immunopathology of aging. *Federation Proceedings* 33:2053–2056.

Good, R. A., and Bach, F. H. (1974) Bone marrow and thymus transplants: Cellular engineering to correct primary immunodeficiency. Pp. 63–114 in R. A. Good and F. H. Bach, *Clinical Immunology*, Vol. 2. New York: Academic Press.

Goodrick, C. L. (1980) Effects of long-term voluntary wheel exercise on male and female Wistar rats I. Longevity, body weight, and metabolic rate. *Gerontology* 26:22–33.

Gruman, G. J. (1966) A history of ideas about the prolongation of life. *Transactions of the American Philosophical Society* 56(9).

Harman, D. (1978) Free radical theory of aging: Nutritional implications. *Age* 1:143–150.

Hart, R. W., and Setlow, R. B. (1974) Correlation between deoxyribonucleic acid excision-repair and life-span in a number of mammalian species. *Proceedings of the National Academy of Sciences, USA* 71:2169–2173.

Hart, R. W., and Trosko, J. E. (1976) DNA repair processes in mammals. Pp. 134–167 in R. G. Cutler, ed., *Cellular Aging: Concepts and Mechanisms. Interdisciplinary Topics in Gerontology*, Vol. 9. Basel: Karger.

Hathway, D. E. (1966) Metabolic fate in animals of hindered phenolic antioxidants in relation to their safety evaluation and antioxidant function. *Advances in Food Research* 15:1–56.

Havighurst, R. J., and Sacher, G. A. (1977) Prospects of lengthening life and vigor. In B. L. Neugarten and R. J. Havighurst, eds., *Extending the Human Life-Span: Social*

Policy and Social Ethics. Chicago: Committee on Human Development, University of Chicago. (USGPO Stock No. 638–000–00337–2.)

Hirokawa, K., Albright, J. W., and Makinodan, T. (1976) Restoration of impaired immune functions in aging animals II. Effect of syngeneic thymus and bone marrow grafts. *Clinical Immunology and Immunopathology* 5:371–376.

Hochschild, R. (1973) Effects of various drugs on longevity in female C57BL/6J mice. *Gerontologia* 19:271–280.

Horita, A. (1977) Neuropharmacology and aging. Pp. 171–186 in J. Roberts, R. C. Adelman, and V. J. Cristofalo, eds., *Pharmacological Intervention in the Aging Process.* New York: Plenum Press.

Hughes, J. R., Williams, J. G., and Currier, R. D. (1976) An ergot alkaloid preparation (Hydergine) in the treatment of dementia. *Journal of the American Geriatric Society* 24:490–497.

Johnson, J. E., and Cutler, R. G. (1980) Effects of hypophysectomy on age related changes in the rat kidney glomerulus: Observations by scanning and transmission electron microscopy. *Mechanisms of Aging and Development* 13:63–74.

Jones, M. L. (1968) Longevity of primates in captivity. *International Zoo Yearbook* 8:183–192.

Jose, D. G., and Good, R. A. (1973a) Quantitative effects of nutritional essential amino acid deficiency upon immune responses to tumors in mice. *Journal of Experimental Medicine* 137:1–9.

Jose, D. G., and Good, R. A. (1973b) Quantitative effects of nutritional protein and calorie deficiency upon immune response to tumors in mice. *Cancer Research* 33:807–812.

Jose, D. G., Stutman, O., and Good, R. A. (1973) Long term effects on immune function of early nutritional deprivation. *Nature* 241:57–58.

Kanungo, M. S. (1975) A model for ageing. *Journal of Theoretical Biology* 53:253–261.

Kay, M. M. B., and Makinodan, T. (1976) Immunobiology of aging: Evaluation of current status. *Clinical Immunology and Immunopathology* 6:394–413.

Kayser, C. (1961) *The Physiology of Natural Hibernation.* New York: Pergamon Press.

Kent, S. (1976) A look at gerovital—the "youth" drug. *Geriatrics* 31:95, 96, 101, 102.

Kent, S. (1977a) Can drugs increase the immune response? *Geriatrics* 32:101, 105, 109, 110, 112–114.

Kent, S. (1977b) Can cellular therapy rejuvenate the aged? *Geriatrics* 32(8): 92, 93, 95, 99.

Kent, S. (1977c) Can nucleic acid therapy reverse the degenerative processes of aging? *Geriatrics* 32:130, 132, 134, 136.

Kent, S. (1978) Body temperature and life-span. *Geriatrics* 33(9):109, 110, 112, 116.

Kibler, H. H., Silsby, H. D., and Johnson, H. D. (1963) Metabolic trends and life-span of rats living at 9°C and 28°C. *Journal of Gerontology* 18:235–239.

Kohn, R. R. (1971) Effect of antioxidants on life-span of C57BL mice. *Journal of Gerontology* 26:378–380.

Kohn, R. R. (1978) *Principles of Mammalian Aging.* New York: Prentice-Hall.

Kohn, R. R., and Leash, A. M. (1967) Long term lathyrogen administration to rats, with a special reference to aging. *Experimental and Molecular Pathology* 1:354–361.

Kormendy, C. G., and Bender, A. D. (1971a) Chemical interference with aging. *Gerontologia* 17:52–64.

Kormendy, C. G., and Bender, A. D. (1971b) Experimental modification of the chemistry and biology of the aging process. *Journal of Pharmacological Sciences* 60:167–180.

LaBella, F., and Vivian, S. (1978) Beta-aminopropionitrile promotes longevity in mice. *Experimental Gerontology* 13:251–254.

Lamb, M. J., ed. (1977) *Biology of Aging*. New York: J. Wiley and Sons.

Leibovitz, B. E., and Siegel, B. V. (1980) Aspects of free radical reactions in biological systems: Aging. *Journal of Gerontology* 35:45–56.

Lekholm, G. C. (1939) *En Alderstigen Al*. Halsingborg, Sweden: Halsingborgs Museum Arsskrift.

Leto, S., Kokkonen, G. C., and Barrows, C. H. (1976a) Dietary protein, life-span and biochemical variables in female mice. *Journal of Gerontology* 31:144–148.

Liu, R., and Walford, R. (1972) The effect of lowered body temperature on life-span and immune and non-immune processes. *Gerontologia* 18:363–388.

Liu, R., and Walford, R. (1975) Mid-life temperature-transfer effects on life-span of annual fish. *Journal of Gerontology* 30:129–131.

McCay, C. M., Crowell, M. F., and Maynard, L. A. (1935) The effect of retarded growth upon the length of life-span and upon the ultimate body size. *Journal of Nutrition* 10:63–79.

McCay, C. M., Maynard, L. A., Sperling, G., and Barnes, L. L. (1939) Retarded growth, life-span, ultimate body size, and age changes in the albino rat after feeding diets restricted in calories. *Journal of Nutrition* 18:1–13.

McCay, C. M., Maynard, L. A., Sperling G., and Barnes, L. L. (1962) Retarded growth, life-span, ultimate body size and age changes in the albino rat after feeding diets restricted in calories. *Journal of Nutrition* 77:439–442.

Makinodan, T. (1977) Immunity and aging. Pp. 379–408 in C. E. Finch and L. Hayflick, eds., *Handbook of the Biology of Aging*. New York: Van Nostrand Reinhold Co.

Makinodan, T. (1979) Control of immunologic abnormalities associated with aging. *Mechanisms of Ageing and Development* 9:7–18.

Manes, C. (1979) Current concepts in onco-developmental gene expression. Pp. 1–6 in F. G. Lehmann, ed., *Carcino-Embryonic Proteins*, Vol. I. Amsterdam: Elsevier/North-Holland Biomedical Press.

Martin, G.M. (1979) Genetic and evolutionary aspects of aging. *Federation Proceedings* 38:1962–1967.

Martin, P. (1974) Can hyperbaric oxygen add years to your life? *Consumers Digest* 1:(Sept./Oct.)19–21.

Massie, H. R., Baird, M. B., and Piekielniak, M. J. (1976) Ascorbic acid and longevity in *Drosophila*. *Experimental Gerontology* 11:37–42.

Maynard-Smith, J. (1962) Review lectures on senescence I. The causes of aging. *Proceedings Royal Society, London, Series B* 157:115–127.

Maynard-Smith, J. (1966) Theories of aging. Pp. 1–27 in P. L. Krohn, ed., *Topics in the Biology of Aging*. New York: Interscience.

Medical World News (1977) Medicine 2000. January 24:44–48, 53–59, 63, 67, 74–76, 81, 84, 100.

Medvedev, Z. A. (1975) Aging and longevity. *The Gerontologist* 15:196–201.

Meredith, P. J., and Walford, R. L. (1979) Autoimmunity, histocompatibility, and aging. *Mechanisms of Aging and Development* 9:61–78.

Miller, E. C. (1978) Some current perspectives on chemical carcinogenesis in humans and experimental animals: Presidential addresses. *Cancer Research* 38:1479–1496.

Miller, J. K., and Bolla, R., Denckla, W. D. (1980) Age-associated changes in initiation of ribonucleic acid synthesis in rat liver nuclei. *Biochemical Journal* 188:55–60.

Miquel, J., Lundgren, P. R., Gensch, K. G., and Atlan, H. (1976) Effects of temperature on the life-span, vitality and fine structure of *Drosophila melanogaster*. *Mechanisms of Ageing and Development* 5:347–370.

Mittal, C. K., and Murad, F. (1977) Properties and oxidative regulation of guanylate cyclase. *Journal of Cyclic Nucleotide Research* 3:381–391.

Montesano, R., Bresil, H., and Margison, G. P. (1979) Increased excision of O^6-methylguanine from rat liver DNA after chronic administration of dimethylnitrosamine. *Cancer Research* 39:1798–1802.

Moore, C. J., and Schwartz, A. G. (1978) Inverse correlation between species life-span and capacity of cultured fibroblasts to convert benzo(a)pyrene to water-soluble metabolites. *Experimental Cell Research* 116:359–364.

Munkres, K. D. (1976a) Aging of *Neurospora crassa* III. Induction of cellular death and clonal senescence of an inositol-less mutant by inositol starvation and the protective effect of dietary antioxidants. *Mechanisms of Ageing and Development* 5:163–170.

Munkres, K. D. (1976b) Ageing of *Neurospora crassa* IV. Induction of senescence in wild type by dietary amino acid analogues and reversal by antioxidants and membrane stabilizers. *Mechanisms of Ageing and Development* 5:171–191.

Munkres, K. D., and Colvin, H. J. (1976) Ageing of *Neurospora crassa* II. Organic hydroperoxide toxicity and the protective role of antioxidant and the antioxigenic enzymes. *Mechanisms of Ageing and Development* 5:99–108.

Munkres, K. D., and Minssen, M. (1976) Ageing of *Neurospora crassa* I. Evidence for the free radical theory of ageing from studies of a natural-death mutant. *Mechanisms of Ageing and Development* 5:79–98.

Napier, J. R., and Napier, P. H. (1967) *A Handbook of Living Primates.* New York, N.Y.: Academic Press.

Neugarten, B. L., and Havighurst, R. J. (1977a) *Extending the Human Life-Span: Social Policy and Social Ethics.* Chicago: Committee on Human Development, University of Chicago. (USGPO Stock No. 038–00337–2.)

Neugarten, B. L., and Havighurst, R. J. (1977b) *Social Policy, Social Ethics and the Aging Society.* Chicago: Committee on Human Development, University of Chicago. (USGPO Stock No. 038–002996.)

Ono, T., and Cutler, R. G. (1978) Age-dependent relaxation of gene repression: Increase of endogenous murine leukemia virus-related and globin-related RNA in brain and liver of mice. *Proceedings of the National Academy of Sciences, USA* 75:4431–4435.

Ordy, J. M., and Brizzee, K. R., eds. (1975) *Neurobiology of Aging.* New York: Plenum Press.

Ostfeld, A., Smith, C. M., and Stotsky, B. A. (1977) The systemic use of procaine in the treatment of the elderly: A review. *Journal of the American Geriatric Society* 25:1–19.

Parker, R., Berkowitz, B., Lee, C. -H., and Denckla, W. D. (1978) Vascular relaxation, aging and thyroid hormones. *Mechanisms of Ageing and Development* 8:397–405.

Pearl, R. (1928) Experiments on longevity. *Quarterly Review of Biology* 3:391–407.

Petell, J. K., and Lebherz, H. G. (1979) Properties and metabolism of fructose diphosphate aldolase in livers of "old" and "young" mice. *Journal of Biological Chemistry* 254:8179–8184.

Peter, C. P., Perkins, E. H., Peterson, W. J., Walburg, H. E., and Makinodan, T. (1975) The late effects of selected immunosuppressants on immunocompetence, disease incidence, and mean life-span. *Mechanisms of Ageing and Development* 4:252–262.

Pitot, H. C., and Heidelberger, C. (1963) Metabolic regulatory circuits and carcinogenesis. *Cancer Research* 23:1694–1700.

Pryor, W. A. (1976) The role of free radical reactions in biological systems. In W. A. Pryor, ed., *Free Radicals in Biology*, Vol. 1. New York: Academic Press.

Reiss, U. (1979) Enzyme repair system in mouse liver. *Israel Journal of Medical Sciences* 15:62.

Reiss, U., and Gershon, D. (1978) Methionine sulfoxide reductase: A novel protective enzyme in liver and its potentially significant role in aging. Pp. 55–64 in K. Kitani, ed., *Liver and Aging.* Amsterdam: Elsevier/North-Holland Biomedical Press.

Robertson, O. H. (1961) Prolongation of the life-span of Kokanee salmon (*Oncorynchus nerka kennerlyi*) by castration before beginning of gonad development. *Proceedings of the National Academy of Sciences, USA* 47:609–621.

Robertson, O. H., and Wexler, B. C. (1960) Histological changes in the organs and tissues of migrating and spawning Pacific salmon (Genus *Oncorhynchus*). *Endocrinology* 66:222–239.

Ross, M. H. (1961) Length of life and nutrition in the rat. *Journal of Nutrition* 75:197–210.

Ross, M. H. (1976) Nutrition and longevity in experimental animals. Pp. 43–57 in M. Winick, ed., *Nutrition and Aging*. New York: J. Wiley and Sons.

Roth, G. S. (1979) Hormone receptor changes during adulthood and senescence. Significance for aging research. *Federation Proceedings* 38:1910–1914.

Rubner, M. (1908) Probleme des wachstums und der lebensdauer. *Gesellschaft fur Innere Medizine und Kinderheilkunde*, Vol. 7. Wien: Mitteilungen, Beiblat.

Sacher, G. A. (1959) Relation of life-span to brain and body weight in mammals. Pp. 115–133 in G. E. W. Wolstenholme and C. M. O'Connor, eds., *Ciba Foundation. Colloquia on Aging, Vol. 5, The Life-span of Animals*. London: Churchill.

Sacher, G. A. (1975) Maturation and longevity in relation to cranial capacity in hominid evolution. Pp. 417–441 in R. R. Tuttle, ed., *Primate Functional Morphology and Evolution*. The Hague: Mouton.

Sacher, G. A. (1977) Life table modification and life prolongation. Pp. 582–638 in C. E. Finch and L. Hayflick, eds., *Handbook of the Biology of Aging*. New York: Van Nostrand Reinhold.

Sacher, G. A., and Hart, R. W. (1978) Longevity, aging and comparative cellular and molecular biology of the house mouse, *Mus musculus*, and the white-footed mouse, *Peromyscus leucopus*. Pp. 71–96 in D. Bergsma and D. E. Harrison, eds., *Genetic Effects on Ageing*. New York: Alan R. Liss, Inc.

Schwartz, A. G. (1975a) Correlation between species life-span and capacity to activate 7, 12-dimethylbenz(a)anthracene to a form mutagenic to a mammalian cell. *Experimental Cell Research* 94:445–447.

Schwartz, A. G. (1975b) Inhibition of spontaneous breast cancer formation in female C3H(Avy/a) mice by long-term treatment with dehydroepiandrosterone. *Cancer Research* 39:1129–1131.

Schwartz, A. G., and Perantoni, A. (1975) Protective effect of dehydroepiandrosterone against aflatoxin B_1 and 7,12-dimethylbenz(a)anthracene-induced cytotoxicity and transformation in cultured cells. *Cancer Research* 35:2482–2487.

Schwartz, A. G., and Moore, C. J. (1977) Inverse correlation between species life-span and capacity of cultured fibroblasts to bind 7, 12-dimethylbenz(a)anthracene to DNA. *Experimental Cell Research* 109:448–450.

Schwartz, H. L., Forciea, M. A., Mariasch, C. N., and Oppenheimer, J. H. (1979) Age related reduction in response of hepatic enzymes to 3,5,3'triiodothyronine administration. *Endocrinology* 105:41–46.

Scott, M., Bolla, R., and Denckla, W. D. (1970) Age-related changes in immune function of rats and the effect of long-term hypophysectomy. *Mechanisms of Ageing and Development* 11:127–136.

Segall, P. E., and Timiras, P. S. (1975) Age-related changes in thermoregulatory capacity of tryptophan deficient rats. *Federation Proceedings* 34:83–85.

Segall, P. E., and Timiras, P. S. (1976) Patho-physiologic findings after chronic tryptophan deficiency in rats: A model for delayed growth and aging. *Mechanisms of Ageing and Development* 5:109–124.

Shamberger, R. J. (1970) Relationship of selenium to cancer I. Inhibitory effect of selenium on carcinogenesis. *Journal National Cancer Institute* 44:931–936.

Shock, N. W. (1952) Ageing of homeostatic mechanisms. Pp. 415–446 in A. I. Lansing, ed., *Cowdry's Problems of Ageing*. Baltimore, Md.: Williams and Wilkins Co.

Shock, N. W. (1961) Physiological aspects of aging in man. *Annual Review of Physiology* 23:97–122.

Shock, N. W. (1970) Physiologic aspects of aging. *Journal of the American Dietetic Association* 56:491–496.

Sims, P., and Grover, P. L. (1974) Epoxides in polycyclic aromatic hydrocarbon metabolism and carcinogenesis. *Advances in Cancer Research* 20:165–274.

Smith, G. S., and Walford, R. L. (1977) Influence of the main histocompatibility complex on aging in mice. *Nature* 270:727–729.

Smith-Sonneborn, J. (1979) DNA repair and longevity assurance in *Paramecium tetraurelia*. *Science* 203:1115–1117.

Sohal, R. S., and Donato, H. (1978) Effects of experimentally altered life-spans on the accumulation of fluorescent age pigment in the housefly, *Musca domestica*. *Experimental Gerontology* 13:335–341.

Stegink, A. J. (1972) The clinical use of piracetam, a new nootropic drug. The treatment of symptoms of senile involution. *Arzneim-Forschung* 22:975–977.

Strehler, B. L. (1977) *Time, Cells and Aging*. New York: Academic Press.

Stuchlikova, E., Juricova-Horakova, M., and Deyl, Z. (1975) What is the role of obesity in aging? *Experimental Gerontology* 10:141–144.

Sun, A. Y., and Samorajski, T. (1975) The effects of age and alcohol on (Na^+K^-)-ATPase activity of whole homogenate and synaptosomes prepared from mouse and human brain. *Journal of Neurochemistry* 24:161–165.

Sun, A. Y., and Seaman, R. N. (1977) The effect of aging on synaptosomal Ca^2; transport in the brain. *Experimental Aging Research* 3:107–116.

Sun, G. Y., and Samorajski, T. (1973) Age differences in the acyl group composition of phosphoglycerides in myelin isolated from the brain of the Rhesus monkey. *Biochemica Biophysica Acta* 316:19–27.

Tam, C. F., Smith, G. S., and Walford, R. L. (1979) Resting and concanaualin-A stimulated levels of cyclic nucleotides in splenic cells of aging mice with spontaneous cancers. *Life Sciences* 24:311–322.

Tam, C. F., and Walford, R. L. (1978) Cyclic nucleotide levels in resting and mitogen-stimulated spleen cell suspensions from young and old mice. *Mechanisms of Ageing and Development* 7:309–320.

Tannenbaum, A., and Silverstone, H. (1953) Nutrition in relation to cancer. *Advances in Cancer Research* 1:451–501.

Tappel, A. L. (1968) Will antioxidant nutrients slow aging processes? *Geriatrics* 23:97–105.

Tappel, A. L. (1973) Lipid peroxidation damage to cell components. *Federation Proceedings* 32:1870–1874.

Tappel, A. L., Fletcher, B., and Deamer, D. (1973) Effect of antioxidants and nutrients on lipid peroxidation fluorescent products and aging parameters in the mouse. *Journal of Gerontology* 28:415–424.

Timiras, P. S. (1978) Biological perspectives on aging. *American Scientist* 66:605–613.

Tolmasoff, J., Ono, T., and Cutler, R. G. (1980) Superoxide dismutase: Correlation with life-span and specific metabolic rate in primate species. *Proceedings of the National Academy of Sciences, USA*, in press.

Totter, J. R. (1980) Spontaneous cancer and its possible relationship to oxygen metabolism. *Proceedings of the National Academy of Sciences, USA* 77:1763–1767.

Trosko, J. E., and Chang, C. -C. (1978) Relationship between mutagenesis and carcinogenesis. *Photochemistry and Photobiology* 28:157–168.

Upton, A. C. (1977) Pathobiology. Pp. 513–535 in C. E. Finch and L. Hayflick, eds.,

Handbook of the Biology of Aging. New York: Van Nostrand Reinhold Co.

Walford, R. L. (1969) The Immunologic Theory of Aging. Baltimore, Md.: Williams and Wilkins Co.

Walford, R. L. (1974) Immunological theory of aging: Current status. *Federation Proceedings* 33:2020–2027.

Walford, R. L. (1975) Immune function and survival in a long-lived mouse strain subjected to undernutrition. *Gerontologia* 21:184–202.

Walford, R. L. (1979) Multigene families, histocompatibility systems, transformation, meiosis, stem cells, and DNA repair. *Mechanisms of Aging and Development* 9:19–26.

Walford, R. L., and Bergmann, K. (1979) Influence of genes associated with the main histocompatibility complex on deoxyribonucleic acid excision repair capacity and bleomycin sensitivity in mouse lymphocytes. *Tissue Antigens* 14:336–342.

Walford, R. L., Liu, R. K., Troup, G. M., Hsiu, J. (1969) Alterations in soluble/insoluble collagen ratios in the annual fish, *Cynolebias bellottii,* in relation to age. *Experimental Gerontology* 4:103–109.

Walford, R. L., Meredith, P. J., and Cheney, K. E. (1977) Immunoengineering: Prospects for correction of age-related immunodeficiency states. Pp. 183–201 in T. Makinodan and E. Yunis, eds., *Immunology and Aging.* New York: Plenum Press.

Wattenberg, L. W., Lam, L. K. T., Speier, J. L., Loub, W. D., and Borchert, P. (1977) Inhibitors of chemical carcinogenesis. Pp. 795–799 in H. H. Hiatt, J. D. Watson, and J. A. Winsten, eds., *Origins of Human Cancer. Book B. Mechanisms of Carcinogenesis.* Cold Spring Harbor, New York: CSH Press.

Weber, A., Gregori, C., and Schapira, F. (1976) Aldolase B in the liver of senescent rats. *Biochemica Biophysica Acta* 444:810–815.

Weindruch, R. H., Cristie, J. A., Cheney, K. E., and Walford, R. L. (1979) Influence of controlled dietary restriction on immunologic function and aging. *Federation Proceedings* 38:2007–2016.

Wodinsky, J. (1977) Hormonal inhibition of feeding and death in octopus: Control by optic gland secretion. *Science* 198:948–951.

Wulf, J. H., and Cutler, R. G. (1975) Altered protein hypothesis of mammalian aging processes I. Thermal stability of glucose-6-phosphate dehydrogenase in C57BL/6J mouse tissue. *Experimental Gerontology* 10:101–118.

Young, V. R. (1978) Nutrition and aging. Pp. 85–100 in J. Roberts, R. C. Adelman, and V. J. Cristofalo, eds., *Pharmacological Intervention in the Aging Process.* New York: Plenum Press.

Young V. R. (1979) Diet as a modulator of aging and longevity. *Federation Proceedings* 38:1994–2000.

Yunis, E. J., and Greenberg, L. J. (1974) Immunopathology of aging. *Human Pathology* 5:122–125.

Zeman, W. (1974) Studies in the neuronal ceroid-lipofuscinoses. *Journal of Neuropathology and Experimental Neurology* 33:1–12.

chapter 4

Environment and Biology in Aging: Some Epidemiological Notions

MERVYN SUSSER

Epidemiology begins with the existence and discovery of variation in health states. Traditionally epidemiology is a public health science, and epidemiologists have sought environmental sources for such variation. The means to look at these environmental sources in interaction with heredity are coming to hand, and epidemiologists have begun to share this ground with population geneticists moving from the opposite direction. Epidemiologists now proceed from and must begin to study this assumption of interaction of heredity and environment. In this discussion, I shall assume that the variation of aging, and with aging, comprises an intrinsic biological component and an extrinsic environmental component, which are combined in unknown weights that probably vary under different conditions.

A scientifically productive definition of aging is of a condition that begins with conception. In the past, I have subscribed to and used a definition (proposed by Comfort 1956) that characterizes aging as a deteriorative process in an organism, essentially the obverse of differentiation, organogenesis, and development. This is a process that implies decrement and loss. One cannot deny that in industrialized western societies, deterioration is the social connotation of aging: once across the aging threshold—ill-defined and changeable though that may be—it is all

AGING
Biology and Behavior

downhill. For purposes of scientific study, however, development and aging are indissolubly linked by the chronological idea at the core of the aging construct: an infant is older than an embryo, a child older than an infant. Aside from chronology, there is no unique criterion by which we can mark the onset of the downward trajectory of this unidirectional process. We must either forge a compound of multiple criteria or use singular criteria limited to a specific dimension of the aging process. The epidemiological approach rests on some form of quantification and demands the designation of the criteria to be measured. The differentiation of criteria includes levels of organization.

DIFFERENTIATION OF LEVELS OF ORGANIZATION

It is necessary to distinguish among a hierarchy of levels in the process of aging: social, psychological, and physical; organs, tissues, cells, and molecules. Each level has its own developmental timetable and momentum. Thus, the onset of deterioration at one level, while linked with other levels, need not be strictly concurrent. These variations give the promise of maneuverability, leverage to work with, when we face the question of what can be done about aging.

Epidemiology is mainly engaged at the social, psychological, and organic levels. Most plastic is the social role. Men have led societies in their eighties (Mao Tse-Tung, Konrad Adenauer, Ho Chi Minh, and the Ayatollah Khomeini) as well as in their forties (John Kennedy, Olaf Palme, and Pierre Trudeau). The psychological component has considerable plasticity, too. Great artists and scientists have been creative in their eighties as in their twenties; others have burned out by middle age. From common observation we can say that the physical component, while also variable, has less plasticity in the developmental timetable than the social or psychological. Thus, for each level and for the elements within a given level, the pace of change and the trajectory through the life-cycle need not be the same. Elements within the same level, even different measures of ostensibly the same elements, can exhibit dissimilar trajectories. This is apparent and obvious to any observer who notes the uneven deterioration or specific failure in individuals of the heart, brain, joints, or senses. Epidemiology, however, is concerned with population measures.

Mortality is the most definitive of epidemiologic measures and was the first to be applied by John Graunt in the seventeenth century. Overall mortality in populations exhibits with uncanny consistency the Gompertz curve. After a sharp decline from infancy to the nadir at pubescence, there follows an exponential rise. What varies among societies, social classes, and other social groups is the slope of the curve (Susser and Watson 1977).

Overall morbidity does not display the same consistency as mortality. First, much depends on what diseases are measured. Specific disorders, physical and mental, have characteristic age patterns. For example, the incidence of schizophrenia peaks in the third and fourth decade; the incidence of adult depressive illness also peaks in the fourth decade, but the curve is bimodal and rises to a second peak in the seventh decade; the incidence of coronary heart disease resembles the Gompertz mortality curve. Acute and chronic sickness also vary by age: Acute illnesses predominate in the young, chronic in the old.

Second, when we examine the relationship of morbidity to aging, much depends on what aspect of morbidity is measured. Results differ with the measure, whether rates of incidence, prevalence, or lifetime prevalence.[1] Results also differ with the definition of the dependent variable. To describe health states, Elinson (1967) invented a hierarchy of Ds—dissatisfaction, discomfort, disease, disability, and death—each of which has a distinct pattern of variation. For social and epidemiological purposes, we must, at the least, separate a hierarchy of three broad levels. First is the objective perception of disorder—that is, at the organic and physiological level, which is expressed in its dynamic aspect as disease, and in its stable analogue as impairment. Second is the subjective perception of disorder—that is, psychological awareness of dysfunction, which is expressed in its dynamic aspect as illness and in its stable analogue as disability. Third is the social perception of disorder—that is, role and status recognized at the social level, which is expressed in its dynamic aspect as sickness, and in its stable analogue as handicap.

We can expect different degrees of variation in the life trajectories of each level with changes in the sociocultural and economic environment. Each level is accessible and sensitive to different forces of change or different instruments of intervention. Most biological approaches have inclined toward seeing the organic infrastructure as fundamental and the psychosocial level as superstructure; they view intervention and change at the molecular or cellular and individual level as essential to change in the aging process at higher levels in the hierarchy. From a broad social

[1] The rate of incidence is a measure, over a defined time period and in a defined population, of specified happenings or events, usually the onset of disease. Prevalence is the ratio of specified manifestations existing at a given point in time to the defined population in which they are observed. Prevalence is a function of incidence and the duration of a manifestation. Lifetime prevalence is the frequency of specified happenings through the lifetime of a given population, preferably a birth cohort but sometimes the population existing at a point in time.

view, however, change and intervention at the social and population level have certainly wrought change in the aging process. Habits and physical capability, musculature, blood pressure and cardiac function, and measured mental performance all vary in the rate and manner in which they deteriorate across societies or social groups. It is not too much to hypothesize that pathways from the psychosocial down to the cellular and molecular levels allow the intrinsic aging process to be influenced.

SEPARATION OF HISTORY AND THE LIFE-CYCLE

The readiest perception of history is that the impact of a given period is seen in the population existing at the time. As times change, so the immediate impact of change is sought in that existing population. Both suicide and mental hospital admission rates rise with alienating catastrophes, like the depression following the stock market crash of 1929, and fall with collective response to disasters, like World War II (MacMahon et al. 1963, Murphy 1959, Susser 1968b) in accord with the findings Durkheim produced long ago to buttress his theoretical predictions (Durkheim 1951). Mortality seems to rise with unemployment after a lag of 2 or 3 years (Brenner 1971)—a conclusion of ecological analysis that, it must be admitted, has been strongly challenged. The imprint of period exposure, however, can also be carried over by the survivors into subsequent periods. So the population existing at a given period will manifest effects special to that period, combined with all the effects carried forward or deferred from earlier periods. Changes in manifestations over time are owing both to effects on an array of generations of different ages existing at a given point in time and to effects carried forward by each successive birth cohort or generation as a consequence of its own distinctive experience.

Therefore, in an age distribution for any attribute of a population, either or both of these components—period and generation—may have contributed. In addition, a third component of signal interest to this discussion, chronological age, is structurally linked to period and generation effects. Intrinsic age effects are the fundamental and built-in complement of the developmental life-cycle; they cannot be inferred, however, simply, from an age-specific distribution without taking account of period and generation effects. The need for such analysis is discussed later in this chapter.

Changes over time or across societies in mortality and morbidity at any age are of obvious and vital importance to the quality of life of the population surviving into later and older ages. Much less obvious is the direction and desirability of these changes; that is, whether declines in mortality and the increased life expectancy that characterize the past century in industrialized societies lead only to less morbidity and not to more.

Pessimists tend to point to the absolute increase in disability that follows from the increment in the aged population because of the disproportionate rate of disability found at older ages. Or they emphasize the absolute increase in handicap that has followed from the increased life expectancy of severely handicapped persons. As we shall see, absolute increases can occur even in the face of an actual decline in incidence rates.

Early and influential predictions of this kind were made by Karl Pearson, a founding father of biostatistics. Many nineteenth-century thinkers were obsessed with ideas of racial or social degeneration, each rationalizing the idea in a different way (Lombroso 1911, Morel 1857). Pearson, a social Darwinist and eugenicist (Semmel 1958) believed that the decline in infant mortality that began in England and Europe at the turn of the century was the herald of racial degeneration; the weak as well as the strong now survived to flout natural selection, and in their adult years they could only add to the general debility of the population.

These fears were put to rest by one of the first generation or cohort analyses to be applied to a health problem: Kermack, McKendrick, and McKinley in 1934 analyzed British and Swedish mortality trends (Kermack et al. 1934). They showed quite clearly that as the infant mortality of each successive birth cohort declined, so, equally regularly, the age-specific mortality of each of these cohorts at successive ages declined. Figures 4.1 and 4.2 illustrate their analyses for Britain.

Some other grounds for pessimism can also be discarded. In the first half of this century, the substantial and continuing decline in infectious and childhood diseases was accompanied by a rise—virtually epidemic in character—in the now familiar chronic diseases of adulthood; peptic ulcer, ischemic heart disease, and lung cancer are notable examples (Morris 1955). These diseases were most often seen as degenerative and "competing" causes of death, the ineluctable accompaniment of aging. Epidemiological research has changed that paradigm of chronic disease. Following the dramatic discovery of cigarette smoking as the predominant cause of lung cancer, environmental causes of other cancers and chronic diseases are routinely postulated and searched for. Meanwhile, deaths from many so-called diseases of aging have been in decline, particularly peptic ulcer, coronary heart disease, hypertension, and chronic renal disease. These epidemics began to wane without benefit of direct

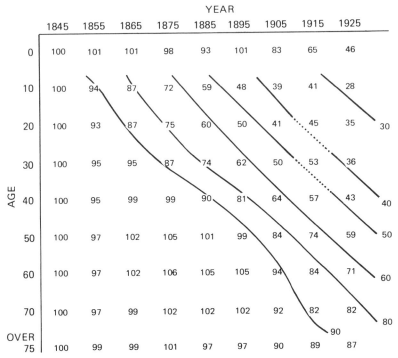

Figure 4.1. England and Wales: relative mortalities. (The figures in the zero row refer to deaths under 1 year per 1000 births.) (From Kermack *et al.* 1934.)

intervention; cohort analyses demonstrate that the downward curves began before any effective treatments were available, and certainly well before such treatments were widely in use and distributed (Susser and Stein 1962, Krueger *et al.* 1967, Hansen and Susser 1971, Susser and Watson 1977, U.S. Department of Health, Education, and Welfare 1979).

A host of complex biological and health changes proceed together and interact, however, and the consequences may not always be benign.

To follow through on the point that one should study aging from conception, we may note, for instance, the considerable expansion in fecundity over the past century or so: Menarche has occurred at ever younger ages (Tanner 1962), and menopause (probably) at older ages (MacMahon and Worcester 1966).[2] Yet this increase in fecundity has been accompanied by the control of fertility and a sharp decline in births.

---

[2] Smoking may be doing something, by contrast, to accelerate menopause (Jick and Porter 1977).

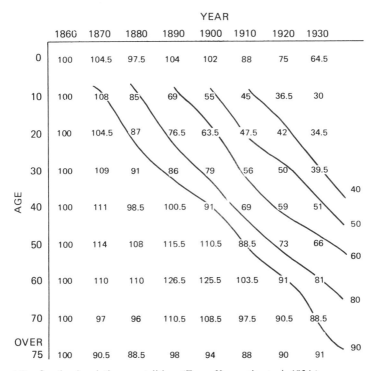

Figure 4.2. Scotland: relative mortalities. (From Kermack *et al.* 1934.)

The technical means to control fertility and the accompanying changes in social relations and values have surely produced numerous consequences for health. Cancer of the breast is a disease of older women, but the extension of the interval between menarche and first pregnancy has put women at higher risk of breast cancer (MacMahon and Yuasa 1970). Cancers of the uterus are affected differently according to their site. Cancer of the *neck* of the uterus has been declining steadily in frequency over recent decades. Yet as women are sexually active at earlier ages and with more partners and use chemical rather than mechanical means of contraception, we can expect to see in their later years a generational increase in cancers of the neck of the uterus. Such a result has been demonstrated for the cohort of British women who became sexually mature around World War II, when there was a characteristic wartime abandonment of sexual restraints (Adelstein *et al.* 1971). With cancer of the *body* of the uterus, the use of estrogens to suppress menopausal symptoms and to sustain genital youth and sexuality has put many postmenopausal women at risk.

MATERNAL AGE AND TRISOMY

The catalogue of secular change in health states is a long one. Since I have elsewhere considered the ways in which such changes impinge on and interact with the aging process (Susser 1968a, Susser 1973, Susser 1975, Susser and Watson 1977), I shall here take a different approach. I turn to a problem related to aging on which our group at Columbia University[3] is at work (Stein et al. 1979). This problem, the relationship of Down's syndrome (more generally, all trisomies) to maternal age, illustrates my opening paradigm of the interaction of genetic and environmental contributions in the epidemiology of aging.

In the first half of the twentieth century, we learned from Penrose (1934) and others that the frequency of Down's syndrome was strongly related to maternal age and to practically nothing else (see Figure 4.3). Paternal age could be fairly confidently ruled out as a factor by statistical analysis. There also seemed to be little variation across populations; in other words, an environmental component in the maternal age factor seemed unlikely. Taking account of these apparently well-founded assumptions, we could estimate that incidence at birth of this condition declined sharply with decline in maternal fertility at older ages through this century. In spite of that decline, there was a concurrent increase in prevalence owing to much improved survival rates (see Figure 4.4).

The prevalence of Down's syndrome is a function of the maternal age composition of the population, of fertility rates by age, and of the individual survival of Down's syndrome cases (Stein and Susser 1971). One approach to the problem of increasing prevalence would be to find what the causes of Down's syndrome are and to try to prevent them. Some of these causes clearly must be connected with maternal age, which focuses attention on mothers.

The chromosome anomaly in Down's syndrome can be of three types, but 95% are standard trisomies owing to nondisjunction (or possibly to precocious separation) of the chromosomes (Magenis et al. 1977). This chromosome pathology is the result of errors in cell division and the splitting of the chromosomes in the germ cell or oocyte at one of two stages. The first meiotic division begins while the future mother is in the womb—all her germ cells are laid down in embryo—and this first division could produce the disorder. The process, however, is long-drawn-out and is not completed for a given oocyte until the time of ovulation in

---

[3] Zena Stein, Jennie Kline, Dorothy Warburton with Ezra Susser have generously allowed me to use unpublished data and ideas in this discussion. Fuller analysis of these data appears in Stein et al. (1980).

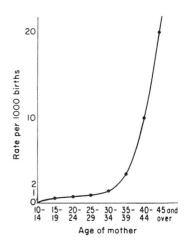

Figure 4.3. Risk of being a mongoloid child according to age of mother. (From Collman and Stoller 1962.)

the sexually mature woman. The second meiotic division of the germ cell is rapid and takes place at fertilization—that is, it cannot be affected before conception in the sexually mature woman. Since maternal age at conception is so strongly related to Down's syndrome, it seems probable that most cases of standard trisomy originate at some time during the prolonged process of the first division. The aging oocyte, which has awaited ovulation and fertilization since prenatal life, is thus the likely source of the trisomies in older women. Other factors may operate more often in younger women.

Mean maternal age is not uniform among different trisomies, and this variation has provided a further clue about mechanisms. The pooling of the largest available series of karyotypes cultured from spontaneous abortions has allowed us to see that the higher the mean maternal age associated with a given trisomy, the smaller the trisomic chromosome tends to be. Smaller chromosomes have fewer chiasmatic "joining" pairs of chromosomes (Henderson and Edwards 1968, Jagielo and Fang 1979). Furthermore, in chromosomes cultured from peripheral blood, it has been inferred that there is a loss of chiasmata with age, since chromosomes from older individuals have fewer of them (Luthardt 1977). The mechanism involved in the association of trisomy with maternal age may thus be a loss of chiasmata.

The question then arises as to whether the malfunction of the germ cell in the first meiotic division is simply the result of intrinsic aging. Alternatively, could there be an environmental component in the aging of the germ cell? Such a component could act on the oocyte at any time during its period of exposure subsequent to the beginning of the first meiotic division in prenatal life. The apparently fixed frequencies of the

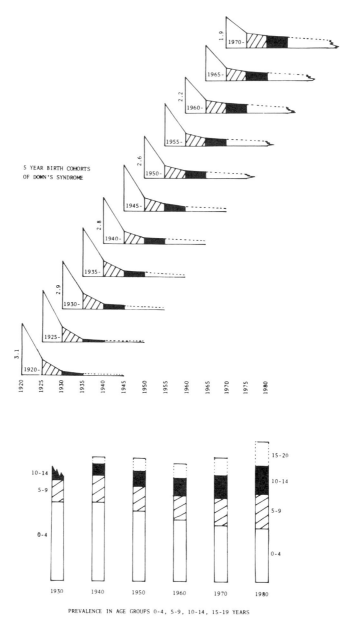

Figure 4.4. A model of the incidence and prevalence of Down's syndrome during the twentieth century, estimated from multiple sources. (From Steing and Susser 1977.)

incidence of Down's syndrome at birth by maternal age seems to point to an intrinsic process. New data have led us to reconsider whether that is the sole factor, however, and give grounds for hope that the whole process may not be entirely intrinsic.

First, the maternal monopoly of Down's syndrome has been challenged. A paternal contribution to Down's syndrome has been recognized. Cytogeneticists have in a proportion of cases been able to trace the parental origin of chromosomes by means of idiosyncratic markers. In a number of these, the anomalous chromosome is paternal and must have its origin in sperm (Hultén 1974). Subsequently, in a Danish study in which mothers were closely matched for age, a higher rate of Down's syndrome was found with very old fathers (Stene and Stene 1977). This relation of Down's syndrome to paternal age (although not the paternal origin of a number of trisomic chromosomes) has once more been rendered uncertain because a subsequent American study (Erickson 1978) has contradicted the Danish result. The crucial link between the idiosyncratic markers of trisomic chromosomes and paternal age has yet to be made, although the data are bound soon to be tested.

Three kinds of data offer more direct challenge to the biological invariance of Down's syndrome:

1. The available evidence points to an increase over time in the incidence of Down's syndrome at birth among older women (Stein and Susser 1977). Such a change suggests that an environmental factor has influenced incidence (see Figure 4.5).

2. There is evidence of an emerging racial difference in the incidence of Down's syndrome, with a higher rate among blacks than whites—a difference not previously observed—again, especially affecting older women. This evidence supports the suggestion of an environmental factor in the incidence of Down's syndrome among older women (Stark and White 1977).

3. Lately it has become obvious that trisomy anomalies found by amniocentesis performed for prenatal diagnosis in women 40 years of age and older occur at frequencies much higher than expected. The high frequency seems not to be mere artifact and is not readily explained by bias toward abnormality among cases selected for amniocentesis. One explanation is that incidence has increased, as the data given above suggest. Another explanation is that the frequency of trisomy 21 at amniocentesis is higher than frequency at birth because of a substantial loss through late spontaneous abortions between amniocentesis (at 16 to 20 weeks gestation) and birth (Kline 1979). This explanation turns us back to the prenatal period and the problem of spontaneous abortions.

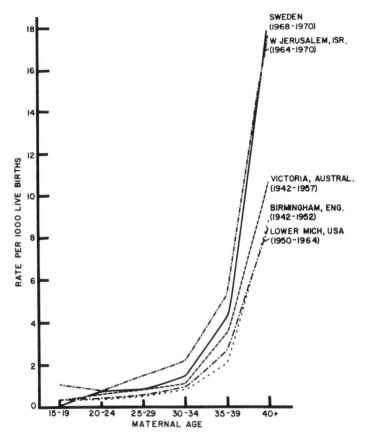

Figure 4.5. Maternal age-specific incidence rates of Down's syndrome. (From Stein and Susser 1977.)

SPONTANEOUS ABORTION AND AGING

We turned to the study of spontaneous abortions in our search for causes of congenital anomalies. In attempting to study congenital anomalies in newborns, the low survival rate in the period from conception to birth of anomalies, including trisomy 21, frustrates the epidemiological principle that all cases of a disorder should be accounted for if its natural history is to be understood. As a result of the high loss rate during pregnancy, the concentration of anomalies among spontaneous abortions is about a hundred times that at birth. About 95% of chromosomal anomalies abort. Trisomy 21 is more viable than most, and even of these about 70% abort (see Figure 4.6).

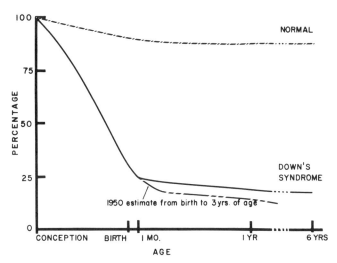

Figure 4.6. Survival model for Down's syndrome: conception through childhood. (From Stein and Susser 1977.)

With such attrition, the potential for confounding and bias at birth is large. Factors associated with anomalies at birth could be associated with their survival rather than with their genesis. Such a factor might be the malfunction of a normal maternal screening device that culls out fetal anomalies (Stein *et al.* 1975).

To examine such questions we developed a simple mathematical model that would enable us to separate abortions of normal and abnormal fetuses and to infer the operation of maternal factors as well as fetal factors (see Figure 4.7).

Gestational Age

In the course of such studies, we have begun to learn about aging in the prenatal phase by analyzing gestational age in spontaneous abortions, particularly the survival span of anomalies (Stark and White 1977). Many have a very short survival span. Some never go to term as live births; for example, trisomy 16, which comprises about half of all recognized trisomies. One could argue also that specific anomalies have a modal age of survival (see Figure 4.8). Such regularities and modalities may have meaning for the construct of specific age, in the sense of a modal or maximum age attainable by a species.

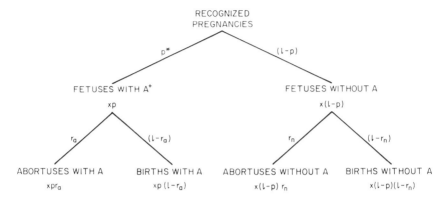

* p could be taken as a function of gestational time.

+ For the moment only one A per fetus is assumed.

Figure 4.7. Relationships between incidence of anomalies, fetal loss, and birth defects among recognized pregnancies. (From Stein, Susser, Warburton, Wittes, and Kline. Spontaneous abortion as a screening device: Effect of fetal survival on the incidence of birth defects. *American Journal of Epidemiology* 1975, 102:275–290.)

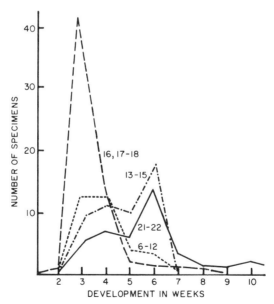

Figure 4.8. Frequency of various chromosomal anomalies found in abortus fetuses at given gestational age (development in weeks). Each curve represents frequency for the chromosome numbers indicated. (From Stein *et al.* 1977.)

Maternal Age

In the course of our studies, we have also come to understand something about maternal age as a factor in spontaneous abortions and anomalies (Stein *et al.* 1979). The rate of all forms of trisomy (not just trisomy 21) is fairly constant up to the mid-thirties; it then rises steeply with age to more than threefold at age 40. This age pattern is similar to that of Down's syndrome at birth. The rate of spontaneous abortion without chromosome anomalies (euploid) is also fairly constant up to the mid-thirties; then the rate again rises steeply with age, to more than threefold at age 40 (see Figures 4.9, 4.10, 4.11). The maternal age distribution does not go in the same direction for all the anomalies, however; for instance, the XO anomaly (of which about ± 0.2 % reach term and are born with Turner's syndrome) is associated with younger ages (Warburton *et al.* 1980).

There is some evidence about an environmental component in the maternal age distribution of trisomy. Radiation exposure both years before conception (Uchida 1971, Watanabe 1971, Alberman *et al.* 1972)

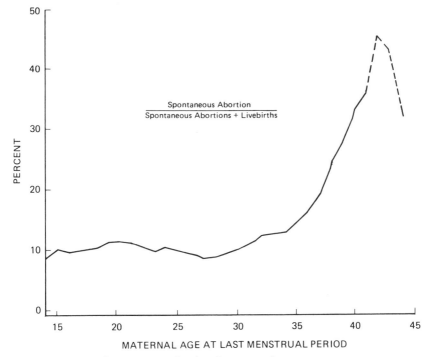

Figure 4.9. Rate of spontaneous abortion, by maternal age.

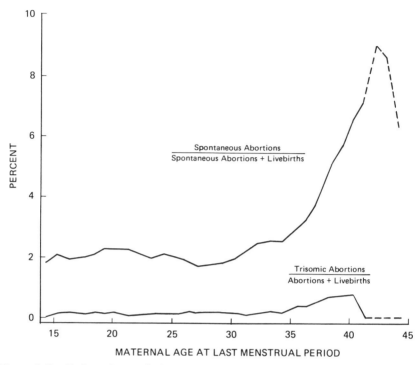

Figure 4.10.   Estimated rate of trisomic conceptions, by maternal age.

and around conception (Uchida 1971, Cohen *et al.* 1977) has been related
to Down's syndrome and trisomies in several studies. (A few studies
have failed to confirm the result.) The effect is confined to older women.

The first hint we ourselves found of an environmental factor in trisomies was not related to age. This was the observation of a cluster of
trisomies in time—in other words, a small epidemic (Warburton *et al.*
1977) (see Figure 4.12). We then began to identify antecedent risk factors
in spontaneous abortions, among them drug abuse, alcohol, and smoking.
To drink the equivalent of one ounce of alcohol twice a week (on average)
more than doubles the risk of spontaneous abortion. This effect is con-
centrated in euploid conceptions, most of which, unlike the aneuploidies,
do not abort (Kline *et al.* 1979a). Women who smoke have a relative
risk (strictly, an odds ratio) of 1.7 in spontaneous abortion (Kline *et al.*
1978), almost doubling the risk. The ready hypothesis was that here, too,
the incremental risk would be found in euploid conceptions. This hypothesis has not been so easily confirmed. So far, the most feasible
model is that younger smokers alone fit the expectation of an excess risk
of euploid abortions. Among older smokers, there seems to be an excess
risk of abortions with trisomies as well as of those without anomalies.

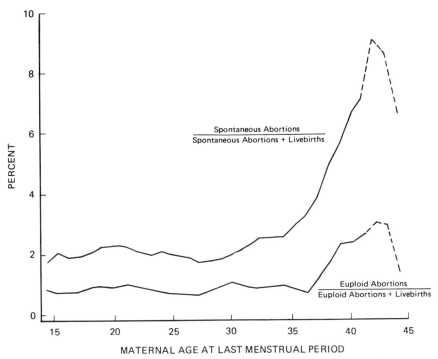

Figure 4.11. Estimated rate of abortion for euploid conceptions, by maternal age.

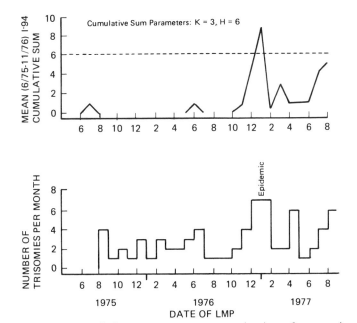

Figure 4.12. Frequency of trisomy among spontaneous abortions of pregnancies with last menstrual period June 1975 through August 1977 in three New York hospitals. Surveillance by cumulative summation techniques.

If the result holds—and it might not do so as we assemble the very large numbers of spontaneous abortion cases needed to narrow the confidence limits—we could have grounds for believing that this chromosomal anomaly is caused by an environmental factor that is conditional on age. Fortunately, the practical outcome in terms of incidence of Down's syndrome at birth is not alarming. Smoking seems to increase the spontaneous abortion rate of both trisomic and euploid fetuses, and older women who smoke have, if anything, a relative deficiency of trisomic births (Kline *et al.* 1979b).

Should results like these be confirmed, we shall have to open our minds to possibilities of the interaction of environment and cytogenetic structure at levels more fundamental than we have been accustomed to entertain.

REFERENCES

Adelstein, A. M., Hill, G. B., and Maung, L. (1971) Mortality from carcinoma of the cervix. *British Journal of Preventive and Social Medicine* 25:186–191.

Alberman, E., Polani, P. E., Fraser-Roberts, J. A., Spicer, C. C., Elliott, M., and Armstrong, E. (1972) Parental exposure to x-irradiation and Down's syndrome. *Annals of Human Genetics* 36:195–208.

Brenner, M. H. (1971) Economic changes in heart disease mortality. *American Journal of Public Health* 61:606–611.

Cohen, B. H., Lilienfeld, A. M., Kramer, S., and Human, L. C. (1977) Parental factors in Down's syndrome—results of the second Baltimore case-control study. Pp. 301–352 in E. B. Hook and I. H. Porter, eds., *Population Cytogenetics: Studies in Humans.* New York: Academic Press.

Collman, R. D., and Stoller, A. (1962) A survey of mongoloid births in Victoria, Australia, 1942–1957. *American Journal of Public Health* 53.

Comfort, A. (1956) The biology of aging. *Lancet* ii:772–778.

Durkheim, E. (1951) *Suicide: A Study in Sociology.* J. A. Spalding and G. Simpson, trans. (First published in 1897.) Chicago: Free Press.

Elinson, J. (1967) Effectiveness of social action programs in health and welfare. Assessing the effect of child health services. Ross Foundation Conference in Pediatric Research.

Erickson, J. D. (1978) Down's syndrome, paternal age, maternal age, and birth order. *Annals of Human Genetics* 41:289–298.

Hansen, H., and Susser, M. W. (1971) Historic trends in deaths from chronic kidney disease in the United States and Britain. *American Journal of Epidemiology* 93:413–442.

Henderson, S. A., and Edwards, R. G. (1968) Chiasma frequency and maternal age in mammals. *Nature* 218:22–28.

Hultén, M. (1974) Chiasma distributions at diakinesis in the normal human male. *Hereditas* 76:55–78.

Jagiello, G., and Fang, J. S. (1979) Analyses of diplotene chiasma frequencies in mouse oocytes and spermatocytes in relation to aging and sexual dimorphism. *Cytogenetics and Cell Genetics* 23:53–60.

Kermack, W. O., McKendrick, A. G., and McKinlay, P. L. (1934) Death-rates in Great Britain: Some general regularities and their significance. *Lancet* i:698–703.

Kline, J. (1979) The proportion of Trisomy 21 fetuses at amniocentesis compared to the proportion at birth. *Down's Syndrome: Papers and Abstracts for Professionals* 2:1–2.

Kline, J., Stein, Z. A., Susser, M. W., and Warburton, D. (1978) Smoking: A risk factor in spontaneous abortion. *New England Journal of Medicine:* 297:793–796.

Kline, J., Stein, Z. A., Susser, M. W., and Warburton, D. (1979a) Environmental influences on early reproductive loss in a current New York City study. In *Proceedings, New York State Symposium on Human Reproductive Loss,* Albany.

Kline, J., Stein, Z. A., Susser, M. W., and Warburton, D. (1979b) New insights into the epidemiology of chromosomal disorders: Their relevance to the prevention of Down's syndrome. In *Proceedings, Internation Association for the Scientific Study of Mental Deficiency,* Jerusalem.

Krueger, D. E., Williams, J. J., and Paffenbarger, R. (1967) Trends in death rates from cerebrovascular disease in Memphis, Tennessee, 1920–1960. *Journal of Chronic Diseases* 20:129–137.

Lombroso, C. (1911) *Crime: Its Causes and Remedies.* H. P. Horton, trans. Boston: Little, Brown.

Luthardt, F. W. (1977) Cytogenetic analyses of human oocytes. *American Journal of Human Genetics* 29:71A.

MacMahon, B., Johnson, S., and Pugh, T. F. (1963) Relation of suicide rates to social conditions. *Public Health Reviews* 78:287–293.

MacMahon, B., and Worcester, J. (1966) Age at menopause: United States, 1960–1962. *National Health Survey, Vital and Health Statistics,* Series 11, No. 19. Washington, D.C.: U.S. Department of Health, Education, and Welfare.

MacMahon, B., and Yuasa, S. (1970) Lactation and reproductive histories of breast cancer patients in Tokyo, Japan. *Bulletin of the World Health Organization* 42:185–194.

Magenis, E., Palmer, C. G., Wang, L., Brown, M., Chamberlin, J., Parks, M., Merritt, A. D., Rivas, M., and Yu, P. L. (1977) Heritability of chromosome banding variants. Pp. 179–188 in E. B. Hook and I. H. Porter, eds., *Population Cytogenetics: Studies in Humans.* New York: Academic Press.

Morel, B. A. (1857) Traité des dégénérescences physiques, intellectuelles, et morales de l'espèce humaine. Paris: Baillière.

Morris, J. N. (1955) Uses of epidemiology. *British Medical Journal* 2:395–401.

Murphy, H. B. M. (1959) Social change and mental health. In *Causes of Mental Disorders: A Review of Epidemiological Knowledge.* New York: Milbank Memorial Fund.

Penrose, L. S. (1934) *Mental Defect,* 1st ed. New York: Farrar.

Semmel, B. (1958) Karl Pearson, socialist and Darwinist. *British Journal of Sociology* 9:111–125.

Stark, C. R., and White, N. B. (1977) Cluster analysis and racial differences in risk of Down's syndrome. In E. B. Hook and I. H. Porter, eds., *Population Cytogenetics: Studies in Humans.* New York: Academic Press.

Stein, Z. A., Kline, J., Susser, E., Shrout, P., Warburton, D., and Susser, M. W. (1979) Maternal age and spontaneous abortion. In *Proceedings, New York State Symposium on Human Reproductive Loss,* Albany.

Stein, Z. A., Kline, J., Susser, E., Shrout, P., Warburton, D., and Susser, M. W. (1980) *Reproductive Loss: Human Embryonic and Fetal Death.* New York: Academic Press.

Stein, Z. A., and Susser, M. W. (1971) The preventability of Down's syndrome (mongolism). *HSMHA Rep.* 650–658.

Stein, Z. A., and Susser, M. W. (1977) Recent trends in Down's syndrome. Pp. 45–54 in P. Mittler, ed., *Research to Practice in Mental Retardation,* Vol. III. Baltimore, Md.: University Park Press.

Stein, Z. A., Susser, M. W., Kline, J., and Warburton, D. (1977) Amniocentesis and selective abortion for Trisomy 21 in the light of the natural history of pregnancy and fetal survival. In E. B. Hook and I. H. Porter, eds., *Population Cytogenetics: Studies in Humans*. New York: Academic Press.

Stein, Z. A., Susser, M. W., Warburton, D., Wittes, J., and Kline, J. (1975) Spontaneous abortion as a screening device: Effect of fetal survival on the incidence of birth defects. *American Journal of Epidemiology* 102:275–290.

Stene, J., and Stene, E. (1977) Statistical methods for detailing a moderate paternal age effect on incidence of disorder when a maternal one is present. *Annals of Human Genetics* 40:343–353.

Susser, M. W. (1968a) Aging and the field of public health. Pp. 114–160 in M. W. Riley and M. E. Johnson, eds., *Aging and Society*, Vol. II. New York: Russell Sage Foundation.

Susser, M. W. (1968b) *Community Psychiatry: Epidemiologic and Social Themes*. New York: Random House.

Susser, M. W. (1973) *Causal Thinking in Health Sciences: Concepts and Strategies in Epidemiology*. New York: Oxford University Press.

Susser, M. W. (1975) Demography of aging. Pp. 83–96 in A. M. Ostfeld and D. C. Gibson, eds., *Epidemiology of Aging*. Bethesda, Md.: U.S. Department of Health, Education, and Welfare.

Susser, M. W., and Stein, Z. A. (1962) Civilization and peptic ulcer. *Lancet* i:115–119.

Susser, M. W., and Watson, W. (1971) *Sociology in Medicine*, 2nd ed. London: Oxford University Press.

Tanner, J. M. (1962) *Growth at Adolescence*, 2nd ed. Oxford: Blackwell Scientific Publications.

Uchida, I. A. (1971) Trisomy associated with diagnostic X-rays. *Southern Medical Journal* 64:81–84.

U.S. Department of Health, Education, and Welfare (1979) National Heart, Lung and Blood Institute, Working Group on Heart Disease Epidemiology. National Institute of Health publication #79–1667. Bethesda, Md.: U.S. Department of Health, Education, and Welfare.

Warburton, D., Kline, J., Stein, Z. A., and Susser, M. W. (1977) Trisomy cluster in New York. *Lancet* ii:20.

Warburton, D., Kline, J., Stein, Z. A., and Susser, M. W. (1980) Monosomy X: A chromosomal anomaly associated with young maternal age. *Lancet* 1:167–169.

Watanabe, G. (1971) Environmental determinants of birth defects prevalence. Pp. 91–100 in M. A. Klingberg and J. A. C. Weatherall, eds., *Epidemiologic Methods for Detection of Teratogens, Contributions to Epidemiology and Biostatistics*, Vol. 1. Basel: S. Karger.

chapter 5

Some Economic Implications of Life-Span Extension

This chapter is concerned with the question: What would the economy look like if we suddenly discovered the fountain of youth? Though this question may seem fanciful, a growing number of contemporary Ponce de Leons with impressive scientific credentials would argue that there is a significant chance of unraveling the mystery of aging in the near future. The search for the famed fountain of youth has moved from the swamps of Florida to the laboratories of biologists, chemists, and physicians. These gerontologists are not, however, searching for some magical elixir; they are instead exploring the biochemical nature of aging with the goal of ultimately stopping, if not reversing, the aging process.

The scientific community appears to differ about the near-term likelihood of discovering a drug that would prevent or at least retard aging. While the probability of quickly finding such a youth drug may be small, the socioeconomic consequences of such a discovery could be enormous. The expected value of social science research on this type of life-span extension may be very large from the perspective of a cost–benefit calculation. Until some very basic social science research is done on the subject, however, it will be difficult to judge how much of the nation's scientific as well as social science research support should be devoted to life-span extension.

AGING
Biology and Behavior

I concentrate here on the implication of life-span extension for aggregate factor supply and economic welfare. While this is the major focus, I also consider the impact of life-span extension on the economy's skill composition and on existing economic institutions, particularly the social security system.

The major conclusion I draw from my analysis is that the expansion of work-span and total life-span should significantly increase economic welfare, which is measured as average consumption per year over an individual's lifetime; increasing the length of life, including productive life, appears to permit a higher level of consumption in every year that an individual is alive.

Life-span extension is taken to mean keeping people young for longer periods of time. This is quite different from what one conventionally means by life-span extension—keeping old people alive for longer periods.

The youthful extension of life with which I am here concerned represents a true expansion of the lifetime leisure and consumption opportunities of individuals. Assuming that both consumption and leisure are normal goods, this increase in individuals' life-spans permit them to purchase more commodities as well as to enjoy more leisure during their elongated lives. The purchase of additional commodities does require, however, additional earnings. Hence, at least some fraction of the increased number of years resulting from the youth drug will be devoted to additional work.

In the stylized economic models examined below, I consider equal increases in the age at retirement and the age at death as well as proportionate increases in age at retirement and age at death. Since the potency of the youth drug is as much in doubt as the availability of the drug itself, I attempt to distinguish the economic consequences of short extensions of life from those of long extensions.

In the first section I investigate how life-span extension affects our per capita output and economic welfare, assuming a fixed stock of capital in the economy. The section demonstrates that even if output per worker falls due to diminishing returns to increases in the labor force, output per capita and economic welfare may still rise.

The second section considers the impact of longer lives on aggregate capital accumulation and the economy's capital–labor ratio. This analysis indicates that capital intensity is likely to rise or at least not to fall as life-spans and work-spans are extended. This in turn implies that output per worker and wages per worker will not be adversely affected by longer life-spans. Combining the results of these two sections I arrive at a fairly optimistic assessment of the economic welfare consequences of the extension of life.

The third section explores how the skill composition of the labor force and the relative wages of skilled and unskilled workers are likely to change as a result of the youth drug; the fourth section is concerned with the impact of life-span extension on the social security system and other economic institutions.

PER CAPITA OUTPUT AND ECONOMIC WELFARE ASSUMING A FIXED STOCK OF CAPITAL

Assuming that total annual births remain unchanged and that after a transition period total annual deaths are also unchanged, life-span extension will be associated with an increase in total population. While the total stock of people who are alive will rise, assumptions about births and deaths indicate that the long-run growth rate of population is unaffected by life-span extension. The discovery of the youth drug will lead initially to a decline in total deaths as the number of physically old people declines. Assuming the drug is potent for only a fixed period of time, the number of physically old people will eventually return to its former level, as the early users of the drug reach the limits of its effectiveness. During this transition period, the population growth rate will exceed its long-term rate and the total population will rise.

Practitioners of the "dismal science" have long been concerned with population increases. Population increases arising from life-span extension have quite a different impact on per capita output and economic welfare from that of population growth arising from, for example, higher birth rates.

Population growth due to life-span extension involves an increase in the ratio of productive persons to dependent persons. The change in this dependence ratio can potentially reverse the dismal Malthusian prescription that population growth is immiserating. The Malthusian argument that population growth reduces economic welfare relies on the law of diminishing returns. For a fixed stock of nonlabor inputs, output as a function of labor input is subject to diminishing returns, that is, the level of output per worker will decline as the number of workers increases.

An interesting feature of life-span and work-span extension is that although output per worker could fall as the total work force rises, output per person in the economy may still rise because the ratio of workers to total population increases.

Per capita output seems to be a good measure of economic well-being because it indicates the level of consumption that each member of society could enjoy for each year of his or her life if output were uniformly distributed. While total lifetime utility would surely rise from the introduction of the drug (this would be evidenced simply by the voluntary purchase of the drug), it seems interesting to inquire whether this lifetime utility increase represents a higher or lower yearly level of economic well-being. Per capita income seems to be a good measure of potential yearly economic welfare.

To examine precisely the changes in per capita income, let us consider a very simple economy in which each person lives D years, is unproductive for C years (reflecting, for example, childhood, schooling, and retirement years), and works for $(D-C)$ years. Let us further assume that conventional population growth is zero and that the number of people at each age equals N. The total population of this economy is then DN, and the work force is $(D-C)N$.

Per capita output, y, may be written as:

$$y = \frac{F[(D-C)N]}{DN},$$
(1)

where F is the economy's production function that relates output to labor input. The assumption of positive but diminishing marginal productivity means that $F' > 0$ and $F'' < 0$. Differentiating y with respect to D yields:

$$\frac{\delta y}{\delta D} = \frac{F'N}{DN} - \frac{F}{D^2N} = \frac{F'DN-F}{D^2N}.$$
(2)

Equation (2) allows us to consider how per capita output responds to equal increases in life-span and work-span. The technological assumptions that $F' > 0$ and $F'' < 0$ imply that:

$$F > F'(D-C)N \qquad \text{or} \qquad F + F'CN > F'DN.$$
(3)

Condition (3) does not suffice to determine the sign of Eq. (2), that is, whether life-span extension increases or decreases per capita output. While nothing definitive can be said about the impact of small increases in life-span and work-span on per capita output, for very large increases in life-span the force of diminishing returns holds sway, and per capita output definitely declines. To see this, consider the inequality:

$$\frac{F}{F'} > DN.$$
(4)

While inequality (4) may not hold for small values of D, as D increases the inequality must hold; the right side of (4) increases at a rate N as D increases, while the left side increases at rate

$$\frac{\delta F/F'}{\delta D} = N - \frac{FF''N}{F'^2},$$

which exceeds N since $F'' < 0$.

For our economy, the sign of Eq. (2) seems clearly to be positive. Using the conventional Cobb–Douglas description of United States' production:

$$F = [(D-C)N]^\alpha,\tag{5}$$

where α is labor's share in total output equal to about .7. Using Eq. (5) and expressing Eq. (2) in terms of the percentage change in per capita output due to a percentage change in life-span, I arrive at:

$$\frac{\delta y}{\delta D}\frac{D}{y} = \left(\frac{\alpha D}{D-C} - 1\right).\tag{6}$$

In our economy, a working-span $(D-C)$ of 45 years, from age 20 to age 65, and a life-span (D) of 75 years seems to be the norm.

Applying these numbers to Eq. (6) yields a value of .17, suggesting that a 10% increase in life-span gives rise to a 1.7% increase in per capita output. The increase in per capita income would, of course, be much greater if output per worker did not fall. In this case, a 10% increase in life-span would give rise to a 6.7% increase in per capita output. One should keep this fact in mind when reading the next section, which indicates that output per worker could easily rise when capital accumulation is considered.

The prognosis for per capita output is less sanguine if, instead of assuming that the total increase in life-span is devoted to work, we assume that a constant fraction of the total life-span is spent working as longevity is extended. Per capita output in this case definitely falls. The change in per capita output for this case is given in Eq. (7), which from Eq. (3) is negative:

$$\frac{\delta y}{\delta D} = \frac{F'(D-C)N - F}{D^2N} < 0.\tag{7}$$

Which type of labor supply response seems most likely to occur—a year-for-year increase in the work-span, or a smaller, proportionate increase in working lives? A year-for-year increase in work-span as total life-span rises means that there is no desire for additional lifetime leisure as income rises. Evidence about retirement patterns in this century seems to rule out the year-to-year increase in work-span. As real wages have risen, there has been a dramatic increase in early retirement of men. In 1920, 60.1% of men over age 65 were in the labor force. The comparable number in 1977 was 20.1%. If the real wage were the only thing that had changed during this period, we could unambiguously conclude that life-time leisure was a normal good; since the substitution effect of a higher wage leads to a larger labor supply, the reduction in labor supply must reflect a positive income effect for lifetime leisure. The counter argument is that much of the increase in early retirement may reflect social security's implicit taxation of the labor supply of older workers (see Kotlikoff 1978). Another potentially important consideration is that this historic increase in lifetime leisure has occurred only for ages at which physical stamina and general health are poorest. If the youth drug permits individuals to remain highly energetic for years and years, desired lifetime leisure could actually fall; the preference for leisure appears to be strongly dependent on one's state of physical well-being, even for individuals who are adjudged to be medically healthy relative to their age cohort.

Another factor involved in thinking about changes in $(D - C)$ is that much of C reflects childhood and old age, periods during which work is physically impossible. The fraction of the lifetime that represents nondiscretionary leisure will certainly fall with the advent of the youth drug. Hence, even if the period of discretionary leisure increases proportionately with the period of work, the work-span as a fraction of total life-span will rise.

Population growth due to life-span extension is special in that it increases the ratio of productive to nonproductive people in society (i.e., it increases the fraction of each person's life that is productive). For a fixed stock of capital, population increases lead to a reduction in output per worker because of diminishing returns. Output per capita can, however, still rise if the ratio of productive to nonproductive years increases, an event that I perceive as highly likely.

CAPITAL STOCK, CAPITAL INTENSITY, AND OUTPUT PER WORKER

The capital–labor ratio determines output per worker; if the capital–labor ratio does not fall as a consequence of life-span extension, output per worker will not decline. If the capital–labor ratio rises, output per worker will rise as well. The message of this section is that diminishing returns to additional labor input need not occur, provided there are concomitant increases in the capital stock arising from life-span extension.

To make the analysis as intuitive as possible, I first present a very simplified life-cycle model of capital accumulation that ignores intertemporal discounting, conventional population growth, and various types of economic uncertainties. Consider then, an economy in which individuals live for D years and work for the first R years. Letting e stand for the earnings per year of work, lifetime earnings equal eR. I assume equal consumption per year over one's life; consumption per year is then eR/D. Conventional population growth is zero. There are N individuals at each age. The total capital stock for this economy consists of the capital (wealth) owned by workers plus the capital owned by retirees (i.e., those older than R). Each person saves $e(1 - R/D)$ per year until retirement; thereafter, he or she dissaves an amount eR/D each year until death at age D. A preretirement worker of age x has saved $e(1 - R/D)$ for x years and thus has a net worth of $e(1 - R/D)x$. The total assets of workers, Aw, is given by the integral over workers from age zero to age R of assets held at age x times N, the population at each age:

$$Aw = \int_0^R e\left(1 - \frac{R}{D}\right)Nx\,dx = e\left(1 - \frac{R}{D}\right)N\frac{R^2}{2}. \tag{8}$$

Assets for retirees equal their net worth at retirement age, $e(1 - R/D)R$, less their accumulated dissaving from age R to their current age x. Assets for a retiree age x can thus be written as $e(1 - R/D)R - eR/D(x - R)$, or $eR - (eR/D)\,x$. Total assets of retirees, A_R, equal the integral over ages R to D of retiree's assets at age x:

$$A_R = \int_R^D \left(eR - \frac{eR}{D}x\right)N\,dx = eR(D-R)N - \frac{eR}{D}\left(\frac{D^2 - R^2}{2}\right)N. \tag{9}$$

Adding Eqs. (8) and (9) gives the total capital stock, K, in this economy:

$$K = Ne\frac{(D-R)R}{2}. \tag{10}$$

Let us now consider equal increases in life-span D and retirement age R, that is, the differential $D - R$ is constant. The change in the capital stock is thus $Ne(D - R)/2$, which is clearly positive. There appear to be two opposing forces involved here. On one hand, simultaneously increasing D and R reduces the relative length of the retirement period. This reduces the annual savings of each worker, $e(1 - R/D)$, and increases the annual dissaving of each retired person, eR/D. On the other hand, there is an absolute increase in the number of workers, while the number of retirees stays constant. Although each worker saves less, there are so many additional workers that total savings of workers as well as the capital stock rise. To obtain some notion of the magnitude of these capital stock increases, I present the elasticity of the capital stock with respect to this type of life-span and work-span extension:

$$\frac{\delta K}{\delta D}\left(\frac{D}{K}\right) = \frac{D}{R}. \tag{11}$$

Since D exceeds R, this elasticity exceeds unity. Values of D of 55 and R of 45 give an elasticity of 1.22. In our model, a value of 55 corresponds to a real-world age of death of 75, since the age at which work begins (e.g., 20) is normalized to zero. An elasticity of 1.22 implies that a 10% increase in life-span would increase the capital stock by 12.2%.

If, rather than assuming that $D-R$ stays constant, we assume that $(D - R)/R$ stays constant as D increases, the elasticity of capital to D equals 2.

Since the labor force equals NR, the capital labor ratio, K/L, is easily computed:

$$\frac{K}{L} = \frac{Ne(D-R)\,R/2}{NR} = e\,\frac{(D-R)}{2}. \tag{12}$$

Note that equal increases in life-span and work-span leave the capital-labor ratio unaltered, while equal proportionate increases in D and R increase the capital-labor ratio by the same percentage.

Proportionate increases in retirement and death ages that increase the absolute length of retirement lead to more capital per worker, while changes in life-span that leave the length of retirement unaltered do not alter capital intensity. Equation (12) paints a rosy picture of the impact of life-span extension on per capita output independent of whether the work-span increases year-for-year with life-span or increases proportionally. If work-span increases *pari passus* with life-span, output per worker will remain fixed, but per capita output will rise due to the increase in workers per person in the economy. If the extension of the work-span is proportionate, per capita output will rise because output per worker increases, although the ratio of workers to the population remains fixed.[1] Since the real wage, e, is also an increasing function of capital intensity, the same story can be told for yearly consumption, which is eR/D. When R/D rises, e remains fixed; when R/D is fixed, e rises. Yearly consumption rises in either case.

The analysis to this point has assumed that each worker is fully em-

---

[1] It can be demonstrated that these per capita output results hold in a model in which there is an initial nonproductive period of B years, followed by $(R-B)$ years of work, and $(D-R)$ years of retirement.

ployed for each year prior to retirement. I now permit the quantity of labor supplied each year to be chosen by the individual and ask whether this type of labor supply response to life-span extension will alter the economy's capital intensity. To begin, let us assume that each person works for the same fraction of each year. As life-span is extended, the increases in potential lifetime resources discussed above might lead individuals to reduce their labor supply, l, during each working year, as well as alter the total number of years, R, spent working. This type of labor supply reduction, by reducing earnings, will reduce savings and the capital stock. Although the capital stock falls, the capital–labor ratio is unaffected.[2]

To see this, let $e = wl$, where w is the wage per year. The economy's labor supply, L, in this case is NRl. Rewriting the capital–labor equation (12) for this situation of variable labor supply gives:

$$\frac{K}{L} = \frac{Nwl(D-R)R/2}{NRl} = \frac{w(D-R)}{2}. \tag{13}$$

In Eq. (13) it is clear that the capital–labor ratio is independent of annual labor supply l. Intuitively one knows that the yearly labor supply falls by the same percentage as the capital stock falls, leaving the capital–labor ratio unaltered. Even if labor supply differs from one period to the next, as long as the percentage reduction in the labor supply in each period is the same, the capital–labor ratio will be unaltered. To the extent that labor supply when young falls (rises) by a greater (lesser) percentage than labor supply when old, the capital–labor ratio will fall (rise).

The conclusion that emerges from this very simplified model is that the economy's capital intensity is likely to rise or at least remain constant in response to life-span extension.

It is important to determine whether those results hold for a more realistic and correspondingly more complex model of economic growth. I therefore constructed a more detailed steady-state life-cycle model that takes into account interest rates, population and productivity growth, and intertemporal optimal consumption choice. Rather than consuming at a constant level each year, individuals choose a consumption path that maximizes an intertemporal utility function, U, of the form:

$$U = \int_0^D \log C_t e^{-\rho t}. \tag{14}$$

[2] Martin Feldstein (1974) investigates the impact of the long-run labor supply elasticity on capital intensity. A related paper is Kotlikoff and Summers (1978).

In Eq. (14), ρ is the rate-of-time preference that indicates the consumer's relative preference for consumption today rather than consumption tomorrow. C_t is consumption at time t. Individuals choose the path of C_t that maximizes Eq. (14) subject to the lifetime budget constraint:

$$\int_0^D C_t e^{-rt} dt \leq \int_0^R w_t e^{-rt} dt \tag{15}$$

Equation (15) indicates that the present value of the consumption path chosen must not exceed the present value of lifetime earnings. The interest rate at which dollar values are discounted back to time zero is r; R and D are, respectively, ages of retirement and death; and w is the real wage in year t. The real wage is assumed to grow at a constant rate, g, due to labor augmenting technological change. To make the model somewhat more realistic, I incorporate a 30% tax on wage income and a 50% tax on interest income in the analysis.

Given the optimal consumption and earnings paths, one can compute savings and wealth holdings at each age for a representative individual in this economy. Aggregating the wealth holdings of each person at each age, I arrive at Eq. (15) which indicates the total supply of capital at time t in the economy, K_t^s, corresponding to different parameter values of the model.

$$K_t^s = \frac{w_t}{rg} \left(H_1 + H_3 H_4 \right),$$

where

$$H_1 = \left(\frac{1 - e^{(r-u)R}}{u - r} \right) - \left(\frac{1 - e^{-nR}}{n} \right),$$

$$H_3 = \left[\left(\frac{e^{zD} - 1}{z} - \frac{1 - e^{(r-u)R}}{u - r} \right) - \left(\frac{e^{(r-u)R} - e^{(r-u)D}}{u - r} \right) e^{-\rho D} \right], \tag{16}$$

$$H_4 = \frac{1 - e^{(g-r)R}}{1 - e^{-\rho D}},$$

$$u = n + g,$$

$$z = (r - u) - \rho.$$

In Eq. (16), n and g are respectively rates of population and productivity growth.

The demand for capital by firms corresponding to given after-tax factor prices, w_t and r, is derived from the Cobb–Douglas production function:

$$K_t^D = \frac{\alpha w_t (1 - tr)}{(1 - \alpha) r (1 - tw)} \frac{1 - e^{-nR}}{n}, \tag{17}$$

where α is capital's share in total income (taken here to be .3), tr is the tax rate on interest income (.5), and tw is the tax rate on wage income (.3).

To investigate how changes in life-span D and work-span R influence the capital stock in general equilibrium, I first solve for the equilibrium value of K, which equates capital supply and demand for initial values of D and R. I then change D and R and compute the new equilibrium value of K. To find equilibrium solutions for Eqs. (16) and (17), I eliminate K_t/w_t from both equations, leaving an equation in r. This equation was solved using a computer. The solution is unique because in Eq. (16) K_t/w_t is a decreasing function of r, while in Eq. (17) K_t/w_t is an increasing function of r. Given the equilibrium value of r, Eq. (15) or (16) may be used to solve for the equilibrium value of K_t/w_t.

Table 5.1 reports general equilibrium capital–labor ratios for a range of different retirement ages and death ages. By general equilibrium I mean that all changes in the optimal consumption path that arise due to changes in wages and interest rates are taken into account. Since age zero in this model corresponds to the age of entrance into the labor force, an age of death of 50 and a retirement age of 40 should be thought of as corresponding to real-world ages of 70 and 60. The table also reports real net wage rates corresponding to the different capital–labor ratios, for which the net wage for a death age of 50 and a retirement age of 40 is normalized to one.

The numerical values in Table 5.1 support the finding from the more simplified model that proportionate growth in retirement and death ages will raise capital intensity. An increase in retirement age from 40 to 80 concomitant with an increase in the age of death from 50 to 100 raises capital intensity from 6.89 to 10.15, or 47.3%. At the same time the real wage rises by 14% and per capita output rises by 18%. An interesting feature underlying these proportionate changes is that although the ratio of the retirement age to the death age stays constant, the ratio of productive to nonproductive workers rises. This reflects the positive rate of population growth, that is, there are few people aged 80–100 relative

TABLE 5.1
General Equilibrium Capital–Labor Ratios and Wage Rates for Various Life-Spans and Work-Spans[a]

Age of retirement	Age of death										
	50	60	70	80	90	100	110	120	130	150	200
40	6.89 / 1	10.25 / 1.15	13.29 / 1.28	15.99 / 1.37	18.32 / 1.50	20.46 / 1.59	22.16 / 1.66	23.95 / 1.74	25.12 / 1.79	27.19 / 1.88	30.90 / 2.04
50		7.42 / 1.02	10.23 / 1.14	11.27 / 1.19	14.92 / 1.35	17.02 / 1.44	18.86 / 1.52	20.43 / 1.59	21.89 / 1.65	24.47 / 1.76	27.80 / 1.91
60			8.02 / 1.05	10.13 / 1.14	12.27 / 1.23	14.22 / 1.32	15.86 / 1.39	17.49 / 1.46	19.06 / 1.53	21.30 / 1.63	25.09 / 1.79
70				8.36 / 1.05	10.23 / 1.14	11.85 / 1.22	13.59 / 1.29	15.00 / 1.35	16.56 / 1.42	18.73 / 1.51	22.66 / 1.69
80					8.80 / 1.08	10.15 / 1.14	11.60 / 1.20	13.27 / 1.28	14.16 / 1.32	16.40 / 1.41	19.93 / 1.57
90						9.00 / 1.09	10.33 / 1.15	11.57 / 1.20	12.62 / 1.25	14.47 / 1.33	18.30 / 1.50
100							9.23 / 1.10	10.23 / 1.14	11.39 / 1.20	13.56 / 1.29	16.12 / 1.40

[a] Top number in each cell is capital–labor ratio; bottom number is the wage rate. The wage rate for a retirement age of 40 and a death age of 50 is normalized to 1. The table assumes 1% growth in population 2% growth in productivity, and a 1% rate of time preference.

to people under 80 due to population growth. Even at a low 1% rate of population growth there are only .37 100-year-olds for every 1-year-old in the population.

The table indicates some nonlinearities with respect to equal increases in retirement and death ages. Holding the retirement period at 10 years, increases in life-span from 50 to 100 raises capital intensity from 6.89 to 9.00, the real wage by 9%, and per capita output by 21%. On the other hand, for a 20-year retirement period, raising the age of death from 60 to 110 leads to very little change in capital intensity; it rises from 10.25 to 10.33. Per capita output rises, however, by 22% primarily because of the increase in the ratio of productive to nonproductive citizens.

THE SKILL COMPOSITION OF THE LABOR FORCE

The extension of the age of retirement will affect career choices and human capital investment (training) decisions. Increases in the age of retirement will make careers that require an initial period of training relatively more attractive than careers that involve no initial training because the lengthened work-span permits a longer period of amortization on the initial training investment. If there is no change in the length of training received in these careers, an increased number of workers will choose skilled careers; the growth in skilled workers relative to unskilled workers in the economy will continue until skilled wages are depressed relative to unskilled wages to the point that marginal workers are again indifferent to a choice between unskilled and skilled careers.

This increase in the skill composition of the labor force and fall in the relative wages of skilled and unskilled workers need not, however, occur. The increase in the retirement period makes additional training desirable. If each skilled worker engages in additional training, the returns to the career paths can be realigned with the same proportion of skilled to unskilled workers in the economy, although with an increase in the ratio of effective skilled workers to unskilled workers. By effective skilled workers I mean the number of skilled workers adjusted for their degree of training. In this scenario, the wage per unit of skilled human capital falls, although annual earnings of skilled workers could actually rise because of the greater amount of human capital per skilled worker.

These points are illustrated in the following simple model. I assume that the economy's output, F, can be described by a Cobb–Douglas production function in effective skilled labor, S^*, and unskilled labor, U:

$$F(S^*, U) = S^{*\alpha} U^{1-\alpha}, \tag{18}$$

where α is the share of effective skilled labor in total income. I let W_S denote yearly earnings per skilled worker and W_U yearly earnings per unskilled worker; competitive choice of career paths will ensure an equalization of lifetime earnings in both careers:

$$W_S(R - E) = W_U R . \tag{19}$$

The effective stock of skilled labor is related to the number of skilled workers, S, by:

$$S^* = SH(E) . \tag{20}$$

In Eq. (20), $H(E)$ is the human capital production function that indicates the number of effective skill units of labor provided by a worker with E years of training. I assume that $H'(E) > 0$ and $H''(E) < 0$; W_S and W_U are determined in competition factor markets and equal, respectively, the marginal products of skilled and unskilled workers:

$$W_S = \frac{\alpha F}{S} ; \qquad W_U = (1 - \alpha)\frac{F}{U} . \tag{21}$$

Equations (19) and (21) imply:

$$\frac{\alpha}{1 - \alpha} \frac{R - E}{E} = \frac{S}{U}. \tag{22}$$

If one holds E, the length of training, constant, then increases in R definitely raise the economy's skill composition. However, this need not occur because E will increase with R.

The length of training is chosen to maximize lifetime earnings in a career as a skilled worker:

$$W_S(R - E) = W_{S^*} H(E)(R - E). \tag{23}$$

In Eq. (23) W_{S^*} is the wage per unit of skilled human capital. Individuals take W_{S^*} as given by the market when they determine their optimal amount of training, E. Optimal choice of E satisfies:

$$H'(E)(R - E) = H(E) . \tag{24}$$

It is also clear that:

$$\frac{dE}{dR} = -\frac{H'(E)}{H''(R - E) - 2H'(E)} > 0. \tag{25}$$

Equation (25) indicates that the length of training unambiguously rises with increases in the age of retirement, R. The greater the age of retirement, the longer is the period of time that a skilled worker can amortize his or her training investment. Hence, increases in the retirement age make additional training more desirable. The skill composition, S/U, determined in Eq. (22), may, however, remain unchanged. If the elasticity of the training period, E, with respect to the retirement age, R, is unity, E will rise in the same proportion as R, and S/U will be unaltered. In every case, the wage per unit of skilled human capital, W_{S^*}, falls relative to the unskilled wage, W_U:

$$\frac{W_{S^*}}{W_U} = \frac{R}{H(E)(R-E)} \tag{26}$$

and

$$\frac{dW_{S^*}/W_U}{dR} = -\frac{H(E)E}{H(E)^2(R-E)^2} < 0. \tag{27}$$

In the case of zero population growth, the ratio of trainees, T, to skilled workers, S, is:

$$\frac{T}{S} = \frac{E}{R-E} \tag{28}$$

Taking N to be the population at each age, the total labor force, RN, is divided between trainees, skilled workers, and unskilled workers:

$$RN = S + U + T. \tag{29}$$

If E and R move in equal proportions, Eqs. (22), (28), and (29) dictate a proportionate growth in the number of skilled workers, unskilled workers, and trainees. If E rises less than in proportion to R, the skilled work force will rise relative to the unskilled work force, and the number of trainees will fall relative to the number of skilled workers.

While I know of no empirical study that has investigated the elasticity of the training period with respect to the age of retirement, my own impression is that this elasticity is likely to be less than unity. This impression is based on the observation that in many areas there is a fixed body of knowledge that can be digested in a few years, and that additional training time will be subject to severe diminishing returns.

Although it will influence the skill mix, the length of training, and relative wages of skilled and unskilled workers, life-span extension will not necessarily increase the number of people choosing to have multiple careers during their lifetimes. Leaving aside the issue of boredom, the decision to pursue a single career over one's lifetime rather than to pursue multiple careers will always generate greater lifetime earnings. To see this, consider an individual who at the beginning of his or her working life must choose between careers A, B, and C. Let us assume that each of these careers requires some period of training and that each career provides the same present value of lifetime earnings. Suppose the individual chooses career A. Is it ever optimal in the sense of income maximizing for the individual to switch careers at some time during his or her working life after he or she has received training in career A? The answer is no; while each career offers the same present value of earnings for an individual who has received no training, once the individual has received training in career A, remaining in career A will always generate a higher present value of earnings because no additional training is required to remain in A, while training would be required in careers B or C. Except for the increase in boredom for remaining in a single career over an extended period I would not expect to see a marked increase in the percentage of the work force that engages in multiple careers.

THE SOCIAL SECURITY SYSTEM AND OTHER ECONOMIC INSTITUTIONS

The past two decades have witnessed an enormous growth in the social security system and old-age health insurance. During this period, the number of social security recipients has more than doubled, and benefits—including retirement, disability, and old-age health insurance payments—have almost quadrupled in real terms. Since 1960 the combined employee and employer social security tax rate has doubled from 6% to 12.1%. The 1977 legislation calls for even higher social security taxes in the near future; between 1978 and 1982, social security taxes for a middle-income worker will rise in real terms by about 52%, about $1000 1978 dollars. Even these massive tax increases may prove quite insufficient to finance the program through the first half of the twenty-first century. Robertson (1978), Chief Actuary of the Social Security Administration, projects that if the current law is maintained up to the year 2025, tax rates will have to increase by more than 8% to meet scheduled benefit payments. Projecting far into the future is, of course, a hazardous business; still, forecasts of a 23% or greater social security tax in 2025 do not augur well for the future of the social security's system.

A large part of recent increases in the tax burden reflects healthy legislated increases in real social security benefits for the elderly. Much of the problem down the road reflects the enormous recent reductions in fertility rates; in 1957, the fertility rate reached a postwar high of 3.7 children born per woman; in 1976, the figure was 1.8. The lower fertility rates imply that the ratio of workers to retired beneficiaries will fall from a current level of 3.2 to about 2 by the middle of the next century.

Increases in life-span and work-span could greatly relieve our social security problems. Our system is set up on a pay as you go basis, in which young workers pay taxes that are handed over to old people as retirement benefits. If, through life-span extension, we can markedly increase the ratio of workers to retired people, the tax burden per worker will be greatly alleviated.

Certain features of the social security program will have to be changed to permit the extension of life to improve the financial status of the system; if structural changes in the program are not implemented, life-span extension could greatly exacerbate our funding problems. The main change that would need to be made is to eliminate implicit taxation of the work efforts of the elderly. Prior to age 72 (age 70 after 1981, under the new law), the social security earnings test reduces or eliminates benefits for many working aged people. Not only do aged workers lose their benefits by working, but they also receive, in most instances, little return on the social security taxes they continue to pay. The earnings test represents an implicit 50% tax rate on the labor earnings of the elderly over a wide range of potential earnings.

If we maintain the earnings test in its current form in the face of extended life-spans, we could quickly create a situation in which most physically young people were induced by social security to retire because they were old in calendar time and ran into the social security tax bite. Surely we will want to either eliminate the earnings test altogether or raise the minimum age at which benefits can be received. If we are responsive to the need for institutional change in the social security system when the youth drug is discovered, the extension of life will undoubtedly greatly relieve our social security problems.

There are other economic institutions that would be dramatically affected by life-span extension. Certainly the medical profession and health delivery system would suffer a relative if not an absolute decline as the percentage of physically old people declines. Insurance companies and pension funds with annuity obligations would face severe financial problems if their beneficiaries suddenly stopped dying, perhaps for 40 years. The economy would presumably become much more youth-oriented with corresponding increases in the demand for physical recreational activities.

The list of potential changes in the structure of the economy is indeed a long one. I have focused on just a few important economic issues involved in life-span extension. My analysis leads me to be highly optimistic about the economic gains from life-span extension; life-span extension is likely to raise per capita income and the economic welfare of a vast majority of people. In addition, life-span extension can greatly relieve the financial crunch of our social security and old-age health insurance programs.

REFERENCES

Feldstein, M. S. (1974) Tax incidence in a growing economy with variable factor supply. *Quarterly Journal of Economics* 88:551–573.
Kotlikoff, L. J. (1978) Social security, time to reform. Pp. 119–144 in M. Boskin, ed., *Federal Tax Reform*. San Francisco, Calif.: Institute for Contemporary Studies.
Kotlikoff, L. J., and Summers, L. H. (1978) Long Run Tax Incidence and Variable Labor Supply Revisited. U.C.L.A. working paper no. 111, February 1978.
Robertson, A. H. (1978) Financial status of the social security program after the social security amendments of 1977. *Social Security Bulletin* 14 (March):21–36.

chapter 6

Old Age in Tzintzuntzan, Mexico

GEORGE M. FOSTER

Urban dwellers, beset by the stresses of city life since classical times, have turned to the countryside to find their models of the ideal social system. Western civilization has believed, or wanted to believe, that rural life is marked by a virtuous quality that sets it off from city life, that it encapsulates the fundamental moral qualities of every society— in opposition to the city, with its impersonality, disorganization, anomie, and vices. Aristophanes (?448–?380 B.C.) in *The Clouds* contrasted the two ways of life: Strepsiades was a pious, industrious man who loved country life, while his wife and son were city people "addicted to all sorts of diversions, extravagance and superfluities [Caro Baroja 1963, pp. 27–28]." Aristophanes, says Caro Baroja, was repeating the common view of Athenians of his time "yet this commonplace has lasted to our day; in the city are found vice, corruption and artifice; in the country the ancient virtues, and still more than in the countryside of one's own land, in the countryside of distant regions which have a smaller number of cities [p.28]."

This stereotypic view of the contrast between the moral qualities of rural and urban life has profoundly influenced American life, from the time of Jefferson (and earlier) to the present. For generations, it has shaped our national agricultural policy: Without millions of single-family

115

AGING
Biology and Behavior

farms, we reason, democracy cannot flourish. More recently it has taken
new forms in the commune movement and in the flight from the city.
Among intellectuals, this image of the ideal society is apparent in the
widespread belief that psychological stress and its attendant ills exist
only at low levels in technologically simple societies that, in their collective wisdom, have developed holistic approaches to illness that treat
patients in the context of family and society. By many, these approaches
are deemed superior to contemporary "impersonal," disease-oriented
therapy.

Clearly, an implicit premise of great power—the virtues of a simple
rural life—underlies our quest for solutions to social and health problems.
Much of what we read about the status of the aged in nonindustrial
societies contributes to this premise. Thus, about the Sidomo of southwest Ethiopia we read "For both sexes old age is highly esteemed
[Hammer 1972, p. 15]." "The lifecycle for both sexes involves emphasis
on the importance and prestige of old age. According to the Sidomo
hierarchy of values youth is not a highly esteemed time of life [Hammer
1972, p. 24]." The power of the aged is apparent among the Ibo, by
whom aged men as a class are referred to as "those who rule" or "those
who are headmen," appellations "reflecting the social roles of old men
[Shelton 1972, p. 32]." And for the southern African Bantu we learn that
"the Bantu regard for gray beards and white heads is quite universal.
So deeply engrained is the assumption that wisdom goes with age that
Africans have tended to give automatic expressions of respect to the
elderly in cultures other than their own [Fuller 1972; p. 58]." "Almost
every elder, in most Bantu tribes, unless made incompetent through
physical or mental disorder, has a respected role as a wise counsellor
[Fuller 1972, p. 67]." In Samoa, "Old age is almost universally referred
to as the 'best time of life' by both old and young Samoans [Holmes
1972, p. 75]."

Accounts such as these lead to the common stereotype of old age in
simple societies as a happier and more satisfactory period of life than
in contemporary America. Certainly societies in which the aged live
comfortably in the bosom of a loving family, their every psychological
and economic need met, rich in prestige and honor, consulted for their
views on community policy, and respected and envied by all, present
an attractive alternative to the reality of old age for vast numbers of
Americans. Whether or not there are lessons to be learned that can be
incorporated into contemporary social policy from such societies is another matter.

It is notable that in societies in which the conditions just described
prevail or are believed to prevail, we find very few elderly people. For

the stereotype often fails to point out that, in the absence of modern preventive and curative medicine—and despite the virtues of holistic traditional therapies—very few people survive into the advanced years. A few aged people can be supported and even cherished in almost any society, but it may be another matter when they constitute 10% or more of the total population. It is also notable that in these societies great cultural stability, with little change from generation to generation, has prevailed until recently. But the stable society in which the elderly are fountains of wisdom no longer exists; the striking thing about the modern world is the rapidity with which the "classical" communities of anthropological studies have been transformed into the rural dimension of nation states. Whatever the truth of the common picture of the status and role of the aged in simple societies, it seems likely that concomitant with socioeconomic changes, changes are also occurring in such societies.

TZINTZUNTZAN, MICHOACÁN, MEXICO

It is against this stereotypic background that I describe what it is like to grow old in a traditional Mexican community currently experiencing rapid socioeconomic change. The primary question in my mind is not a simple "Is it better to grow old in this community or in contemporary United States?" Rather, I am concerned with such matters as the extent to which the common anthropological picture of the status of the aged in simple societies holds true in this case as well as with the aspects of the lives of the aged that I consider to be strengths—and weaknesses—of the social system of that community.

Tzintzuntzan, Michoacán, Mexico is a Spanish-speaking village of about 2600 people on the shores of Lake Pátzcuaro in highland Mexico, about 230 miles west of Mexico City. Prior to the Spanish conquest of Mexico, it was a major city, capital of the Tarascan Indian Empire, but since about 1540, it has been a humble village of potters, farmers, and fishermen. Today, only 10% of the population can be classed as Indian, largely on the basis of ability to speak the Tarascan language. In prior publications (e.g., Foster 1967), I have described Tzintzuntzan and analyzed its institutions and the behavior of its people within the conceptual framework of peasantry models. But because of the rapidity with which the community is modernizing, I am no longer sure this approach is appropriate for the present, and certainly it will be inappropriate for the future.

My formal study of the community, which began early in 1945, is now in its thirty-fifth year. During this period, great changes have occurred.

Population has increased from 1231 in 1945, to 1877 in 1960, to 2253 in 1970, to an estimated 2600 in 1979. Accelerating emigration has slowed the growth of the village during the past two decades. Preventive and curative modern medicine, both little known in 1945, are now the first choice of almost everyone, except for several "folk" illnesses such as *bilis, empacho,* and the evil eye, and longevity has increased significantly. Primary education, little esteemed 35 years ago, is now nearly universal, and large numbers of young people seek, and often complete, higher education as teachers, doctors, lawyers, and even computer technicians. Most of these young professionals are lost to the community. Tourist demand for local arts and crafts and the remissions of villagers living legally and illegally in the United States have increased standards of living significantly over the years, and surprisingly large numbers of people say, in effect, "Times have never been better."

The observations that follow are both synchronic and diachronic: I describe what it is like to be elderly in Tzintzuntzan today, and I trace the changes that have occurred during the past 35 years.

Demographic Characteristics of the Aged

Unlike many nonwestern societies, in Tzintzuntzan there is no commonly agreed on age-grading system. When asked about age categories, most informants reply that childhood (*la niñez*) extends from birth to physiological maturity. Infancy (*la infancia*) is a subcategory of childhood that ends at 5 or 6 years of age. Childhood is followed by youth (*la juventud*), which lasts until 25 or 30 years of age. Some, but not all, informants recognize maturity (*la madurez*) as the period between the end of youth until the onset of old age (*la vejez*). Most informants set as the onset of old age the decade of the fifties, with 60 being the single most common answer; no informant has given a later age. Since my census data are divided into 5-year units (i.e., 0–5, 6–10) arbitrarily I have chosen to label people 61 years of age and over as *viejo* ("old").

Over the years, the proportion of old people in Tzintzuntzan has increased significantly, as Table 6.1 shows. This striking increase in the proportion of the aged to the total population is due in part to emigration (especially since 1960) and in part to rapidly increasing longevity. Kemper (1977) has calculated that, during the 15-year period of 1945–1959, a total of 183 villagers moved away, an average of only 12 per year. In contrast, during the decade 1960–1969, 492 left the community, an average of 49 per year. Had these emigrants remained in the village, the proportion of the aged would have remained lower: in 1960, about 4.0 (versus the actual 4.4), and in 1970, 5.6 (versus the actual 6.9).

TABLE 6.1
Percentage, in Selected Years, of Tzintzuntzan's Aged Population

Year	Village population	Number of aged	Percentage of population
1945	1231	46	3.7
1960	1877	82	4.4
1970	2253	155	6.9
1979 (estimated)	2600	230	9.0

From this evidence, we conclude that of the increase in the percentage of the aged between 1945 and 1970, almost 2% (the difference between 5.6 and 3.7) can be explained by greater longevity. The vastly improved health status of Tzintzuntzeños today, compared with that of 30 years ago, is apparent from death records. During the decade 1940–1949 when the population averaged 1200 people, 257 deaths occurred. During the decade 1969–1978 when the population averaged 2400, only 156 deaths occurred. Table 6.2 gives the breakdown by years and sex for deaths during these two decades.

During the earlier decade, the crude death rate appears to have been a little over 20 per 1000; during the latter decade, this figure dropped to about 6.5 per 1000. Equally striking as this dramatic decrease in crude death rates and correlated with it is the upward shift in the age of death, shown in Table 6.3.

During both decades, the first 5 years of life were marked by the most deaths, but during the earlier period children died four times as frequently as during the later period when the percentage of all deaths, while still

TABLE 6.2
Tzintzuntzan Deaths by Sex, 1940–1949 and 1969–1978

Year	Male	Female	Total	Year	Male	Female	Total
1940	18	12	30	1969	10	8	18
1941	12	20	32	1970	10	6	16
1942	17	13	30	1971	7	5	12
1943	20	13	33	1972	5	11	16
1944	7	15	22	1973	12	8	20
1945	10	10	20	1974	10	6	16
1946	5	10	15	1975	8	8	16
1947	11	19	30	1976	8	8	16
1948	9	11	20	1977	5	10	15
1949	14	11	25	1978	8	3	11
Totals	123	134	257	Totals	83	73	156

TABLE 6.3
Tzintzuntzan Deaths by Age, 1940–1949 and 1969–1978

Age bracket	1940–1949		1969–1978	
	Number	Percentage	Number	Percentage
0– 5	142	55	62	40
6–10	9	3.5	3	2
11–20	15	6	5	3
21–30	18	7	4	2.5
31–40	8	3	7	4.5
41–50	10	3.5	11	7
51–60	15	6	11	7
61–70	21	8	15	10
71–80	14	6	22	14
80 +	5	2	16	10
Totals	257	100%	156	100%

very high, had declined by nearly one-third. At the other end of the life-span, during the earlier period only 16% of all deaths were of the elderly, while during the second period the percentage more than doubled to 34%. Most of this increase can be thought of as children who formerly would have died in infancy, for death rates in the intervening years have changed very little. Such shifts as have occurred represent age–class deferment of deaths from "youth" to "maturity." It is apparent that, quite apart from emigration, normal demographic processes reflected in increasing longevity will raise the present estimated 9% of the total population to an even higher figure in the near future.

Changing Patterns of Causes of Death

Patterns of causes of death have changed significantly during the interval between the 2 sample decades. Unfortunately, precise comparison is impossible because during the earlier period, almost all "diagnoses" represent the guesswork of family members. Some causes, such as whooping cough and other bronchial ailments, are quite clear. Malaria and typhoid fever probably were also diagnosed accurately. General gastroenteric causes are recorded as diarrhea, vomiting, and the like. Hence, we can speak with some certainty about broad categories of causes of death. Only in the category *bilis* is there considerable uncertainty. *Bilis* is a "folk" disease said to be caused by a strong emotional experience, sometimes pleasant but more often unpleasant. A majority of cases of *bilis* are attributed to anger or fright, which are believed to cause the bile to overflow the gall bladder and drip into the bloodstream. Common symptoms are yellowish eyeballs, a sallow complexion, intense headache, lack of appetite, dizziness, a bitter taste in the mouth, and great fatigue and sleepiness. Recovery with herbal remedies often takes several weeks. The evidence suggests possible hepatic infection; it is possible, too, that *bilis* is a catchall label for various illnesses. The age epidemiology is interesting: Of our sample of 35 deaths, one-third ($N = 12$) cluster in the 2–5 years bracket, while one-fourth ($N = 8$) cluster in the 55–60 years bracket.

Since about 1970, Mexican law has required a medical certificate stating the cause of death. Today, most people have been attended by a physician during their last illness, so stated causes are reasonably accurate. In other cases, family members, to conform to the law, have described symptoms after death to a physician who then lists his best guess on the death certificate. Despite the limitations of the data, notable changes in causes of death can be seen in Table 6.4.

Among the conclusions to be drawn from these figures (and other data) is that the common childhood infectious killers have been con-

TABLE 6.4
Causes of Death in Tzintzuntzan, 1940–1949 and 1969–1978

	Numbers	
Cause	1940–1949	1969–1978
Gastroenteric	67	33
Pulmonary	43	27
Bilis	35	—
Hepatitis	—	3
Old age[a]	24	7
Fever	24	3
Whooping cough	15	2
Accident	6	6
Cardiovascular disease	5	34
Measles	5	1
Rheumatism	5	—
Homicide	4	3
Tumor (cancer)	3	3
Epilepsy	3	1
Liver, cirrhosis	—	3
Renal failure	—	3
All other	18	27
Totals	257	156

[a] Exhaustion (*agotamiento*), weakness (*debilidad*), and "ancientness" (*ancianidad*).

quered as the result of immunization. The last recorded death from smallpox was about 1920; the most recent death from whooping cough occurred in 1970. Pure water and improved environmental sanitation have contributed to a significant decrease in deaths attributable to gastroenteric causes, while the decrease in pulmonary deaths is probably due to the widespread and often indiscriminate use of antibiotics. In contrast to these gains, and as is predictable with a growing population of the elderly, cardiovascular deaths have mushroomed. Surprisingly, this increase has not been paralleled by cancer deaths: Can this be due to the relative absence of environmental insults in a community where industrial pollution is unknown and agricultural pesticides are little used? Since *bilis* is not recognized by physicians as a disease, it is not surprising that people no longer die of it. Still, it would be interesting to know to what causes physicians assign deaths that are said to be due to *bilis* by the villagers. *Bilis* is still a very common complaint.

One gains a more precise idea of what the elderly die of in Tzintzuntzan today from Table 6.5, in which the causes of death are given for the 44 people who in 1970 were 61 years of age or older and who have subsequently died. Most striking is the fact that cardiovascular problems account for one-third of all deaths of the aged. Differences in sex-specific causes appear to be few, but the sample is too small to be meaningful on this score. One concludes that as Tzintzuntzan enters the contemporary world, it acquires most (but perhaps not all) of the health problems posed by modern industrial life.

TABLE 6.5
Causes of Death in Tzintzuntzan among the Elderly, 1970–1979

| Causes | Numbers | | |
	Males	Females	Totals
Cardiovascular	7	8	15
Pulmonary	4	3	7
Gastroenteric	2	2	4
Old age	3	1	4
Hepatitis	1	2	3
Tumor	—	2	2
Anemia	1	—	1
Paralysis	—	1	1
Renal failure	1	—	1
Malnutrition and dehydration	—	1	1
Unknown	3	2	5
Totals	22	22	44

THE VIEW OF OLD AGE IN TZINTZUNTZAN

In contrast to the oft-quoted accounts of the attractions of old age in nonwestern societies, to become old is no more appealing to the people of Tzintzuntzan than it is to contemporary Americans. It is seen as a time of declining vitality and energy, aches and pains, gray hairs, wrinkles, hearing loss, and dimming vision. Above all, most people regret old age because they are unable to work with the same intensity as before. In part, this regret is economic: less work, less income. But in part it reflects what in other societies would be called a Protestant ethic: People feel happier when they are working hard. To be unable to work as formerly is the single most common complaint about old age. A 70-year-old woman once said to me, "If I cease working for a week, I feel as if . . . my body aches, as if with the flu, that's how my body feels. . . . But when I am working, I am very happy." Elderly people often describe themselves in deprecatory terms: "I feel useless, I don't serve for anything." When living with their children, as many do, they feel sad that they are no longer able to carry their full share of the household chores and economic burden.

Many aging women are embarrassed by gray hair and wrinkles. They can and often do take action about the former: They dye their hair. But nothing can be done about the latter. As the proverb says.

> *La cana sale de ganas*
> *La arruga saca de dudas*
>
> The gray hair appears when it wants to
> The wrinkle removes doubt as to age

The meaning is that young people frequently have gray hairs, and elderly people may conceal theirs; hence gray hair is not a guide to age. But wrinkles remove doubt; they are the mark of only the aged, and nothing can be done about them.

The importance of avoiding the appearance of old age is clearly stated in attitudes toward the *bordón*, the cane. To use a walking stick for pleasure is unthinkable; to be forced to hobble about on a stick is the absolute symbol of decrepitude. Recently, I was returning from a 2-mile walk into the countryside, swinging my walking stick. Nearing my house, I encountered a middle-aged friend. "*¿Que le pasó?*" he asked solicitously. "What happened to you?" He simply could not conceive of a man in good health voluntarily assuming the symbol of physical incapacity. The union of decrepitude and cane is symbolized by the proverb,

"*Cada viejo alaba su bordón*,""Every old man praises his cane" (i.e., he makes the best of a bad situation). Doña Micaela González, in whose home I have lived for the last 20 years, in talking about the cane once said "We say of an old man who walks with a cane, *Ya no sirve para nada, ya es una gente inútil.*" ("He no longer serves for anything, now he is a useless person.")

The physical symptoms old people complain of most frequently, apart from general loss of vitality, are the rheumatic aches and pains known to the elderly the world over. In recent years, diabetes and high blood pressure have become common complaints. Loss of teeth is not particularly considered a sign of old age, perhaps because teeth begin to disappear during the mid-teens. Despite increasing use of dentists, people today say the teeth of young people are much less good than in their youth. The tremendous consumption of soft drinks, candy, and cheap pastries leads one to believe this observation is probably correct.

Loss of hearing to a greater or lesser degree characterizes many elderly people, but hearing aids are unknown. Glasses, however, are fairly common. My impression is that problems of vision specifically due to aging are less marked than in contemporary American life. A few people give evidence of cataracts, but retinal problems appear to be few. Strokes are increasingly common, but most seem not to result in permanent paralysis. The speech of one elderly victim is unintelligible, but otherwise she seems physically normal. Senility is conspicuous by its near absence. One elderly woman, recently deceased at age 89, who spent the last 4 years of her life in bed, blind, deaf, and nearly oblivious to what went on around her, is the only case of true senility I have encountered. When I try to explain senility to friends, most of their reactions have to do with inability to work. One 65-year-old woman spoke thus: "A person feels useless. . . . Now I am *tonta*, foolish. At times I don't hear. My vigor is not adequate to the job, so I feel useless. I want to lift something; I can't. I want to work; I can't. Then I feel useless, and because of this uselessness, I feel *tonta*. I want to do something, and I can't."

Respect and Power

In Tzintzuntzan, old age brings few valued perquisites. Young people take a rather pragmatic attitude toward the aged, considering them somewhat like any item of material culture that is wearing out: As long as they still "serve" (i.e., can do the job), they are appreciated, but when they no longer work, they lose much of their value. In an earlier time, institutionalized prestige automatically was conferred on elderly people who had "served" the community in the elaborate ritual system formerly widespread in Middle America. Men and their wives who as young newlyweds began to accept religious *mayordomías* (fiesta sponsorships) and who systematically worked their way up the ladder with increasingly difficult, time-consuming, and costly obligations, by the age of 45 or 50 became *principales* ('principals,' or village elders). The full-blown *mayordomía* system disappeared about 1925, but reports of elderly people who knew it as youngsters agree that an elderly *principal* and his wife did indeed enjoy widespread community respect.

At the same time, *principales* were not automatically civil authority figures; in fact, the last, in the mid-1920s, apparently never were political leaders. Conversely, during the same period, political leaders seem not to have participated to a major degree in the religious ritual system. In 1930, Tzintzuntzan and a number of adjacent villages were elevated to the political category of *municipio*, with the right to elect a mayor and community council (with authority over all communities). During the subsequent 49 years, 27 of the 33 mayors have been Tzintzuntzeños. Relative youth, rather than age, characterizes this group. Their average age upon assumption of office for the first time (several have served more than once) was 37 years. Only three were 50 years of age or older: Two were 58 and one was 55. In contrast, six were in their late twenties, the youngest only 26. Thirteen were in their thirties, and five in their forties. In short, youth predominates insofar as acceptability for highest political office is concerned, and I am inclined to believe that this has been true for many decades.

Such respect as the elderly enjoy is conferred on the basis of personal qualities. Elderly people who continue to work as best they can, do not drink to excess, and are "serious" (i.e., respectful, marked by proper behavior) are respected by younger people. Those who stop working, drink to excess, use foul language, and fail to show respect to others, do not enjoy community respect. In asking informants about specific elders, only one pattern emerged: Those few people who still know something about traditional medical practices, who treat the childhood illnesses of *empacho* and fallen fontenelle and victims of witchcraft and the evil eye and who know how to *sobar* (to massage 'displaced nerves') are respected for their knowledge as well as for their serious behavior. But this seems to be the only traditional wisdom that is appreciated by members of the younger generation. Otherwise, the aged are not regarded as repositories of useful experience. People recognize that life is changing so rapidly that useful knowledge of 50 years ago serves little purpose today. The elderly, in fact, know much less that is useful than do many 20-year-olds who have completed advanced schooling, have grown up with radio and television, and have traveled widely.

An important fact emerges from these data: The traditional wisdom of the elderly is of value to the community only in an essentially stable society. In a rapidly changing society, knowledge is quickly outdated, and the elderly are the least knowledgeable about what is desirable, appropriate, adaptive behavior under current conditions. Hence, at least insofar as prestige and status are concerned, technological change is the worst enemy of the aged. Their wisdom is, in the eyes of the young, apt to be mere foolishness, something to be tolerated at best, laughed at at worse.

Proverbs reflect this evaluation:

> *Entre más viejo, más pendejo.*
> The older the person, the more stupid.

> *A los mayores de edad*
> *Con un palo se les da.*
> Older people must be struck with
> a stick.

That is, they must be hit from time to time (figuratively rather than literally) to keep them going straight.

The elderly feel that youth no longer shows respect for the aged. In earlier years, a grown man neither smoked nor drank in the presence of his father until the latter invited him to do so. This usually occurred after the birth of the son's first child, an event bringing recognition of full adult status. Godchildren routinely knelt and kissed the hands of their godfathers when they met them, in homes or on streets. These practices have long since gone. The elderly also feel that today's young people are less serious than they themselves were, that they sleep late, and that they do not know how to work hard.

The Happiest Time of Life

Despite their cynical view of today's youth, the elderly most often name their own *juventud* as the happiest time of their lives. The question, which I have asked of many old people, is hypothetical, and most informants have never thought about the idea in specific terms. Yet all have grasped its import and given good answers. The years from 15 to 30, they feel, are marked by psychological and personal freedom from the constraints of childhood. In the words of one informant, before the age of 15, one is like a tree, still growing, not fully formed. After 15, one begins to think independently, to evaluate, and to make personal decisions. Intellectual maturity is what he seemed to have in mind. Above all, these are the years of physical vitality and energy. With appropriate gestures, this man told how he would pick up 150 pound loads without a thought, even though he is physically slight; but now in his mid-fifties, no more.

One woman in her mid-fifties, the mother of 10 children, considered her childhood her best years, a surprising answer, since adults often describe the "suffering" they experienced as children, the frequent hunger, the parental beatings. Her father never beat her, her mother, once or twice, "but probably I deserved it." Her father, a cobbler, hunted squirrels, rabbits, and badgers, and they ate meat every day, "which is probably why we were never sick." Above all, she liked the lack of *preoccupaciones*, of preoccupations and worries, which for her have been the main concern of more recent years.

One woman in her early seventies said that for her the best years were from 30 to 50. During those years, she said, one lives *con su gusto completo*, with zest for everything, for a husband, for children, for work, for dancing—*para todo* ('for everything.')

Only one informant, a woman also in her seventies, said she would not like to relive these happy earlier years. This woman, highly intelligent and greatly respected for her curing talents, reflected a moment and then said no, it is probably best to "continue on the same path," since one does not know what might happen the second time around.

Although the earlier years are viewed as the happiest time of life, old age is not without its pleasures. Since, as we will see, the great majority of elderly people have children and grandchildren in the village, there is the satisfaction of family fiestas of baptism, marriage, and saints' days. On these occasions, dancing is appropriate behavior for the elderly of both sexes, and septuagenarians not infrequently are applauded for their skill in dancing the *jota*, which has been displaced among younger people by ballroom steps. The pleasures of dancing are also symbolized in the local Tarascan "Dance of the Little Old Men," one of the most famous of Mexican folkloric dances. Masked boys with false hair, suitably bent over their canes, dance in lively style to the music of guitars in one of the most animated of Mexican dances.

About the sexual habits of the aged I know nothing. Tzintzuntzeños are a prudish people, not given to talking lightly about sexual matters even among age mates. Elderly people presumably continue in varying degree to enjoy sexual activities. An elderly man teased by a younger friend may reply:

> *Viejo los cerros, y cada año se enverdecen.*
> The hills may be old, but every year they become green.

The younger man is reminded that there is still life in the old body. An elderly man who shows excessive interest in younger women is described as *un viejo rabo verde*, 'an old man with a green tail.' Of him it may be said:

También de viejo, viruelas.
Smallpox can also strike the aged.

The idea is that when the time is long past for a particular activity or event, it may nonetheless occur. Normally, smallpox was a disease of childhood, but a few people who escaped it then subsequently were struck in later life.

Attitudes toward Death

Beliefs about what follows life on earth strongly influence the attitudes toward death of many people. If warriors who die in battle enjoy a favored status in the hereafter, they presumably fight with greater abandon. If one expects to be reunited with friends and loved ones, death can be faced with less fear than if the future is uncertain. Since Tzintzuntzan is a strongly Catholic community in which literally no one doubts the Christian belief in an afterlife, one might expect the elderly to face death with equanimity. There is reason to doubt that this is true. "Everyone fears death," says Doña Micaela González. "No one really wants to die." They fear physical suffering and the thought of leaving their children and grandchildren. They are also apprehensive about the consequences of their moral defects. A few regret having to leave their worldly goods behind.

The fear of death and the reluctance to leave this life can partially be explained by the fact that heaven is not viewed as a particularly attractive alternative to life. It is distinctly second-best; although most people would not put it in these words, they see it as a deadly, dull place. Most people believe that at death the departing soul must revisit all the places it has known in life, which is why ghosts are particularly likely to make their presence known the night after a death occurs. Some say the soul remains near the body until burial, again an observation based on the propensity of ghosts to appear in the hours immediately following death.

When the soul sets out on its final journey, it must first cross the River Jordan. Some people of Indian ancestry believe that a black dog helps the soul across; for this reason they feel it unwise to abuse black dogs during their lifetimes. Other, more sophisticated people say it is the guardian angel who does the favor. On the far side of the River Jordan, one is judged, but exactly how no one knows. Real sinners, for whom there is no hope, are picked off by the devil's minions and taken to hell, where they burn forever. Most adults go to purgatory, where they are purified by fire but spared the temptations of demons. Ideas vary about the length of time spent in purgatory, but most believe it is a relatively short one, depending on the seriousness of one's sins. Devotees of the Virgen del Carmen are said to be taken out of purgatory by their patron on the first Saturday following arrival, a belief that seems to explain a widespread devotion to this virgin.

As in Spain and other Latin American countries, it is believed that a young person who dies without carnal knowledge of another goes straight to heaven, an *angelito* (a 'little angel'). Entry to *la gloria* ('heaven'), is marked by few formalities. Although Saint Peter is at the gate holding the keys, he does not judge people. Ideas vary concerning heaven. For some, the soul again takes human form, but not that of the body it has left behind. It finds itself in a place sometimes described as a huge cathedral with chapels and oratories where people spend their time listening to celestial choirs and praising God. One neither eats nor works. Upon entry to heaven, deceased relatives may welcome the soul, but otherwise there appears to be no family interaction.

Other informants paint a more somber picture of heaven. The soul, upon arrival, is a mere *soplo* (a 'breath'), a butterfly drifting through space. Souls are garbed in *el vestido de la gracia* ('the clothing of grace,' 'a little white cloud'). One does not know who the little white clouds are, except that, somehow, one recognizes baptismal co-godparents, the *compadres* who are so important in the formal friendship network of the village. Whenever *compadres* meet they acknowledge each other by bowing in the silent *caravana* greeting, the same term used to describe the greetings penitents exchange when making their rounds with great crosses on Good Friday night. Souls listen to choruses of angels all day and sing God's praises themselves.

Even the most optimistic view of heaven provides a poor second to earthly life with all of its pain and sorrow. This view enforces a belief that the souls of the departed are anxious to return to earth once a year, on the occasion of All Souls' night to be welcomed with food, drink, flowers, and candles by their survivors. One elderly woman compared this visit to the vacation an industrial worker takes, as "recreation" granted by Our Lord. No one expresses the hope that death will relieve earthly suffering. Hence, even though a person obviously is dying, well wishers try to cheer the patient by pretending that he or she will get better. Patients are reminded that

El enfermo se levanta de la cama,
Y el bueno y sano cae muerto.

The sick person arises from his bed,
and the hail and hearty falls dead.

LIFE FOR THE AGED

In Tzintzuntzan, in the absence of formal retirement, retirement communities, nursing homes, and other institutional devices to cater to the needs of the aged, life-long activities and living arrangements change less drastically in later years than in the United States. Almost without exception, elderly couples, sometimes alone but often with a married son and his children, continue to occupy the home in which they have lived since their early married years. Widows and widowers may also continue on in their old homes, often until advanced ages. Although Mexico has social security for government and industrial workers, this system to date has played a very small role in village life. The aged are dependent on their own earnings and the support of their children for most expenses. Very few people have inherited sufficient wealth so as not to worry about food, clothing, and shelter in old age.

Fortunately, the nature of village life is such that as people grow older they are still able to engage in many customary tasks, albeit at lower levels of activity. Potters continue to make pots, even into their nineties. No longer able to mine clay, they buy it from neighbors or perhaps are supplied by their children. When the firing of a kiln surpasses their strength, they sell greenware they have molded to other potters or fire in the kiln of a son or daughter. Elderly men milk cattle, and during the rainy season follow them, on foot or horseback, to the pastures where they graze. Well into their seventies and early eighties, both men and women may travel by bus to deliver arts and crafts to distant cities, and some own stores or roadside shops in which they sell to passing tourists.

Elderly women cook for themselves and their husbands, clean house, and do laundry just as they have done for most of their lives. Those who live in three-generation households may help care for their grandchildren in addition to doing a wide variety of household tasks. Middle-aged women who are members of religious orders assume the responsibility 1 day a month to clean and adorn with flowers the two churches and to keep an eye on them lest visitors cause damage. Burdened with more pressing tasks, these women often arrange for older women to substitute for them, feeding them, and giving them 10 or 15 pesos.

The striking feature is not that there are a few older people, mostly men, who do nothing, but rather that so many struggle to continue with productive tasks. No one suffers the trauma of retirement. This is not to say that all elderly people eat well or that they have sufficient clothing and shelter. Yet they do get by, and most seem pleased that they contribute significantly to their own support.

Patterns of Inheritance

Inheritance patterns and inheritance strategies are central to living arrangements for the elderly. Responsible parents feel a strong compulsion to provide a house for each of their sons. The first son to marry usually lives in the parental home for several years until the birth of one or two children or until the marriage of the second son. At that time, the parents have two options: If they own a large house and yard they may 'divide', that is, split off a part of the yard and/or house to be given to the eldest son. If the property is insufficient for this, they may buy another house or building lot for the son. The second and subsequent sons in turn receive houses or additional pieces of the original plot, down to the youngest, who remains in what is left of the homestead to inherit it upon the death of the parents. Parents occasionally provide houses for their daughters, but since it is assumed they will marry men who receive property from their parents, a settlement in cash or kind, usually less in value than real estate, is the common pattern. It is likely that many, perhaps a majority of parents, are unable fully to conform to this ideal inheritance pattern.

Inheritance quarrels may embitter sibling relationships, for parents often favor one child over another. Life is particularly difficult for the youngest son who remains at home; until he inherits, he and his wife are subject to an often onerous paternal control. The young couple, modern in outlook, may want to improve the house with cement floors, windows, and perhaps a sewer connection. But in the absence of clear title, they are reluctant to spend the money. Elderly parents, in turn, are reluctant to surrender the last vestige of their control of life: their property. Enough instances of ungrateful children who cast out aged parents are known so that the prudent course, most elderly owners feel, is to divest only as death approaches. Thus, when elderly parents live with married children, tension seems to prevail frequently. Some cases of elderly couples, widows, and widowers living alone are due to the desire to reduce friction with their children as much as possible.

Grown children, then, look upon aged parents with ambivalence. In many instances, real affection is felt for them, and it is assumed that financial and psychological support for them is a just obligation for the sacrifices they made for their children. Only very rarely do elderly people have sufficient means not to require help from their children. The norm of filial help was made apparent to me when, after the death of my father, Doña Micaela González asked if my three siblings and I supported our mother, who she knew lived alone. She found it difficult to understand that a husband could leave a wife in such circumstances that would not require her children's contribution to her support.

Siblings also know they are in competition with each other for their parents' property; hence, it is highly important to be at the bedside when a parent dies. In 1970, I had just arrived in the village when word came that my father was dying. I left at once. When I returned 10 days later, I was asked, even before sympathy was expressed, ¿le alcanzó? ("Did you reach him [before he died]?"). When I told them no, they showed distress. I assumed they were thinking of filial love and respect and the emotional satisfaction of a last reunion. But at supper on the night of my return, Doña Micaela remarked, El hijo ausente no ve la muerte de su padre ("The absent son [child] is not in on the death of his father"). She spoke not so much of sympathy as of the fact that in a society without written testaments, the deathbed is often the scene of inheritance decisions. An absent child, she reasoned, is apt not to receive his share.

Living Arrangements

With these general patterns and attitudes in mind, I turn to an examination of the actual living arrangements of the 111 individuals (54 men, 57 women) in Tzintzuntzan who, on April 1, 1979, were 70 years of age or older. The social, economic, and residential arrangements that characterize these people tell us much about the practical problems faced by the aged. For analytical purposes, I have divided the 111 people into eight categories of unequal size:

1. Nineteen couples, both members over 70	38
2. Twenty-five couples, wives under 70	25
3. One couple, husband under 70	1
4. Widows	33
5. Widowers	9
6. Single women, never married	3
7. Abandoned wife	1
8. Abandoned husband	1
Total	111

The basic living arrangements of these 111 people are shown in Table 6.6. The table does not, of course, reveal all variations, and brief comment on the most important categories will add depth to the picture.

HUSBAND AND WIFE BOTH OVER SEVENTY

Of the 38 people in this category, two men and four women live with second spouses. The other 32 live with first partners, a statistic showing remarkable conjugal stability. One of the nine couples in this group living alone is childless, but the spouses are not totally devoid of family ties since they have siblings in the village. A second couple has but a single child, a resident of California, while a third has a schoolteacher son in another village who often visits and helps support them. The remaining six couples living alone have one or more children in Tzintzuntzan on whom they rely in time of need. Of the five couples living with a married son, in only one instance has the father relinquished control and ownership of the house to his son and heir; the other four sons, the youngest of their families, await to inherit. Of the 19 men in this category, 18 are household heads and property owners.

HUSBAND OVER SEVENTY, WIFE UNDER SEVENTY

Households of this type often reflect a second (or third) marriage by a husband following the death of his first wife. Of the 25 cases in this category, 13 men live with a second, and 2 with a third wife. Only 10 men live with their first wife. In the latter cases, the age differential is relatively slight, a matter of 5 to 10 years. But in a number of instances the husband has remarried a much younger wife, thus starting a second family. This accounts for the four households with minor children in which the father is 70 years or older. Of the seven couples living with a married son, in six the elderly husband continues to be property owner and household head. Upon the death of one or both parents, the sons will inherit the property. Four couples live alone: One is childless, a second has children in Tijuana, and the other two have grown children in the village.

WIDOWS

When both elderly parents are living, in all cases of three-generation households it is a married son who lives with them. This arrangement, as we have seen, reflects the ultimogeniture inheritance pattern whereby the youngest son remains at home after marriage to take over the household when his parents die. In contrast, widows are more than twice as

TABLE 6.6
Living Arrangements of the Elderly in Tzintzuntzan

	Categories					
	Couples					
Household arrangement	Spouses both 70+	Husband 70+ wife 70-[a]	Widows[b]	Widowers[c]	Unmarried women	Totals
Live alone	9 (18)	4	4	2	—	19 (28)
With married son	5 (10)	7	4	4	—	20 (25)
With married daughter	—	—	9	3	—	12
With minor children	—	4	—	—	—	4
With unmarried adult son	—	2	2	—	—	4
With unmarried adult daughter	4 (8)	5	6	—	—	15 (19)
With minor grandson(s)	—	3	2	—	—	5
With minor grandaughter(s)	1 (2)	—	2	—	—	3 (4)
With widowed daughter	—	1	2	—	—	2
With widowed son	—	—	1	—	—	2
Other	—	—	2	1	3	6
Totals	19 (38)	26	34	10	3	92 (111)

[a] Includes one case of wife 70+ and husband 70-.
[b] Includes one abandoned wife.
[c] Includes one abandoned husband.

likely to live with married daughters than with married sons. This living pattern reflects the widespread recognition that the relationship between mothers-in-law and daughters-in-law is fraught with peril. While it may be difficult for a mother to live with a daughter, it is deemed almost impossible for a mother-in-law to live happily under the same roof with her son's wife. The two roles are seen as structurally incompatible. While widows who live with married children almost always are dependent on them, those who have inherited property and who may live with unmarried children or with grandchildren, tend to continue as household heads.

WIDOWERS

Although widowers can (and a few do) live alone, the majority live with married children to whom they have relinquished their role as household head. Of the two in this sample who live alone, the only son of one resides in the United States, regularly sending his father money; the whereabouts of the son of the other is unknown.

UNMARRIED WOMEN

Elderly unmarried women are tucked into almost any family niche that seems feasible, or bearable, to the particpants. Of the three females in this category, one lives with a married brother, a second with a married sister, and the third with an unmarried niece.

The most striking fact in Tzintzuntzan, in contrast to the United States, is that real loneliness—in the sense of living an isolated life, with few or no friends and relatives with whom to interact—is rare. Even most of those who in Table 6.6 are shown as living alone are not isolated. In the case of widows, more often than not a grandchild or grandchildren come to spend the night. Sometimes a married daughter lives next door, with a connecting gate between patios. The mother technically lives alone and cooks for herself, but she sees her daughter many times a day, and should she fall ill the daughter can spend the night with her without abandoning her husband.

CONCLUSION

For most elderly people there is, obviously, a good deal of social, psychological, and economic support. But this is not to say that there is little or no resentment between older and younger relatives. Intergenerational friction is common, particularly in three-generation households. A common way to reduce friction between two women a generation apart in age is to build each her own kitchen; if this is not feasible, each prepares meals apart from separate food budgets. This is a particularly important safety valve when mothers-in-law and daughters-in-law are under the same roof. Yet in spite of friction, most people assume that elderly parents have a moral claim to the help of children. Village estimates vary widely as to the percentage of children who do in fact contribute. Yet I know of enough instances in which schoolteacher children or successful laborers in Mexico City or the United States help their parents, so that we can speak of a norm of filial help.

TO BE OLD IN TZINTZUNTZAN: THE PROS AND CONS

It is clear that many positive things can be said for Tzintzuntzan as a place in which to grow old. The awful loneliness so often a part of the aging process in the United States is avoided to a large degree. Furthermore, there is no trauma of retirement as such: Both men and women continue in constructive tasks almost to the time of their death. The elderly, too, join in the social and religious life of the community. Mass and the care of the churches is an important outlet for many women. At baptismal and wedding fiestas the elderly are included, just as are the very young; social activities are not age-graded as in the United States. The elderly have the satisfaction of seeing, day after day, in stores, on the streets, and in church, people they have known and appreciated all of their lives. They have the satisfaction, too, of being known by name and as family members, whether they enjoy particular respect or not. They are not faceless wraiths on busy city streets or in centers for the aged.

There are also negative aspects to old age in Tzintzuntzan. Medical care on average is less good than in the United States. A few well-to-do families seek the best medical care for aging relatives, but there is a tendency in most families not to spend money for expensive care for the elderly. This is a realistic approach; medical care is costly, and such expenses are more profitably directed to younger, more productive people. As time goes by, the role of the aged may become less and less attractive. Large numbers of young people with professional training, as we have seen, are leaving the community. Although today only a few older people are without children at hand, in the future this number certainly will grow. Whether distant children will continue to support aged parents is hard to determine. Young schoolteachers tend to be very helpful, but when they marry and begin their own families, they find it harder and harder to spare money for aged parents. If families are reduced in size and if social security is not extended to rural areas, the economic position of the elderly may become more precarious than at present.

To conclude with a value judgment, given the standard of living most Tzintzuntzeños have known during their lives, the social and religious forms they have experienced, and the relative homogeneity of the community, I think old age is no more painful than in the United States; very possibly, it is a better place in which to face one's last years. At the same time, I see no way in which the Tzintzuntzan experience can be taken as a model in part or in whole, for the development of policy for the care of the aged in the United States. Cultures and standards of living are too distinct; in both countries answers must be found within respective contemporary cultures.

REFERENCES

Caro Baroja, J. (1963) The city and the country: Reflections on some ancient commonplaces. Pp. 27–40 in J. Pitt-Rivers, ed., *Mediterranean Countrymen*. Paris/LaHaye: Mouton.

Foster, G. M. (1967) *Tzintzuntzan: Mexican Peasants in a Changing World*. Boston: Little, Brown.

Fuller, C. E. (1972) Aging among southern African Bantu. Pp. 51–72 in D. O. Cowgill and L. D. Holmes, eds., *Aging and Modernization*. New York: Appleton-Century-Crofts.

Hammer, J. H. (1972) Aging in a gerontocratic society: The Sidamo of southwest Ethiopia. Pp. 15–30 in D. O. Cowgill and L. D. Holmes, eds., *Aging and Modernization*. New York: Appleton-Century-Crofts.

Holmes, L. D. (1972) The role and status of the aged in a changing Samoa. Pp. 73–89 in D. O. Cowgill and L. D. Holmes, eds., *Aging and Modernization*. New York: Appleton-Century-Crofts.

Kemper, R. V. (1977) *Migration and Adaptation: Tzintzuntzan Peasants in Mexico City*. Beverly Hills, Calif.: Sage Publications.

Shelton, A. J. (1972) The aged and eldership among the Ibo. Pp. 31–49 in D. O. Cowgill and L. D. Holmes, eds., *Aging and Modernization*. New York: Appleton-Century-Crofts.

PART II

AGING BRAIN AND BEHAVIOR

chapter 7

The Neurobiological Basis of Age-Related Changes in Neuronal Connectivity

WILLIAM BONDAREFF

In 1889, Ramon y Cajal demonstrated that the brain is composed of individual cells separated from one another. This has since been amply confirmed by twentieth-century electron microscopists who leave little room to doubt that not only neurons (the subject of Cajal's original thesis) but also the neuroglia are structural entities. Nonetheless, a peculiar tendency for neurobiologists to interpret narrowly Cajal's enlightened observations has persisted since Freud did it in 1901. Freud failed to see each nerve cell as dependent on its own metabolism for the electrochemical properties of its own membrane. Why he might have done this and why this interpretation might have lead to a clinically useful theory of the mind with little relationship to the real brain is discussed by McCarley and Hobson (1977).

Neurons and neuroglia are, of course, separate entities. They are geometrically complex cells with long, often intricately branched processes. Each cell is an individual metabolic unit and all its parts—its cell body or perikaryon, its processes, and the terminals of each process—are metabolically dependent upon the same machinery of cellular metabolism. Nonetheless, neurons and neuroglia are unique in that metabolic changes in one cell typically affect other cells, and only small energy transfers from one neuron to another are required to cause major

AGING
Biology and Behavior

changes in neuronal membranes already polarized as a result of ongoing metabolic processes. Such interneuronal activities are affected by neighboring neuroglia that appear to exert generalized controlling influences. Although these influences are not understood, they are exemplified by two hypotheses: (1) astrocytes create regional states of relative excitability caused by regional differences in the 5'-nucleotidase activity of astrocytic plasma membranes (Kreutzberg, Barron, and Schubert 1978); and (2) astroglia maintain the constancy of the neuronal microenvironment by controlling local extraneuronal concentrations of neuroactive substances such as K^+ (Grossman and Seregin 1977) and GABA (Martinez-Hernandez, Bell, and Norenberg 1977). Neurons and neuroglia, therefore, exist as functional individuals and groups dependent on the metabolic activities of individual cells, whose changing metabolic activities can be anticipated to result in functional changes. Whether these changes will have behavioral counterparts will depend on the nature and number of the neurons involved and the extent of the involvement.

It is well known that changes in the relative numbers and distributions of neurons and neuroglia in the brains of vertebrates occur during normal development and maturation. Such changes also occur as a consequence of aging and, depending on the amount and kind of brain tissue involved, may interrupt functionally important neuronal circuitry and significantly alter behavior. But neuronal circuitry may also be interrupted by less severe age-related changes, which are dynamic and result neither in neuronal death nor in alteration in relative numbers of nerve cells. These changes involve neuronal metabolism, which if sufficiently compromised can no longer maintain the structural and functional integrity of neurons, especially at sites distant from the metabolic machinery of the perikaryon. These sites, where transmission from one neuron to another involves electrochemical interaction between two neurons along a region of interneuronal contact, are known as synapses. In vertebrate brains, interactions are generally mediated by transmitter substances that react with receptor sites on synaptic membranes to affect permeability to various ions. Synaptic membranes are modified segments of neuronal plasma membranes and their integrity and special properties in different types of neurons depend on cellular events occurring largely in the perikaryon. Although neuronal processes—axons and dendrites—may terminate at relatively great distances from the center of metabolic activity (the perikaryon), they and the synaptic membranes associated with them depend on the same cellular metabolism.

The neurobiological substrata of synaptic events that appear to change in senescence are discussed under four headings: changes in the actual number of synapses; changes in the organization of brain that result in relative, though not necessarily absolute, changes in the number and/or distribution of synapses; changes in the microenvironment of neurons that affect synaptic function; and changes in the metabolism of neurons that result in the loss of synaptic structure and/or function.

CHANGES IN THE NUMBER OF SYNAPSES

Loss of synapses will, of course, result from a loss of neurons and it is a long-taught maxim of neuropathology that the number of neurons declines with age. This decline, which is reflected by the general pessimism of agism (Butler and Lewis 1973), is not ubiquitous and in some cases not even certain. Thus, the loss of cerebral cortical neurons reported by Brody (1955, 1973) is difficult to evaluate because tissue shrinkage caused by tissue preparation was not adequately controlled. Nonetheless, the age-related loss of neurons has been reported in certain parts of the cerebral cortex and perhaps more reliably in the cerebellar cortex (Hall, Miller, and Corsellis 1975). In the hippocampus and, with the possible exception of the locus coeruleus (Brody 1973), in brainstem nuclei generally, no such loss of neurons is found (cf. review by Bondareff 1980a). If technical problems encountered in an enumeration of neurons may be prohibitive, they are considerably less likely to be so than is an enumeration of synapses, which because of their smaller size require electron optics to be adequately visualized. Studies of synaptic numbers are, therefore, understandably few. Cragg (1975) found no loss of synapses (nor of neurons) in a study of human cerebral cortex in which brains from a group of people aged 65 to 89 years were compared with brains from mentally defective and neurosurgical patients. Cragg (1975) also found no relationship between numbers of synapses (nor of neurons) and mental deficiency in selective areas of cerebral cortex.

In an attempt to circumvent the myriad problems in studies of human brains, I undertook a study of a well-defined area of the hippocampus in the aged Fischer-344 rat. The hippocampus was chosen for study because of its presumed relationship to memory and learning functions. A specific region of the hippocampus, the molecular layer of the dentate gyrus, was chosen because its anatomy is well known (see Lynch and Gerling, Chapter 9 in this volume). The animals, bred under pathogen-free conditions, were commercially available and their natural history and pathology have been characterized (Coleman *et al.* 1977). Their 50% mean survival age is reported to be 29 months and their maximal survival age appears to be about 36 months. A comparative study of 3-

to 4-month-old animals and 24- to 25-month-old animals, which differ in size but appear to be of comparable health, seemed to offer a reasonably meaningful approach to problems of aging in human beings.

Attention was focused initially on axo-dendritic synapses (Table 7.1). The postsynaptic component of these synapses appears to consist primarily of dendrites of dentate gyrus granule cells, but the presynaptic component is less well defined. Synapses were first counted in electron micrographs of the middle third of the molecular layer (Bondareff and Geinisman 1976). When compared with synaptic counts of the same region of 3-month-old rats, a 27% decrease in the number of synapses per unit of square area of neuropil was found in the 24-month-old animals. Unfortunately, it was difficult to determine whether this loss of synapses reflected an antecedent age-related insult to the presynaptic or postsynaptic neurons involved in the synapses. There was, however, no age-related change in the number of postsynaptic granule cell bodies nor in the length of the postsynaptic or subsynaptic plate (Geinisman and Bondareff 1976). Similarly, the length of the postsynaptic density of axo-dendritic synapses did not decline in the cerebellar cortex of senescent rats (Glick and Bondareff 1979). It appears, therefore, that the loss of synapses depends primarily on changes to the presynaptic neuron. A loss of synapses, almost identical to that found in the middle third part,

TABLE 7.1
Loss of Axo-Dendritic Synapses per Unit Square Area of Adult and Senescent Male Fischer-344 Rats

	Percentage of 3-month-old animals	Percentage of loss
Dentate gyrus molecular layer[a]		
Shaft	65.3	34.7
Spine	74.1	25.9
Total	73.3	26.7
Supragranular layer[b]		
Shaft	65.4	34.6
Spine	75.7	24.3
Total	74.1	25.9
Cerebellum[c]		
Shaft	102.2	0.0
Spine	66.8	33.2
Total	75.8	24.2

[a] From Geinisman and Bondareff 1976.
[b] From Geinisman, Bondareff, and Dodge 1977.
[c] From Glick and Bondareff 1979.

has been found in the supragranular portion of the dentate gyrus molecular layer in senescence (Geinisman *et al.* 1978a). The presynaptic elements have been shown to be of different origin in these two regions of the dentate gyrus.

A loss of axo-dendritic synapses has also been found in the visual area of the cerebral cortex (Feldman 1976) and in the cerebellar cortex (Glick and Bondareff 1979) of the Fischer-344 rat. In the latter, a 33% decrement in the axo-dendritic synapses of 25-month-old rats was found to involve axo-spinous synapses selectively. The number of these synapses, between parallel fibers (axons) and Purkinje cell dendritic spines, seemed to decline in senescence while those between climbing fibers and dendritic shafts were spared (Table 7.1).

Lest the impression be given that synaptic loss in the senescent brain involves only axo-dendritic synapses and that there is some property of the axo-dendritic synapse that makes it uniquely susceptible to the aging process, it should be noted that axo-somatic synapses may also be lost (Table 7.2), and there appears again to be no age-related decrease in the length of the postsynaptic density (Bondareff 1980b). These synapses were counted in an electron microscope study of dentate gyrus granule cells, which accumulate lipofuscin pigment but appear otherwise normal in 25-month-old Fischer-344 rats (Bondareff 1980b). Their numbers as compared with those of 3- to 4-month-old young adults appeared to be constant. There was, nevertheless, a 15% decrease in synapses per unit length of plasma membrane surface, which amounted to a 22% decrease in the percentage of the granule cell surface covered by synapses in senescent animals. The age-related loss of synapses appears well established, particularly in the dentate gyrus, where synapses of more than one type, in more than one locus, and of more than one afferentation are involved. It is not, however, incontrovertible. Cotman and Scheff (1979), who analyzed a segment of dentate gyrus similar to that studied by my colleagues and me, found no loss of synapses in 24-month-old

TABLE 7.2
Loss of Synapses per Unit Length of Neuronal Surface in the Dentate Gyrus of Senescent Male Fischer-344 Rats

	Percentage of 3-month-old animals	Percentage of loss
Axo-dendritic[a]	60.3	39.7
Axo-somatic[b]	85.1	14.9

[a] From Geinisman, Bondareff, and Dodge 1977.
[b] From Geinisman, 1979; see also Bondareff 1980b.

Fischer rats. There is, as yet, no satisfactory explanation for this discrepancy.

Assuming that there is a loss of synapses with age, it is noteworthy that degenerating synapses are not found in the dentate gyrus of the 24-month-old Fischer-344 rat and that the fate of the lost synapses is unknown. There is no increase in the number of microglia in the dentate gyrus although an increase in microglia has been found in the cerebral cortex of senescent rats (Vaughan and Peters 1974). There is, therefore, no indication that synaptic remains have been cleared away by phagocytes unless, of course, the entire process of degeneration and removal of degenerated material from the dentate gyrus has been completed prior to the twenty-fourth month. In this regard, it is interesting that Sotelo and Palay (1971) found degenerating synapses in the lateral vestibular nuclei of apparently healthy adult rats. Perhaps, as these authors suggest, synapses are continually remodeled throughout the course of an animal's life. If so, regenerative capacity appears to decline with age, although the capacity to form new synapses seems to persist in the hippocampi of senescent Fischer-344 rats (Scheff et al. 1978), and, interestingly, in the brains of demented humans afflicted with Alzheimer's disease (Scheibel and Tomiyasu 1978). With regard to the former, it has been shown that the capacity of adrenergic neurons to sprout following partial deafferentation of the septal area and dentate gyrus is present but diminished at 24 months (Scheff et al. 1978). This suggests that if the distribution of synapses continually changes during life, that is, if synapses are continually being formed, destroyed and reformed, then the formative process must fail in senescence.

CHANGES IN THE ORGANIZATION OF THE BRAIN

Although a voluminous literature might lead to the assumption that synaptic loss is associated with an antecedent loss of neurons, available data do not substantiate it. The data, however, are conflicting. On one hand, counts of granule cells in senescent Fischer-344 rats have failed to demonstrate any significant age-related decrease (Bondareff and Geinisman 1976). On the other hand, a whittling away of dendritic trees of neurons appears to be a fairly generalized characteristic of aging and has been described for several areas of the brain.

In selected areas of the cerebral cortex of a group of 10 human patients aged 58–96 years, Scheibel et al. (1975) found a progressive loss of horizontally oriented dendrites. Similar changes were found in human hippocampus (Scheibel et al. 1976). These changes seemed to be associated with a variety of degenerative changes involving cell bodies and dendritic trees, more particularly, a striking loss in the number of dendritic spines. A loss of dendritic spines as well as a loss of dendritic substance has been found in the visual region of the cerebral cortex of senescent Fischer-344 rats (Feldman and Dowd 1975, Feldman 1976, Vaughan 1977). A similar loss of dendritic substance, found in the auditory region of the cerebral cortex of the senescent Fischer-344 rat, suggests a preferential loss of distal segments of selective dendrites with a progressive attenuation of dendritic trees. A loss of dendrites was found also in the olfactory bulb of senescent rats by Hinds and McNelly (1977). These authors reported a decrease in the total volume of mitral cell dendrites apparently compensated for by an increase in the volume of individual mitral cell dendritic trees and the reorganization of the entire olfactory bulb.

To characterize more thoroughly the extent of reorganization in the senescent brain, an analysis of all cellular elements remaining in the dentate gyrus of the senescent Fischer-344 rat was undertaken. Decreases in both the volume fraction and surface area of dendrites, coincident with the age-related decrement in numbers of synapses already described, were demonstrated and shown to reflect an absolute loss of dendrites (Table 7.3). That the decrements in dendritic volume fraction and surface area were disproportionately more severe than the decrement in numbers of dendrites (Geinisman *et al.* 1978a) probably indicates a selective loss of smaller diameter, distally located dendritic branches in the dentate gyrus, as might have been predicted from the findings of others in other parts of the brain. The mechanism of this loss is unknown but it does not appear to depend on the clogging of the proximal portions of dendrites with neurofibrils or other cytoplasmic organelles, which was believed (Scheibel and Tomiyasu 1978) to initiate the process of dendritic atrophy in pyramidal cells of the human cerebral cortex. It also does not appear to be a prerequisite for synaptic loss in the rat dentate gyrus because the loss of synapses is significant whether it is determined relative to

TABLE 7.3
Dendritic Atrophy in Dentate Gyrus of Senescent Male Fischer-344 Rats[a]

	Percentage of 3-month-old animals	Percentage of loss
Volume fraction	87.6	12.4
Surface area	72.6	27.4
Number of profiles	75.6	24.4

[a] From Geinisman, Bondareff, and Dodge 1978a.

the square area of neuropil or to a unit length of surviving dendrites found in the senescent dentate gyrus (Table 7.2).

The loss of synapses and dendrites appears not to lead to a measurable change in the width of the dentate gyrus. This suggests a compensatory growth of nonneuronal tissue elements and structural reorganization. Contributors to this reorganization appear to be cellular, there being no apparent increases in the volume of the extracellular space or the vascular compartment and no increases in the numbers of any types of cells. In particular, there is no evidence that the number of microcytes increases in the senescent dentate gyrus and no evidence of microcytes laden with phagocytized remains of synapses or dendrites.

What appeared to compensate for the loss of neuronal cytoplasm in the senescent dentate gyrus was a significant increase in the volume fraction of astrocytes. Our electron microscopic analysis of the supragranular region of dentate gyrus demonstrated no increase in the number of astrocyte cell bodies but did show a 45% increase in the volume fraction of astrocytic processes (Geinisman et al. 1978b). The light microscopic study of Landfield et al. (1977), although not so readily interpreted, suggests a comparable degree of astrocytic hypertrophy. It appears, then, that there is a notable redistribution of cellular components with no associated change in overall dimensions of the hippocampus in senescence. It is not known whether a comparable redistribution without apparent tissue degeneration occurs in other parts of the brain. One would assume that reorganization of neural tissue and the associated rearrangement of synaptic connections as found in the senescent dentate gyrus would result in functional changes, presumably with adaptive advantage. It seems reasonable to predict that the capacity to modify the distribution of synapses in compensation for maladaptive age-related changes in brain structure would be adaptively advantageous to the aging animal. Senescent rats do possess the capacity to redistribute synapses (Scheff et al. 1978) and although the length of synaptic contacts appears fixed throughout adult life (Table 7.4), Greenough et al. (1978) have suggested recently that the number of perforations in the subsynaptic plate, which have been thought to indicate reactive sites of the synapse, may change with maturation and environmental complexity.

CHANGES IN THE MICROENVIRONMENT OF NEURONS

Synaptic function depends on ionic transactions across an extracellular gap, the synaptic cleft. This cleft appears in electron micrographs to be a specialized part of the extracellular compartment of the brain, and

TABLE 7.4
Length of Postsynaptic Density of Synapses Involving Dendritic Shafts and Spines in Brains of Adult and Senescent Fischer-344 Rats

| Tissue/age | Mean length of postsynaptic density (nm) + S.E.M. | |
	Shafts	Spines
Dentate gyrus[a]		
3 months	300.8 ± 5.8	208.2 ± 1.4
25 months	295.6 ± 7.1	200.2 ± 1.8
Cerebellum[b]		
12 months	378.3 ± 12.9	443.5 ± 11.8
25 months	358.7 ± 8.7	435.1 ± 9.8

[a] Molecular layer, middle third. From Geinisman and Bondareff 1976.
[b] Cerebellar cortex, molecular layer immediately adjacent to Purkinje cell layer, vermian lobule V. From Glick and Bondareff 1979.

various substances introduced into the extracellular space of a living animal from either the cerebral vasculature or the cerebrospinal fluid can be shown to gain access to the synaptic clefts. The composition of synaptic clefts, however, is unknown although their histochemical properties suggest that they contain charged molecules, perhaps glycoproteins or glycosaminoglycans, some of which may be constituents of the plasma (i.e., synaptic) membranes bordering synaptic clefts (Bondareff and Lin-Liu 1977). Because ions and neurotransmitters move across these clefts it is reasonable to assume that astrocytes and neurons, which appear to contribute to the composition of synaptic clefts, may (by altering their composition) affect molecular transport across the clefts. Similarly, such mechanisms might be operative in the extracellular compartment through which ionic transactions occur and through which metabolites and ions appear to be transported between neurons and the vascular and cerebrospinal fluid compartments. The formation and maintenance of synaptic membranes depend on adequate neuronal metabolism. Neuronal metabolism in turn depends on a physiological relationship between neurons, blood vessels supplying them, and the extracellular spaces through which neuronal–vascular exchanges occur. Mechanisms might also exist, in addition to those affecting ionic transactions, whereby the passage of metabolites through the extracellular space might be modified and the metabolism of neurons thereby controlled. There is some reason to believe that alterations of the brain vasculature and/or extracellular space might result in age-related changes in the neuronal microenvironment.

Little is known about the vascular compartment of the aging brain. For human beings the data are few and controversial. In the aging rat, age-related structural changes appear to be minimal, but it has been recently shown that the blood–brain barrier, at least to [^{14}C]sucrose is intact in the 28-month-old Fischer-344 rat. Rapoport *et al.* (1979) found no age-related change in cerebrovascular permeability and little if any change in regional blood volume, but they found a 45 percent decline in the volume of the [^{14}C]sucrose distribution space. The magnitude of this decrease in the volume of extracellular space in the rat brain is remarkably similar to that measured directly in electron micrographs by Bondareff and Narotzky (1972). The latter found a 50% reduction in the volume fraction of extracellular space in the rat cerebral cortex. In the Fischer-344 rat it has been shown, in addition, that the depth of penetration of ruthenium red from the free ventricular surface into the substance of the dentate gyrus decreases in the 25-month-old Fischer-344 rat (Bondareff and Lin-Liu 1977).

Ruthenium red is a highly charged cation, whose penetration into the brain depends on its electrostatic interaction with intercellular polyanions in the extracellular space, in which ruthenium is distributed selectively. Its decreased depth of penetration, therefore, suggests an age-related change in the charge density of intercellular polyanions in the extracellular space in senescence. Although macromolecular events underlying this apparent change in charge density are uncertain, they may include both a relative decrease in the amount of keratan sulfate in brain proteoglycans (Vitello *et al.* 1978) and a decrease in water content in the senescent brain (Samorajaski and Ordy 1972).

CHANGES IN THE METABOLISM OF NEURONS

Normal neuronal metabolism, on which all neuronal functions (synthetic, transport, electrochemical, etc.) depend, requires a constant, adequate exchange between blood and brain. It can be assumed that the age-related reorganization of brain tissue may affect exchange mechanisms and adversely affect neuronal metabolism. In addition to such extrinsic factors, neuronal metabolism may be adversely affected by any number of age-related changes intrinsic to the neuron. Although many such changes have been described, few are supported adequately by experimental data.

That which has become most frequently associated with intracellular aging, almost a *sine qua non* of the aging process in neurons (for review see Bondareff 1976) is the accumulation of lipofuscin pigment. The occurrence of lipofuscin and the rate of its accumulation with chronological time varies in different types of neurons. Its composition and its effect on cellular metabolism have long been debated and are further confused by recent attempts to equate lipofuscin found in senescent brains with similar materials found in that rare group of human neuronal storage diseases known as neuronal ceroid-lipofuscinosis (Goebel *et al.* 1979). Lipofuscin appears to be a lysosomal derivative (Sekhon and Maxwell 1974); tertiary lysosomes or intracellular residual bodies resulting from lipid peroxidation. It has been suggested that cellular materials such as lipoproteins are sequestered in lysosomes and modified by peroxidation (Barden 1970). The resulting residue, which is undigested by the lysosome, then accumulates with time.

Lipofuscin progressively accumulates in huge amounts. In selective neurons, such as those of the inferior olivary nucleus of human beings, it is found eventually in almost all neurons (Brody 1973). As the amount of lipofuscin accumulates, it displaces cytoplasmic structures and the amount of RNA declines (Mann and Yates 1974). Yet there is no decline in the number of inferior olivary nucleus neurons with age (Monagle and Brody 1974), and in the rat there is no age-related decline in the number of olivo-cerebellar synapses (Glick and Bondareff 1979).

In the Fischer-344 rat, Brizzee and Ordy (1979) further find that the increase in lipofuscin is not associated with a decline in numbers of neurons in the visual area of the cerebral cortex and hippocampus. The question of whether lipofuscin accumulation benefits neurons, in the sense that it protects neurons against potentially noxious or otherwise harmful substances that it sequesters, or damages neurons by crowding out the machinery of normal metabolism, remains moot.

Although an age-related decline in neuronal RNA has been shown in the human inferior olivary nucleus (Mann and Yates 1974) as well as in neurons of the human spinal cord (Hyden 1967) and hippocampus (Ringborg 1966), it is of questionable significance. On one hand, the rate of protein turnover, at least by neurons isolated from the spinal cord, was shown not to differ in young and senescent rats (Jakoubek *et al.* 1968). On the other hand, a decline in neuronal protein synthesis is suggested by the decreased capacity of cerebellar and spinal cord neurons to incorporate [^{3}H] cytidine in old mice (Wulff *et al.* 1965). Although in themselves they may not be convincing, several studies collectively suggest rather strongly that neuronal metabolism in general, and protein metabolism in particular fail in the senescent brain. From this conclusion, one would predict a decline in the synthesis of at least certain neuroactive substances—which has, in fact, been shown. Gamma aminobutyric acid (Davis and Himwich 1975), acetylcholine esterase activity (Samorajaski *et al.* 1971), and catecholamines and indolamines (Finch 1973, Samorajaski *et al.* 1971) have all been shown to decline with age.

There has as yet been no systematic attempt to elucidate how a decline of neuronal metabolic processes might adversely affect neuronal interactions at synapses or lead to a loss of synapses such as is found in the hippocampus in senescent rats. One might hypothesize a change in protein metabolism such as to affect the composition of fibrillar proteins, for example, tubulin and the neurofilament protein that was isolated from the microtubules (neurotubules) and microfilaments (neurofilaments) of neurons. Changes in these neurofibrils (so-called neurofibrillary change) have long been associated with aging (see review by Bondareff 1959), and various human dementias including senile dementia of the Alzheimer's type. More recently, neurofibrillary tangles, similar to those typically found in the hippocampus of senescent human beings, have been induced in selected animals by aluminum salts (Crapper 1976) and viruses (Wisniewski 1978). Because intraneuronal transport mechanisms appear to depend on neurofilaments and neurotubules (Watson 1976) it is reasonable to speculate that structural alterations in neurofibrils secondary to changes in neurofibrillary proteins might cause changes in neuronal connectivity. Such changes have not been shown. There is evidence, however, of an age-related change in intraneuronal transport mechanisms of neurons of the rat septal nucleus. These neurons, which contribute presynaptic cholinergic afferents to synapses in the dentate gyrus, take up and incorporate [^{3}H] fucose into glycoproteins similarly in senescent and young adult Fischer-344 rats. This was shown by labeling the medial septal nucleus of young adult and senescent rats with [^{3}H] fucose and comparing the arrival times of ^{3}H-labeled glycoproteins in the hippocampus as a function of age (Geinisman, Bondareff, and Telser 1977). The arrival times differed significantly, reflecting a 30% reduction in the rate of axonal transport of glycoproteins to synapses remaining in the dentate gyrus of senescent rats. Since glycoproteins are components of presynaptic membranes, such an age-related decrement in the amount and/or the rate of glycoproteins transported to axonal terminals probably indicates a failure of presynaptic neurons to maintain the integrity of their synaptic membranes in senescence.

Although no conclusive data indicate that faulty intraneuronal transport of glycoproteins adversely affects neuronal interactions in senescence, two recent findings support the speculation that the faulty intraneuronal transport of glycoproteins might be more than merely temporally related to structural alterations of synaptic membranes. First, a change in Conconavalin A binding patterns of neurons isolated from the lateral vestibular nuclei of senescent rats was demonstrated by fluorescence microscopy (Bennett and Bondareff 1977). Second, a decrease in the sensitivity of cationized ferritin binding capacity of synaptosomes iso-

lated from the brains of senescent rats was demonstrated to neuramini-
dase (Lin-Liu 1978). Both observations suggest age-related changes in
glycoprotein composition and are compatible with structural changes in
presynaptic membranes. It is not known whether such changes are related
to functional impairment or to the reorganization of structural components known to be taking place in the dentate gyrus of senescent rats.

In this chapter, I have attempted to review age changes in the brain
that appear not to be species-specific, have been reliably and repro-
duceably demonstrated, and appear more related to the process of aging
than to disease. These changes, which have been demonstrated in relatively healthy animals, are generally reversible and not catastrophic.
Their etiology, like the etiology of age-related changes in other organs,
is uncertain. They may be genetic, that is, they may be programmed into
the genomes of neurons and neuroglia. They might as well result from
nongenetic, time-related changes in the genome. Such changes might
involve the brain selectively or, if the result of some more generalized
cellular phenomenon, they might occur throughout the body of aging
organisms. And they need not be exclusively cellular, although they are
undoubtedly cellular in origin. They might affect the extracellular macromolecules found in connective tissues, including those occurring in
blood vessels and extracellular ground substance. Such nonspecific, age-
related changes could have unique consequences in the brain.

It is apparent that the functions of some neurons change with age but
that most neurons continue to function and remain capable of adaptational change throughout life. One example of this is the retention of the
capacity of axons to sprout and form new synapses in response to synaptic loss resulting from environmental trauma in senescent rats (discussed by Lynch and Gerline, Chapter 9 in this volume). The capacity
of neurons to respond to experience by changes in dendritic distribution
(discussed by Greenough and Green, Chapter 8, this volume) indicates
further adaptational response. Both these responses appear to be less
efficient than those of younger animals, suggesting a decreased adaptational response of the nervous system in senescence. This was suggested some 20 years ago when it was noted that in old rats forced to
swim to the point of exhaustion neurons of spinal ganglia were less able
to replace depleted Nissl substance (cytoplasmic RNA) than were those
of young animals (Bondareff 1962). Should this age-related loss of metabolic reserve of peripheral neurons prove more generally applicable it
can be predicted that central nervous system neurons are not only vulnerable in old age but may become progressively more vulnerable due
to the cumulative effects of disease and toxic substances. The vulnerability of neurons generally to the environmental insults that besiege

older members of a species may result from this progressive, age-related metabolic failure, not apparent until metabolic systems are severely tested by insult added to injury. A consequence of such compromised neuronal functioning vis-à-vis psychological functions in human beings is the prediction that intellectual functioning will fail discontinuously in senescence. Predictably, age changes in psychological functions do seem to be characterized by a discontinuity, in that they are related to neuronal variables only when the latter lie in an abnormal range as in disease (cf. Birren *et al.* 1963).

The relationship between disease and intellectual functioning in senescent human beings is complex, and with the exception of cardiovascular disease (discussed by Steuer and Jarvik, Chapter 10, this volume) is poorly understood. Elderly human beings are beset also by insults, which, if less injurious, appear to be more pervasive, as they relate more directly to constraints of social living, and are perhaps less escapable. In elderly human beings such insults may result from self-imposed dependence (discussed by Langer, Chapter 10, this volume), secondary to the fear of growing old in a society with negative attitudes toward the elderly or to multiple object loss. In either case, the resulting adaptational failure may have a neuronal substrate. In the sense that this adaptational failure does not result directly from neuronal pathology but is in response to some complex, socially related insult, the ills of old age may be artifactual. If this is so and if the age-related decline in intellectual functioning turns out to be preventable or at least treatable, the words of Robert Browning will have real meaning—the last of life may indeed prove to be that for which the first of life was made.

REFERENCES

Barden, H. (1970) Relationship of Golgi thiamine pyrophosphatase and lysomal acid phosphatase to enruomelanin and lipfuscin in cerebral neurons of the aging rhesus monkey. *Journal of Neuropathology and Experimental Neurology* 29:225–240.

Bennett, K. D., and Bondareff, W. (1977) Age-related differences in binding of Conconavalin A to plasma membranes of isolated neurons. *American Journal of Anatomy* 150:175–184.

Birren, J. E., Butler, R. N., Greenhouse, S. W., Sokoloff, L., and Yarrow, M. R. (1963) Interdisciplinary relationships: Interrelations of physiological, psychological, and psychiatric findings in healthy elderly men. Pp. 283–308 in J. E. Birren, R. N. Butler, S. W. Greenhouse, L. Sokoloff, and M. R. Yarrow, eds., *Human Aging: A Biological and Behavioral Study*. Washington, D.C.: U.S. Government Printing Office.

Bondareff, W. (1959) Morphology and the aging nervous system. Pp. 187–215 in J. E. Birren, ed., *Handbook of Aging and the Individual*. Chicago: University of Chicago Press.

Bondareff, W. (1962) Distribution of Nissl substance in neurons of the rat spinal ganglia as a function of age and fatigue. In *Proceedings of the Fifth Congress of the International Association of Gerontology: Aging Around the World*. New York: Columbia University Press.

Bondareff, W. (1967) An intercellular substance in rat cerebral cortex: Submicroscopic distribution of ruthenium red. *Anatomical Record* 157:527–536.

Bondareff, W. (1976) The neural basis of aging. Pp. 157–176 in J. E. Birren and K. W. Schaie, eds., *Handbook of the Psychology of Aging*. New York: Van Nostrand Reinhold.

Bondareff, W. (1980a) Neurobiology of aging. In J. E. Birren and R. B. Sloan, eds., *Handbook of Mental Health and Aging*. New York: Van Nostrand Reinhold.

Bondareff, W. (1980b) Changes in synaptic structure affecting neural transmission in senescent brain. In *Proceedings of the Naito International Symposium on Aging*. New York: Plenum Press.

Bondareff, W., and Geinisman, Y. (1976) Loss of synapses in the dentate gyrus of the senescent rat. *American Journal of Anatomy* 145:129–136.

Bondareff, W., and Lin-Liu, S. (1977) Age-related change in the neuronal microenvironment: Penetration of ruthenium red into extracellular space of brain in young adult and senescent rats. *American Journal of Anatomy* 148:57–64.

Bondareff, W., and Narotzky, R. (1972) Age changes in the neuronal microenvironment. *Science* 176:1135–1136.

Brizzee, K. R., and Ordy, J. M. (1979) Age pigments, cell loss and hippocampal function. *Mechanisms of Ageing and Development* 9:143–162.

Brody, H. (1955) Organization of the cerebral cortex. III. A study of aging in the human cerebral cortex. *Journal of Comparative Neurology* 102:511–556.

Brody, H. (1973) Aging of the vertebrate brain. Pp. 121–134 in M. Rockstein, ed., *Development and Aging in the Nervous System*. New York: Academic Press.

Butler, R. N., and Lewis, M. I. (1973) Pp. 123–142 in *Aging and Mental Health: Positive Psycho-Social Approaches*. St. Louis: C. V. Mosby.

Coleman, G. L., Barthold, S. W., Osbaldiston, G. W., Foster, S. J., and Jonas, A. M. (1977) Pathological changes during aging in barrier-reared Fischer-344 male rats. *Journal of Gerontology* 32:258–278.

Cotman, C. W., and Scheff, S. W. (1979) Compensatory synapse growth in aged animals after neuronal death. *Mechanisms of Ageing and Development* 9:103–118.

Cragg, B. G. (1975) The density of synapses and neurons in normal, mentally defective and aging human brains. *Brain* 98:81–90.

Crapper, D. R. (1976) Functional consequences of neurofibrillary degeneration. Pp. 405–432 in R. D. Terry and S. Gershon, eds., *Neurobiology of Aging*. New York: Raven Press.

Davis, J. M., and Himwich, W. A. (1975) Neurochemistry of the developing and aging mammalian brain. Pp. 329–359 in J. M. Ordy and K. R. Brizzee, eds., *Neurobiology of Aging*. New York: Plenum Press.

Feldman, M. L. (1976) Aging changes in the morphology of cortical dendrites. Pp. 211–227 in R. D. Terry and S. Gershon, eds., *Neurobiology of Aging*. New York: Raven Press.

Feldman, M. L., and Dowd, C. (1975) Loss of dendritic spines in aging cerebral cortex. *Anatomy and Embryology* 148:279–301.

Finch, C. (1973) Catecholamine metabolism in the brains of aging male mice. *Brain Research* 52:261–276.

Geinisman, Y. (1979) Loss of axosomatic synapses in the dentate gyrus of the senescent rat. *Brain Research* 168:485–492.

Geinisman, Y., and Bondareff, W. (1976) Decrease in the number of synapses in the senescent brain: A quantitative electron microscopic analysis of the dentate gyrus molecular layer in the rat. *Mechanisms of Ageing and Development* 5:11–23.

Geinisman, Y., Bondareff, W., and Dodge, J. T. (1977) Partial deafferentation of neurons in the dentate gyrus of the senescent rat. *Brain Research* 134:541–545.

Geinisman, Y., Bondareff, W., and Dodge, J. T. (1978a) Dendritic atrophy in the dentate gyrus of the senescent rat. *American Journal of Anatomy* 152:321–330.

Geinisman, Y., Bondareff, W., and Dodge, J. T. (1978b) Hypertrophy of astroglial processes in the dentate gyrus of the senescent rat. *American Journal of Anatomy* 153:537–544.

Geinisman, Y., Bondareff, W., and Telser, A. (1977) Transport of (^{3}H) fucose labeled glycoproteins in the septo-hippocampal pathway of young adult and senescent rats. *Brain Research* 125:182–186.

Glick, R., and Bondareff, W. (1979) Loss of synapses in the cerebellar cortex of the senescent rat. *Journal of Gerontology* 34(6):818–822.

Goebel, H. H., Zeman, W., Patel, V. K., Pullarkat, R. K., and Lenard, H. G. (1979) On the ultrastructural diversity and essence of residual bodies in neuronal ceroid-lipofuscinosis. *Mechanisms of Ageing and Development* 10:53–70.

Greenough, W. T., West, R. W., and DeVoogd, T. J. (1978) Synaptic plate perforations: Changes with age and experience in the rat. *Science* 202:1096–1098.

Grossman, R. G., and Seregin, A. (1977) Glial-neural interaction demonstrated by the injection of Na$^+$ and Li$^+$ into cortical glia. *Science* 195:196–198.

Hall, T. C., Miller, A. K. H., and Corsellis, J. A. N. (1975) Variations in the human Purkinje cell population according to age and sex. *Neuropathology and Applied Neurology* 1:267–292.

Hinds, J. W., and McNelly, N. A. (1977) Aging of the rat olfactory bulb: Growth and atrophy of constituent layers and changes in size and number of mitral cells. *Journal of Comparative Neurology* 171:345–367.

Hyden, H. (1967) Dynamic aspects on the neuron-glia relationship—a study with microchemical methods. Pp. 179–220 in H. Hyden, ed., *The Neuron*. Amsterdam: Elsevier.

Jakoubek, B., Gutmann, E., Fischer, J., and Babicky, A. (1968) Rate of protein renewal in spinal motorneurons of adolescent and old rats. *Journal of Neurochemistry* 15:633–641.

Kreutzberg, G. W., Barron, K. D., and Schubert, P. (1978) Cytochemical localization of 5′-nucleotidase in glial plasma membranes. *Brain Research* 158:247–257.

Landfield, P. W., Rose, G., Sandles, L., Wohlstadter, R. C., and Lynch, G. (1977) Patterns of astroglial hypertrophy and neuronal degeneration in the hippocampus of aged, memory-deficient rats. *Journal of Gerontology* 32:3–12.

Lin-Liu, S. (1978) Surface charge of synaptosomes in young adult and senescent rat brain. Dissertation, Northwestern University.

Mann, D. M. A., and Yates, P. O. (1974) Lipoprotein pigments—their relationship to aging in the human nervous system. I. The lipofuscin content of nerve cells. *Brain* 97:481–488.

Martinez-Hernandez, A., Bell, K. P., and Norenberg, M. D. (1977) Glutamine synthetase: Glial localization in brain. *Science* 195:1356–1358.

McCarley, R. W., and Hobson, J. A. (1977) The neurobiological origins of psycholoanalytic dream theory. *American Journal of Psychiatry* 134:1211–1221.

Monagle, R. D., and Brody, H. (1974) The effects of age upon the main nucleus of the inferior olive in the human. *Journal of Comparative Neurology* 155:61–66.

Rapoport, S. I., Ohno, K., and Pettigrew, R. D. (1979) Blood–brain barrier permeability in senescent rats. *Journal of Gerontology* 34:162–169.

Ringborg, U. (1966) Composition and content of RND in neurons of rat hippocampus at different ages. *Brain Research* 2:296–298.

Samorajaski, T., and Ordy, J. M. (1972) Neurochemistry of aging. P. 45 in C. M. Gaitz, ed., *Aging and the Brain*. New York: Plenum Press.

Samorajaski, T., Rolsten, C., and Ordy, J. M. (1971) Changes in behavior, brain, and neuroendocrine chemistry with age and stress in C56B1/10 male mice. *Journal of Gerontology* 26:168–175.

Scheibel, M. E., Landsay, R. D., Tomiyasu, U., and Scheibel, A. B. (1975) Progressive dendritic changes in aging human cortex. *Experimental Neurology* 47:392–403.

Scheibel, M. E., Lindsay, R. D., Tomiyasu, U., and Scheibel, A. B. (1976) Progressive dendritic changes in the aging human limbic system. *Experimental Neurology* 53:420–430.

Scheibel, A. B., and Tomiyasu, U. (1978) Dendritic sprouting in Alzheimer's presenile dementia. *Experimental Neurology* 60:1–8.

Scheff, S. W., Bernardo, L. S., and Cotman, C. W. (1978) Decrease in adrenergic axon sprouting in the senescent rat. *Science* 202:775–778.

Sekhon, S. S., and Maxwell, D. S. (1974) Ultrastructural changes in neurons of the spinal anterior horn of aging mice with particular reference to the accumulation of lipofuscin pigment. *Journal of Neurochemistry* 3:59–72.

Sotelo, C., and Palay, S. L. (1971) Altered axons and axon terminals in the lateral vestibular nucleus of the rat: Possible example of axonal remodelling. *Laboratory Investigation* 25:653–671.

Vaughan, D. W. (1977) Age-related deterioration of pyramidal cell basal dendrites in the rat auditory cortex. *Journal of Comparative Neurology* 171:501–516.

Vaughan, D. W., and Peters, A. (1974) Neuroglial cells in the cerebral cortex of rats from young adulthood to old age: An electron microscope study. *Journal of Neurocytology* 3:405–429.

Vitello, L., Breen, M., Weinstein, H. G., Sittig, R. A., and Blacik, L. J. (1978) Keratan sulfate-like glycosaminoglycan in the cerebral cortex of the brain and its variation with age. *Biochemica and Biophysica Acta* 539:305–314.

Watson, W. E. (1976) *Cell Biology of Brain*. London: Chapman and Hall.

Wisniewski, H. M. (1978) Possible viral etiology of neurofibrillary changes and neuritic plaques. Pp. 555–558 in R. Klatzman, R. D. Terry, and K. Bick, eds., *Alzheimers Disease: Senile Dementia and Related Disorders*. New York: Raven Press.

Wulff, V. J., Quastler, H., Sherman, F. G., and Samis, H. V. (1965) The effect of specific activity of H^3-cytidine on its incorporation into tissues of young and old mice. *Journal of Gerontology* 20:34–40.

chapter **8**

Experience and the Changing Brain[1]

WILLIAM T. GREENOUGH
EDWARD J. GREEN

A simple statement of contemporary thought regarding brain development over the human life-span suggests that the brain goes through three stages. During the initial stage of relatively rapid development, the brain appears uniquely receptive to certain experiences at certain times; in the adult stage, the brain retains its capacity to store information from the environment, but the effects of specific experiences are considerably less profound than during early development; in the stage of aging (which may, in fact, begin quite early) the brain becomes increasingly less capable of directing many kinds of mental and physical performance, and the ability to store and retain information from the environment gradually (or sometimes precipitously) declines.

Rather striking differences in the manner in which the brain interacts with experience during these three stages have led to the postulation that different biological mechanisms are operative. The developing brain is thought to exhibit a very high degree of plasticity or ability to change

[1] Work described in this chapter and not reported elsewhere was supported by NSF BNS7723660 and NSF SER7618255.

AGING
Biology and Behavior

in the face of experience, which is reflected in anatomical and physiological as well as behavioral measures. The adult brain is thought of as relatively stable from an anatomical and physiological point of view, and information storage as a relatively minor process in terms of the metabolic activity of the brain as a whole (although the assumption by many investigators that metabolic consequences of a single training experience may be discovered suggests an expectation of relatively major involvement of the brain at least for short periods).

The aging brain has been seen to decline in terms of anatomical, physiological, and metabolic as well as behavioral measures, and it has been widely assumed that this relatively inevitable physiological decay underlies the decline of behavioral performance. Thus the developing brain has been viewed as relatively dynamic, adding to its structures and potential; the adult brain as relatively stable; and the aging brain as again dynamic, in the reverse direction, irrevocably declining at rates that apparently vary widely across individuals.

Recently, experimental evidence has begun to challenge these views. First, it has become quite clear that degeneration, including both loss of cells and elimination of cellular processes, is inherent in normal development. Thus, early development is not merely a process of adding to the structure of the brain. Second, there is increasing evidence that the adult brain may remain remarkably plastic from an anatomical perspective. That is, experience appears to continue to modulate the structure of the brain and its cellular components. Third, there is a limited amount of evidence that suggests that the aging brain may retain a considerable degree of flexibility in structure. Although the evidence is far from complete, we can begin to speculate that the structure (and correspondingly the function) of the brain at any point may reflect the historical and current state of a dynamic interplay of growth and degeneration of neuronal processes, with the relative weight of the degeneration aspect increasing in the older years.

This model suggests somewhat different mechanisms whereby experience affects the brain during early development and also suggests that experience may continue to affect the brain in much the same way throughout life. If so, the organism's experience may play an important role in the aging process. In this chapter, we first review briefly the evidence for this newer view of early development; then consider data that indicate continuing effects of experience on the adult brain; and finally examine the small amount of evidence suggesting that brain plasticity of a functionally appropriate type may continue in the aging brain.

EXPERIENCE AND SELECTIVE PRESERVATION
IN EARLY DEVELOPMENT
Early Influences on Brain and Behavior

VISUAL SYSTEM DEVELOPMENT

In higher mammals such as rats, cats, and monkeys, visual experience appears to be necessary to the development of a normally functioning visual system. The effects of experience are seen clearly in the anatomy and physiology of the visual system as well as in behavior. Mammals reared in the dark or with both eyes sutured closed are deficient in a variety of visual behaviors, including depth perception, pattern discrimination, and visual acuity (e.g., Tees 1976, Chow and Stewart 1972, Loop and Sherman 1977, Smith *et al.* 1978). Even more severe deficits are seen when only one of the eyes is occluded, apparently due to the mechanisms involved in the development of stereoscopic depth perception, in animals with overlapping central nervous system visual projections (e.g., Dews and Wiesel 1970, Chow and Stewart 1972, Ganz and Fitch 1968).

Electrophysiological studies of single cells in the visual system have provided clues to the mechanisms by which these deficits are generated. In dark-reared or binocularly occluded kittens, for example, neurons in the visual cortex do not exhibit the fine tuning of the receptive field to a particular orientation, which is seen in normally reared cats. Rather, the bulk of cells lack this "orientation specificity," and the system appears to degenerate as deprivation is prolonged. In the case of monocular deprivation, the deprived eye appears actually to relinquish its control over single neurons in the visual cortex such that stimulation of the experienced eye causes most neurons to fire, whereas stimulation of the nonexperienced eye fires very few cells (e.g., Hubel and Wiesel 1963).

Anatomical comparisons of animals that have been visually deprived with normally reared subjects indicate differences in the number, the pattern, and the fine structural features of the synaptic connections between nerve cells in the visual system. Studies using Golgi-staining procedures, a technique that stains entire neurons so that their processes can be followed (see Figure 8.1), indicate that there are fewer synapses on neurons in the visual cortex of animals that have been deprived of vision. Valverde (1971), for example, reported that mice reared in the dark had fewer spines (the postsynaptic element of one type of connection) on the neurons he studied in visual cortex than did light-reared animals. An even more important type of change may involve the pattern

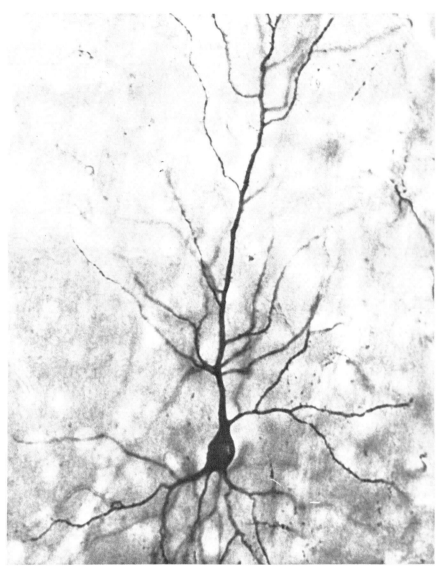

Figure 8.1. A pyramidal neuron from rat visual cortex stained by the rapid Golgi method. Processes extending from the cell body are dendrites, the major recipients of input from other neurons (the axon is out of focus). The small spots along the dendrites are spines, sites of the majority of synapses on the dendrites.

of synaptic connections. Valverde (1970) and Borges and Berry (1976) reported that the dendrites (receptive portions, see Figure 8.1) of some types of neurons were positioned differently in the visual cortex of dark-reared rodents relative to light-reared controls. Similarly, Hubel *et al.* (1977) reported that the axons of neurons connected to the deprived eye in monocularly deprived monkeys were constrained to a relatively small area while those connected to the experienced eye were expanded, relative to the pattern in the normally reared cat. (Changes of the fine structure of synapses are not reviewed in this paper.)

PROPOSED MECHANISMS

Of particular interest to our purpose is the manner in which these differences in number and pattern of synaptic connections arise as a result of differential visual experience. One historically popular view argued that experience somehow stimulates and/or directs the formation of new connections (e.g., Valverde 1971). Valverde's work provides strong evidence for some form of stimulation of anatomical growth by visual experience. When animals are placed in the light after dark-rearing, a rapid acceleration of development of postsynaptic spines appears to occur. Electron microscopic evidence for a similar phenomenon has been presented by Cragg (1967).

An alternative view, arising both from studies of the periphery and from a few reports on central nervous system development, suggests that selective preservation of a subset of synaptic connections from a larger pool of connections generated during development is involved in visual system development. This concept has arisen as a consequence of two primary lines of research. The first suggests that in the periphery of neonatal rats, spinal motor neurons are typically connected to a number of subunits (motor units) of the muscles they innervate, and similarly the muscles are typically innervated by several motor neurons. During early postnatal development in the rat, these multiple connections degenerate, probably as a result of neuronal activity, leaving behind the one-neuron-to-one-motor-unit pattern of connectivity of the adult (Brown *et al.* 1976). An analogous process appears to occur in the development of the peripheral autonomic nervous system (Lichtman 1977). Thus these peripheral neurons appear to generate excess connections during development, only one or a few of which survive. It has been proposed (Brown *et al.* 1976, Changeaux and Danchin 1977) that the axons compete for control of postsynaptic cells and that some consequence of their normal impulse-carrying and synaptic transmission activity determines the degree to which they are favored in the competition. Ultimately, the axon of one neuron appears to be preserved while other axons innervating the motor unit degenerate.

The second line of research suggests that there is increasing evidence for a similar process in central nervous system development. For example, Booth *et al.* (1979) examined neurons in monkey visual cortex at various ages from late fetal stages to adulthood. They found (see Figure 8.2) that the number of postsynaptic spines on various neurons

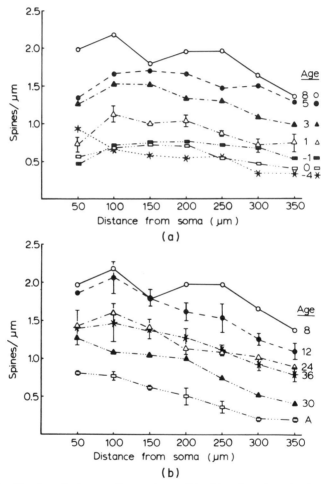

Figure 8.2. Number of spines per linear micron of dendrite of monkey visual cortex Layer III B pyramidal cells as a function of age and distance from the soma, or cell body. (a) Spine numbers increase up to 8 weeks after birth. (b) Spine numbers decrease from 8 weeks of age to adulthood, with the most pronounced decrease occurring before 30 to 36 weeks of age. (Reprinted from Boothe *et al.* 1979, by permission of Alan R. Liss, Inc.)

reached a peak relatively early in development, following which the number decreased to a relatively stable adult level. The peak in several cell populations occurred as early as eight weeks of age, and the decline that followed was definitely not an aspect of what we typically consider to be the aging process. Cragg (1975) has presented similar results for cat visual cortex using electron microscopy. This suggests that visual system neurons overproduce synapses in early development and that a significant proportion of this overproduction is discarded as a part of the development process. Evidence that experience can affect the retention of connections is provided by Hubel *et al.* (1977). Recall that in the monocularly deprived cat and monkey, axons from the deprived eye are constricted to relatively narrow bands in the visual cortex, whereas those from the experienced eye are relatively expanded. Examining the sequence of development in the monkey, Hubel *et al.* (1977) found that the regions of axon termination of the two eyes in early development were extensive and overlapping. As a result of experience, the open eye appeared to retain and embellish its wide pattern of connections, while the closed eye's connections appeared to undergo marked degeneration, such that only a narrow band remained.

These and other studies suggest that normal neuronal development may often involve a pattern of overproduction of synaptic connections followed by a selective loss of connections, perhaps because they are unused or otherwise inappropriate. Since there is some evidence that the use of the connection may preserve it from loss, we have chosen to term this theoretical process *selective preservation* (Greenough 1978). Changeaux and Danchin (1977) used the term *selective stabilisation*.

Selective preservation alone probably cannot account for all experience-dependent developmental phenomena. For example, as we noted in a preceding paragraph, there is evidence in the work of Valverde (1971) and Cragg (1967) that the sudden onset of light can trigger a burst of synapse formation in rodent visual cortex. Other studies have shown rapid metabolic changes in the visual system following light onset (e.g., Rose 1967, Richardson and Rose 1972). Whether the formation of synapses is somehow directed appropriately by experience or whether it merely provides a basis for a further selection process remains uncertain.

Environmental Complexity and Brain Development

Evidence that the role of experience in the modulation of brain development extends beyond early sensory system organization has been provided by studies in which animals have been reared following weaning in environments differing in complexity. Following initial demonstrations by Hebb and his students (e.g., Hebb 1949, Hymovitch 1952) that animals reared under differing conditions of environmental complexity differed in learning ability, several investigators have begun to examine correlates of this process in the structure and metabolism of the brain. The pioneering work of the Berkeley group (e.g., Krech *et al.* 1962, Bennett *et al.* 1964, Rosenzweig *et al.* 1972b) indicates rather striking differences between the brains of animals reared in isolation and those reared in enriched or complex environments (Figure 8.3). Their early work indicates that various regions of rat cortex, particularly the visual cortex, were heavier and thicker in animals reared in complex environments than in litter mates reared individually in standard laboratory cages or in groups in larger laboratory cages. In addition, a higher ratio of RNA to DNA indicates that the brains of animals from complex environments are metabolically more active. Light microscopic studies indicate that nerve cell bodies in the visual cortex are larger and that more glial cells are present.

Further light microscopic studies as well as electron microscopic studies have produced conflicting results regarding the number, or frequency per unit volume, of synapses in the visual cortex of these animals. Moll-gaard *et al.* (1971) and Diamond *et al.* (1975) reported that the frequency of synapses per unit volume in the visual cortex measured in electron micrographs is greater in isolated animals than in animals reared in complex environments. This result is especially striking, since the synapses of the animals reared in complex environments are larger than those of the isolates, and the frequency figures were not corrected for these size differences. (West and Greenough [1972] also reported larger synapses in animals reared in complex environments, although the size of the difference was much smaller.) Hence these studies probably contain a relative overestimate of the number of synapses per unit volume in the animals reared in complex environments. More recently, Cummins and Walsh (1976) reported a higher frequency/volume of synapses in the visual cortex of rats reared in environmental complexity. Of course, the number of synapses per unit volume in tissue in which other elements are also expanding (e.g., neuronal cell bodies and glia) may not be an accurate estimator of the number of synapses per neuron. That is, it remains possible that there are more synapses *in toto* in the visual cortex of the animals reared in a complex environment.

Light microscopic studies, estimating the number of synapses per neuron from the size of the dendritic tree and the frequency of postsynaptic spines, have generated more consistent results. Our laboratory has quantified the branching of neuronal dendrites in various cortical

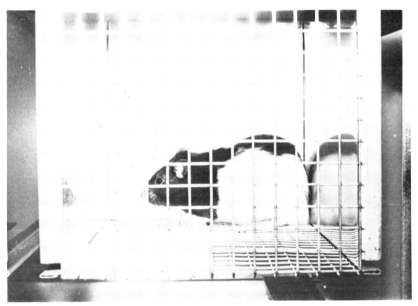

Figure 8.3. *Top:* Rats explore a typical toy filled field as part of the environmental complexity procedure. *Bottom:* The isolation condition, with which complex rearing is compared, involves individual housing in laboratory cages.

areas and the hippocampus of rats reared under conditions of environmental complexity, isolated in individual laboratory cages, and, in some cases, of animals reared in pairs in laboratory cages. Camera lucida tracings of the dendritic tree of Golgi-stained neurons were used in most of this work, but more recently we have developed a computer system (DeVoogd 1979), in which the three-dimensional coordinates of points along dendrites are recorded as the operator tracks the neuron in the microscope. In both cases, neurons are analyzed in essentially the same manner. To examine the amount and distribution of dendritic material, a reflection of the amount of space for synapses, the intersections between dendrites and an overlay of concentric rings (for drawings) or spheres (for computer-stored neurons) is counted (see Figure 8.4). To analyze more specifically the ways in which neurons differ, the number and length of branches at each order away from the cell body are recorded. Measures of total ring intersections and total dendritic length correlate very highly and provide an overall estimate of neuronal growth,

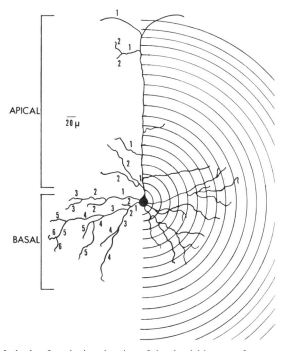

Figure 8.4. Methods of analyzing the size of the dendritic tree of a neuron. The left side indicates the numbering system for dendritic branches. Branches arising from the cell body or main ascending dendrite are termed order 1, those arising from a bifurcation order 2, etc. The right side demonstrates the ring intersection method of Sholl (1956).

while measures of intersections with individual rings and measures of branches of individual orders indicate the pattern of growth within the neuron.

These measures revealed that Layer II, IV, and V pyramidal neurons as well as Layer IV stellate neurons in the visual cortex of animals reared in complex environments had as much as 15% more dendritic material than those in animals reared in isolation (Volkmar and Greenough 1972, Greenough and Volkmar 1973). Socially reared animals were intermediate between these two groups. The magnitude and some details of the pattern of these effects vary across later replications, but the basic finding, that animals reared in environmental complexity exceed their less elegantly housed litter mates in dendritic tree dimensions, appears quite reliable in the visual cortex. In the temporal region of the cortex associated with audition, the magnitude of the difference was smaller, but again animals from complex environments had more extensive dendritic branching in pyramidal neurons from deep cortical layers (Greenough et al. 1973). In a frontolateral region of the cortex associated with motor activity, there were no differences in dendritic branching among the three groups (Greenough et al. 1973). This latter finding suggests that the effects are less likely to be of a hormonal or metabolic nature, since hormonal or metabolic effects might be expected to occur relatively generally throughout the brain. These differences are not limited to the cerebral cortex. Fiala et al. (1978) found that granule cells of the dentate gyrus of the hippocampus were more highly branched in animals reared in a complex environment than in rats reared in isolation.

While these findings suggest greater dendritic space for synapses, they do not necessarily indicate that more synapses are, in fact, present. As stated in the previous section, the frequency with which spines, representing synapses, occur along dendrites can vary with age and experience. However, Globus et al. (1973) have shown that the frequency of spines along dendrites of at least the deep pyramidal cell populations in the occipital cortex is greater overall in animals from complex environments than in animals from isolated rearing conditions in the basal dendritic region, and that the complex environment animal does not have fewer spines than the isolated animal in any part of the neuron. Thus these studies do indicate that in the sensory cortical areas examined, neurons from animals reared in a complex environment have more dendritic spine synapses than neurons from animals reared in isolation.

Similar findings have been reported in species other than rodents. Struble and Riesen (1978; see also Riesen et al. [1980]) examined the cerebral cortex of monkeys that were reared individually but that had differing amounts of space for activity and in one case a cage equipped with various play objects. Animals reared with mothers served as controls. While primary visual cortex was not affected, the amount of stellate cell dendritic branching increased in somatosensory and motor cortex as the opportunity for interaction with the environment increased. Animals reared with play objects surpassed even those reared with the mother in dendritic branching in most areas.

In similar work, Floeter and Greenough (1979) examined the branching of Purkinje and granule cells in the cerebellum of differentially reared monkeys. The cerebellum is a structure involved in the coordination of motor activity. Monkeys were raised in isolation, in laboratory cages allowing daily social contact, or in a large two-room colony containing adults, juveniles, and infants as well as various play objects and structures. In several cerebellar areas associated with vestibular sensation (movement of the body in space), the spiny portions of the Purkinje cell dendritic tree were more extensive in the animals from the colony condition. There were no consistent differences between isolation and socially reared animals. The dendritic fields of the granule cells did not differ across groups. Since only one of these two simultaneously developing cell populations showed this effect, it seems unlikely to have arisen from general metabolic differences. Moreover, the point at which the plasticity occurred, the Purkinje cell spiny branchlets, is the point at which several theorists, such as Marr (1969), have predicted cerebellar plasticity based on mathematical models of cerebellar function. Pysh and Weiss (1979) reported a very similar finding in rats. Motorically restricted rats had less extensive Purkinje cell dendritic branching than did rats reared in a motorically enriched environment.

Taken together, these studies demonstrate that the number of connections of a variety of different types of central nervous system neurons depends to a significant degree on the experience of the organism during its development. This plasticity appears to be widespread in the nervous system—in fact it may well be the rule, rather than the exception. (Even cells in the seemingly "hard-wired" regulatory regions of the brain appear to show a form of developmental plasticity. For example, various aspects of the morphology of neurons in the preoptic area associated with reproductive activity appear to be influenced by the hormonal environment during infancy [Gorski et al. 1978, Greenough et al. 1977, Hsu et al. 1978, Raisman and Field 1973a].)

There is evidence to suggest that a selective preservation process similar to or identical with that described in visual development may be involved in generating these differences. In monkey visual cortex, for example, the time period during which spines, and in some cases apparently dendritic branches, are being lost extends beyond 9 months of age for at least some cell populations. Whether additional synapses are also being generated during that period is uncertain, but evidence supporting this possibility, at least in the rat, is described later in this chapter. Hence, some morphological effects of experience could result from selective preservation of synapses against some otherwise preprogrammed loss (informally we term this a *sunset law* for synapses). Similarly, while our data regarding the course of cerebellar development are fragmentary, Weiss and Pysh (1978) have shown that the extent of the dendritic tree of rat cerebellar Purkinje cells reaches a peak near the age of weaning and then declines to stable adult values. Hence, again, experience appears to be acting on a background of gradual loss of synaptic connections in such a manner that selective preservation would be a quite plausible mechanism for the ultimately greater size of the Purkinje cell dendritic tree. In rat visual cortex, Parnavelas *et al.* (1978) reported that stellate cells (the most affected cell type in the Volkmar and Greenough 1972, and Greenough and Volkmar 1973, studies) reached an apparent peak in terms of the frequency of spines and other indications of maturity during the third postnatal week, and then declined to adult levels. The rate of the decline is somewhat uncertain, since the observations of Parnavelas *et al.* were not quantified. While the case for involvement of a selective preservation mechanism is as yet only circumstantial, the preservation hypothesis appears to fit the facts better than historically more popular suggestions that experience or neuronal activity acts only to direct the formation of synapses. Further tests of the hypothesis will require sequential developmental studies of the effects of experience on the developmental baseline.

At this point, we know that various apparently appropriate types of experience at appropriate times during development yield differences in the number, and in some cases the pattern, of nerve cell connections ultimately seen in the adult. The preservation hypothesis holds that these differences arise at least in part because the neuronal activity caused by experience preserves connections that are activated (or are in some other way affected by the processing of information associated with experience). Some mechanisms whereby such a preservation process could act have been outlined by Changeaux and Danchin (1977).

EXPERIENCE AND PLASTICITY IN THE ADULT BRAIN

The Critical Period Concept

As the foregoing suggests, the bulk of demonstrations of functional and anatomical plasticity have involved young organisms. The relative sensitivity of the developing nervous system to extrinsic events is often described in terms of critical or sensitive periods—times at which the organism is uniquely susceptible to certain events. Some research suggests that critical periods may be delimited by natural fluctuations in hormones or neurotransmitters (e.g., Kasamatsu and Pettigrew 1979, Kasamatsu et al. 1979, Lauder and Krebs 1978, Nicholson and Altman 1972). While much behavioral and physiological research supports the notion that the effects of differential experience may be greater during development, there is increasing evidence that at least some plasticity of a type quite similar to that found in early development may exist in adult animals.

As indicated earlier, the sensitivity of the visual system to deprivation appears age-dependent. However, the deprived visual system appears to respond to light, both behaviorally and anatomically, well after the time at which visual experience normally begins to occur (e.g., Tees 1976, Cragg 1967, Smith et al. 1978, Valverde 1971).

At least some of the phenomena discussed above are apparently age-dependent. For example, monocular eye closure after about 12 weeks of age in kittens seems to have little effect on the control of visual cortex neurons by the closed eye (e.g., Wiesel and Hubel 1965), although, perhaps surprisingly, partial reversal of the effects of earlier monocular closure by reverse suture (closing the previously opened eye and vice versa) appears possible later than this (e.g., Spear et al. 1980, Ganz and Fitch 1968, Wiesel and Hubel 1965). Sensitivity to monocular deprivation can be induced in adult cats by local administration of norepinephrine (Kasamatsu et al. 1979), suggesting that levels of neurotransmitters may govern the critical period. Similarly, Fiala et al. (1978) reported that the effects of complex environment versus isolation rearing on hippocampal granule cell dendrites seen in animals placed in the environments at weaning were not seen in animals placed in the environments at 145 days of age.

On the other hand, it is quite clear that adult animals do show plasticity. Not only do adult animals learn and remember, in some cases much better than infants (e.g., Campbell and Spear 1972), but they also appear to show relatively general behavioral consequences of a complex environment experience, although the effects are less broad than those seen in animals placed in the environments after weaning (e.g., Rosenzweig et al. 1972b). (It is interesting to note that some behaviors that are not affected by adult exposure to environmental complexity versus isolation but are facilitated by infant exposure are also impaired by lesions of the hippocampus [Fiala et al. 1978].)

Physiological Plasticity

Electrophysiological studies have also described plasticity in the adult brain. For example, the long-term potentiation of the postsynaptic response to afferent stimulation, following a brief burst of high-frequency afferent stimulation, described by Lynch and Gerling (Chapter 9, this volume) and others suggests that the strength of connections between neurons in the adult brain is susceptible to modification by ongoing neuronal activity. Similarly, the "kindling" phenomenon, in which regular stimulation of a brain region (particularly in the limbic system) at low levels gradually decreases its seizure threshold (e.g., Goddard *et al.* 1969), indicates that activity in the central nervous system can alter its functional organization. An older related phenomenon, the mirror focus (Morrell 1961), in which an independent region of epileptic neurons develops in the hemisphere opposite an experimentally induced epileptic focus, may reflect a similar process.

The recovery that does occur following visual deprivation, while incomplete, likewise indicates physiological plasticity in the adult brain. In particular, the fact that reverse suture can, over time, shift control over neurons back to the previously deprived eye suggests that the brain remains sensitive to functionally appropriate reorganization by experience well after the critical period for disorganization by experience has ended. Taken with other work, these few studies indicate that the adult brain may be much more dynamic than earlier theories had anticipated. Relatively massive changes in neuronal activity induced artificially or through normal sensory channels appear capable of significantly altering the brain's functional organization.

Anatomical Substrates of Adult Plasticity

Until quite recently, there was only limited evidence to indicate that these forms of plasticity might be associated with anatomical changes similar to those seen in early development. In a relatively early study along these lines, Sotelo and Palay (1971) described a pattern of changes in axon terminals in the adult lateral vestibular nucleus that was consistent with a possible continuing process of degeneration and regeneration of synaptic connections. They proposed that "axonal remodeling" might be a mechanism of nervous system adjustment to functional demand in the adult organism.

Support for continuing synapse formation in adult brain is provided by Hinds and McNelly (1979), who found continuing increases in the number of perikaryal synapses on olfactory bulb mitral cells until 27 months of age in rats. Another indication that the rat brain continues to grow in adulthood is that overall brain weight increases through adulthood in rats and mice (Brizzee *et al.* 1968, Ordy and Schjeide 1973).

Further evidence that the adult mammalian nervous system is capable of such change has come from the now quite extensive literature on axonal sprouting into regions denervated by damage elsewhere (discussed in Chapter 9 of this volume by Lynch and Gerling). It has been proposed that sprouting may be a unique response to damage, triggered perhaps by the presence of open postsynaptic sites (Raisman and Field 1973b) or some other aspect of the pathological response to denervation (e.g., Lynch *et al.* 1975). However, it is possible that sprouting instead reflects a continuing process of generation of new axonal branches that is somehow amplified or made more evident by the removal of other afferents. Hence, these studies provide some basis for the suggestion that the generation of new synapses may be a continuing process in adulthood if not throughout the life of the organism.

If such new connections were to function appropriately with regard to the overall pattern of brain organization, some mechanism for either directing their growth to appropriate sites or selecting those that have grown to appropriate sites would be necessary. Numerous mechanisms have been suggested whereby the growth of axons may be directed to appropriate locations (see, e.g., Jacobson 1978, Kappers 1971). Whether such mechanisms could direct growth with the precision that might be necessary to appropriately modify what we believe to be relatively specific patterns of brain organization remains uncertain. In development, many of these neuronal specification mechanisms appear to be combined with some form of selective preservation or removal of apparently inappropriate growth.

Selective preservation does provide an attractive alternative to the notion that experience acts only to direct growth. In this case, if functional activity were somehow involved in determining which connections survive, then the resultant pattern of added connections could conceivably be precisely tuned to functional demand. Moreover, if connections depend on continuing use or on some minimum cumulative total amount of use for their survival (often termed maintenance), then no longer appropriate structures arising from earlier developmental demand or from unusual environmental circumstances could be eliminated.

Independent of the viability of these or other models, several relatively recent findings indicate that behavioral experience or neuronal activity may alter synaptic connections in adult organisms. In comparatively early work, the Berkeley group reported that exposure to environmental complexity in adulthood could alter the weight and thickness of the cerebral cortex in a manner quite similar to that found when subjects were placed in the environments at weaning (Rosenzweig *et al.* 1972a, 1972b, Diamond *et al.* 1972). In animals as old as 285 days of age, 90 days of exposure to a complex environment appeared to trigger an increase in cortical weight of roughly the same magnitude seen in the infants (Riege 1971). Comparisons with (socially reared) baseline measures on animals at the time of entry into the complex environment in early adulthood indicate that the cortex actually does grow thicker in animals placed in complex environments, while there is a slight tendency for cortical thickness to decline in animals maintained in the social condition (Uylings, Kuypers, Diamond, and Veltman 1978). Thus by this relatively gross measure, which presumably includes both neuronal and glial responsiveness, cortical plasticity appears not to decline for at least the first year of life in the rat.

More recently, parallel effects have been reported at the level of the structure of individual visual cortical nerve cells. Uylings *et al.* (1978a) placed rats in complex environments at 112 days of age (rats were socially housed until this time in all the experiments described in this section). Comparisons were made with "baseline" animals killed at the onset of the exposure period and with animals maintained in social environments during the exposure period. After 30 days of differential housing, they found increases in the number of higher-order basal dendritic branches in pyramidal cells from Layers II and III of occipital cortex in both social and "enriched" groups, relative to the baseline group. The lengths of first-order and terminal basal dendritic branches were greatest in the rats from complex environments, intermediate in those maintained socially, and shortest in the baseline group. Uylings *et al.* suggest that the differential experience effect is greatest in terminal dendrites, while lowest-order dendrites change more with age alone. Intermediate basal segment length did not differ across groups. Preliminary data suggest a similar pattern in terminal segments of oblique dendrites from the apical shaft (Uylings *et al.* 1978b). In support of these results, Connor *et al.* (1980) reported that exposure to complex or novel social environments beginning as late as 444 or 600 days of age can increase the number of branches of visual cortical neuronal dendrites above the level seen in a pre-exposure socially-reared baseline group.

We (Juraska *et al.*, 1980) have carried out an experiment similar to that of Uylings *et al.* Rats were raised in social conditions to 145 days of age and were then placed in either environmental complexity or isolation for 12 weeks. Dendritic branching of pyramidal and stellate neurons in occipital cortex was examined. Apical dendrites of Layer V pyramidal neurons did not differ statistically between conditions. Layer IV stellate and Layer III pyramidal neurons had greater overall dendritic length (Figure 8.5) and longer terminal branches (Figure 8.6) in the rats placed in the complex environment. There were no effects on the number of pyramidal branches at any order, but stellates had slightly more first-order branches. The relative similarity of results from two laboratories with different procedures gives us confidence in the reliability of the effects of experience on the adult brain.

Recent studies in our laboratory involving the effects of maze training on the adult brain provide further evidence of plasticity in response to experience and also strongly suggest that these effects are related to the processing of experiential information *per se*, rather than to some more generalized (e.g., hormonal, metabolic) effect of the experience. In the first of these experiments (Greenough *et al.* 1979), litter mate pairs of rats reared socially until 80 days of age were assigned to one of two conditions. Rats in the training condition were subjected to an extensive regimen of training on the Hebb–Williams (1946) maze. This maze has movable barriers, such that a very large number of different problems can be presented. We trained the animals on a new problem each day for a total of 25 days. Each animal received at least 25 trials each day. If it reached a criterion of two errorless trials prior to achieving this minimum, the animal was retrained on problems from previous days.

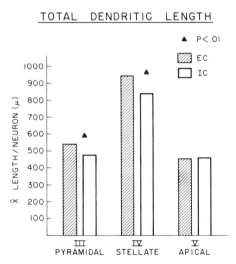

Figure 8.5. Mean total linear length of dendrite for the three types of neurons examined after adult exposure to environmental complexity (EC) or isolation conditions (IC). (From Juraska *et al.* 1980.)

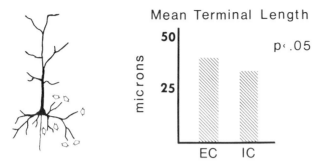

Figure 8.6.   Mean length of terminal dendrites (as indicated by arrows at left) in the basilar portion of the Layer III pyramidal neurons. (After Juraska *et al.* 1980.)

The handled condition control group procedure consisted of removing the animal from its cage several times a day and giving it a small drink from a bottle held in the experimenter's hand. (Both groups were water-deprived and water was used as the reward in the maze.) At the end of training, dendritic branching was examined in pyramidal cells from Layers IV and V of occipital cortex. In both cell populations, there were clear-cut differences between the trained and handled animals in the distal regions of apical dendrites. These differences were evident in both the concentric ring analysis and in measures of dendritic length and branching (see Figure 8.3), and occurred in the parts of these deep pyramidal cells that pass through upper cortical layers (Layers III and IV). There were no apparent effects on Layer IV stellate neurons, and the effect on Layer V apical dendrites contrasts with the adult environmental complexity study (Juraska *et al.* 1980). At this point, we do not know whether this difference in the pattern of effects represents an alteration in the part of the neuron susceptible to experience in the adult animal or whether it represents a qualitative difference in the way in which the brain responds to different experiences. However, the lack of effect on apical dendrites of Layer V [deep] pyramidal cells in our adult environmental complexity study suggests that this response may be selectively enhanced by training. (However, the orientation of sections was better in the training study and hence the apical dendrites were longer, on average, in this study.) In either case, this study, taken with the demonstrations of neuroanatomical plasticity in the adult brain described above, clearly indicates that the number or pattern of synaptic connections in the adult rat can be modified by the animal's experience.

   A second maze training study (Chang and Greenough 1978, Chang and Greenough 1980) suggests that the changes seen in the brain after training really are associated with the processing of information from the training experience. In this experiment, the "split-brain" procedure (sectioning the corpus callosum throughout its length) was utilized to produce relative independence of the cerebral hemispheres prior to training. Opaque contact occluders were then used to direct the visual input associated with training experience primarily to a single hemisphere. (In the rat, 90–95% of the fibers originating in the eye cross to the other side of the brain. Hence a relatively limited amount of the visual system activity associated with the training experience would be projected to the side of the brain having the contact occluder.) Using these procedures, members of socially reared litter mate triplet sets were assigned to one of three groups. Training procedures were essentially identical to those in the preceding experiment, except, due to the time necessary for recovery from surgery, the animals were about 10 days older (approximately 90 days old) at the beginning of maze training. Unilaterally trained animals had the contact occluder placed in one eye (the same eye each day, position determined by coin toss) just prior to the beginning of training, such that the visual information associated with the training experience was directed primarily to the hemisphere ipsilateral to the occluder. In bilaterally trained animals, the occluder was alternated from one eye to the other on subsequent days so that, on the average, both hemispheres received equivalent amounts of afferent visual activity from the training situation. Members of the nontrained group received a handling procedure as in the Greenough *et al.* experiment above. For half of these animals, the occluder was placed in the same eye each day; for the other half it was alternated. In all cases, the occluders were removed at the end of the approximately 4–6-hour training session.

The results of this experiment are shown in Figure 8.7. (Note that this figure presents results for the concentric-ring analysis of entire Layer V pyramidal neurons, including both basal and apical portions of the dendritic tree. Hence the inner rings [approximately rings 1–10] make the bulk of their intersections with basal dendrites. Very few basal dendrites intersect with rings beyond approximately 250 microns from the cell body [approximately ring 12].) Here, as in the preceding study, the differences between the hemispheres exposed to visual information from training and those not so exposed appear in the more distal rings—those that intersect distal regions of the apical dendrite. The difference between the bilaterally trained and the nontrained or handled group replicates the result of Greenough *et al.* (1979) and indicates greater distal apical dendritic branching of deep pyramidal neurons in visual cortex in animals subjected to extensive maze training. The difference between hemispheres within the unilaterally trained group indicates that visual afferent activity associated with the training experience is important in generating

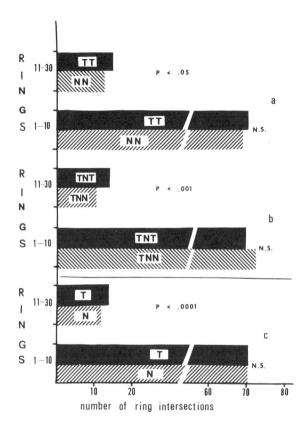

Figure 8.7. Mean ring intersections for dendrites of Layer V pyramidal neurons in the split brain experiment. TT = bilaterally exposed; NN = nontrained; TNT = hemisphere opposite open eye in unilaterally trained animals; TNN = hemisphere opposite occluded eye; T = mean for all exposed trained hemispheres; N = mean for all nonexposed or nontrained hemispheres. (From Chang and Greenough, in preparation.)

these effects. Distal apical dendritic branching was consistently greater in the hemisphere opposite the eye exposed to the training experience. (Consistent with these findings, Bennett *et al.* [1979] have reported biochemical and brain weight effects of maze training.)

A final experiment, the procedures of which are reminiscent of the mirror focus and kindling results described previously, involves a training paradigm in which electrical stimulation of the suprasylvian gyrus of cats was used as the conditioned stimulus in a Pavlovian aversive conditioning procedure (Rutledge 1976, Rutledge *et al.* 1974). The unconditioned stimulus was electrical shock to the foreleg, and the conditioned response a flexion of the foreleg. The cats were extensively trained, receiving 20 trials per day for approximately 90 days. Analysis of Golgi-stained neurons indicated effects of both the electrical stimulation and the conditioning procedure. Electrophysiologically, electrical stimulation over a prolonged period combined with the conditioning procedure resulted in the appearance of a maintained evoked potential to test stimuli that did not occur to test stimulation in the opposite interhemispheric direction. That is, the response evoked by the electrical stimulation procedure used in training was potentiated on the side contralateral to that stimulated. This response was not seen in animals that had been stimulated but not trained (foreleg shock was explicitly unpaired with stimulation). Anatomically, effects of both the stimulation procedure and of the conditioning procedure were apparent. Dendritic branching was examined in the apical dendrites of pyramidal cells from upper layers of the cortex. These dendrites receive multisynaptic extracallosal projections from the contralateral homologous area. Stimulation, whether or not accompanied by conditioning, increased the branching of dendrites in this upper apical region. The differences, using the stimulated side as a control and the contralateral side as "experimental," indicated relative increases of more than 150% in some measures. The effect of the addition of the conditioning procedure appeared to be on the frequency of spines on apical dendrites. Spine frequency averaged about 15% higher on vertical and oblique dendrites in Layer II and III pyramidal cells in cats that had received stimulation plus conditioning relative to cats receiving stimulation alone (i.e., no foreleg shock). There were no differences in basal dendrites of these same neurons, which apparently do not receive afferents from the contralateral homologous region. Thus these data further support the notion that neuronal activity can modify the number or pattern of connections in adult animals. Moreover, they suggest that the pattern of modification may depend in part on the behavioral relevance of the neuronal activity.

The foregoing studies provide strong evidence that naturally and artificially induced alterations in neuronal activity can modify dendritic structure, and consequently the number and pattern of synaptic connections, in the adult nervous system. (Additional support is presented in the sections on the aging brain which follow.) Whether these results arise from growth that is actively stimulated by neuronal activity, preservation of growth from a constitutive process, both, or some other mechanism, remains uncertain.

It is curious that some life-span studies indicate that animals are, on the average, losing synaptic connections during ages relatively comparable to those at which these experiments were taking place. Feldman and Dowd (1975) have reported a continuing process of decreased spine frequency accompanied by dendritic shrinkage in rat visual cortex during adulthood and aging. Feldman and Dowd's rats appeared to have been housed in a manner similar to that of the controls in the above environmental complexity experiments. Hence, they might be considered "experientially degenerate," relative to the experimental rats in the foregoing studies, and all groups might be considered degenerate relative to those in the wild. Thus the decline in synapses seen by Feldman and Dowd may represent an extreme case, in which the experience available to the animals was insufficient to generate, preserve, or maintain a complement of synapses equivalent to that expected in the feral situation. In fact, the use of standard laboratory rats in aging studies might be comparable to studies in which human beings imprisoned for life are used as subjects. In passing, then, we might recommend that a better rodent model for aging would be one in which the animals are reared in an environment that somewhat more closely approximates conditions likely to be experienced in the natural situation.

As we return to our discussion of aging *per se*, we should reiterate the possible roles of experience with regard to synaptic connectivity in development and pre-adulthood. First, experience may act to stimulate, and potentially to direct the formation of new synapses. Second, experience may modify existing synapses, a point we have not discussed in detail in this paper. Third, experience may act to selectively preserve a subpopulation of synapses from a larger population, which may be generated independently of experience or alternatively may depend to some degree on experience for its generation. Finally, experience may be involved in the continued maintenance of synaptic connectivity, such that aspects of neural organization for which there have been no further use are eliminated by attrition. While firmer conclusions await further data, a reasonably strong case can be made for preservation and/or maintenance roles of experience from the data described in the preceding sections.

CHANGES IN THE AGING BRAIN AND BEHAVIOR

As we indicated at the outset, the aging organism, like the developing one, goes through some rather dramatic changes. The purpose of this section is to briefly review age-related neuroanatomical changes, placing particular emphasis on neuronal connectivity. (For more complete reviews see, e.g., Terry and Gershon 1976.)

Human Aging

Perhaps the most obvious change in the human brain that occurs with advancing age is a decrease in overall weight. Reduction in weight occurs progressively, with losses in the range of 10–20% between the ages of 20 and 90 (Feldman and Peters 1975). This weight reduction occurs regardless of brain pathology although it appears to be less severe in healthy subjects (Tomlinson 1972).

Neuronal death may be a major contributing factor in this weight loss. Neuron loss is variable, depending on the brain region and particular cell type involved. For instance, most brainstem regions that have been examined show no detectable cell loss with advancing age. Konigsmark and Murphy (1972) found no evidence of cell loss in the ventral cochlear nucleus, and cell counts in the abducens (Vijayashankar and Brody 1971), trochlear (Vijayashankar and Brody 1973), and facial nuclei (Van Buskirk 1945) have also revealed no age-related cell loss. Significant cell loss has been detected in the locus ceruleus (Brody 1976).

In contrast to the above findings in brainstem, the cerebral cortex appears particularly susceptible to neuron loss. Studies by Brody (1955, 1970) have indicated a decrease in cell number with age that varies with regard to the cortical area examined. While no significant cell loss took place in the postcentral or inferior temporal gyri, significant loss was found in such areas as precentral gyrus, superior temporal gyrus, and superior frontal gyrus. Many of these results have been confirmed by other investigators (e.g., Colon 1972). Cragg (1975), however, did not find evidence for neuron loss in the neocortex of normal, healthy, aged human beings. Even within a given area, cells in certain layers or of certain types may be selectively lost. Brody (1970) notes that in his study, loss of Golgi type II cells in Layers II and IV is more prominent than of other cells in different layers.

More common than neuron death, and perhaps more important, are the losses in neural connectivity that have often been reported in aged individuals, particularly in pathological cases. In a series of qualitative Golgi studies, Scheibel's group has described degeneration of pyramidal cells in the aging human limbic system (1976), superior temporal and prefrontal (1975) and precentral cortex (1977). Throughout the regions studied, they noticed a sequence of changes that, in a sense, resemble a reversal of the initial (pre-preservation) developmental process, or an analogue of the post-peak declines in connectivity in development. This sequence includes loss of dendritic spines to a variable degree, followed by a rather drastic disappearance of the horizontal, then the vertical components of the dendritic tree. Irregular swellings along the cell soma and dendrites were noted as well. Surprisingly, when examining the Golgi-stained brains of several patients previously diagnosed as having Alzheimer's presenile dementia, Scheibel and Tomiyasu (1978) observed clusters of new dendritic growth on degenerating cortical neurons, suggesting that the capacity for growth, albeit abnormal, may not be absent in an aging brain.

Using the electron microscope, Huttenlocher (1979) has also found evidence for decreased connectivity in the senescent brain. Counting the number of synapses in Layer III of frontal cortex, he found essentially no difference between human beings aged 16–72 years. From subjects aged 74–90 years, however, a significant decline in synapse density was noted. In the only other study of this type reported to date, Cragg (1975) could find no difference in synapse number between two groups of people averaging 38˙and 73 years of age.

Buell and Coleman (1979) have performed quantitative Golgi studies in the parahippocampal gyri of adult, aged, and demented humans (using coded tissue to prevent bias). Layer II pyramids were randomly selected for quantification. Apical dendrites of pyramids from aged subjects had more extensive dendritic trees than those of adults. Adults, in turn, possessed dendritic trees that were more extensive than those of the demented subjects. Other measures indicated that this was not a function of differential loss of smaller cells in the aged. This suggests that some neurons may continue to grow relatively normally in the aging brain, a point we return to later. Similar losses in demented patients have been reported in third and fifth layer pyramids in the cingulate gyrus (Mehraein *et al.* 1975), and in Purkinje cells in the vermis of the cerebellum (Mehraein *et al.* 1975). They found reduced levels of dendritic arborization and spine density in tissue from patients with Alzheimer's disease and other senile dementia.

The foregoing studies make a convincing case for a net loss of connectivity in the surviving neurons in the brain in senile human beings. Whether this connectivity loss merely reflects degeneration of connections from afferent neurons that have been lost, or whether some connectivity loss is independent of afferent neuron loss remains an open question. There is, however, a strong suggestion that this connectivity loss is more apparent, if not exclusively apparent, in cases showing behavioral pathology.

Animal Aging

The extent to which animals exhibit age-related neuron loss is not clear. There are several older reports of decreases in the number of neurons, but these need to be confirmed. In many cases, appropriate corrections for changes in cell size and tissue volume, which can affect apparent density, were not made. However, the work published to date suggests that animals as well as human beings may exhibit neuron loss that is variable, depending on the brain region and the neuron type.

With respect to neuronal connectivity, the same kinds of changes seen in the aging human brain can also be found in brain tissue from aging animals. Mervis (1978) has used the Golgi technique to qualitatively assess morphological alterations of pyramidal cells in the frontal cortex of aged dogs. His studies reveal cortical morphology very similar to the type described for aged human subjects. That is, he observed cell body distortion, loss of spines, atrophy of horizontal and vertical dendrites, and senile plaques. In addition, Mervis reports occasional "dendritic tufting," an outgrowth of filamentous processes from dendrites somewhat reminiscent of the dendrite sprouting described by Scheibel and Tomiyasu (1978).

In a series of qualitative Golgi studies of aging mice, Machado-Salas *et al.* have described soma distortion, spine loss, and dendritic deterioration in the brainstem and spinal cord (1977b), hypothalamus (1977a), and limbic system (1979). Similar pathology was seen in a quantitative Golgi study of Layer V pyramids in rat auditory cortex (Vaughan 1977). Feldman and Dowd (1975) reported a monotonic decrease in the density of dendritic spines in Golgi stained rat visual cortex with increasing age, and this loss was later confirmed with the electron microscope (Feldman 1976). In addition to spine loss, Feldman (1977) has also reported an age-related reduction in mean dendritic lengths of Golgi-stained Layer III and Layer V pyramidal cells from rat cortex. Hinds and McNelly (1977, 1979) have carried out several quantitative studies of the rat olfactory bulb. Their results reveal a remarkably dynamic mitral cell population. Between 24 and 27 months of age, a sharp decrease in the number of mitral cells occurred. During this time, the size of remaining mitral cell dendritic trees increased, as if to take over the space and, conceivably, some of the function of the lost cells. Also, their data suggest that there may be new synapse formation in the aging mitral cells.

In careful, quantitative electron microscopic studies of 24-month-old rat dentate gyrus, Geinisman and Bondareff found evidence for a decrease in the number of axodendritic and axosomatic synapses (Bondareff and Geinisman 1976, Geinisman 1979, see Bondareff, Chapter 7 of this volume), axon terminals (Geinisman *et al.* 1979), and atrophy of the granule cell dendritic tree (Geinisman *et al.* 1978). Hasan and Glees (1972) in a nonquantitative study also reported that aged rats had fewer axosomatic synapses. However, Cotman and Scheff (1979) found no statistically significant synapse loss in the middle molecular layers of the dentate gyrus in 24-month-old rats.

Because of a lack of knowledge about the specific location of afferent neurons, it has not been feasible in such studies to determine whether synapse losses were independent of afferent neuron loss. Thus the question of whether synapse loss occurs independently of the loss of neurons remains unanswered.

The major difference between human and animal pathology concerns the presence of senile plaques and neurofibrillary tangles. These two types of lesion, while routinely found in human tissue, are not characteristic of most animals. Senile plaques have been observed in aged primate and canine tissue, but are only minimally present in other animals. The most common type of neurofibrillary pathology (specifically, paired helical filaments of the Alzheimer type) has apparently never been observed to occur naturally in tissue other than human brain (Iqbal *et al.* 1977).

The degree to which these pathologies play a role in dementia is not known. It has been established that a significant correlation exists between the degree of morphological change (in terms of plaques and tangles) and the clinical diagnosis of dementia in aged human beings (e.g., Tomlinson and Henderson 1976). Nonetheless, a causal relationship between any of these pathologies and functional deterioration has not yet been established. Furthermore, animals that do not exhibit these types of lesions clearly do exhibit functional impairments comparable in a general sense to those of demented human beings. Rodent studies, for instance, have indicated age-related deficits in a variety of measures, including general activity (Samorajski *et al.* 1971), active and passive avoidance tasks (McNamara *et al.* 1977, Gold and McGaugh 1975), and maze learning (Oliverio and Bovet 1966).

Because of this, we concur with the view of others that an additionally fruitful approach may be to use the pattern and extent of connectivity (in terms of dendritic and synaptic alterations) for correlational purposes (Scheibel *et al.* 1976). Quantitative studies (Buell and Coleman 1979, Mehraein *et al.* 1975) and qualitative observations (Scheibel *et al.* 1975, 1976) have indicated that decreased overall connectivity often occurs in groups that show functional impairment. Moreover, in terms of cell death and general connectivity, there exists a qualitative (if not always quantitative) agreement between the results of human and animal studies. Finally, in previous sections we have presented evidence to underscore the obvious functional implications that alterations in the extent and pattern of connectivity may have. Thus, regardless of etiology, measures of connectivity may be a valuable means of studying the relationship between brain aging, behavior, and the environment.

CONCEPTUAL VIEWS OF LOSSES IN SYNAPTIC CONNECTIVITY

It is clear that a major loss in synaptic connectivity may occur with advancing age and that a variety of behavioral deficits may ensue. But what is the sequence of events that culminates in synapse loss, dendritic atrophy and, in some cases, neuron death? An understanding of the causal relationships among these changes is necessary in order to make meaningful predictions with regard to the potential for preventive measures or clinical treatment.

Of primary importance is whether these changes stem from maladies within the postsynaptic cell structures (i.e., intrinsic factors) or from external influences, such as afferent activity or age-related changes in nonneuronal elements.

Intrinsic Degeneration

There is a wealth of data concerning age-related abnormalities of various cellular structures and functions, such as errors in protein synthesis, lipofuscin accumulation, and vascular atrophy (see Terry and Gershon 1976, Bondareff, Chapter 7 of this volume). Some theories of neuronal degeneration arising from such data make a great deal of intuitive sense. For instance, Terry and Wisniewski (1972) determined that neurofibrillary tangles are intracellular tubules that are abnormal in size and number, and may be the product of abnormal protein metabolism inside the cell. Since dendrites are dependent on materials transported from the cell body (possibly involving tubules), abnormal tubules in sufficient numbers could obstruct the flow of substances necessary to support the dendritic tree (Scheibel *et al.* 1975). It is certainly reasonable to suspect that pathologies such as these would compromise the ability of severely affected neurons to maintain themselves. At this time, however, there is little evidence to allow us to assert a causal relationship between intracellular changes and degeneration of the neuron as a whole.

Transsynaptic Factors (Deafferentation)

Independent of, or in conjunction with, intrinsic factors, degeneration in aging neurons may be due to transsynaptic influences (e.g., Mervis

1978, Terry and Wisniewski 1972). In fact, there is a striking resemblance between some senescent neurons (those that appear to be degenerating) and neurons that have been deprived of afferent input in any of several ways. Deafferentation of a neuron results in a loss of dendritic spines, atrophy of the dendritic tree, and if the deafferentation is severe enough, the result is neuron death. A growing amount of evidence suggests that a process of deafferentation may occur in the aging brain.

Naranjo and Greene (1977) have reported an increased amount of axonal degeneration in the brains of elderly rats, indicating a loss of axons and possibly their cell bodies in these animals. Barondes (1968) has studied the incorporation of intracerebrally injected radioactive leucine into soluble protein of a whole brain and a nerve ending fraction. He found that the specific activities of radioactive protein associated with isolated nerve endings progressively decreased in mice from 3 to 12 months of age. Geinisman *et al.* (1977) have found an age-related decrease in the axonal transport of glycoproteins in the rat septo-hippocampal pathway. Ochs (1973), however, could find no decrement in the rate of axonal transport of proteins in the sciatic nerve of aged dogs and cats. Perhaps this nerve, being a member of the peripheral nervous system, is not affected by age, as are central axons. Alternatively, central axons could be losing a proportion of their terminals, thus requiring reduced metabolic support at the terminals, whereas motoneurons, which connect with single motor units, may maintain a constant number of terminals. Geinisman (1979) has confirmed a relative loss of axon terminals in the hippocampus, without finding evidence for neuron loss. Finally, it is possible that the reduced septo-hippocampal transport reflects axon loss due to neuron death.

The loss of connectivity with aging could involve transsynaptic degeneration taking place across more than one synapse. Thus, damage to or degeneration of a small number of neurons could result in deafferentation and subsequent atrophy of many more neurons, the process "cascading" through the brain. The aged brain may be particularly susceptible to such cascade effects. One role of axon sprouting (see Lynch and Gerling, Chapter 9 of this volume) may be to provide sustaining collaterals to prevent the loss of neurons that have been partially deafferented by damage to neurons elsewhere. A reduced amount of sprouting in the aged brain (see Chapter 9 by Lynch and Gerling) could account for widespread degeneration occurring as a consequence of minor damage, regardless of its cause.

Dynamic Balance between Growth and Loss: Various Views

In previous sections, we have presented evidence to indicate that the brain may be responsive to experience throughout the life of an organism, in terms of both neuronal connectivity and function. Recent research, in particular, has indicated that the mature brain retains the capacity to grow and form new connections to a much greater extent than was previously believed. In the following sections we will use as a primary model the scheme outlined earlier in this chapter—that new connections may be continually generated on a nonsystematic basis in the mature brain, and that some fraction of these tentative connections is preserved (or stabilized) as a result of neuronal activity. However, if the primary role of experience is to trigger the generation of new connections rather than to preserve them, or if both generation and maintenance roles are ascribed, the same basic concepts would apply as long as there exists some intrinsically dependent loss of synapses that is not a direct consequence of neuronal death.

According to the selective preservation hypothesis, the extent and pattern of connectivity of the brain is dependent on the dynamic balance between the formation of new connections and the loss of pre-existing ones. With regard to this, there are a number of conceptual views that may account for age-related losses in synaptic connectivity. These are:

1. An acceleration of the loss process due to:

   Intrinsic factors. This is undoubtedly the most prevalent view, and is typical of many, if not the majority, of articles on the morphology of the aging brain. The basic assumption is that other pathological conditions cause the degeneration of neurons and neuronal processes.

   Preservation/maintenance failure. A view in which the process of preservation of appropriate connections in infancy becomes a process of continued growth, selection, and maintenance of connections in adulthood. During senescence, there may be a reduction in neural activity (for various reasons) or its functional equivalent (i.e., more activity is necessary to "hold" a connection), and hence the maintenance pressure is insufficient to prevent losses of connections.

   Cascade effects. Damage to or degenerative loss of a small number of neurons could, through transsynaptic degeneration, result in deafferentation and subsequent damage to many more neurons than were originally involved.

2. Reduction in new synapse formation due to a reduction in:

   Damage-triggered growth. There may be a reduction in the normal process of recovery from the chronic decay occurring at all ages (Jacobson 1978, Johnson and Almli 1978). Scheff, Bernardo, and Cotman (1978) reported decreased axonal sprouting after brain damage in aged rats (see Chapter 9 by Lynch and Gerling in this volume).

Experience-triggered growth. Experience-triggered growth may occur at a reduced rate with age. This might result from a reduced general capacity for growth or a diminished level of activity in the system (Jacobson 1978, Ordy and Schjeide 1973).

Constitutive growth. A decline in the above-postulated normally occurring, random constitutive growth may occur. This process would presumably act in concert with a preservation/maintenance mechanism, but either or both of these processes could be affected in the aging brain.

Predictions Regarding Experience

From these potential mechanisms of connectivity losses, one can generate predictions regarding the potential for experiential factors to affect age-related losses in connectivity.

1. *Damage-triggered growth,* such as sprouting, could conceivably be influenced by experiential factors. There is evidence to indicate that experience may alter the rate of recovery from brain damage (see Greenough *et al.* 1976), and sprouting could be involved as a precursor to selective preservation, or, conceivably, sprouting or other growth could be stimulated or directed by experience.

2. If *experience or activity-triggered growth* occurs in the senescent brain, as in the younger brain, it would be influenced by changes in neuronal activity. Decrements resulting from a reduced level of activity or from a reduced rate of activity-dependent growth could be offset by increased experience. Constitutive growth, as previously defined, is experience-immutable.

3. *Preservation/maintenance* mechanisms could be operating together with any of the three proposed mechanisms for generating new growth. Preservation/maintenance failure due to an actual or functional diminution of activity could be reversed by increased experience.

4. There is no reason to believe that loss of neuronal processes due to *intrinsic* factors would be attenuated by any experiential factors. However, experience, through any of the mechanisms discussed in this section, could attenuate the cascade of damage that may follow intrinsic damage to a limited number of neurons.

EXPERIENCE AND THE AGING BRAIN

Behavioral Effects

As we noted at the beginning of this chapter, the aging brain has been viewed as relatively rigid—less capable of adapting to the requirements of the environment. To the extent this is so, one might expect the brain and the behavior of aged subjects to be relatively impervious to the environment. While losses in capacity for memory and other measures (see Jarvik and Steuer, Chapter 10 of this volume) support this view, there is also evidence that experience can affect the aging brain measured in terms of behavioral performance.

De Carlo (1971) has carried out longitudinal studies of aging twins, the results of which have been summarized by Jarvik (1975). She reports that physical and, particularly, mental activities were associated with what she deemed "successful" aging. Inactive people did not age as successfully as ones who engaged in cognitive, emotive, and physical activities on a regular basis. Successful aging was judged on the basis of medical, psychiatric, and psychological examinations. Jarvik emphasized that activities of later life, rather than those occurring earlier, were primarily related to successful aging.

With this in mind, it is easy to imagine how an institutional environment could affect the physical and psychological well-being of aged individuals. Nursing homes and other similar institutions are often "impoverished" relative to typical community settings. As such, due to the inopportunity for stimulation, losses in connectivity and hence function could be hastened in persons residing in these environments.

The environment itself need not be physically impoverished in order for functional deprivation to occur. An experiential self-deprivation could have the same effect. Among the most prominent psychological consequences of institutionalization are feelings of apathy and severe withdrawal (e.g., Frankl 1963, Cohen 1953), depression, and a reduced capacity for independent thought and action (e.g., Lakin 1960, Pollack *et al.* 1962). Also interesting in this regard are the studies described by Langer (Chapter 11 of this volume) emphasizing the apparent role played by feelings of helplessness in the physical and psychological well-being of the elderly.

Is there, then, evidence that environmental/experiential variables can influence cognitive functioning in aged human beings? Preliminary data from Winocur (personal communication) indicate that institutionalized old people performed poorly on a standard negative transfer paradigm. In contrast, old people who lived at home performed at a much higher level on this test. Winocur is currently carrying out experiments designed to control for other factors that could be contributing to these differences as well as expanding his behavioral measures.

Lieberman *et al.* (1968) have also investigated the effects that institutionalization may have on various psychological and cognitive measures. This study compared three groups of subjects: 34 people who had lived from 1 to 3 years in either of two institutions; 25 people on the waiting list for the same institutions; and 40 community residents. Since effects ascribed to institutional settings may actually result from biased samples (i.e., those needing care), the waiting list group represents a thoughtful control that may eliminate this type of bias. The results of a battery of tests indicated that, in general, institutionalized subjects showed a deficit in cognitive functioning relative to the community dwelling and the waiting list groups.

It has previously been reasonably well established that environmental variables, including institutionalization, can have dramatic motivational and behavioral effects on aging individuals, independent of any population differences (see Lieberman *et al.* 1968 for a discussion). Studies such as the one above suggest that there may be cognitive effects as well. It should be noted that these studies are only suggestive, as it is often very hard, perhaps impossible, to control for other factors, such as motivation, etc., in attempts to measure cognitive performance.

If these cognitive differences are real, it is tempting to speculate that they may be due, at least in part, to differences in brain structure resulting from environmental stimulation.

Anatomical Effects

There is limited though increasing evidence to indicate that the aging brain, like its younger counterpart, may retain the capacity for anatomical growth and plasticity. For example, Cummins *et al.* (1973) subjected rats that had been raised in either an isolated or an enriched environment for 509 days to training on various problems for 21 days in a Hebb-Williams maze. At this point, the animals were killed and their brains were removed and weighed. The brains of animals that had been raised in an isolated environment and subsequently had the maze experience were significantly larger (length × width) and heavier than those of isolation-reared rats that had not been exposed to the maze.

Studies of the aging rat olfactory bulb mentioned previously (Hinds and McNelly 1977, 1979) also suggest that a remarkable amount of new growth may occur in the senescent brain. Their careful, quantitative electron microscopic studies indicate that a constant increase in the size of individual mitral cell dendritic trees as well as all layers of the olfactory bulb occurs in animals from 3 to 24 months of age. From 3 to 27 months of age there is also a significant increase in the number of somato-dendritic, mitral-to-granule cell synapses on the mitral cell perikaryon. The authors also noted that while a precipitous loss of mitral cells occurred between 24 and 27 months of age, there was a sharp, significant increase in the volume of individual remaining mitral cell dendritic trees, as well as perikaryal and nuclear size. It should be noted that the authors have determined that this increase in volume is not due to a sampling bias that could result from a population of smaller cells dropping out. Thus the remaining cells' dendritic trees had actually grown larger. These results strongly suggest that dendritic growth and synapse formation continues throughout the life of the rat, even into senescence. Hinds and McNelly argue that the "hypertrophy" of the individual mitral cell dendritic trees may compensate for the loss of cells that occurs at that time. Thus, the aging olfactory bulb may have the capacity to recoup some of the connections (and corresponding functions) that are lost through cell death.

Buell and Coleman (1979) have described quantitative Golgi results that lend support to the view that continued dendritic growth may occur in the aging brain. They examined Layer II pyramidal cells in the parahippocampal gyri of 15 human beings previously diagnosed as normal adults (average age 51.2 years), nondemented aged (average age 79.6 years), or demented aged (average age 76.0 years). In the nondemented aged group, dendritic trees were clearly more extensive than in the adult group, with the majority of the difference resulting from increases in the number and average length of terminal dendritic segments of the apical portion of the dendritic tree. This result parallels the Uylings *et al.* (1978a) and Juraska and Greenough results in adult brain presented above. The demented group possessed dendritic trees that were less extensive than the adult group, again, the difference being in the terminal dendrites. Buell and Coleman suggest that while some degenerating cells were present in every brain, the dominant population of cells in nonsenile aged human beings is actually growing.

We have, following pilot work in collaboration with Donald G. Stein of Clark University, completed a preliminary study that strongly suggests that neural connectivity in middle-aged rats, like their younger counterparts, is also sensitive to the animals' experiences. Female hooded rats (ex-breeders) that had been housed socially from weaning to 15 months of age (450 days) were transferred to either complex or isolated environments for a period of 45 days. Layer IV stellate neurons from visual cortex of Golgi-Cox stained brain tissue were analyzed as described

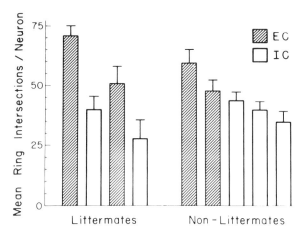

Figure 8.8.   Mean ring intersections for dendrites of Layer IV stellate neurons examined after 45 days of differential housing, beginning at 450 days of age.

above. Figure 8.8 presents the number of intersections of concentric rings with the dendritic tree for individual animals. (Unlike our prior studies, only two litter mate pairs were used.) While we have data for only nine animals, all four complex-environment rats had more intersections than any isolated rat (Mann-Whitney U-test $p < .01$). Although we cannot at this time determine whether experience promotes synapse formation, prevents loss, or both, these results indicate that differential housing differentially affected brain structure in these animals. While these rats, about 500 days old at the end of the experiment, should not be considered "elderly," they are certainly very mature. Thus they provide hope that the aging brain may retain responsiveness to experience and that studies of the effects of the environment on elderly animals may ultimately lead us to new approaches to human brain aging.

REFERENCES

Barondes, S. H. (1968) Further studies of the transport of protein to nerve endings. *Journal of Neurochemistry* 15:343–350.

Bennett, E. L., Diamond, M. C., Krech, D., and Rosenzweig, M. (1964) Chemical and anatomical plasticity of brain. *Science* 146:610–619.

Bennett, E. L., Rosenzweig, M. R., Morimoto, H., and Hebert, M. (1979) Maze training alters brain weights and cortical RNA/DNA ratios. *Behavioral and Neural Biology* 26(1):1–22.

Bondareff, W., and Geinisman, Y. (1976) Loss of synapses in the dentate gyrus of the senescent rat. *American Journal of Anatomy* 145:129–136.

Boothe, R. G., Greenough, W. T., Lund, J. S., and Wrege, K. (1979) A quantitative investigation of spine and dendritic development of neurons in visual cortex (area 17) of Macaca nemestrina monkeys. *Journal of Comparative Neurology* 186:473–490.

Borges, S., and Berry, M. (1976) Preferential orientation of stellate cell dendrites in the visual cortex of the dark-reared rat. *Brain Research* 112:141–147.

Brizzee, K. R., Sherwood, N., and Timiras, P. S. (1968) A comparison of cell populations at various depth levels in cerebral cortex of young adult and aged Long-Evans rats. *Journal of Gerontology* 23:289–297.

Brody, H. (1955) Organization of the cerebral cortex III. A study of aging in the human cerebral cortex. *Journal of Comparative Neurology* 102:511–556.

Brody, H. (1970) Structural changes in the aging nervous system. Pp. 9–21 in H. T. Blumenthal, *Interdisciplinary Topics in Gerontology*, Vol. 7. Munchen: Karger, Basel.

Brody, H. (1976) An examination of cerebral cortex and brainstem aging. Pp. 177–181 in R. D. Terry and S. Gershon, eds., *Neurobiology of Aging*. New York: Raven Press.

Brown, M. C., Jansen, J. K. S., and Van Essen, D. (1976) Polyneuronal innervation of skeletal muscle in new-born rats and its elimination during maturation. *Journal of Physiology* 261:387–422.

Buell, S. J., and Coleman, P. D. (1979) Dendritic growth in the aged human brain and failure of growth in senile dementia. *Science* 206:854–856.

Campbell, B. A., and Spear, N. E. (1972) Ontogeny of memory. *Psychological Review* 79:215–236.

Chang, F. L. F., and Greenough, W. T. (1978) Increased dendritic branching in hemispheres opposite eyes exposed to maze training in split-brain rats. *Society for Neuroscience Abstracts* 4:469.

Chang, F. L. F., and Greenough, W. T. (1981) Lateralized effects of monocular training on dendritic branching in adult split-brain rats. In preparation.

Changeaux, J.-P., and Danchin, A. (1977) Biochemical models for the selective stabilization of developing synapses. Pp. 705–712 in G. A. Cottrell and P. N. R. Usherwood, eds., *Synapses*. New York: Academic Press.

Chow, K. L., and Stewart, D. L. (1972) Reversal of structural and functional effects of long-term visual deprivation in cats. *Experimental Neurology* 34:409–433.

Cohen, E. A. (1953) *Human Behavior in the Concentration Camp*. New York: W. W. Norton.

Colon, E. J. (1972) The elderly brain. A quantitative analysis of cerebral cortex during aging, senile and vascular dementia in Pick's and Alzheimer's disease. *Neuroscience and Behavioral Physiology* 6:319–324.

Connor, J. R., Diamond, M. C., and Johnson, R. E. (1980) Occipital cortical morphology of the rat: Alterations with age and environment. *Experimental Neurology* 68:158–170.

Cotman, C. W., and Scheff, S. W. (1979) Compensatory synapse growth in aged animals after neuronal death. *Mechanisms of Ageing and Development* 9:103–117.

Cragg, B. G. (1967) Changes in visual cortex on first exposure of rats to light. Effect on synaptic dimensions. *Nature* 215:251–253.

Cragg, B. G. (1975) The density of synapses and neurons in normal, mentally defective and aging human brains. *Brain* 98:81–90.

Cummins, R. A., and Walsh, R. N. (1976) Synaptic changes in differentially reared mice. *Australian Psychologist* 2:229.

Cummins, R. A., Walsh, R. N., Budtz-Olsen, O. E., Konstantinos, T., and Horsfall, C. R. (1973) Environmentally-induced changes in the brains of elderly rats. *Nature* 243:516–518.

DeCarlo, T. J. (1971) *Recreational participation patterns and successful aging: A twin study*. Unpublished Ph.D. dissertation, Columbia University.

DeVoogd, T. J. (1979) Effects of dark rearing and enucleation on the development of visual cortex in rats. Unpublished Ph.D. dissertation, University of Illinois at Urbana-Champaign.

Dews, P. B., and Wiesel, T. N. (1970) Consequences of monocular deprivation on visual behavior in kittens. *Journal of Physiology* (London) 206:437–455.

Diamond, M. C., Lindner, B., Johnson, R., Bennett, E. L., and Rosenzweig, M. R. (1975) Differences in occipital cortical synapses from environmentally enriched, impoverished, and standard colony rats. *Journal of Neuroscience Research* 1:109–119.

Diamond, M. C., Rosenzweig, M. R., Bennett, E. L., Lindner, B., and Lyon, L. (1972) Effects of environmental enrichment and impoverishment on rat cerebral cortex. *Journal of Neurobiology* 3:47–64.

Feldman, M. L. (1976) Aging changes in the morphology of cortical dendrites. In R. Terry and S. Gershon, eds., *Neurobiology of Aging*. New York: Raven Press.

Feldman, M. L. (1977) Dendritic changes in aging rat brain: Pyramidal cell dendrite length and ultrastructure. In K. Nandy and I. Sherwin, eds., *Advances in Behavioral Biology*, Vol. 23. New York: Raven Press.

Feldman, M. L., and Dowd, C. (1975) Loss of dendritic spines in aging cerebral cortex. *Anatomy and Embryology* 148:279–301.

Feldman, M. L., and Peters, A. (1975) Morphological changes in the aging brain. Pp. 5–21 in G. J. Maletta, ed., *Survey Report on the Aging Nervous System*. Washington, D.C.: U.S. Department of Health, Education, and Welfare, 74–296.

Fiala, B. A., Joyce, J. N., and Greenough, W. T. (1978) Environmental complexity modulates growth of granule cell dendrites in developing but not adult hippocampus of rats. *Experimental Neurology* 59:372–383.

Floeter, M. K., and Greenough, W. T. (1979) Cerebellar plasticity: Modification of Purkinje cell structure by differential rearing in monkeys. *Science* 206:227–229.

Frankl, V. E. (1963) *Man's Search for Meaning*. New York: Washington Square Press.

Ganz, L., and Fitch, M. (1968) The effects of visual deprivation on perceptual behavior. *Experimental Neurology* 23:638–660.

Geinisman, Y. (1979) Loss of axosomatic synapses in the dentate gyrus of aged rats. *Brain Research* 168:485–492.

Geinisman, Y., Bennett, K. D., and Yates, M. E. (1979) Loss of axon terminals in the dentate gyrus of senescent rats. *Society for Neuroscience Abstracts* 5:5.

Geinisman, Y., Bondareff, W., and Dodge, J. T. (1978) Dendritic atrophy in the dentate gyrus of the senescent rat. *American Journal of Anatomy* 152:321–330.

Geinisman, Y., Bondareff, W., and Telslar, A. (1977) Transport of [3-H]-fructose labelled glyco-proteins in the septo-hippocampal pathway of young adult and senescent rats. *Brain Research* 125:182–186.

Globus, A., Rosenzweig, M. R., Bennett, E. L., and Diamond, M. C. (1973) Effects of differential experience on dendritic spine counts in rat cerebral cortex. *Journal of Comparative and Physiological Psychology* 82:175–181.

Goddard, G. V., McIntyre, D. C., and Leech, C. U. (1969) A permanent change in brain function resulting from daily electrical stimulation. *Experimental Neurology* 25:295–330.

Gold, P. E., and McGaugh, J. L. (1975) Changes in learning and memory during aging. Pp. 145–158 in J. M. Ordy and K. R. Brizzee, eds., *Neurobiology of Aging*. New York: Plenum Press.

Gorski, R. A., Gordon, J. H., Shryne, J. E., and Southam, A. M. (1978) Evidence for a morphological sex difference within the medial preoptic area of the rat brain. *Brain Research* 148:333–346.

Greenough, W. T. (1978) Development and memory: The synaptic connection. Pp. 127–145 in T. Teyler, ed., *Brain and Learning*. Stamford, Conn.: Greylock Publishers.

Greenough, W. T., Carter, C. S., Steerman, C., and DeVoogd, T. J. (1977) Sex differences in dendritic patterns in hamster preoptic area. *Brain Research* 126:63–72.
Greenough, W. T., Fass, B., and DeVoogd, T. J. (1976) Influence of experience on recovery following brain damage in rodents: Hypotheses based on development research. In R. N. Walsh and W. T. Greenough, eds., *Environments as Therapy for Brain Dysfunction.* New York: Plenum Press.
Greenough, W. T., Juraska, J. M., and Volkmar, F. R. (1979) Maze training effects on dendritic branching in occipital cortex of adult rats. *Behavioral and Neural Biology* 26(3):287–297.
Greenough, W. T., and Volkmar, F. R. (1973) Pattern of dendritic branching in occipital cortex of rats reared in complex environments. *Experimental Neurology* 40:491–504.
Greenough, W. T., Volkmar, F. R., and Juraska, J. M. (1973) Effects of rearing complexity on dendritic branching in frontolateral and temporal cortex of the rat. *Experimental Neurology* 41:371–378.
Hasan, M., and Glees, P. (1972) Ultrastructural age changes in hippocampal neurons, synapses and neuroglia. *Experimental Gerontology* 8:75–83.
Hebb, D. O. (1949) *The Organization of Behavior.* New York: Wiley.
Hinds, J. W., and McNelly, N. A. (1977) Aging of the rat olfactory bulb: Growth and atrophy of constituent layers and changes in size and number of mitral cells. *Journal of Comparative Neurology* 171:345–368.
Hinds, J. W., and McNelly, N. A. (1979) Aging in the rat olfactory bulb: Quantitative changes in mitral cell organelles and somato-dendritic synapses. *Journal of Comparative Neurology* 184:811–820.
Hsu, C.-H., Carter, C. S., and Greenough, W. T. (1978) Postnatal development of hamster preoptic area: A Golgi study. *Society for Neuroscience Abstracts* 4:115.
Hubel, D. H., and Wiesel, T. N. (1963) Receptive fields of cells in striate cortex of very young, visually inexperienced kittens. *Journal of Neurophysiology* 206:419–436.
Hubel, D. H., Wiesel, T. N., and Levay, S. (1977) Plasticity of ocular dominance columns in monkey striate cortex. *Philosophical Transactions of the Royal Society of London, Series B* 278:377–409.
Huttenlocher, P. R. (1979) Synaptic density in human frontal cortex—developmental changes and effects of aging. *Brain Research* 163:195–205.
Hymovitch, B. (1952) The effects of experimental variations on problem solving in the rat. *Journal of Comparative and Physiological Psychology* 45:313–321.
Iqbal, K., Wisniewski, H. M., Grunde-Iqbal, I., and Terry, R. D. (1977) Neurofibrillary pathology: An update. In K. Nandy and I. Sherman, eds., *Advances in Behavioral Biology,* Vol. 23. New York: Plenum Press.
Jacobson, M. (1978) *Developmental Neurobiology.* New York: Plenum Press.
Jarvik, L. F. (1975) Thoughts on the psychobiology of aging. *American Psychologist* 30:576–583.
Johnson, D., and Almli, C. R. (1978) Age, brain damage, and performance. Pp. 115–134 in S. Finger, ed., *Recovery from Brain Damage.* New York: Plenum Press.
Juraska, J. M., Greenough, W. T., Elliott, C., Mack, K. J., and Berkowitz, R. (1980) Plasticity in adult rat visual cortex: An examination of several cell populations after differential rearing. *Behavioral and Neural Biology* 29:157–167.
Kappers, C. U. A. (1971) Further contributions on "neurobiotaxis" IX. An attempt to compare the phenomena of neurobiotaxis with other phenomena of taxis and trophism. *Journal of Comparative Neurology* 27:261–298.
Kasamatsu, T., and Pettigrew, J. D. (1979) Preservation of binocularity after monocular deprivation in the striate cortex of kittens treated with 6-hydroxydopamine. *Journal of Comparative Neurology* 185:139–162.

Kasamatsu, T., Pettigrew, J. D., and Ary, M. (1979) Restoration of visual cortical plasticity by local microperfusion of norepinephrine. *Journal of Comparative Neurology* 185:163–182.

Konigsmark, B. W., and Murphy, E. A. (1972) Volume of the ventral cochlear nucleus in man: Its relationship to neuronal population and age. *Journal of Neuropathology and Experimental Neurology* 31:304–316.

Krech, D., Rosenzweig, M. R., and Bennett, E. L. (1962) Relations between brain chemistry and problem-solving among rats raised in enriched and impoverished environments. *Journal of Comparative and Physiological Psychology* 55:801–807.

Lakin, M. (1960) Formal characteristics of human figure drawings by institutionalized and noninstitutionalized aged. *Journal of Gerontology* 15:76–78.

Lauder, J. M., and Krebs, H. (1978) Serotonin as a differentiation signal in early neurogenesis. *Developmental Neuroscience* 1:15–30.

Lichtman, J. W. (1977) The reorganization of synaptic connexions in the rat submandibular ganglion during postnatal development. *Journal of Physiology* (London) 273:155–177.

Lieberman, M. A., Prock, V. N., and Tobin, S. S. (1968) Psychological effects of institutionalization. *Journal of Gerontology* 23:343–353.

Loop, M. S., and Sherman, S. M. (1977) Visual discriminations during eyelid closure in the cat. *Brain Research* 128:329–340.

Lynch, G., Rose, G., Gall, C., and Cotman, C. W. (1975) The response of the dentate gyrus to partial deafferentation. Pp. 305–317 in R. Santini, ed., *The Golgi Symposium.* New York: Raven Press.

Machado-Salas, J., and Scheibel, A. B. (1979) Limbic system of the aged mouse. *Experimental Neurology* 63:347–355.

Machado-Salas, J., Scheibel, M. E., and Scheibel, A. B. (1977a) Morphologic changes in the hypothalamus of the old mouse. *Experimental Neurology* 57:102–111.

Machado-Salas, J., Scheibel, M. E., and Scheibel, A. B. (1977b) Neuronal changes in the aging mouse: Spinal cord and lower brain stem. *Experimental Neurology* 54:504–512.

Marr, D. (1969) A theory of cerebellar cortex. *Journal of Physiology* (London) 202:437–470.

McNamara, M. C., Benignus, G., Benignus, V. A., and Miller, A. T. (1977) Active and passive avoidance learning in rats as a function of age. *Experimental Aging Research* 3(1):3–16.

Mehraein, P., Yamoda, M., and Tarnowska-Ozidusko, E. (1975) Quantitative study on dendrites and dendritic spines in Alzheimer's disease and senile dementia. Pp. 453–458 in G. W. Kreutzberg, ed., *Advances in Neurology,* Vol 12. New York: Raven Press.

Mervis, R. (1978) Structural alterations in neurons of aged canine neocortex: A Golgi study. *Experimental Neurology* 62:417–432.

Mollgaard, K., Diamond, M. C., Bennett, E. L., Rosenzweig, M. R., and Lindner, B. (1971) Qualitative synaptic changes with different experience in rat brain. *International Journal of Neuroscience* 2:113–128.

Morrell, F. (1961) Lasting changes in synaptic organization produced by continuous neuronal bombardment. Pp. 375–392 in J. F. Delafresnaye, ed., *Brain Mechanisms and Learning.* Oxford: Blackwell.

Naranjo, N., and Greene, E. (1977) Use of reduced silver staining to show loss of connections in aged rat brain. *Brain Research Bulletin* 2:71–74.

Nicholson, J. L., and Altman, J. (1972) Synaptogenesis in the rat cerebellum: Effects of early hypo- and hyper-thyroidism. *Science* 176:530–532.

Ochs, S. (1973) Effect of maturation and aging on the rate of fast axoplasmic transport in mammalian nerve. Pp. 349–362 in D. H. Ford, ed., *Progress in Brain Research,* Vol. 40. Amsterdam: Elsevier.

Oliverio, A., and Bovet, D. (1966) Effects of age on maze learning and avoidance conditioning in mice. *Life Sciences* 5:1317–1324.

Ordy, J. M., and Schjeide, O. A. (1973) Univariate and multivariate models for evaluating long term changes in neurobiological development, maturity, and aging. Pp. 25–51 in D. H. Ford, ed., *Progress in Brain Research*, Vol. 40. Amsterdam: Elsevier.

Parnavelas, J. G., Bradford, R., Mounty, E. J., and Lieberman, A. R. (1978) The development of non-pyramidal neurons in the visual cortex of the rat. *Anatomy and Embryology* 155:1–14.

Pollack, M., Karp, E., Kahn, R. L., and Goldfarb, A. I. (1962) Perception of self in institutionalized aged subjects. 1. Response patterns to mirror reflection. *Journal of Gerontology* 17:405–408.

Pysh, J. J., and Weiss, G. M. (1979) Exercise during development induces increase in Purkinje cell dendritic tree size. *Science* 206:230–232.

Raisman, G., and Field, P. M. (1973a) Sexual dimorphism in the neuropil of the preoptic area of the rat and its dependence on neonatal androgen. *Brain Research* 54:1–29.

Raisman, G., and Field, P. M. (1973b) A quantitative investigation of the development of collateral reinnervation after partial deafferentation of the septal nuclei. *Brain Research* 50:241–264.

Richardson, K., and Rose, S. P. R. (1972) Changes in 3-H-lysine incorporation following first exposure to light. *Brain Research* 44:299–303.

Riege, W. H. (1971) Environmental influences on brain and behavior of year old rats. *Developmental Psychobiology* 4(2):167–175.

Riesen, A. H., Sonnier, B. J., Struble, R. B., and Lehr, P. (1981) Branching differences in stellate cells related to cortical areas and rearing environments of monkeys. Chapter to appear in J. W. Prescott, ed., *Consequences of Social Isolation on Primate Brain Development and Behavior*. New York: Academic Press.

Rose, S. P. R. (1967) Changes in visual cortex on first exposure of rats to light. *Nature* 215:253–255.

Rosenzweig, M. R., Bennett, E. L., and Diamond, M. C. (1972a) Brain changes in response to experience. *Scientific American* 226(2):22–29.

Rosenzweig, M. R., Bennett, E. L., and Diamond, M. C. (1972b) Chemical and anatomical plasticity of brain: Replications and extensions. Pp. 205–278 in J. Gaito, ed., *Macromolecules and Behavior* 2nd ed. New York: Appleton-Century-Crofts.

Rutledge, L. T. (1976) Synaptogenesis: Effects of synapse use. Pp. 329–339 in M. R. Rosenzweig and E. L. Bennett, eds., *Neural Mechanisms of Learning and Memory*. Cambridge, Mass.: MIT Press.

Rutledge, L. T., Wright, C., and Duncan, J. (1974) Morphological changes in pyramidal cells of mammalian neocortex associated with increased use. *Experimental Neurology* 44:209–228.

Samorajski, T., Rolstens, C., and Ordy, J. M. (1971) Changes in behavior, brain and neuroendocrine chemistry with age and stress in C57 B1/10 male mice. *Journal of Gerontology* 26:169–175.

Scheff, S. W., Bernardo, L. S., and Cotman, C. W. (1978) Decrease in adrenergic axon sprouting in the senescent rat. *Science* 202:775–778.

Scheibel, A. B., and Tomiyasu, U. (1978) Dendritic sprouting in Alzheimer's presenile dementia. *Experimental Neurology* 60:1–8.

Scheibel, M. E., Lindsay, R. D., Tomiyasu, U., and Scheibel, A. B. (1975) Progressive dendritic changes in aging human cortex. *Experimental Neurology* 47:392–403.

Scheibel, M. E., Lindsay, R. D., Tomiyasu, U., and Scheibel, A. B. (1976) Progressive dendritic changes in the aging human limbic system. *Experimental Neurology* 53:420–430.

Scheibel, M. E., Tomiyasu, U., and Scheibel, A. B. (1977) The aging human betz cell. *Experimental Neurology* 56:598–609.

Sholl, D. A. (1956) *Organization of the Cerebral Cortex.* London: Methuen.

Smith, D. C., Spear, P. D., and Kratz, K. E. (1978) The role of visual experience in post critical-period reversal of the effects of monocular deprivation in cat striate cortex. *Journal of Comparative Neurology* 178:313–328.

Sotelo, C., and Palay, S. L. (1971) Altered axons and axon terminals in the lateral vestibular nucleus of the rat: Possible example of axonal remodelling. *Laboratory Investigation* 25:653–671.

Spear, P. D., Langsetmo, A., and Smith, D. C. (1980) Age-related changes in effects of monocular deprivation on cat striate cortex neurons. *Journal of Neurophysiology* 43:559–580.

Struble, R. G., and Riesen, A. H. (1978) Changes in cortical dendritic branching subsequent to partial social isolation in stumptailed monkeys. *Developmental Psychobiology* 11(5):479–486.

Tees, R. C. (1976) Perceptual development in mammals. Pp. 281–326 in G. Gottleib, ed., *Studies on the Development of Behavior and the Nervous System.* New York: Academic Press.

Terry, R. D., and Gershon, S., eds. (1976) *Neurobiology of Aging.* New York: Raven Press.

Terry, R. D., and Wisniewski, H. M. (1972) Ultrastructure of senile dementia and of experimental analogs. In C. M. Gaitz, ed., *Aging and the Brain.* New York: Plenum Press.

Tomlinson, B. E. (1972) Morphological brain changes in non-demented old people. In H. M. van Praag and A. F. Kalverboer, eds., *Ageing of the Central Nervous System.* Bohn: Haarlem.

Tomlinson, B. E., and Henderson, G. E. (1976) Some quantitative cerebral findings in normal and demented old people. Pp. 183–204 in R. Terry and S. Gershon, eds., *Neurobiology of Aging.* New York: Plenum Press.

Uylings, H. B. M., Kuypers, K., Diamond, M. C., and Veltman, W. A. M. (1978a) Effects of differential environments on plasticity of dendrites of cortical pyramidal neurons in adult rats. *Experimental Neurology* 62:658–677.

Uylings, H. B. M., Kuypers, K., and Veltman, W. A. M. (1978b) Environmental influences on neocortex in later life. Pp. 261–274 in M. A. Corner, R. E. Baker, N. E. van de Poll, D. F. Swabb, and H. B. M. Uylings, eds., *Progress in Brain Research,* Vol. 48. Amsterdam: Elsevier.

Valverde, F. (1970) The Golgi method: A tool for comparative structural analyses. Pp. 12–31 in W. J. H. Nauta and S. O. E. Ebbesson, eds., *Contemporary Research Methods in Neuroanatomy.* New York: Springer-Verlag.

Valverde, F. (1971) Rate and extent of recovery from dark rearing in the mouse. *Brain Research* 33:1–11.

Van Buskirk, C. (1945) The seventh nerve complex. *Journal of Comparative Neurology* 82:303–333.

Vaughan, D. W. (1977) Age-related deterioration of pyramidal cell basal dendrites in rat auditory cortex. *Journal of Comparative Neurology* 171:501–516.

Vijayashankar, N., and Brody, H. (1971) Neuronal population of the human abducens nucleus. *Anatomical Record* 169:447.

Vijayashankar, N., and Brody, H. (1973) The neuronal population of the nuclei of the trochlear nerve and the locus coeruleus in the human. *Anatomical Record* 172:421–422.

Volkmar, F. R., and Greenough, W. T. (1972) Rearing complexity affects branching of dendrites in the visual cortex of the rat. *Science* 176:1445–1447.

Weiss, G. M., and Pysh, J. J. (1978) Evidence for loss of Purkinje cell dendrites during late development: A morphometric Golgi analysis in the mouse. *Brain Research* 154:219–230.

West, R. W., and Greenough, W. T. (1972) Effect of environmental complexity on cortical synapses of rats: Preliminary results. *Behavioral Biology* 7:279–284.

Wiesel, T. N., and Hubel, D. H. (1965) Extent of recovery from the effects of visual deprivation in kittens. *Journal of Neurophysiology* 28:1060–1072.

chapter **9**

Aging and
Brain Plasticity[1]

GARY LYNCH
SARA GERLING

Brain scientists have long struggled with the question of how the nervous system modifies itself to store information and adapt behavior to the changing contingencies of the environment. Brain circuits appear to possess remarkable capacities for growth and change, even in the mature animal, and it seems reasonable that one or more of these capacities accounts for behavioral effects such as learning. These findings are pertinent to neurogerontology because recent work suggests that certain forms of brain plasticity may be reduced or altered during the course of aging. Thus along with the structural and biochemical disturbances that accompany aging, it may be the case that the modifiability of brain changes as well. If so, then the explanation of a number of age-related shifts in behavior may require a characterization of changes in brain plasticity as well as some insight into the etiology of those changes. These issues form the subject matter of this review.

Before turning to this specific question, it is perhaps appropriate to outline some of the recent theories of aging and consider how these might direct investigation into the origins of any age-related changes in brain plasticity. Though space considerations necessitate an abbreviated account of the vast literature on cellular theories of brain aging, this material will serve to focus our discussion of the data needs and problem areas associated with the specific topic of aging and brain plasticity.

[1] Supported by NIA grant AG00538.

AGING
Biology and Behavior

THEORIES OF AGING AND THEIR APPLICATION TO
THE CENTRAL NERVOUS SYSTEM

In general, theories of aging can be rather neatly divided into intrinsic or "genetic" and extrinsic or "nongenetic" theories. Intrinsic theories have emphasized the probable consequences of breakdowns in the crucial DNA–RNA–protein sequence and the extent to which this process occurs independently in each cell. Extrinsic theories have emphasized the consequences of various external biochemical and biophysical mechanisms operating on cells. The emphasis is on forces that cause cells to age, rather than a focus on internal mechanisms that would theoretically cause cells to age even in an optimal environment.

Intrinsic Theories of Aging

REPLICATION ERROR

One popular theory of aging is that in cells that undergo continuous mitosis throughout an individual's life, replication errors gradually accumulate. Over time, these accumulated sequence errors result in decreased ability on the part of individual cells to fulfill their specialized functions, or even to survive (Lewis and Holiday 1970, reviewed in Sinex 1977).

Clearly, this theory cannot be applied directly to the central nervous system (CNS). After a very brief postnatal stage, neurons simply do not show the kind of constant proliferation and cell loss that characterizes most other tissues. Other cells in the neuropil, particularly the specialized glial populations, divide only very slowly after adolescence, although brain lesions can induce proliferation (but see Timiras 1972 for another view).

ERROR ACCUMULATION

A second hypothesis concerning DNA alteration and aging suggests that errors can accumulate in nuclear chromatin through a variety of agencies other than replication error (Medvedev 1964, Orgel 1963, Szilard 1959). The accumulation of errors over the intracycle life of the cell is argued to result in an exponential increase in the frequency of errors in protein synthesis, resulting in eventual cell death through "error catastrophe" (Orgel 1963).

This idea is considerably more appealing in its reference to CNS cells than is the theory of replication error. For two reasons, neurons might be even more sensitive to such accumulated somatic mutations than other cells in the body. First, because they are amitotic and long-lived, errors could gradually accumulate in these cells; second, neurons may be more highly specialized than cells in other tissues and hence more readily disturbed in their operation. Several investigators have reported that more of the unique sequences of DNA (as opposed to multiple-copy genes such as those for rRNA) are transcribed in brain than in any other tissue (Bantle and Hahn 1976, Brown and Church 1971, Grouse *et al.* 1973). These findings may reflect the presence in the brain of many small populations of cells, each with its own activated set of DNA sequences. Loss of a critical number of the differentiated cells could affect both the capacity of the specialized population and that of other cells in the CNS with which they communicate.

The data bearing on this hypothesis are, unfortunately, somewhat incomplete and contradictory. Cell death, whether mediated by DNA incapacity or otherwise, seems not to be the major causal factor in brain aging. There is a decline in the number of neurones in some areas of the human brain (reviewed in Brody and Vikayashankar 1977, Bondareff, in Chapter 7 of this volume) and possibly in rat and mouse (Landfield *et al.* 1977, Johnson and Erner 1972), but these changes are frequently minor in extent until quite late in life. This would seem to suggest that neuron loss is more likely to be the result of other age-related events than the cause of them. Synapse loss may be a more widespread and early phenomenon (Bondareff, in Chapter 7 of this volume), but its relationship to changes in DNA is unclear.

Marked changes in DNA and RNA also fail to appear. The amount of DNA and RNA relative to protein in brain tissue shows little decrease over the life-span, according to several researchers (Chaconas and Finch 1973, Finch 1976, Gaubatz *et al.* 1976, Hollander and Barrows 1968), although Chaconas and Finch (1973) noted a decrease in RNA content in the neostriatum of mice. Johnson *et al.* (1972) reported a loss of rRNA genes in the brains of aging dogs, but no such age-related loss was found in the human brain (Gaubatz *et al.* 1976). A recent study demonstrated that, in rats, the quality and quantity of DNA–RNA hybridization did not decrease with age between 12 and 24 months (Colman *et al.* 1980). It is tempting to suggest on the basis of these observations that aging DNA does not produce dramatically different RNA molecules from younger DNA.

TRANSLATION ERROR

Another genetic theory of aging presents the idea that the locus of decreased function in aging cells is at the level of RNA translation to polypeptide sequences or even at the posttranslational level. The mechanisms by which this interference might be mediated are reviewed by Adelman (1977).

The evidence for alterations in CNS protein synthesis patterns with age is somewhat stronger than that for changes in the DNA itself but, again, hardly conclusive. Cutler (1972, 1975) has reported a decrease in the total number of unique DNA sequences transcribed in mouse brain during aging and suggested that some genes may be selectively repressed during the aging process. A similar possibility is suggested by the work of Gordon and Finch (1974). These investigators found the incorporation of leucine into total protein to be unchanged in the aged brain, although gel electrophoresis did indicate reduced synthesis of some proteins. Cicero, *et al.* (1972) also reported regional changes in the levels of two brain-specific proteins, S100 and 14-3-2. Another pattern of age-related changes in proteins has been demonstrated by Klug and Adelman (1977), who found that the level of a high molecular weight protein that resembled thyrotropin immunologically but actually inhibited thyroid activity was higher in old than in young rats. At this point, the possibility of changes in protein synthesis efficiency or patterning as a central mechanism in aging cannot be ruled out, but more data would be welcome.

It has also become popular to attribute the process of aging in the CNS to "genetically programmed death." Much of the support for the idea of an intrinsic genetic program for senescence comes from the study of cell cultures, in which the phenomenon of a limited number of mitotic divisions per cell line has repeatedly been observed (reviewed in Hayflick 1977, for another viewpoint, see Bell *et al.* 1978). Obviously, this situation has little direct relevance to CNS cells for reasons already summarized. It has, however, been suggested that the observed death of neurons in the larval–prenatal–neonatal brain may represent an aspect of this "programmed loss." It is assumed, then, that cell loss in aging is a consequence of some similar process.

The major difficulty with this idea is that the concept of genetically programmed death is often used as if it has explanatory value in itself. One of the challenges of neurogerontology is the development of ideas about mechanisms by which such genetically based changes could be triggered.

Extrinsic Theories of Aging

Among the theories of aging lumped into this category, two general classes of approaches can be distinguished. These can be called "wear-and-tear" and "physiological" theories.

WEAR AND TEAR THEORIES

Theories of general wear and tear emphasize the centrality of accumulated insults over time throughout all cells of the body as a major mechanism of aging. Rather like the Deacon's wonderful one-hoss shay, the aging organism does not decline because one component fails, but because many specialized tissues disintegrate simultaneously.

Deprivation theory. Several mechanisms have been suggested as primary sources of generalized changes. One of these is deprivation of a vital material. A popular nominee for the crucial nutrient in this paradigm has been oxygen. Since the transport of oxygen through the vascular system is accessible to monitoring, and since the importance of oxygen to brain function in particular is obvious, this idea seems to have possibilities as a mechanism of brain aging.

At present, however, it is difficult to come to firm conclusions as to the causal relationships between cerebrovascular changes and age-related changes in brain function. There is no doubt that serious atherosclerosis leading to cerebrovascular ischemia has dramatic and debilitating effects on brain function. It is also apparent that in many patients with Alzheimer's disease or other forms of dementia cerebral blood flow is distinctly abnormal (Perez *et al.* 1977). Nevertheless, dementia can also appear without atherosclerosis, suggesting that vascular changes alone are neither a necessary nor a sufficient explanation for loss of capacity in the elderly.

The question also arises whether Alzheimer's disease represents a dramatic intensification of the normal aging process or whether it is a different sort of entity, one that does not necessarily lie at the end of the continuum of normal aging.

Vascular changes, on the other hand, do seem to be part of the typical aging process, at least for Americans. It has been estimated that the incidence of atherosclerosis in Americans over the age of 70 may be higher than 95% (Masoro 1972). If atherosclerosis leads inevitably to a decrease in oxygen availability to the brain and this decrease results in damaging cell or synapse loss, it is possible that the changes in the arteries are indeed the major force behind changes in the CNS.

It still is not clear, however, just what the linkage is between atherosclerotic changes and degenerative changes in the brain, since there seems to be a lack of certainty as to whether there are significant changes in oxygen transport in the brains of healthy older individuals. Two recent anatomical studies demonstrated that both in normotensive aged humans (Hunziker *et al.* 1978) and aged rats (Bar 1978), the density of capillaries in the aged cortex increased as a consequence of cortical atrophy, and the authors concluded that this increased density results in maintenance of normal oxygen diffusion in the tissue. A study of the brains of senile individuals (Ravens 1978) described destructive changes in the vascular bed; these do not seem to have appeared in tissue from the normal individuals in the other recent studies.

In settling this question, it would be useful to have data that dealt with age-related changes both in cerebral microcirculation and CNS cell organization and structure. Most of the available studies, unfortunately, limit their focus to one or the other.

Waste accumulation theory. Accumulation of metabolic by-products, rather than deprivation of precursors, has also been suggested as a generalized mechanism of aging. In this case, one of the major candidates for study has been lipofuscin, a heterogeneous biochemical containing lipids, carbohydrate, and protein (Bjorkerud 1964). Lipofuscin granules increase intracellularly in both mitotic and amitotic cells, including neurons (Brizzee *et al.* 1974), over the life-span.

The major drawback to the acceptance of lipofuscin accumulation as an underlying cause rather than a symptom of aging has been the inability of researchers to demonstrate any effect of lipofuscinosis on the operation or survival of cells. Althougn Mann and Yates (1974) suggested that lipofuscin brings about cell death, others have failed to find an association between the presence of lipofuscin and metabolic rate within the brain (Ferrendelli *et al.* 1971) or between lipofuscin accumulation and cell death (Moatamed 1966, Monagle and Brody 1974, Zeman 1971), unless the accumulation of lipofuscin reaches extreme proportions (Zeman 1971). It should perhaps be noted that the degeneration of the dendritic apparatus described as characteristic of neurons overloaded with lipofuscin is at least grossly similar to the dendritic stunting observed in pathologic human brains (Scheibel *et al.* 1975, Scheibel and Scheibel 1975). The absence of physiological data on the effects of lipofuscin accumulation in otherwise healthy individuals indicates that the verdict on the significance of lipofuscin must be left open at this time.

PHYSIOLOGICAL THEORIES

The second family of extrinsic theories to be considered are classed as physiological theories; that is, they emphasize changes at the tissue or whole-body level over those occurring within the cell itself.

Many of these theories of aging have emphasized the importance of a single organ in determining the course of aging in an individual; this critical organ may be the heart, the brain, or even the liver. Although these ideas are attractive, they suffer from the same problems as the general theory of genetically programmed cell death; it is necessary to approach the question of why the critical organ fails to function with age.

Immunological theories of aging. A variant of physiological theory emphasizes changes not in a single organ but in a functional system. One such theory describes aging as a function of changes in the immune system. This immunological hypothesis of aging can be further subdivided into two types. One subtheory proposes that aging is the consequence of the gradual decline in the responsiveness of the immune system with age. Any such decline exposes the individual to the invasion of pathological antigens and their disruptive effects (Mackay 1972, Makinodan 1977). In a sense, this idea is diametrically opposed to theories of intrinsic aging; the immune theory implies that if there were no outside antigens or internal neoplasms upsetting the body's ecology, there would be no aging. The other branch of the immunological theory of aging suggests that aging arises from a specific, rather than a general, failure of the immunological system: the loss of the regulatory mechanisms that normally enable the system to differentiate between the body's own components and alien antigens. This results in the onset of autoimmune diseases that lead to age-related loss of function in a variety of systems (Burnet 1970, Phillips and Wegman 1973).

Although both variants of the immunological theory are ingenious and both have prompted considerable research, there seems to be relatively little work specifically applying this theory to aging in the CNS. An intriguing series of experiments by Rapport and Karpiak (1978) demonstrated that, in mice and rats, antibodies to synaptic membranes or specific protein components of synaptic membranes interfered with operant learning, maze learning, and passive avoidance. Deficits in these behaviors are also found in old animals. Antibodies to myelin, galactocerebroside, and the neuronal protein 14-3-2 did not affect behavior, suggesting that the effect was specific to "synaptic" antibodies. A recent survey of the level of antibrain antibody in individuals ranging from 5 to 85 years of age, however, showed that the highest levels of antibody were found in persons between the ages of 15 and 25; the oldest individuals showed the lowest levels (Chaffee *et al.* 1978). Clearly, a great deal of work remains to be done in the areas of characterizing human antibodies to specific CNS components, relating these antibodies to CNS function, and exploring the relative strength of the blood–brain barrier at different ages.

Neuroendocrine theory. Another popular theory of physiological aging suggests that a major mechanism in age-related changes in structure

and function throughout the body is the repeated activation of the adrenal–hypothalamic–pituitary axis and the manifold actions of the adrenal
hormones produced in the stress response. This idea has been developed
by a number of authors and is reviewed in Selye and Tuchweber (1976).

Recently, interest has been focused on an extension of this theory
that may be called the neuroendocrine theory of aging. In this formulation, the process of aging is mediated by the presence of a variety of
hormones and their cyclic changes over the life-span (Finch 1976, Landfield 1979). These hormones, primarily the steroids produced by the
adrenals and gonads but also including thyroid, insulin, and perhaps
others, operate on at least two levels in the body. First, they have direct
effects on an assortment of target tissues. Second, most of them influence
their own synthesis and release through their feedback action on sensitive
cells in the CNS, and thus on the release of hypothalamic and pituitary
releasing and inhibitory factors. It is proposed that age-related changes
in the effect of a hormone on the CNS can result in changes not only
in the release of that hormone, but also in the modulation of the level
of other hypothalamically controlled hormones, which in their turn may
affect the CNS in such a way as to further alter the dynamics of the
initially changed hormone. As these effects on both CNS and hormone-
responsive tissues elsewhere in the body summate, Finch (1976) describes
the consequence as "a cascade (that) could be a major force in mammalian aging."

There is evidence for age-related changes in hormone levels. The
phenomenon of reproductive senescence, which has a time of onset in
females of many species well in advance of maximum life-span (reviewed
in Talbert 1977), is consistently associated with a decline in the synthesis
of ovarian steroids and a reciprocal increase in the levels of circulating
follicle-stimulating hormone (FSH) in both human beings (Tsai and Yen
1971) and rats (Clemens and Meites 1971). Testosterone levels have been
reported to decrease in aging human males (Pirke and Doerr 1973, Vermeulen *et al.* 1972) and in rats (Ghanadian *et al.* 1975, Gray 1979, Reigle
and Miller 1978), although not in healthy elderly mice (Nelson *et al.*
1975). Testosterone-binding globulin shows an increasing ability to bind
testosterone with age (Vermeulen *et al.* 1972) and is stimulated by estrogen (Burke and Anderson 1972). Since aging males show elevated
plasma estradiol (Pirke and Doerr 1973), plasma levels of free testosterone may be further reduced as a consequence.

Studies of the adrenal–hypothalamic–pituitary axis have produced
conflicting evidence. Lewis and Wexler (1974) found elevated plasma
corticosteroids in 19-month-old rats, and Landfield *et al.* (1978c) reported
elevated corticosterone levels in 13-month-old as compared with 4-

month-old animals. In the same study, however, there were no significant differences in steroid levels between 25-month-old and 4-month-old rats, but old rats had heavier adrenals. Several studies on both rats (Britton *et al.* 1975, Hess and Riegle 1970, 1972) and human beings (Blichert-Toft *et al.* 1970) uncovered no differences in basal plasma levels of gluco-corticoids between old and young individuals, although another group of investigators reported that the trough of the diurnal cycle of cortisol secretion was higher in old than in young individuals (Freidman *et al.* 1969). It has been suggested that this may be a consequence of patho-logical changes in the elderly (Grad *et al.* 1971). This again points up the problem of distinguishing normal from abnormal changes, particularly since, if the neuroendocrine hypothesis is true, the abnormal cycles of cortisol release could play a role in the development of the pathology.

The neuroendocrine hypothesis is particularly appealing as a possible explanatory framework for age-related changes in that it offers a link between genetic and physiological theories of aging. Steroid hormones are known to act on target tissues through contact with the genome. The steroid molecule that enters a target cell is bound to a specific protein receptor in the cytosol and translocated with its receptor into the nucleus. There, it interacts with chromatin to derepress synthesis of specific pro-teins (Chan and O'Malley 1976, Thrash *et al.* 1974). The sites of adrenal and gonadal steroid uptake in the brain have been mapped, and numerous studies have indicated that the sites of steroid-binding cells are also the sites in which these steroids act to induce physiological and behavioral responses (Brown and Uphouse 1979, McEwen *et al.* 1976, McEwen *et al.* 1977, Pfaff and Keiner 1973, Tedeschi and Uphouse 1979).

Steroid hormones are also known to act on the brain early in the development to affect the later responsiveness of sensitive sites to these same hormones. The most intensively studied example of this is, of course, the process of sexual differentiation of the brain. During the critical period for differentiation, exposure to gonadal steroids induces a ''masculine'' differentiation of the brain in a variety of species. This results in the development of tonic secretion of gonadotrophins following puberty as well as a variety of other effects (reviewed in Gorski 1974).

The process of sexual differentiation appears to be capable of graded responses. Female rats given low doses of testosterone in infancy differ in their phenotype as adults from females given higher doses (Barraclough and Gorski 1962, Whalen *et al.* 1969); differences in the degree of mas-culinization of behavior between females exposed to differing levels of circulating fetal androgens from their siblings *in utero* have also been reported (Clemens 1974).

A similar process of early differentiation appears in the development of responsiveness to stress: Rats that have been mildly stressed in infancy (leading to corticosterone release) show lesser responses to mild stress and more intense responses to strong stressors than do rats that did not experience stress in infancy (Levine *et al.* 1967). Corticosterone responses in general appear to be relatively sensitive indicators of the intensity of stress experienced by an individual (Hennessy *et al.* 1979).

Steroid hormones, then, have interesting properties as possible mediators of age-related changes in the brain as well as in the rest of the body. They interact with specific sites in the brain by interacting with the genetic material itself, they elicit graded as well as all-or-none responses, they affect their own synthesis and that of their intracellular receptors, they interact with one another and with a variety of target tissues, and they can apparently exert their effects over a long period of time. This is most obvious in the case of sexual differentiation, where most of the effects of neonatal hormone exposure are demonstrated only after puberty.

APPROACHING THE PROBLEM OF BRAIN AGING

Temporal Patterns in Aging

A major problem in attempting to link specific manifestations of brain aging with one or more of the theoretical positions outlined above is that the chronology of age-related disturbances in the brain are, with very few exceptions, unknown. Logically, there are three time courses that a given effect might follow:

1. It may be the result of a normal developmental trend that simply continues in a linear fashion throughout life. In this case, age-related changes are not a function of a specific process called aging, but the result of a steady accumulation of normal developmental events that eventually become deleterious.

2. It may result from a process that goes to a limiting value and the decreases from that value, giving a U-shaped function for the process viewed over time. "And so from hour to hour we ripe and ripe, and then from hour to hour we rot and rot [*As You Like It*]." This type of pattern appears in the gross measures of body and brain weight (Appell and Appell 1942, Lindop 1961); it also seems to be implied in the observation that in examining various types of learning and of neurological skills, those that appear latest in development also disappear earliest

with age. For example, the capacity for passive avoidance learning appears later than the capacity for active avoidance in several species (Campbell and Campbell 1962, Riccio *et al.* 1968, Davis and Jensen 1976), and deficits in passive avoidance appear in old rats at an age when active avoidance is still within normal ranges (Campbell 1978).

3. It may result from a sudden decrease in a stable level of function that has been maintained throughout the greater part of adulthood. Sudden declines of this type have been reported for neuron number in mice (Johnson and Erner 1972) and human beings (Brody 1970). It is also characteristic of the course of reproductive senescence of the female mammal.

The different patterns of these chronologies suggest different possible cellular mechanisms underlying the phenomenon of age-related change in each case. For any aspect of aging, then, it may be important to establish the developmental history of the trait in order to explore its cause or causes.

Separating Interactive Systems into Their Constituents

A second major problem involved in the study of brain aging is consequent to the complexity of the CNS and the multitude of interactions between CNS and other tissues and organs. The image of the brain as computer has been a popular one for many years, but it is possible that the connotations of such an image are limiting when applied to problems of neurogerontology. We may be able to represent the brain more accurately by symbolizing it as an ecological system in which many constantly varying populations of species (neurons, glia, hormones, nutrients, cerebrovascular vessels, etc.) exist in a balanced state of tensions. Such a system, like any ecology, can be visualized as having certain powers of adaptation to changing circumstances (as perhaps exemplified by the increases in capillary density with age that are thought to compensate for possibly decreased efficiency of oxygen transport). The image of the brain as ecosystem also emphasizes the importance of thinking of obvious changes in brain morphology as very possibly caused by some less apparent antecedent, as in the ecological homily about the disappearance of the ducks from a farmers' pond. In this system, the ducks disappear because the farmer's sons trap the skunks living near the pond. The skunks no longer eat the eggs of snapping turtles, and the burgeoning turtle population consumes all the ducklings. In seeking the causes of degenerative changes in synapses, then, it may be more useful to explore calcium levels in the glia than to limit one's area of interest to the synaptic cleft.

Strategies in Neurogerontology

These problems of chronology and complexity suggest certain strategies for the exploration of brain aging. First, it is critical to focus on specific regions of the brain in describing age-related changes. Since many effects appear to be region-limited and may even occur only in specialized cell populations within a region, studies of whole-brain physiology or biochemistry may run a real risk of overshadowing important changes in critical sites by diluting affected with unaffected tissue. Further, a pattern of related disturbances in aging should show up more clearly against a well-defined background, and the analysis of such patterns will assist in determining the causal relationship among their elements.

Second, the quantification of age-related changes and the characterization of such changes over the life-span should become a major focus of gerontology. In most cases, we do not yet know what types or temporal patterns of changes are predictive, coexistent, or postdictive of senescence. Again, in order to decide which elements are critical in the patterns of aging, we need a better idea of what the patterns actually are.

Third, the process of quantifying changes in brain loci must be associated with the generation and testing of hypotheses about the underlying mechanisms of aging. At this point, it can almost be said that the number of ideas about the causes of aging outnumber the tests of these same ideas.

In the remainder of the chapter, we will focus on one possible model system in neurogerontology, the hippocampus. This structure has been the site of a great deal of recent research in neurobiology for a variety of reasons. Many of these aspects of the hippocampus also make it an intriguing area from the point of view of the gerontologist. The hippocampus is fascinating because of its apparent relationship to the storage and retrieval of memory and particularly useful as a model because of its precisely laminated architecture and specialized cell populations (Figure 9.1). In the following sections, we will discuss age-related changes in the hippocampus, the possible relationships between the changes of old age and those of early development, and the plausibility of the hypothesized involvement of steroid hormones in the aging process within this region.

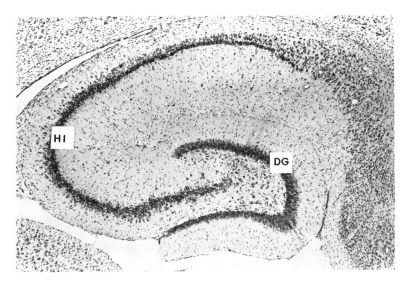

Figure 9.1. A low power photomicrograph of a section through the hippocampus of a rat stained so as to reveal the cell bodies of the neurones. Note that there are but two rows of neurones (the dentate gyrus "DG" and hippocampus "HI") and that these are physically separate from each other. This arrangement is quite rare in the vertebrate brain and, combined with other simplifying features of its anatomy, accounts for the surge in popularity of the hippocampus as a model for investigations into basic neurobiological questions (e.g., aging).

AGE-RELATED CHANGES IN HIPPOCAMPAL PHYSIOLOGY AND FUNCTION

Changes in Physiology of Synapses

Any discussion of the possible effects of aging on brain physiology must begin with a consideration of synaptic physiology, and it is indeed surprising to find that so little work has been done in this area. Recently, Barnes (1979) reported that, for a given stimulation voltage, the size of the postsynaptic potential in hippocampus was smaller in 28-month-old rats than in animals 10–12 months of age. Further work of this type is badly needed; if Barnes's results are replicated for other monosynaptic systems, it would seem that the aging process acts at the most fundamental level of CNS operation.

Complex stimulation paradigms also reveal functional decrements in aged rats. In Barnes's study, the facilitation of the response to a stimulation pulse given within milliseconds of a primary pulse (paired-pulse stimulation) appeared to be essentially unaffected in older animals. Repetitive stimulation at high frequencies, however, produced less facilitation in old rats than in younger ones, although age-related differences did not appear following low-frequency stimulation trains. Furthermore, when lengthy trains of 5 sec^{-1} were given, the synaptic responses of aged rats appeared to become exhausted more rapidly and remained depressed longer than did those of young rats (Landfield and Lynch 1977, Landfield et al. 1978b. These phenomena were demonstrated both in anesthetized acute rats and in the in vitro slice preparation, suggesting that the effects are not simply due to interactions between age and a particular experimental technique.

Two possible mechanisms could account for these findings. It may be that some type of depletion (exhaustion) overtakes the synapses in the older rats more quickly and completely than is the case in young animals. Alternatively, it is possible that the balance of depressive and facilitatory processes brought into action by repetitive stimulation (see Creager et al. 1980, Lynch et al. 1978) is different in the older animals.

Finally, old rats differ from young ones in their ability to produce a fascinating type of physiological response that thus far has been found only in the hippocampus. Essentially all synaptic systems exhibit transient increases in response strength following high-frequency stimulation (posttetanic potentiation), but these effects usually disappear within seconds or minutes. In the hippocampus, response facilitation following very brief trains of high-frequency stimulation continues for hours, days, even weeks (Bliss and Gardner-Medwin 1973, Douglas and Goddard 1975). Thus this type of response facilitation (long-term potentiation or LTP) is a physiological phenomenon that resembles memory in that it is induced by modest and very brief events and, once present, persists indefinitely—it is not surprising that it has become the subject of intense physiological and biochemical research.

Landfield and Lynch (1977) reported that old rats demonstrated less LTP than young ones following long trains of repetitive stimulation. This, however, could be partly due to the depressive effect of long stimulus trains on old rats (see above) rather than a simple impairment of the potentiation process. Barnes (1979) induced LTP with brief bursts of high-frequency stimulation, a procedure that apparently does not activate the depression mechanism (Dunwiddie and Lynch 1978). She found that the strength and persistence of LTP following a single stimulation episode did not show age-related differences. LTP elicited by three successive daily sessions of stimulation, however, was less pronounced and declined much more quickly in old than in young rats.

Old rats, then, seem to show impairments in hippocampal synaptic operations as reflected in the response to single stimuli as well as to repetitive trains.

Two fundamental questions are raised by these data. First, are these age-related changes associated with behavioral deficits? Second, what are the cellular mechanisms responsible for them?

Possible Consequences

The answer to the first question may be yes. Barnes (1979) correlated the fractional change in evoked response following high-frequency stimulation (the LTP phenomenon) with behavioral performance in a circular platform maze. For both old and young rats, there were significant negative correlations between the strength of LTP after three or four stimulation sessions and the numbers of errors and/or amount of distance traveled in the maze. That is, rats that showed strong LTP did well in the maze, whether they were old or young. Old rats were generally poor on both measures. Barnes makes a plausible case that the deficiency in maze performance seen in old (and some young) rats was not due to motivational, locomotor, or sensory impairment, but to a deficit in spatial memory formation. This is particularly exciting in that it has been suggested that the formation of "environmental maps" is one function of the hippocampus (O'Keefe and Nadel 1978); furthermore, the characteristics of LTP, as previously mentioned, are analogous to those of memory. These results, then, suggest a possible relationship between the loss of synaptic plasticity with age and the loss of the ability to form new memories.

Possible Mechanisms

A definitive answer to the second question must await progress in uncovering the cellular mechanisms responsible for the LTP effect. It has been found that the stimulation trains that induce LTP also change the phosphorylated state of specific synaptic proteins (Browning et al. 1979a), and something has been learned of the chemistry responsible for this effect (Browning et al. 1979b). Beyond this, recent work has suggested the startling conclusion that LTP is accompanied by structural changes (Fifkova and Van Harreveld 1977, Lee et al. 1979). It may be the case that long-lasting changes in the operating characteristics of brain circuitries involve synaptic chemistries of a type quite different from those responsible for transmission and that these chemistries control the micro-organization of synaptic systems. Investigation of the ways in which aging affects these cellular processes may offer new insights into the origins of the subtle behavioral alterations that appear with age.

ANATOMICAL PLASTICITY IN THE HIPPOCAMPUS: CHANGES OVER THE LIFE-SPAN AND SOME POSSIBLE REGULATORY FACTORS

It has become increasingly evident over the past several years that the capacity for growth and change in the CNS is not restricted to the period of early development but instead is retained well into adulthood. Certain electron microscopic studies, in fact, suggest that degeneration and regeneration of synaptic connections are part of the normal operation of the mammalian brain (Sotelo and Palay 1971). This raises the possibility that losses in synaptic numbers as described by Bondareff (Chapter 7 of this volume) as well as of neurones may reflect age-related changes in growth processes or the appearance late in life of factors that tend to impede such processes. Furthermore, there is evidence that anatomical growth participates in the functional plasticity of brain (see above) and behavior (see Greenough and Green, Chapter 8 of this volume); alterations in growth responses may therefore have significant impact on the ability of an organism to deal with changing environmental circumstances. For these reasons, it is of some importance to establish whether aging decreases the capacity of neuronal circuitry to undergo structural rearrangement.

Age-Related Changes in the Sprouting Response of Hippocampal Fiber Projections

The use of the hippocampus as a model system for studies of anatomical as well as functional plasticity has increased dramatically in recent years, largely because of the relative simplicity of its structure. As shown in Figure 9.1, the hippocampus possesses but two major subdivisions—the pyramidal cell field (hippocampus proper) and the granule cell zone (the denate gyrus). The major fiber systems traveling into these two regions as well as between hippocampal subdivisions are strictly laminated. Granule cells receive three sets of projections. Axons from the ipsilateral entorhinal cortex enter the hippocampus through the perforant path and synapse on the distal portion of the dendrites of the granule cells. The proximal portion of the dendrites receives two sets of fibers. One group (the associational system) is generated by the pyramidal cells of the ipsilateral hippocampus; the other (the commissural fibers) project from the pyramidal cells of the contralateral hippocampus. There is virtually no overlap between the projection sites of the entorhinal system and those of the commissural–associational fibers in normal adult animals (Lynch *et al.* 1978).

Destruction of one of these projections to the dentate gyrus causes the remaining undamaged inputs to begin emitting new branches and to invade and contact the deafferented zones. Figure 9.2 illustrates a typical experiment. Following lesions of the entorhinal cortex, the outer two-thirds of the granule cell dendrites lose the great majority of their connections; these are shortly replaced in part by invading fibers from the adjacent commissural–associational inputs (see Lynch *et al.* 1975 for a review). Several experiments using a variety of anatomical techniques have been conducted using this paradigm and have indicated that the commissural and associational axons in the fully mature dentate gyrus

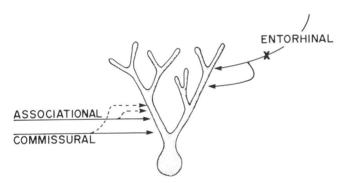

Figure 9.2. A schematic to illustrate an experiment intended to test the growth capacities of the axonal inputs to the mature hippocampal formation. The neurone in the drawing is a granule cell of the dentate gyrus ("DG" in Figure 8.1) and, as illustrated, receives most of its input from three sources. The hippocampus ("HI" in Figure 8.1) contributes the "commissural" and "associational" projections while a cortical area, the "entorhinal" region, is responsible for the third input. Note that these connections are *laminated;* that is, the entorhinal projections terminate exclusively in the outer portions of the dendrites of the granule cells and do not overlap the inputs from the hippocampus which are restricted to the inner dendritic regions. This severe segregation of inputs is again most atypical and greatly facilitates studies of anatomical plasticity. Several experiments have shown that if the entorhinal projections are surgically eliminated (note the "x" in the figure) the undamaged commissural-associational fibers will emit new branches (dotted lines in the drawing) which invade the dendritic zones that have lost connections (see Lynch *et al.* 1975 for a review). This "sprouting" response begins some 5–6 days after the lesion of the entorhinal cortex in the fully mature rat but is much more rapid and vigorous in 2- to 3-week-old animals; furthermore, recent research suggests that it is somewhat retarded in aged rats.

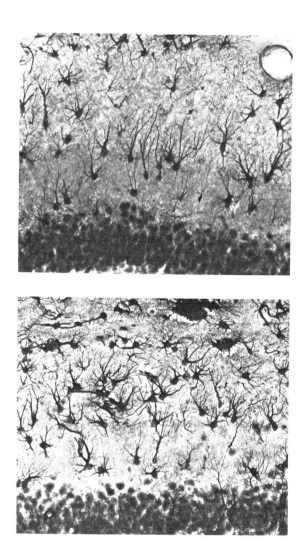

Figure 9.3. Photomicrographs of histological sections which have been treated so that only the astrocytes are stained. The upper panel shows a population of cells from the dentate gyrus of a normal adult rat while the lower micrograph shows the same region 4 days after removal of the entorhinal inputs (see Figure 9.2). Note that in the latter case the astroglial processes are more numerous and extensive and that, in general, the cells have undergone a structural transformation. This effect suddenly reverses itself on the fifth and sixth days after the lesion, at essentially the same time that the sprouting response begins (see Rose *et al.* 1976 for a complete description). As described in the text, the astroglial cells undergo distinctive age-related changes. (For purposes of clarity, the upper panel from the normal brain was photographed at a slightly higher magnification than was the lower picture.)

218

possess a surprising capacity for growth. It has also been found that the sprouting response begins 5 to 6 days after a lesion and requires about 40–60 days to replace the lost synapses.

It is only recently that attempts have been made to establish whether age influences the sprouting response of axons, but the available results strongly suggest that this is indeed the case. Cotman and Scheff (1979) found that the extent and speed with which commissural and associational projections sprouted after lesions of the entohrinal cortex was significantly reduced in 24-month-old rats compared with younger animals.

It is not known if this loss in sprouting capacity represents an effect that appears only late in life or if it is due to a steady loss of capacity beginning at some point early in the life of the animals. It bears mention in this context, however, that there is a striking parallel between the apparent decline in anatomical plasticity in the old as compared with the young rats and a similar decrease in plasticity seen in comparisons of adult and neonatal rats. In 14-day-old rats, entorhinal lesions induced sprouting within 24 hours of the lesion and the axons spread through a much greater area of the denervated region than they did after lesions in adults (Lynch and Gall 1979). Subsequent work has shown that the decline in rate and magnitude of the response occurs gradually over the course of development from infancy to adulthood.

Thus it appears that the sprouting response is reduced in rate and extent first during postnatal development and then again from adulthood to old age. Whether a period of stability is achieved during adulthood is a subject for further research.

Age-Related Changes in Astroglia: Possible Origins and Relationships to Neuronal Plasticity

As stressed earlier, age-related changes in a particular CNS element may not be intrinsic to that element but may be extrinsic, a function of aging in an intimately related system. Thus the decrease in vigor of the sprouting response that appears first in the comparison of neonate and adult and again in the comparison of the adult and elderly rat might be caused by changes in the constituents of the neuropil that modulate sprouting rather than by an alteration in the axons themselves. In the following section, we will explore this possibility, first discussing the postulated relationship of the glia to sprouting and then considering the effects of age on this poorly understood cell type.

Astrocytes undergo radical transformation in brain regions that have lost afferent input, and these changes show an intriguing correlation with the sprouting response. Astrocytes undergo a marked hypertrophy within 24–48 hours after the removal of input (see Figure 9.3). At that time or shortly thereafter, they begin to engulf and consume the degenerating boutons of the lesioned fibers. On the fifth and sixth day after the lesion, this activity decreases dramatically and the astroglial hypertrophy begins to subside; this abrupt change in the behavior of the astrocytes parallels the onset of the sprouting response. These observations have led to the suggestion that the sprouting response is retarded by the hypertrophied (and hyperactive) astrocytes (Lynch *et al.* 1975). If indeed the astroglia do play this role, then it is conceivable that age-related decrements in axonal plasticity may be secondary to gradual changes in the astrocyte population over the life of the animal.

Longitudinal studies of the astroglia provide some support for this idea. Astrocytes in the rat undergo their final divisions between the second and fifth days of postnatal life and by the sixth day are present in essentially adult numbers. Between the fifth and fourteenth days, the astrocytes migrate to the various subfields of the hippocampus; after the fourteenth day, their numbers in any particular subfield remain constant for the life of the animal. Once in place, the astroglia begin to emit and elaborate dendritic processes, which become progressively larger and thicker (Gall, Ishibashi and Lynch, unpublished data).

There is reason to suspect that, unlike neurones, astrocytes continue their development beyond the second and third months of life. A comparison of hippocampal astrocytes in 4-, 13-, and 25-month-old Fischer rats indicated that an increasing percentage of the cells of older animals exhibited well-developed processes (Lindsey *et al.* 1979). Earlier work had also shown that astrocytic processes in the aged hippocampus were more extensive and thicker than those in young adult rats (Landfield *et al.* 1978c), and electron microscopic studies have indicated that the percentage of the neuropil occupied by astrocytic processes was elevated in the hippocampus of the aged Fischer rat (Bondareff, Chapter 7, this volume). While the results of light microscopic studies of astrocytes need to be confirmed with electron microscopy, they do strongly suggest that the development of astrocytic processes that begins in the second week of life continues on through adolescence into mid-life and old age. If so, the glial hypertrophy seen in the aged brain may not be a sign of pathology but may be the simple extension of a process that was begun in the earliest stages of postnatal life. To the extent that astrocytes inhibit axonal growth, these results suggest an explanation for the reduction in the vigor of the sprouting response seen between neonate and adult and again from adult to old age.

A question then arises: Why do astrocytes continue their development over such an extended period? One hypothesis arises from the observation that, in both middle-aged and old rats, considerable individual differences in the degree of apparent astrocyte hypertrophy were observed (Lindsey *et al.* 1979). This observation suggests that events occurring during the life of the rat may influence the course of astroglial development. As previously discussed, it has been argued that endocrine systems, including the pituitary–adrenal axis, may participate in brain aging. Furthermore, there is evidence that glucocorticoids may influence astroglial biochemistry (deVellis and Inglish 1968)—hence it is possible that some aspects of astroglial changes observed over the course of aging could reflect glucocorticoid effects. The high concentration of corticosterone receptors in the hippocampus (McEwen *et al.* 1975) also indicates the possibility that hippocampal cells could respond to corticosterone.

Data that support this hypothesis come from several sources. First, Landfield *et al.* (1978c) reported a significant correlation between serum levels of plasma corticosterone and the number of "reactive" cells (showing well-developed dendritic processes) in 13-month-old rats and between adrenal weight and the number of reactive cells in 25-month-old rats. Second, preliminary results suggest that corticosterone injections induce astrocyte hypertrophy (Landfield *et al.* 1978a), a result that has recently been confirmed in another laboratory (Cotman, personal communication). Finally, recent experiments using *in vitro* slices of hippocampus have provided evidence that corticosterone increases the synthesis of a protein or proteins with a molecular weight of 54,000 daltons (Etgen *et al.* 1979). While several protein species are found in this weight range, it is of interest that the glial fibrillary acidic protein, a constituent of the astrocyte cytoskeleton, has a molecular weight of about 54,000 daltons. While further work is clearly needed for solid conclusions, the available data are consonant with the hypothesis that corticosterone levels influence the morphology of hippocampal astroglia.

According to this model, astrocytes continue to elaborate their processes throughout adulthood, a phenomenon that is modulated by the experiences of the individual organism and its adrenal response to those experiences. This is not to say that developmental programs and glucocorticoid levels alone suffice to explain the status of these glial cells, which could also be responsive to the vascular elements and synaptic terminal to which they are so intimately related, or that all the age-related changes in the hippocampus are due to the activities of the glia. The hypothesis does, however, suggest a manner in which intrinsic developmental patterns and extrinsic factors could intereact to influence one characteristic of the aged brain. And, to the extent that astrocytes themselves mediate sprouting and other forms of synaptic plasticity in the hippocampus, the hypothesis may explain the development of individual differences in synaptic efficacy, hippocampal function, and behavior.

SUMMARY AND CONCLUSIONS

The study of brain aging is currently an exciting field, but also a difficult one. As this review points out, many of the existing theories of aging are difficult to apply to the central nervous system; the intrinsic cellular mechanisms that are hypothesized to mediate aging cannot play the same role in the brain that they do in continuously mitotic tissues. Yet because we recognize the general role of genetic differences in aging, we can assume that the genome must also be somehow involved in brain aging. The challenge is to characterize the internal and external factors that are involved.

It is for that reason that the examination of age-related changes in the hippocampus is of great interest. The study of the relationships among steroid levels, astroglial biochemistry and morphology, neuronal plasticity, and behavior offers the possibility of comprehending these aspects of CNS structure and function within the framework of, for example, the neuroendocrine theory of aging. The neuroendocrine hypothesis is particularly attractive because it offers a means of linking the intracellular process of protein synthesis with extrinsic endocrine processes and with an organism's life history. If, as we speculate, astroglial hypertrophy may be provoked by the stimulus of steroid derepression of protein synthesis, and if this astroglial response inhibits the responsiveness of neurons, leading to changes in hippocampal functional capacities, we can begin to describe the relations between genotype, experience, and aging processes as an interactive function.

The problem of delineating the pattern of age-related changes in brain organization presents another challenge. Is the process of aging continuous with earlier developmental processes, or does it reflect the induction of novel mechanisms? Approaching neurogerontology as an aspect of developmental neurobiology implies different research strategies and conclusions from approaching it as a form of disease.

Overall, these studies are based on an eclectic model of the aging process. Their result, it is hoped, will be a better understanding of aging as a consequence of the interaction between cell populations and the ways in which they are capable of modulating one another's functions within the larger ecosystem of the body.

REFERENCES

Adelman, R. C. (1977) Macromolecular metabolism during aging. Pp. 63–72 in C. E. Finch and L. Hayflick, eds., *Handbook of the Biology of Aging*. New York: Van Nostrand Reinhold Co.

Appell, F. W., and Appell, E. M. (1942) Intracranial variation in the weight of the human brain. *Human Biology* 14:235–250.

Bantle, J. A., and Hahn, W. E. (1976) Complexity and characterization of polyadenylated RNA in the mouse brain. *Cell* 8:139–150.

Bar, T. (1978) Morphometric evaluation of capillaries in different laminae of rat cerebral cortex by automatic image analysis: Changes during development and aging. Pp. 1–9 in J. Cervos-Navarro, E. Betz, G. Ebhardt, R. Ferszt, and R. Wullenweber, eds., *Advances in Neurology*, Vol. 20. New York: Raven Press.

Barnes, C. A. (1979) Memory deficits associated with senescence: A neurophysiological and behavioral study of the rat. *Journal of Comparative and Physiological Psychology* 93:74–104.

Barraclough, C. A., and Gorski, R. A. (1962) Studies on mating behavior in the androgen-sterilized female rat in relation to the hypothalamic regulation of sexual behavior. *Journal of Endocrinology* 25:175–182.

Bell, E., Marek, L. F., Levinstone, D. S., Merrill, C., Shery, S., Young, I. T., and Eden, M. (1978) Loss of division potential *in vitro:* Aging or differentiation? *Science* 202:1158–1163.

Bjorkerud, S. (1964) Studies of lipofuscin granules of human cardiac muscle. II. Chemical analysis of isolated granules. *Experimental and Molecular Pathology* 3:377–389.

Blichert-Toft, M., Blichert-Toft, B., and Jensen, H. K. (1970) Pituitary–adreno–cortical stimulation in the aged as reflected in levels of plasma cortisol and Compound S. *Acta Chirurgica Scandinavica* 136:665–670.

Bliss, T. V. P., and Garner-Medwin, A. T. (1973) Long-lasting potentiation of synaptic transmission in the dentate area of the unanesthetized rabbit following stimulation of the perforant path. *Journal of Physiology* (London) 232:357–374.

Britton, G. W., Rotenberg, S., Freeman, C., Britton, V. J., Karoly, K., Ceci, L., Klug, T. L., Lacko, A. G., and Adelman, R. C. (1975) Regulation of corticosterone levels and liver enzyme activity in aging rats. *Advances in Experimental Medicine and Biology* 61:209–227.

Brizzee, K. R., Ordy, J. M., and Kaack, B. (1974) Early appearance and regional differences in intraneuronal and extraneuronal lipofuscin accumulation with age in the non-human primate *(Macaca mulatta). Journal of Gerontology* 29:366–381.

Brody, H. (1970) Structural changes in the aging nervous system. Pp. 121–133 in H. T. Blumenthal, ed., *Interdisciplinary Topics in Gerontology*, Vol. 7. Basel, Switzerland: S. Karger.

Brody, J., and Vikayashankar, N. (1977) Anatomical changes in the nervous system. Pp. 241–261 in C. E. Finch and L. Hayflick, eds., *Handbook of the Biology of Aging*. New York: Van Nostrand Reinhold Co.

Brown, J., and Uphouse, L. (1979) Corticosterone effects on rat brain template active chromatin. *Behavior Genetics* 9:441.

Brown, I. R., and Church, R. B. (1971) RNA transcription from nonrepetitive DNA in the mouse. *Biochemical, Biophysical Research Communications* 42:850–854.

Browning, M., Bennett, W., and Lynch, G. (1979a) Phosphorylase kinase phosphorylates a brain protein which is influenced by repetitive synaptic activation. *Nature* (London) 278:273–275.

Browning, M., Dunwiddie, T., Bennett, W., Gispen, W., and Lynch, G. (1979b) Synaptic phosphoproteins: Specific changes after repetitive stimulation of the hippocampal slice. *Science* 203:60–62.

Burke, C. W., and Anderson, D. C. (1972) Sex-hormone-binding globulin is an estrogen amplifier. *Nature* 240:38–40.

Burnet, F. M. (1970) *Immunological Surveillance.* Oxford: Pergamon Press.

Campbell, B. A. (1978) Paper presented at International Society for Developmental Psychobiology meetings, St. Louis, Mo.

Campbell, B. A., and Campbell, E. H. (1962) Retention and extinction of learned fear in infant and adult rats. *Journal of Comparative and Physiological Psychology* 51:488–492.

Chaconas, E., and Finch, C. E. (1973) The effect of aging on RNA/DNA ratios in brain regions of the C57BL/6 male mouse. *Journal of Neurochemistry* 21:1469–1473.

Chaffee, J., Nassef, M., and Bobin, S. (1978) Cytotoxic autoantibody to the brain. Pp. 61–72 in K. Nandy, ed., *Senile Dementia: A Biomedical Approach.* New York: Elsevier North-Holland.

Chan, L., and O'Malley, B. W. (1976) Mechanism of action of the sex steroid hormones. *New England Journal of Medicine* 294:1322–1328.

Cicero, T. J., Ferrendelli, J. A., Suntzeff, V., and Moore, B. W. (1972) Regional changes in CNS levels of the S100 and 14-3-2 proteins during development and aging of the mouse. *Journal of Neurochemistry* 19:2119–2125.

Clemens, L. G. (1974) Neurohormonal control of male sexual behavior. Pp. 23–53 in W. Montagna and W. A. Sadler, eds., *Advances in Behavioral Biology,* Vol. 2. New York: Plenum Press.

Clemens, J. A., and Meites, J. (1971) Neuroendocrine status of old constant-estrous rats. *Neuroendocrinology* 7:249–256.

Colman, P. D., Kaplan, B. B., Osterburg, H. H., and Finch, C. E. (1980) Brain poly (A)RNA during aging: Stability of yield and sequence complexity in two rat strains. *Journal of Neurochemistry* 34:335–345.

Cotman, C., and Scheff, S. W. (1979) Compensatory synapse growth in aged animals after neuronal death. *Mechanisms of Ageing and Development* 9:103–117.

Creager, R., Dunwiddie, T., and Lynch, G. (1980) Paired-pulse and frequency facilitation in the CA1 region of the *in vitro* rat hippocampus. *Journal of Physiology* (London) 299:409–424.

Cutler, R. G. (1972) Transcription of reiterated DNA sequence classes throughout the lifespan of the mouse. Pp. 219–231 in B. L. Strehler, ed., *Advances in Gerontological Research,* Vol. 4. New York: Academic Press.

Cutler, R. G. (1975) Transcription of unique and reiterated DNA sequences in mouse liver and brain tissues as a function of age. *Experimental Gerontology* 10:37–60.

Davis, J. L., and Jensen, R. A. (1976) The development of passive and active avoidance learning in the cat. *Developmental Psychobiology* 9:175–179.

deVellis, J., and Inglish, D. (1968) Hormonal control of glycerol phosphate dehydrogenase in the rat brain. *Journal of Neurochemistry* 15:1061–1070.

Douglas, R. M., and Goddard, G. V. (1975) Long-term potentiation of the perforant path-granule cell synapse in the rat hippocampus. *Brain Research* 86:205–215.

Dunwiddie, T., and Lynch, G. (1978) Long-term potentiation and depression of synaptic responses in the rat hippocampus: Localization and frequency dependency. *Journal of Physiology* (London) 276:353–367.

Etgen, A. M., Lee, K. S., and Lynch, G. (1979) Glucocorticoid modulation of specific protein metabolism in hippocampal slices maintained *in vitro*. *Brain Research* 165:37–45.

Ferrendelli, J. A., Sedgwick, W. G., and Suntzeff, V. (1971) Regional energy metabolism and lipofuscin accumulation in the mouse brain during aging. *Journal of Neuropathology and Experimental Neurology* 30:638–649.

Fifkova, E., and Van Harreveld, A. (1977) Long-lasting morphological changes in dendritic spines of dentate granular cells following stimulation of the entorhinal area. *Journal of Neurocytology* 6:211–230.

Finch, C. E. (1973) Catecholamine metabolism in the brains of aging male mice. *Brain Research* 52:261–276.

Finch, C. E. (1976) Physiological changes of aging in mammals. *Quarterly Review of Biology* 51:49–83.

Friedman, M., Green, M. F., and Sharland, D. E. (1969) Assessment of hypothalamic–pituitary–adrenal function in the geriatric age group. *Journal of Gerontology* 24:292–297.

Gaubatz, J., Prashad, N., and Cutler, R. G. (1976) Ribosomal RNA gene dosage as a function of tissue and age for mouse and human. *Biochemica and Biophysica Acta* 418:358–375.

Ghanadian, R., Lewis, J. G., and Chisholm, G. D. (1975) Serum testosterone and dihydrotestosterone changes with age in rat. *Steroids* 25:753–759.

Gordon, S. M., and Finch, C. E. (1975) An electrophoretic study of protein synthesis in brain regions of senescent male mice. *Experimental Gerontology* 9:269–273.

Gorski, R. A. (1974) The neuroendocrine regulation of sexual behavior. Pp. 1–56 in G. Newton and A. H. Riesen, eds., *Advances in Psychobiology*, Vol. 2. New York: John Wiley and Sons.

Grad, B., Rosenberg, G. M., Liberman, H., Trachtenberg, J., and Kral, V. A. (1971) Diurnal variation of the serum cortisol level of geriatric subjects. *Journal of Gerontology* 26:351–357.

Gray, G. D. (1979) Age-related changes in penile erections and circulating testosterone in middle-aged male rats. *Advances in Experimental Medicine and Biology* 133:149–158.

Grouse, S., Omenn, G. A., and McCarthy, B. J. (1973) Studies by DNA–RNA hybridization of transcriptional diversity in human brain. *Journal of Neurochemistry* 20:1063–1073.

Hayflick, L. (1977) The cellular basis for biological aging. Pp. 159–170 in C. E. Finch, and L. Hayflick, eds., *Handbook of the Biology of Aging*. New York: Van Nostrand Reinhold Co.

Hennessy, M. B., Heybach, J. P., Vernikos, J., and Levine, S. (1979) Plasma corticosterone concentrations sensitively reflect levels of stimulus intensity in the rat. *Physiology and Behavior* 22:821–825.

Hess, G. D., and Riegle, G. D. (1970) Adrenocortical responsiveness to stress and ACTH in aging rats. *Journal of Gerontology* 25:354–358.

Hess, G. D., and Riegle, G. D. (1972) Effects of chronic ACTH stimulation on adrenocortical function in young and aged rats. *American Journal of Physiology* 222:1458–1461.

Hollander, J., and Barrows, C. H. (1968) Enzymatic studies in senescent rodent brain. *Journal of Gerontology* 23:174–179.

Hunziker, O., Abdel'Al, S., Schulz, U., and Schweizer, A. (1978) Architecture of cerebral capillaries in aged human subjects with hypertension. Pp. 471–477 in J. Cervos-Navarro, E. Beta, G. Ebhardt, R. Ferezt, and R. Wullenweber, eds., *Advances in Neurology*, Vol. 20. New York: Raven Press.

Johnson, H. A., and Erner, S. (1972) Neuron survival in the aging mouse. *Experimental Gerontology* 7:111–117.

Johnson, R., Chrisp, C., and Strehler, B. (1972) Selective loss of ribosomal genes during the aging of postmitotic tissues. *Mechanisms of Ageing and Development* 1:183–198.

Klug, T. L., and Adelman, R. C. (1977) Evidence for a large thyrotropin and its accumulation during aging in rats. *Biochemical, Biophysical Research Communications* 77:1431–1437.

Landfield, P. W. (1979) An endocrine hypothesis of brain aging and studies on brain-endocrine correlations and monosynaptic neurophysiology during aging. *Advances in Experimental Medicine and Biology* 113:179–199.

Landfield, P. W., Lindsey, J. D., and Lynch, G. (1978a) Apparent acceleration of brain aging pathology by prolonged administration of glucocorticoids. *Society for Neuroscience Abstracts* 4:118.

Landfield, P. W., and Lynch, G. (1977) Impaired monosynaptic potentiation in *in vivo* hippocampal slices from aged, memory-deficient rats. *Journal of Gerontology* 32:523–533.

Landfield, P. W., McGaugh, J., and Lynch, G. (1978b) Impaired synaptic potentiation in the hippocampus of aged, memory-deficient rats. *Brain Research* 150:85–101.

Landfield, P. W., Rose, G., Landles, L., Wohlstadter, T. C., and Lynch, G. (1977) Patterns of astroglial hypertrophy and neuronal degeneration in the hippocampus of aged, memory-deficient rats. *Journal of Gerontology* 32:3–12.

Landfield, P. W., Waymire, J. C., and Lynch, G. (1978c) Hippocampal aging and adrenocorticoids: Quantitative correlations. *Science* 202:1098–1102.

Lee, K., Oliver, M., Schottler, F., Creager, R., and Lynch, G. (1979) Ultrastructural effects of repetitive synaptic stimulation in the hippocampal slice preparation: A preliminary report. *Experimental Neurology* 65:478–480.

Levine, S., Haltmeyer, G. C., Karas, G. G., and Denenberg, V. H. (1967) Physiological and behavioral effects of infantile stimulation. *Physiology and Behavior* 2:55–59.

Lewis, C. M., and Holliday, R. (1970) Mistranslation and aging in *Neurospora*. *Nature* 228:877–880.

Lewis, B. K., and Wexler, B. C. (1974) Serum insulin changes in male rats associated with age and reproductive activity. *Journal of Gerontology* 29:139–144.

Lindop, P. (1961) Growth rate, lifespan, and causes of death in SAS/4 mice. *Gerontologia* 5:193–208.

Lindsey, J., Landfield, P. W., and Lynch, G. (1979) Early onset and topographical distribution of hypertrophied astrocytes in hippocampus of aging rats: A quantitative study. *Journal of Gerontology* 66:661–671.

Lynch, G., and Gall, C. (1979) Organization and reorganization in the central nervous system: Evolving concepts of brain plasticity. Pp. 125–144 in F. Falkner and J. M. Tanner, eds., *Human Growth*, Vol. 3. New York: Plenum Press.

Lynch, G., Gall, C., and Dunwiddie, T. V. (1978) Neuroplasticity in the hippocampal formation. Pp. 113–128 in *Maturation of the Nervous System: Progress in Brain Research*, Vol. 48. Amsterdam: Elsevier.

Lynch, G., Rose, G., Gall, C., and Cotman, C. W. (1975) The response of the dentate gyrus to partial deafferentation. Pp. 305–317 in M. Santini, ed., *The Golgi Centennial Symposium Proceedings*. New York: Raven Press.

Mackay, I. R. (1972) Ageing and immunological function in man. *Gerontologia* 18:285–304.

Makinodan, T. (1977) Immunity and aging. Pp. 379–408 in C. E. Finch and L. Hayflick, eds., *Handbook of the Biology of Aging*. New York: Van Nostrand Reinhold Co.

Mann, D. N. A., and Yates, P. O. (1974) Lipoprotein pigments—their relation to ageing in the human nervous system. I. The lipofuscin content of nerve cells. *Brain* 97:481–488.

Masoro, E. (1972) Other physiologic changes with age. Pp. 137–155 in A. M. Ostfeld, and

D. C. Gibson, eds., *Epidemiology of Aging*. DHEW Publication No. (NIH) 75–711. Washington, D.C.: U.S. Department of Health, Education, and Welfare.

McEwen, B. S., deKloet, R., and Wallach, G. (1976) Interactions *in vivo* and *in vitro* of corticoids and progesterone with cell nuclei and soluble macromolecules from rat brain regions and pituitary. *Brain Research* 105:129–136.

McEwen, B. S., Gerlach, J. L., Luine, V. N., and Lieberburg, I. (1977) Neural steroid hormone receptors. *Psychoneuroendocrinology* 2:249–255.

McEwen, B. S., Gerlach, J. L., and Micco, D. J. (1975) Putative glucocorticoid receptors in hippocampus and other regions of the rat brain. Pp. 285–322 in R. L. Isaacson and K. H. Pribram, eds. *The Hippocampus*. New York: Plenum Press.

Medvedev, Zh. A. (1964) The nucleic acids in development and aging. Pp. 181–206 in B. L. Strehler, ed., *Advances in Gerontological Research*, Vol. 1. New York: Academic Press.

Moatamed, F. (1966) Cell frequencies in human inferior olivary complex. *Journal of Comparative Neurology* 128:109–116.

Monagle, R. D., and Brody, H. (1974) The effects of age upon the main nucleus of the inferior olive in the human. *Journal of Comparative Neurology* 155:61–66.

Nelson, J. F., Latham, K., and Finch, C. E. (1975) Plasma testosterone levels in C57BL/6J male mice: Effects of age and disease. *Acta Endocrinologica* 80:744–752.

O'Keefe, J., and Nadel, L. (1978) *The Hippocampus as a Cognitive Map*. New York: Clarendon.

Olendorf, W. H., and Kitano, M. (1965) Isotope study of brain blood turnover in vascular disease. *Archives of Neurology* 12:30–38.

Orgel, L. E. (1963) The maintenance of the accuracy of protein synthesis and its relevance to ageing. *Biochemistry* 49:517–521.

Perez, F. I., Mathew, N. T., Stump, D. A., and Meyer, J. S. (1977) Cerebral blood flow and psychological correlates in Alzheimer's disease and multi-infarct dementia. Pp. 35–39 in J. S. Meyer, H. Lechner, and M. Reivich, eds., *Cerebral Vascular Disease*. Amsterdam: Excerpta Medica.

Pfaff, D., and Keiner, M. (1973) Atlas of estradiol-concentrating cells in the central nervous system of the female rat. *Journal of Comparative Neurology* 151:121–158.

Phillips, S. M., and Wegman, T. G. (1973) Active suppression as a possible mechanism of tolerance in tetraparental mice. *Journal of Experimental Medicine* 137:291–300.

Pirke, K. M., and Doerr, P. (1973) Age-related changes and interrelationships between plasma testosterone, oestradiol, and testosterone-binding globulin in normal adult males. *Acta Endocrinologica* 74:792–800.

Rapport, M., and Karpiak, S. E. (1978) Immunological perturbation of neurological functions. Pp. 73–87 in K. Nandy, ed., *Senile Dementia: A Biomedical Approach*. New York: Elsevier North-Holland.

Ravens, J. R. (1978) Vascular changes in the human senile brain. Pp. 487–501 in J. Cervos-Navarro, E. Betz, G. Ebhardt, R. Ferszt, and R. Wullenweber, eds., *Advances in Neurology*, Vol. 20. New York: Raven Press.

Riccio, D. C., Rohrbaugh, M., and Hodges, L. A. (1968) Developmental aspects of passive and active avoidance learning in rats. *Developmental Psychobiology* 1:108–111.

Riegle, G. D., and Miller, A. E. (1978) Aging effects on the hypothalamic-hypophyseal-gonadal control system in the rat. Pp. 159–162 in E. L. Scheider, ed., *The Aging Reproductive System*. New York: Raven Press.

Rose, G., Lynch, G., and Cotman, C. W. (1976) Hypertrophy and redistribution of astrocytes in the deafferented dentate gyrus. *Brain Research Bulletin* 1:87–92.

Scheibel, M. E., Lindsay, R. D., Tomiyasu, U., and Scheibel, A. B. (1975) Progressive dendritic changes in aging human cortex. *Experimental Neurology* 47:392–403.

Scheibel, M. E., and Scheibel, A. B. (1975) Structural changes in the aging brain. Pp. 11–37 in H. Brody, D. Harmon, and J. M. Ordy, eds., *Aging I*. New York: Raven Press.

Selye, H., and Tuchweber, B. (1976) Stress in relation to aging and disease. Pp. 553–569 in A. F. Everitt and J. A. Burgess, eds., *Hypothalamus, Pituitary, and Aging*. Springfield: Charles C. Thomas Co.

Sinex, F. M. (1977) The molecular genetics of aging. Pp. 37–62 in C. E. Finch and L. Hayflick, eds., *Handbook of the Biology of Aging*. New York: Van Nostrand Reinhold Co.

Sotelo, C., and Palay, S. L. (1971) Altered axons and axon terminals in the lateral vestibular nucleus of the rat: Possible example of neuronal remodeling. *Laboratory Investigation* 25:653–673.

Szilard, L. (1959) On the nature of the aging process. *Proceedings of the National Academy of Sciences, U.S.A.* 45:30–45.

Talbert, G. B. (1977) Aging of the reproductive system. Pp. 318–356 in C. E. Finch and L. Hayflick, eds., *Handbook of the Biology of Aging*. New York: Van Nostrand Reinhold.

Tedeschi, B. W., and Uphouse, L. L. (1979) Footshock alters availability of rat brain chromatin for transcription. *Behavior Genetics* 9:481–482.

Thrash, C. R., Ho, T.-S., and Cunningham, D. D. (1974) Structural features of steroids which initiate proliferation of density-inhibited 3T3 mouse fibroblasts. *Journal of Biological Chemistry* 249:6099–6103.

Timiras, P. W. (1972) Degenerative changes in cells. Pp. 429–449 in P. S. Timiras, ed., *Developmental Physiology and Aging*. New York: Macmillan.

Tsai, C. C., and Yen, S. S. C. (1971) Acute effects of intravenous infusion of 17 beta-estradiol on gonadotrophin release in pre- and post-menopausal women. *Journal of Clinical Endocrinology and Metabolism* 32:766–771.

Vermeulen, A., Reubens, R., and Verdonck, L. (1972) Testosterone secretion and metabolism in males. *Journal of Clinical Endocrinology and Metabolism* 34:730–735.

Whalen, R. E., Edwards, D. A., Luttge, W. G., and Robertson, R. T. (1969) Early androgen treatment and male sexual behavior in female rats. *Physiology and Behavior* 4:33–40.

Zeman, W. (1971) The neuronal ceroid lipofuscinosis-Batten-Vogt syndrome: A model for human aging? Pp. 147–169 in B. L. Strehler, ed., *Advances in Gerontological Research*, Vol. 3. New York: Academic Press.

III

COGNITIVE AND
SOCIAL FUNCTIONING

chapter 10

Cognitive Functioning in the Elderly: Influence of Physical Health

JOANNE STEUER
LISSY F. JARVIK

When considering the influence of physical health on cognitive functioning in the elderly, one may simply assume that those who are in better health will show better cognitive performance than those who are ill. Indeed, one could expect this relationship to hold at any age. Someone suffering from an acute illness is unlikely to function optimally in the cognitive or other spheres. And in the elderly, in particular, we could expect cognitive functioning to be markedly depressed when we recall the frequency of acute confusional states associated with physical illness in the older age groups. These assumptions are based on common sense and clinical experience rather than scientific data. It is not surprising that all the data are not available, since it is questionable whether the benefits to be gained from subjecting acutely ill individuals of any age to formal psychological testing outweigh the additional discomfort that would have to be imposed on an already uncomfortable patient.

When we speak, then, of the influence of physical health on cognitive performance in the elderly, we are restricting ourselves to the chronic health impairments found commonly among the older population. Can we assume a priori that the individual with chronic arthritis, long-standing diabetes, cardiovascular disease, hypertension, bronchial asthma, or benign prostatic hypertrophy—to name but a few of the conditions seen

AGING
Biology and Behavior

frequently among the elderly—will show worse cognitive functioning than the matched individual without such physical illness? And what about the cognitive functioning of individuals with impairments in vision and hearing, which are, again, impairments frequently occurring among the elderly? There are some data indicating that such impairments may indeed result in impaired cognitive functioning. But adequate functioning is possible despite marked impairment of vision and hearing; recall the example of Helen Keller.

We also know that adequate cognitive functioning is possible in the face of numerous physical handicaps as well as some of the chronic health impairments mentioned above. Again, we cite just one of the best known examples, Franklin Delano Roosevelt. Although we may say that individuals like Helen Keller and Franklin Roosevelt might have shown better cognitive functioning were it not for their handicaps, their functioning must certainly be considered adequate by any of our definitions. Even though chronic health impairments or physical handicaps are frequent in all age groups, data indicating that chronic physical illness interferes markedly with cognitive and other areas of psychological development, not only for adults but even for children, are remarkable by their absence. Keeping an open mind, we may ask the question whether cognitive functioning appears to be appreciably diminished in the presence of chronic physical impairment and, if so, what aspects of cognition seem to be particularly sensitive to the influence of which particular impairment. Unfortunately, no specific answers are available from the literature published to date.

If we consider the entire area of cognition, we must remember that cognitive functioning has generally been subdivided into three aspects—learning, memory, and intelligence—which are clearly interrelated and overlapping, yet appear in the literature as if they were separate, independent entities. In addition, when it comes to the influence of physical illness or physical handicap, on cognitive function, the only aspect of cognitive functioning in which physical health has been included as a variable in a significant number of studies is that measured by various tests of intellectual functioning. Although there are enormous amounts of data on both learning and memory in the elderly (cf. Arenberg and Robertson-Tchabo 1977, Botwinick 1978, Craik 1977), these have rarely been related to physical health, so the major emphasis of this review concerns the influence of physical health on measures of intellectual functioning. Moreover, the focus is the influence of physical health on intellectual functioning in the "normal" elderly rather than in patients suffering from mental disorders in old age, variously described as senility, dementia, cerebral arteriosclerosis, organic brain syndrome, or some other appellation. Such patients show, in addition to the mental impairment, a high frequency of physical illness and high mortality. By contrast, the evidence accumulated to date indicates that when physical health is good in the normal older person, decline on psychometric tests appears to be limited to specific tasks, particularly speeded psychomotor tasks, at least until age 70 or 75. When performance beyond the eighth decade is compared with that during earlier decades, a general decline does become evident, but it remains unknown whether this decline reflects a biological clock, a life-style, physical tasks, or the interaction of some or all of these variables. Those studies distinguishing between the physically healthy and the physically ill elderly report a decline in intellectual functioning among the physically ill beyond that seen among the physically healthy.

In order to conceptualize the difficulties encountered in studying the association between intellectual functioning, age, and health, it is helpful to have some understanding of the research designs used to date and the variations in results to be expected from them.

RESEARCH DESIGNS

Cross-sectional and longitudinal designs most commonly utilized in development research have been supplemented during the past decade by the cross-sequential design. Cross-sectional investigations involve comparisons of different persons at different ages measured at the same time. These studies have been criticized (Baltes 1968, Schaie 1970) for confounding age differences (cohort effects) with age changes ("true" aging effects). Older people, for example, tend to be less educated and to have experienced cultural environments different from those of younger people. These cohort effects are compounded by the inclusion in cross-sectional samples of large numbers of old persons who are so close to death that they may be experiencing terminal decline. Cross-sectional designs are no longer considered acceptable when developmental change is the subject of investigation (Schaie 1977).

By contrast, longitudinal designs that follow the same individuals over time, thereby eliminating age differences, suffer from subject attrition, especially when dealing with the elderly, in whom death rates are high (Jarvik *et al.* 1973, Siegler and Botwinick 1979). Interpretation of data from longitudinal studies may also be made difficult by regression effects due to lack of reliability of the measuring instruments, and by subjects' reactions to repeated testings (Campbell and Stanley 1963).

Cross-sequential designs, which combine cross-sectional with longitudinal methods, were devised to disentangle age changes from age differences (Schaie 1970). In their simplest version, they carry a minimum of two samples from two different age groups over the same time period, each member of the sample being tested twice (Schaie 1977). In more elaborate versions, attempts are made to cover the major portions of the life-span. Even cross-sequential methods, however, have disadvantages, among them a tendency to produce results biased in favor of generational rather than age effects (Botwinick and Arenberg 1976, Adam 1977).

PATTERNS OF COGNITIVE FUNCTIONING

Does intellectual performance change as a function of age? According to early cross-sectional studies, global intelligence peaked at mid-adolescence and declined thereafter (cf. Jones 1959, Botwinick 1967). In later cross-sectional studies, the same decline has been noted, but the peak age has continued to rise. For example, when the Stanford-Binet was standardized in 1916, 16 was the age at which intelligence reached its zenith; by 1933, the peak had moved to age 20 (Jones and Conrad 1933); and by the 1950s, when the Wechsler Adult Intelligence Scale (WAIS) was standardized, the optimal age for intelligence had moved into the 25–29 year range (Wechsler 1958). As the WAIS-R is being standardized, it will be interesting to discover the age of peak intelligence for the 1970s.

Longitudinal studies show a somewhat different pattern of age changes. Global IQ rises until age 20 or 30 and, instead of declining, appears to stabilize, or even to increase, through the late fifties or sixties (Bailey 1955, Eisdorfer et al. 1959, Owens 1953, 1966, Terman and Oden 1947) until the seventies, when declines are generally expected (cf. Botwinick 1977, Jarvik et al. 1973). Age-related differential changes in verbal and psychomotor abilities (the former rising, the latter declining) appear to account for the stability of global IQ scores in longitudinal investigations.

Schaie and Labouvie-Vief (1974), in a cross-sequential analysis of data from Thurston's Primary Mental Abilities Test, found cross-sectional age differences to be greater than longitudinal age changes. However, as Botwinick (1977) points out, these results could have been predicted, since the longitudinal study spanned only 14 years, while the cross-sectional comparisons covered 40 years. In order to investigate whether cross-sectional sequences show greater or less decline than longitudinal sequences with persons of the same age, Botwinick (1977) reanalyzed

Schaie's data and found that through the mid-forties neither the cross-sectional nor the longitudinal analyses revealed age declines, while both exhibited declines between ages 67 and 81. The largest differences appeared in the age group 53 to 77, with the cross-sectional method showing greater decline than the longitudinal analysis.

It is now generally accepted that for intellectual functioning, the classic pattern of aging is stability or increase of verbal abilities until late in life with concomitant progressive decline on all tasks that require speed. This pattern occurs "regardless of age group . . ., irrespective of intelligence level . . ., and without reference either to socioeconomic status . . . or to residential setting [Jarvik 1973, p. 65]" and "constitutes one of the best-replicated results in the literature [Botwinick 1978]." It is perhaps most clearly formulated by Cattell's (1963) theory of "crystallized" and "fluid" intelligence, in which crystallized intelligence refers to abilities that are learned (related to education and experience), and fluid intelligence to abilities believed to be more closely related to biological processes. According to Horn (1978), one of Cattell's disciples, declines in speed on simple tasks are relatively independent of intellectual abilities.

If intelligence is not a unitary construct, then one would expect differential decline on the 11 Wechsler subtests. Indeed, this appears to be the case, with Verbal subtests (e.g., Information and Vocabulary) showing the smallest, and Performance subtests (e.g., Picture Arrangement and Digit Symbol Substitution) showing the greatest age differences (Botwinick 1967).

There is also the issue of sex differences in intellectual functioning during old age, and information on this topic is minimal. Wechsler (1958) did not find sex differences in IQ for persons aged 60 and older in the WAIS standardization sample, but, in the New York Psychiatric Study of Aging Twins, elderly women performed better than men on Digit Symbol Substitution and Block Design as well as on other tests of immediate recall of unfamiliar verbal and visual material and visual motor coordination. Men were superior to women only on the Digits Forward and Digits Backwards subtests of the Wechsler-Bellevue, tests on which Beard's (1968) male centenarians excelled. Eichorn (1973), reporting data from the Berkeley Growth Study, found women consistently superior to men on Digit Symbol Substitution and Vocabulary. Others have corroborated this trend for middle-aged and elderly samples on Digit Symbol Substitution but not on Vocabulary (Normann 1953, Dopplet and Wallace 1955). Bayley (1970), also reporting on the Berkeley Growth Study, found a leveling off of full-scale Wechsler-Bellevue scores for both sexes by age 36, but increases in Verbal IQ scores for men between ages 26 and

36, and a decrease in Performance IQ scores for women over the same time period.

Many investigations excluded women, and when both men and women were studied sex differences often were not reported. There are several possible interpretations of this omission: researchers may have assumed that men and women do not differ in intellectual abilities; perhaps the financial cost of adding another variable and, therefore, requiring a larger sample, was prohibitive; or the omission of women from these studies may be viewed in political terms as a disregard of female intellectual functioning. Whatever the reasons, when the purpose of research is to study the relationship between physical health and cognition, the omission appears to be an important one. Even if all other differences are ignored, we cannot ignore the fact that women tend to outlive men and that there appears to be an association between nearness to death and intellectual decline, an association that is discussed later in this chapter.

There has been a notable absence in this overview of health variables and their possible influence on intellectual functioning in old age; that is, none of the studies cited so far reported health data. Unfortunately, this dearth of information reflects the current data base in this area. There are few studies relating specific disease to mental functioning and even fewer using general health as an important variable in intellectual functioning in old age.

HEALTH STATUS AND COGNITIVE FUNCTIONING

Even though health status has generally not been considered in gerontological research on cognition, one of the early investigations did specifically examine the relationship between health and intellectual functioning in old age (Birren *et al.* 1963a). The sample consisted of 27 "optimally healthy" men (Group I) and 20 men with mild, asymptomatic disease (Group II). All subjects were community residents over age 65 (mean age 71; range, 65–91 years) who underwent intensive medical, psychological, psychiatric, and social investigation during the course of which 23 tests of psychological functioning (including the 11 WAIS subtests) were administered. Although the entire group of 47 men was superior in health to an unselected sample of men of the same age, the classic pattern of aging was apparent with verbal abilities higher than psychomotor abilities. Indeed, Verbal WAIS scores were nearly twice as high as Performance scores for both of these highly selected groups. Further, Group I scored higher than Group II on all but two tests (Digit Span from the WAIS and a mirror tracing task) and significantly higher

($p<.05$) on four WAIS subtests (Comprehension, Similarities, Block Design, and Picture Arrangement) as well as on WAIS Total IQ and Performance IQ. Differences between groups on Verbal IQ did not quite reach statistical significance (Botwinick and Birren 1963). When the association between chronological age and performance on psychological tests was examined, other differences were also observed, including significant correlations between age, a "stored information" factor, and verbal task performance for Group II but not for Group I.

The authors reasoned that the differences on the psychological tests reflected differences in health and examined the intercorrelations between physiological and psychological variables. They obtained eight statistically significant relationships, all but one for Group II only. For Group II, cerebral metabolic rate was related to a "general intellectual factor," while vital capacity, glucose consumption, and diastolic and systolic blood pressure were all related to a speed factor (lower levels of physiological functioning associated with psychomotor slowness). These findings suggested a "discontinuity hypothesis; i.e., that psychological functions are related to physiological variables when the latter lie in an abnormal range as in disease [Birren et al. 1963b, p. 289]," but not when they lie within the normal range.

From a second study relating health status to intellectual functioning, only preliminary results are available. In this ongoing investigation of performance on Piagetian problems in relation to health (assessed medically), age (40–59, 60–69), and education (LaRue et al., unpublished manuscript), both health and education but not age were significantly related to a composite problem-solving score. An interaction effect between those variables suggested that persons with fewer years of education and greater impairment of health tended to do worse on problem-solving tasks than did their healthier, better educated peers. Significant educational differences were found on the WAIS Similarities subtest and, although neither age nor health differences reached statistical significance ($P<.10$), the implied relationship seemed strong. The early results of this study demonstrate the importance of health in cognitive problem solving and suggest possible cumulative effects of health, education, and aging.

CARDIOVASCULAR DISEASE AND COGNITIVE FUNCTIONING

Patients with cardiovascular disease and hypertension are the ones who have been examined most frequently in the search for relationships between intellectual functioning and disease states. The function most often studied has been reaction time (i.e., speed), despite the debate as to whether speed is (Birren 1952, Botwinick and Storandt 1973) or is not (Lorge 1936, Green 1969) an important component of intellectual functioning. Spieth's (1964, 1965) studies of psychomotor speed are among the first in that literature and cover ages prior to senescence (23–59 years). Utilizing a serial reaction time task (the Trailmaking subtests of the Reitan battery) and two WAIS subtests (DSS and BD), Spieth contrasted the performance of healthy male pilots with that of men (pilots and community volunteers) who had mild-to-moderate symptoms of cardiovascular or cerebrovascular disease but were considered "normally" healthy and were leading normal lives. He found reaction time increased with age, as did the time required to complete the Trailmaking tests. Men with coronary heart disease or arteriosclerotic or cerebrovascular disease did not perform as well on the serial reaction time task or on the WAIS Digit Symbol Substitution or Block Design subtests as did the healthy subjects. Spieth thought that the slowing occurred in the decision phase of the response process and was related to central nervous system (CNS) malfunction, normal function possibly being restored by medication, since hypertensives whose blood pressure was controlled by medication performed almost as well as normotensives, while uncontrolled hypertensives performed tasks more slowly.

In an attempt to replicate Spieth's findings, Light (1975) compared 160 hypertensives (>140/90 mm Hg) with 43 normotensive controls on 12 serial reaction time tasks. Subjects, both male and female (age range 18–59), were tested 1–2 hours after administration of furosemide, a potent diuretic, apparently given to both hypertensives and normotensive controls. Results indicated reaction time increased with age, but there were no significant BP by age interactions. Light found, contrary to Spieth, that reaction time (RT) in medicated (but not unmedicated) hypertensives was significantly slower than in controls. Known duration of the hypertensive disorder was not significantly related to RT, but differences in RT between medicated and unmedicated groups was related to plasma renin levels. For medicated persons, low and normal levels were associated with slower RT, while for unmedicated persons high plasma renin levels were related to even slower RT than for the medicated groups with low or normal levels. Although the sample included men and women, no mention was made of sex differences. Light interpreted differences between her findings and those of Spieth as possibly due to the fact that the administration of the diuretic had reduced the blood pressures of hypertensives to nearly normal levels by the time they were tested in her study. The association with renin levels did not reappear in Light's (1978) own attempted replication of her RT findings, nor was it observed in another investigation of the effects of heightened blood pressure on

WAIS scores (Schultz *et al.* 1979). Schultz's group also failed to find significant differences between hypertensives (above 140/90 mm Hg) and normotensives, ranging in age from 45 to 65. Young hypertensives (21–39 years) however, whether previously medicated or not, scored lower than did controls on the Information, Comprehension, Similarities, and Vocabulary WAIS subtests as well as on Verbal IQ, but not on Performance IQ. When subjects were matched on Verbal IQ, additional differences appeared in favor of controls; the matched controls outperformed young and old hypertensives on Performance IQ and on the Digit Symbol Substitution, Block Design, Picture Arrangement, and Object Assembly subtests. Young hypertensives performed more poorly than either young or old controls, despite the fact that in the normotensive groups, the young performed significantly better than the old, and that diuretics had reduced blood pressure to nearly normal levels in both.

Questions these studies failed to ask are: Was hypertension more severe in persons previously medicated when compared with those who were not receiving medication? How well did medicated hypertensives actually comply with the treatment regime, and did men and women differ in their compliance rates? It is well known that patients frequently do not follow physicians' suggestions, and since impotence is an important side effect of antihypertensive medication, it is possible that men are less likely than women to follow the recommended treatment.

Wilkie and Eisdorfer (1974) studied the relationship between diastolic blood pressure and WAIS scores over a 10-year period. When change scores were computed for subjects initially ages 60 to 69, significant differences were obtained between normal (66–95 mm Hg), borderline (96–105 mm Hg), and high (105 mm Hg) blood pressure groups on WAIS Full Scale and Performance IQ. Over the 10-year period, hypertensives showed the greatest losses, while performance scores actually increased for the borderline group. According to the authors, these data support the thesis first proposed by Birren *et al.* (1963a) that slightly increased blood pressure may act to maintain adequate cerebral functioning in the presence of arteriosclerotic disease. There were no significant changes in verbal scores for any of the groups. For subjects initially aged 70 to 79, results were somewhat different. No person in the high blood pressure group completed the 10-year follow-up, and while change scores on verbal tests were not significantly different for the borderline hypertensives and normal groups, both groups showed significant decreases in Performance IQs. When data were pooled across blood pressure groups, higher blood pressure was found to be related to losses only on Verbal IQ for those individuals initially aged 70 to 79, but to losses on all scales (Verbal, Performance, and Full-Scale) for persons initially aged 60 to 69.

Wilkie *et al.* (1976) also failed to find differences in performance on the Wechsler Memory Scale between high, borderline, and low diastolic blood pressure groups when subjects were aged 60 to 69. Blood pressure groups did not differ significantly in age or socioeconomic status. At a follow-up 6.5 years later, the high blood pressure group performed significantly worse on a visual reproduction task than did persons in the two other groups. Although the high blood pressure group also tended to have lower verbal memory scores and scores for the normal and borderline groups increased on verbal tasks, group differences were not statistically significant. As the hypertensives' poor performance on visual reproduction was found only on specific subtask items and did not appear to be influenced by item difficulty, results were interpreted as suggesting that poorer task performance of hypertensives was not due to memory, but perhaps to performance factors such as test instructions, strategies for learning, or reactions to stress (e.g., test anxiety). Since blood pressure groups did not differ at Time 1 but only at Time 2, the authors also suggest that perhaps prolonged duration of hypertension increased CNS involvement (unfortunately, duration was not reported). This contention, while not supported by Light's (1975) study of young and middle-aged adults, may hold true for the old but not for the young. It is possible the elderly are more vulnerable to deteriorating effects of disease than are younger persons.

In the only study located in the literature of a female sample (age 40–93), Jalavisto (1964) found increased diastolic blood pressure and decreased vital capacity to be associated with longer reaction times and slower "tapping" rates. Diastolic pressure was also inversely related to memory and abstracting ability. Although Jalavisto's report was not very detailed, the results tend in general to support findings from male samples; they do not, however, elucidate interactions between age and blood pressure.

Although their sample was not screened for health status, Botwinick and Storandt (1974) found slow simple auditory reaction time to be associated with self-rated cardiovascular symptoms for young (age range 20–28) and old (age range 64–74) men and women, but when the older group was blocked on education level, there was no longer a main effect for cardiovascular symptoms.

Other data indicative of a relationship between diastolic hypertension and cognitive dysfunction come from a study of middle-aged men (mean age 47.6) by Goldman *et al.* (1974) in which hypertension was defined as a blood pressure of at least 140/95 mm Hg on three occasions. Using the Category subtest of the Halstead-Reitan battery, Goldman's group found a significant association between errors on the Category test and diastolic but not systolic pressure, even when effects of age and IQ were statistically controlled.

By contrast, preliminary analyses indicated a significant relationship between increased systolic (mean 137.6 mm Hg) but not diastolic (mean 77.8 mm Hg) pressure, and decreased scores on the Raven Progressive Matrices, WAIS Similarities, and Piagetian task performance in persons aged 40 to 79 (La Rue, personal communication, 11/1979). The difference between La Rue's and Goldman's findings may be due to the fact that blood pressures were much lower in the former study.

Not only blood pressure but also heart disease has been examined in terms of its effects on intellectual functioning. Thus, Herzog *et al.* (1978), using a cross-sequential design, reported that cardiovascular disease had a negative influence on cognitive functioning independent of age. Wang and Busse (1974), using subjects from the Duke longitudinal investigation, reported that persons with decompensated heart disease were more likely to show brain dysfunction on a neurological examination than were those without heart disease, those with "possible" heart disease, or those with compensated heart disease. Persons with either compensated or decompensated heart disease had significantly lower WAIS Verbal and Performance scores and higher blood pressure readings than persons without heart disease. These data suggest, according to the authors, that brain failure is related to heart failure, possibly through reduction of cerebral blood flow rather than to heart disease *per se*, and increased blood pressure may account for the lack of impairment of the compensated heart disease group on the neurological examination, although it does not account for the lower WAIS scores found in this group.

Another hypothesis, based on the influence of life-style or perceived environmental stress, has been generated from the effects of coronary-prone behavior (Type A) on psychomotor performance of healthy, normotensive males ranging in age from 25 to 29 (Abrahams and Birren 1973). Since Type A men were significantly slower on simple and choice reaction time tasks than were noncoronary-prone (Type B) men, Abrahams and Birren suggested that in coronary-prone persons some portion of the CNS mimics the aging process, possibly through more rapid wear and tear of the CNS due to increased blood pressure, serum lipid concentrations, and catecholamines. All of these physiological variables are known to increase with perceived environmental stress. Abrahams and Birren also found that response latency increased during the third and fourth decade and decreased during the fifth decade, leading the authors to suggest that the decrease may represent the results of selection by health status. Type A behavior is a much more potent predictor of coronary heart disease in the age range 35 to 49 than in age groups older than 50, so that Type A persons in the fifth decade are heavily weighted by those persons who did not develop heart disease before age 40. The increased response latencies in the earlier decades may thus be taken to support the contention that "changes in speed are early manifestations of underlying physiological changes or *disease states* that remain unmeasured [Birren *et al.* 1963b, p. 293]."

The implication that life-style can serve as either a mediating or attenuating factor in the observed cognitive losses associated with cardiovascular disease is also in agreement with the finding of the early NIMH study that those men who had lost environmental supports tended to show decreased cognitive and psychomotor functioning. These declines, not associated with measures of cerebral physiology, may have reflected an interaction between the losses and affective state, e.g., depression (Birren *et al.* 1963b). Data from the Duke group (Busse and Wang 1974) and from the Andrus Gerontology Center (reported in Herzog *et al.* 1978) also support an association between life-style, cardiovascular disease, and cognitive loss. According to the latter group, elderly women with limited activities and few social contacts had a higher frequency of cardiovascular disease and more intellectual deficits than did women with other life-styles.

COGNITIVE FUNCTIONING AND SURVIVORSHIP

The relationship between mortality and prior decline in scores on certain psychometric tests has given rise to the hypothesis of terminal decline or terminal drop (e.g., Jarvik *et al.* 1962a, 1962b, Savage *et al.* 1973, Siegler 1975). This hypothesis views decreases in cognitive functioning in terms of distance from death rather than age *per se* and helps to explain discrepancies in results between cross-sectional and longitudinal studies. It is attractive because its corollary is that intellectual ability remains stable into old age, until a new phase, heralding impending death, is entered. Since the hypothesis assumes that whatever causes death also causes intellectual decline, it should stimulate interest in the relationship between disease and intellectual functioning.

One of the earliest investigations addressing the hypothesis of terminal decline was the New York State Psychiatric Institute Study of Aging Twins. The study, begun in 1946 by Franz Kallmann and Gerhard Sander, consisted of a sample of more than 1900 twins over age 60 living in or near New York State. A subgroup of 268 was selected for psychological examination (Kallmann and Sander 1949, Feingold 1950) and followed to date (for summary of findings, see Bank and Jarvik 1978). The subjects were originally tested in 1947–1949, and varying numbers of them were tested again in 1955, 1957, 1967, and 1973 (Blum and Jarvik 1974). The psychological tests used consistently during the 25-year study were: five subtests of the Wechsler-Bellevue (Wechsler 1944)—Similarities, Digits Forward and Backwards, Digit Symbol Substitution and Block Design; the Vocabulary test from the Stanford-Binet (Terman 1916); and a tapping test to evaluate eye–hand coordination. Other tests were used on only one or two occasions.

By 1955, 100 persons had died and 168 were still living. Survivors had originally scored higher than decedents on each of the subtests, suggesting an association between mortality and cognitive performance (Jarvik *et al.* 1962a, 1962b). Examination of the data indicate that three subtests, Vocabulary, Similarities, and Digit Symbol Substitution might potentially discriminate survivors from nonsurvivors, since the former were significantly more likely to have remained stable or improved on vocabulary scores and to have lower annual rates of decline (ARD) on Similarities and Digit Symbol Substitution (Jarvik 1962). The formula used in computing the ARD is:

$$\frac{T_H - T_L}{T_H \times Y} \times 100$$

with T_H representing the highest score from the first two testings; T_L the score on the last testing; and Y the number of years intervening between the highest score and the last testing. Results were multiplied by 100 to convert the ARD into a percentage. An empirical relationship was found between 5-year mortality and an ARD of at least 10% on Similarities, 2% on Digit Symbol Substitution, and any decline on Vocabulary. If at least two of these three declines occurred, they were termed "critical loss."

These criteria were applied to the scores of the 34 persons who had completed three testings by 1955, and who either were still alive 5 years after the last test session or who had died. The remaining subjects had been tested so recently that 5 years had not elapsed at the time of the data analysis ($N = 28$), or scores from all three critical loss tests were not available for calculating the critical loss ratio ($N = 16$). Of the 11 deceased twins, 7 showed a critical loss, while only 1 of the 23 survivors showed such a loss, a statistically significant difference between groups (Jarvik and Falek 1963). When the remaining 28 persons could be classified by the 5-year survivorship criterion, results were essentially the same, with 11 of the 16 deceased, and only 4 of the 46 surviving twins showing critical loss (Blum *et al.* 1973).

These data offered a unique opportunity to submit the critical loss hypothesis to a perhaps more rigorous and impressive test by affording comparisons of twin partners in the 26 intact twin pairs (Jarvik and Blum 1971). In 16 pairs, both twins were 5-year survivors, in 9 pairs 1 twin had died, and in 1 pair both twins had died within the 5-year period. Monozygotic twins showed somewhat greater concordance (13 of 21 pairs) for critical loss (actually, lack of critical loss) than did dizygotic twins (2 of 5 pairs), but the small number of dizygotic pairs makes this comparison unreliable. In all of the 11 twin pairs discordant for critical loss, it was the twin who showed the critical loss who died first.

In 1973, 22 of the surviving twins (age range 83 to 99) were retested once more and in 1978 it became possible to examine again the relationship between 5-year survivorship and cognitive loss (Steuer *et al.* 1981). By 1978, only 10 of the 22 twins retested 5 years earlier were still alive. When critical loss ratios were calculated for the period 1967 to 1973, three of seven survivors and two of eight decedents showed critical loss (data were not available on one or more of the critical loss tests for three survivors and four decedents). Clearly, in this very old small group critical loss no longer distinguished those who would survive for at least another 5 years (to a mean age of 93.5) from those who would not (mean age at death 91.3). It may well be that for persons in the ninth decade and beyond, new criteria have to be developed, as criteria valid at younger ages no longer hold. This is demonstrated by another finding from the New York State Psychiatric Institute Study of Aging Twins, in which both self-ratings and physician's ratings of health were related to 5-year survival in the "younger" subjects (aged 77 to 84) but neither rating was related to survival in the age group older than 85 (La Rue *et al.* 1979).

In the old-old, dementia appears to predict survival and that applies to all previous studies with a single exception. The exception is the report from the Duke study by Gianturco and Busse (1978), indicating no difference in survival between those diagnosed as with or without OBS. In the New York State Psychiatric Institute twin study, psychiatric evaluations were available for 19 of the 22 twins seen in 1973; only 1 of the 9 survivors, but 5 of the 10 decedents, had been diagnosed as having dementia in 1967 (Jarvik *et al.* 1980). All 4 decedents who were unclassifiable in terms of critical loss had dementia, while none of the 3 unclassified survivors had been so diagnosed. When scores from all previous psychological testings were inspected for the 6 demented persons, only 2 had shown critical loss: at an earlier time and, of these, 1 was alive and the other dead in 1978.

It is of interest that critical loss at an earlier age (between the average ages of 65 and 75) still holds up as a predictor, since none of the seven 1978 survivors on whom adequate data are available showed critical loss at that time. Clearly, what needs to be done is to examine retrospectively the relationship between critical loss and critical age. Remembering Riegel's (1971) observation that in his sample the relationship between longevity and decline in test scores was greater for persons below age 65 than for those above that age, we may postulate a gradual decline in the predictive power of critical loss with advancing age until that power is lost entirely, perhaps somewhere in the ninth decade.

Clearly also, the data need to be examined in terms of sex differences, an analysis that was precluded by the small number of survivors in the study discussed above.

Siegler (1975), reviewing all of the longitudinal studies with data useful for the terminal drop hypothesis, concluded that there was a confusing aspect to these studies, in that speeded tests were age-related (Tapping and Block Design) while Digit Symbol Substitution (also a speeded test) was a critical loss subtest. In support, she cites analyses from the Duke data showing Digit Symbol Substitution strongly correlated with reaction time. However, factor analysis of the New York State Psychiatric Institute data showed high loadings on one factor (VI) for both Digit Symbol Substitution and Similarities, while another factor, which was apparently a speed factor, had relatively low Digit Symbol loading (Jarvik *et al.* 1962b). Botwinick and Storandt (1973), too, found a high correlation between Digit Symbol Substitution and Vocabulary.

CONCLUSIONS

In our review we have listed most, if not all, of the pieces of evidence that can be garnered from the literature, but we have been unable to glean from them even the general outline of the puzzle posed by the relationship between cognitive functioning and health status. Disappointingly, we can answer none of the questions we raised at the beginning of this chapter.

We can conclude that health impairments, even if so mild as to be asymptomatic, may be associated with impaired cognitive functioning in the elderly—not only in the elderly, but also in adults younger than

60. However, we have no clue as to the frequency of this association, its parameters, or its consequences, and we are not in a much better position when it comes to describing specific cognitive impairments. The only oft-repeated finding is a slower reaction time or decreased speed in performing various tasks, and even that has not been entirely consistent. Finally, when we try to distinguish individuals who will show cognitive impairment in the presence of impaired health, or even without noticeable health impairment, from those who will not, our leads are perhaps the most meager.

If, for example, we take the proposed association between limited activities, limited social contacts, cardiovascular disease, and intellectual deficits (cf. Herzog *et al.* 1978), we can ask: "Could we reduce the frequency of cardiovascular disease and/or intellectual deficits by increasing activity or social contacts?" Popular answers to this question are available as reflected in social centers for seniors and exercise for all. There are also some data-based leads. For example, in our longitudinal study of aging twins, successful aging was positively related to both physical and mental activities throughout the life-span and even resumption of activities in old age when activity had been low since early adulthood, appeared to be beneficial. Furthermore, according to the correlational data of Berkman and Syme (1979), people without social and community ties were more likely to die within the 9-year period of their study than were persons with extensive contacts. This association was found to be independent of a variety of health-related items, including self-reported physical health status. Perhaps it is not only the number but the quality of social contacts that are involved in these associations between social contacts, cardiovascular disease, and death. Thus, Lowenthal and her group (Lowenthal and Haven 1968, Lowenthal *et al.* 1975) suggest that an intimate relationship may act as a mediator of an individual's perception of stress, and that persons with complex social networks are more likely to have such a relationship than those with less complex social ties. It may be that the more numerous the social contacts, the greater the likelihood of having a confidant; the presence of a confidant, in turn, may reduce the perceived stress with a concomitant decrease in the probability of developing cardiovascular disease.

We then ask the following question: "Were we to identify two groups of individuals in good health at age 40, 50, or 60 years, matched for all relevant variables other than frequency and quality of social contacts, would we find a significant difference between them—in terms of either cardiovascular disease or intellectual deficits—some 5, 10, or 20 years later?"

Today, we cannot answer that question. It is as likely that the frequency and quality of social contact reflect psychophysiological parameters important in the development of cardiovascular disease and/or cognitive deficits, as it is that the frequency and quality of social contacts themselves play that role. At the moment, at least, we cannot distinguish between those two possibilities, and if we do not want to wait decades for an answer and want to intervene now, in terms of possible preventive measures, at least we should set up four groups equally matched, as described above, for variables other than frequency and quality of social contacts. Then, we could use one of each pair for purposes of control and the other for purposes of intervention. But even that type of experiment, were it feasible, would have to be considered simplistic, since the amount of social stimulation optimal for different individuals may vary widely.

In general, then, the data on the influence of health on cognitive functioning in the elderly are so inadequate that they are insufficient for the deductive hypotheses with the exception of the data on cognitive decline and mortality. And here we may make the following hypotheses:

1. All cognitive decline with age is a function of illness, as opposed to normal aging. The illness may be primary (i.e., located within the brain), or it may be secondary (i.e., physical illness outside the brain) or there may be psychosocial factors that translate into physical illness and eventually affect brain function.

2. Even though cognitive changes with advancing age may be due to illness, there will be cognitive changes as a function of advancing chronological age, even without illness. Thus, we may postulate that wear and tear, error, a biological clock, or some other biological process, such as cellular deprivation, accumulation of deleterious substances, formation of free radicals, or cross-linkage of molecules, result in structural and/or functional changes within the brain that lead to cognitive decline. Then, again, we may localize the age-related changes generally, rather than within the brain (e.g., somatic mutations, DNA, chromosome loss, autoimmunity) changes which secondarily affect the brain.

In assessing the influence of physical illness on cognitive functioning in the elderly, we have observed again and again that the major effect appears to be on psychomotor performance, particularly speeded psychomotor performance (including reaction time). Even though other cognitive functions appear to suffer as well, in the case of both "normal" aging and the organic brain syndromes (primarily Alzheimer type senile dementia and multi-infarct changes dementia), changes in speed and in psychomotor performance are the most prominent. Indeed, we might construct a scale of severity in terms of changes affecting reaction time and psychomotor performance, placing at one end of the scale normal aging, and moving through aging influenced by physical illness to the organic brain syndromes. Our first speculative conclusion is, therefore, that the brain responds in a similar fashion to different age-associated insults.

The meager evidence collected to date allows us to formulate another hypothesis: Barring specific localized brain damage, the brain may be seen as a monitor of the organism's general functioning so that, regardless of the cause of impaired general functioning, similar impairment in cognition will result. We may postulate further that speed of psychomotor reaction is one of the first signs of bodily impairment and that higher cognitive functions are affected later. It would be tempting to speculate further that the highest cognitive functions, corresponding to neocortical functions, are affected first, in line with Fuster's view, "last in, first out" (personal communication, November, 1979), but the evidence is inadequate at this time to substantiate this view. It is equally, if not more likely, that the limbic system may be highly sensitive to age as well as to disease-borne dysfunction, since disturbances of memory seem to be common in both normal and pathological aging. On the other hand, we may speculate that the limbic system is particularly sensitive to age-associated changes—as distinguished from disease associated changes—recalling only that with the approach of the sixth decade, if not earlier, anomia becomes a common phenomenon. First to be affected is the readiness to remember names of less familiar associates, for example, the new stars of stage, screen, or the literary scene. Then comes difficulty in recalling the names of acquaintances not seen for prolonged periods of time or classmates suddenly encountered after an absence of decades. The sensitivity of the memory system may be due either to anatomical, structural, or histochemical changes in the specific brain regions, to biochemical neurophysiological changes in these same regions, or to less redundancy in that system compared with the neocortical system. It is possible also that equally pronounced deficits occur in the neocortical system, but these are more difficult to detect because of the ability of other cortical regions to compensate for any specific deficits, somewhat in line with Lashley's Law of Mass Action. Clearly, these areas warrant further examination.

In general, then, we postulate that cognitive functioning may be regarded as a sensitive indicator system of the human organism's total functioning. Barring localized brain lesions, cognitive dysfunction is taken to reflect not a specific etiology, but rather one or more etiologically distinct disturbances of the human organisms, such as: metabolic, toxic, or neurochemical dysfunctions; decreased blood flow; or general changes induced by physical inactivity, drugs, social isolation, feelings of helplessness and hopelessness, lack of intellectual stimulation, excessive intellectual or social stimulation as well as a variety of systemic diseases.

As a corollary of this postulate, we believe that it will not be productive to look for specific relationships between etiological factors and types of cognitive impairment in the same way that it has not been profitable to look for specific relationships between etiology of mental retardation and type of intellectual dysfunction. On the other hand, patterns of intellectual functioning may give us clues so that disturbances in normal patterns may provide the earliest signs of underlying physiological dysfunction and be most helpful, therefore, in early detection and preventive intervention. We must keep in mind also that, in all likelihood, "normal" patterns of cognitive functioning will be varied, and that different individuals will display differences in these patterns so that a variety of patterns, each suited to the given individual, will have to be considered. Life-span-oriented longitudinal studies seem an obvious first approach to the problem.

Another observation that has emerged from a review of the data is that, given apparently similar physical infirmities, some people respond as previously described, but others do not. Thus, we know that senile dementia is not the inevitable accompaniment of even far advanced old age. According to current guesstimates, at most 25 % of the individuals over age 80 suffer from chronic organic brain syndromes. And we have all observed individuals suffering from far advanced cardiovascular disease whose intellectual functioning is seemingly impervious to the physical insult. But, then, individual variability characterizes the human species, as it does any other, and these days perhaps even more so, as the constraints of natural selection are being loosened by scientific and technological advances. Another conclusion, therefore, is that even though impaired physical health will have predictive value for impaired cognitive functioning in elderly groups, like age itself, it will not necessarily predict intellectual functioning in any given individual.

A final observation is that, in general, physical illness appears to have a very limited influence on intellectual functioning, considering the many areas of cognition that appear to remain unaffected when we compare the physically healthy with the physically ill. The brain exhibits remarkable adaptability; it has the skull protecting it from physical trauma and is likely to have protective mechanisms against other traumata (e.g., the physiological). Our final speculative conclusion, therefore, is that as long as the brain receives adequate stimuli to function, it will adapt to numerous insults and will respond to stimuli as challenges for intellectual activity. There is evidence to suggest that in response to challenges that are too great, or perceived to be too great, the organism tends to become overwhelmed and to function inadequately or not at all. Without challenge, the human organism vegetates. We need but recall the experiments on sensory deprivation and the many tales the literature tells of self-stimulation used by prisoners as a means to maintain their sanity. We speculate, therefore, that for the maintenance of optimal intellectual functioning with advancing age, a constant variety of new stimuli is required. Following the Aristotelian golden mean, however, the challenges presented by these stimuli should neither be too great nor too small. Indeed, if we consider intellectual functioning a vital ingredient of human life, we might conclude that for the maintenance of cognitive abilities into old age, variety is not only the spice of life, but its very essence.

REFERENCES

Abrahams, J. P., and Birren, J. E. (1973) Reaction time as a function of age and behavioral predisposition to coronary heart disease. *Journal of Gerontology* 28(4):471–478.

Adam, J. (1977) Statistical bias in cross-sequential studies of aging. *Experimental Aging Research* 3(4):325–333.

Arenberg, D., and Robertson-Tchabo, E. A. (1977) Learning and aging. Pp. 421–449 in J. E. Birren and K. W. Schaie, eds., *Handbook of the Psychology of Aging*. New York: Van Nostrand Reinhold.

Baltes, P. B. (1968) Longitudinal and cross-sectional sequences in the study of age and generation effects. *Human Development* 11:145–171.

Bank, L. I., and Jarvik, L. F. (1978) A longitudinal study of aging human twins. Pp. 303–333 in E. L. Schneider, ed., *The Genetics of Aging*. New York: Plenum Press.

Bayley, N. (1955) On the growth of intelligence. *American Psychologist* 10:805–818.

Bayley, N. (1970) Development of mental abilities. Pp. 1163–1209 in P. H. Mussen, ed., *Carmichael's Manual of Child Psychology*. New York: Wiley.

Beard, D. B. (1968) Some characteristics of recent memory of centenarians. *Journal of Gerontology* 23:23–30.

Berkman, L. F. and Syme, S. L. (1979) Social networks, host resistance, and morality: A nine-year followup study of Alameda County residents. *American Journal of Epidemiology* 109:186–203.

Birren, J. E. (1952) A factorial analysis of the Wechsler-Bellevue Scale given to an elderly population. *Journal of Consulting Psychology* 16:399–405.

Birren, J. E., Butler, R. N., Greenhouse, S. W., Sokoloff, L., and Yarrow, M., eds. (1963a) *Human Aging: A Biological and Behavioral Study*. Washington, D.C.: U.S. Government Printing Office.

Birren, J. E., Butler, R. N., Greenhouse, S. W., Sokoloff, L., and Yarrow, M. R. (1963b) Interdisciplinary relationships: Interrelations of physiological, psychological, and psychiatric findings in healthy elderly men. Pp. 283–308 in J. E. Birren, R. N. Butler,

S. W. Greenhouse, L. Sokoloff, and M. R. Yarrow, eds., *Human Aging: A Biological and Behavioral Study.* Washington, D.C.: U.S. Government Printing Office.

Blum, J., Clark, E. T., and Jarvik, L. F. (1973) The New York State Psychiatric Institute study of aging twins. Pp. 13–19 in L. F. Jarvik, C. Eisdorfer, and J. Blum, eds., *Intellectual Functioning in Adults.* New York: Springer Publishing Co.

Blum, J. E., and Jarvik, L. F. (1974) Intellectual performance of octogenarians as a function of education and initial ability. *Human Development* 17:364–375.

Botwinick, J. (1967) *Cognitive Processes in Maturity and Old Age.* New York: Springer.

Botwinick, J. (1978) *Aging and Behavior,* 2nd ed. New York: Springer.

Botwinick, J. (1977) Intellectual abilities. Pp. 580–605 in J. E. Birren and K. W. Schaie, eds., *Handbook of the Psychology of Aging.* New York: Van Nostrand Reinhold Co.

Botwinick, J., and Arenberg, D. (1976) Disparate time spans in sequential studies of aging. *Experimental Aging Research* 1(1):55–61.

Botwinick, J., and Birren, J. E. (1963) Cognitive processes: Mental abilities and psychomotor responses in healthy aged men. Pp. 86–100 in J. E. Birren, R. N. Butler, S. W. Greenhouse, L. Sokoloff, and M. R. Yarrow, eds., *Human Aging: A Biological and Behavioral Study.* Washington, D.C.: U.S. Government Printing Office.

Botwinick, J., and Storandt, M. (1973) Speed functions, vocabulary ability, and age. *Perceptual Motor Skills* 36:1123–1128.

Botwinick, J., and Storandt, M. (1974) Cardiovascular status, depressive affect and other factors in reaction time. *Journal of Gerontology* 29(5):543–548.

Busse, E. W., and Wang, H. S. (1974) The multiple factors contributing to dementia in old age. Pp. 151–159 in E. Palmore, ed., *Normal Aging II.* Durham, N.C.: Duke University Press.

Campbell, D. T., and Stanley, J. C. (1963) *Experimental and Quasi-Experimental Designs for Research.* Chicago: Rand McNally College Publishing Co.

Cattell, R. B. (1963) Theory of fluid and crystallized intelligence: A critical experiment. *Journal of Educational Psychology* 54:1–22.

Craik, F. I. M. (1977) Age differences in human memory. Pp. 384–420 in J. E. Birren and K. W. Schaie, eds., *Handbook of the Psychology of Aging.* New York: Van Nostrand Reinhold.

Doppelt, J. E., and Wallace, W. L. (1955) Standardization of the Wechsler Adult Intelligence Scale for older persons. *Journal of Abnormal and Social Psychology* 51:312–330.

Eichorn, D. H. (1973) The Institute of Human Development Studies, Berkeley and Oakland. Pp. 1–6 in L. F. Jarvik, C. Eisdorfer, and J. E. Blum, eds., *Intellectual Functioning in Adults: Psychological and Biological Influences.* New York: Springer.

Eisdorfer, C., Busse, E. W., and Cohen, L. D. (1959) The WAIS performance of an aged sample: The relationship between verbal and performance IQs. *Journal of Gerontology* 14:197–201.

Feingold, L. (1950) A psychometric study of senescent twins. Ph.D. dissertation. Columbia University, New York.

Green, R. F. (1969) Age–intelligence relationship between ages sixteen and sixty-four: A rising trend. *Developmental Psychology* 1:618–627.

Gianturco, D. T., and Busse, E. W. (1978) Psychiatric problems encountered during a long-term study of normal ageing volunteers. Pp. 1–16 in A. D. Isaacs and F. Post, eds., *Studies in Geriatric Psychiatry.* New York: John Wiley and Sons.

Goldman, H., Kleinman, K. M., Snow, M. Y., Tidus, D. R., and Koral, B. (1974) Correlation of diastolic blood pressure and signs of cognitive dysfunction in essential hypertension. *Diseases of the Nervous System* 35:571–572.

Herzog, C., Schaie, K. W., and Gribbin, K. (1978) Cardiovascular disease and changes in intellectual functioning from middle to old age. *Journal of Gerontology* 33(6):872–883.

Horn, J. (1978) Human ability systems. Pp. 212–251 in P. B. Baltes, ed., *Life Span Development and Behavior*. New York: Academic Press.

Jalavisto, E. (1964/65) On the interdependence of circulatory–respiratory and neural–mental variables. *Gerontologia* 10:31–37.

Jarvik, L. F. (1973) Discussion: Patterns of intellectual functioning in the later years. Pp. 65–67 in L. F. Jarvik, C. Eisdorfer, and J. Blum, eds., *Intellectual Functioning in Adults*. New York: Springer Publishing Co., Inc.

Jarvik, L. F. (1962) Biological differences in intellectual functioning *Vita Humana* 5:195–203.

Jarvik, L. F., and Blum, J. E. (1971) Cognitive declines as predictors of mortality in twin pairs. A twenty-year longitudinal study of aging. Pp. 199–211 in E. Palmore and F. C. Jeffers, eds., *Prediction of Life Span*. Lexington, Ky.: D. C. Heath and Co.

Jarvik, L. F., and Falek, A. (1963) Intellectual stability and survival in the aged. *Journal of Gerontology* 18:173–176.

Jarvik, L. F., Eisdorfer, C., and Blum, J. E. (1973) *Intellectual Functioning in Adults: Psychological and Biological Influences*. New York: Springer.

Jarvik, L. F., Kallmann, F. J., and Falek, A. (1962a) Intellectual changes in aged twins. *Journal of Gerontology* 17:289–294.

Jarvik, L. F., Kallmann, F. J., Lorge, I., and Falek, A. (1962b) Longitudinal study of intellectual changes in senescent twins. Pp. 839–857 in C. Tibbits and W. Donahue, eds., *Social and Psychological Aspects of Aging*. New York: Columbia University Press.

Jarvik, L. F., Ruth, V., and Matsuyama, S. S. (1980) Organic brain syndrome and aging: A six-year follow-up of surviving twins. *Archives of General Psychiatry* 37:280–286.

Jones, H. E. (1959) Intelligence and problem solving. Pp. 700–738 in J. E. Birren, ed., *Handbook of Aging and the Individual*. Chicago: University of Chicago Press.

Jones, H. E., and Conrad, H. S. (1933) The growth and decline of intelligence: A study of a homogenous group between the ages of ten and sixty. *Genetic Psychology Monographs* 13:223–294.

Kallmann, F. J., and Sander, G. (1949) Twin studies on senescence. *American Journal of Psychiatry* 106:29–36.

La Rue, A., Steuer, J., and Waltuch, A. (1981) Problem solving in middle aged and older adults. Unpublished manuscript. Department of Psychiatry, University of California, Los Angeles.

La Rue, A., Bank, L., Jarvik, L. F., and Hetland, M. (1979) Health in old age: How do physician's ratings and self-ratings compare? *Journal of Gerontology* 34:687–691.

Light, K. C. (1975) Slowing of response time in middle-aged hypertensive patients. *Experimental Aging Research* 1(2):209–227.

Light, K. C. (1978) Effects of mild cardiovascular and cerebrovascular disorders on serial reaction time performance. *Experimental Aging Research* 4(1):3–22.

Lorge, I. (1936) The influence of the test upon the nature of mental decline as a function of age. *Journal of Educational Psychology* 27:100–110.

Lowenthal, M. F. and Haven, C. (1968) Interaction and adaptation: Intimacy as a critical variable. *American Sociological Review*, 33:20–30.

Lowenthal, M. F., Thurnher, M., and Chiriboga, D. (1975) *Four Stages of Life*. San Francisco: Jossey-Bass Inc.

Norman, R. D. (1953) Sex differences and other aspects of young, superior adult performance on the Wechsler-Bellevue. *Journal of Consulting Psychology* 17:411–418.

Owens, W. A., Jr. (1953) Age and mental abilities: A longitudinal study. *Genetic Psychology Monographs* 48:3–54.

Owens, W. A., Jr. (1966) Age and mental abilities: A second adult follow-up. *Journal of Educational Psychology* 51:311–325.

Riegel, K. F. (1971) The prediction of death and longevity in longitudinal research. Pp. 139–152 in E. Palmore and F. C. Jeffers, eds., *Prediction of Life Span*. Lexington, Mass.: Heath.

Savage, R. D., Britton, P. G., Bolton, N., and Hall, E. H. (1973) *Intellectual Functioning in the Aged*. London: Methuen.

Schaie, K. W. (1970) A reinterpretation of age-related changes in cognitive structure and functioning. Pp. 486–508 in L. R. Goulet and P. B. Baltes, eds., *Life-Span Developmental Psychology: Research and Theory*. New York: Academic Press.

Schaie, K. W. (1977) Quasi-experimental research designs in the psychology of aging. Pp. 39–58 in J. E. Birren and K. W. Schaie, eds., *Handbook of the Psychology of Aging*. New York: Van Nostrand Reinhold Co.

Schaie, K. W., and Labouvie-Vief, G. (1974) Generational versus ontogenetic components of change in adult cognitive behavior: A fourteen-year cross sequential study. *Developmental Psychology* 10:305–320.

Schultz, N. R., Dineen, J. T., Elias, M. F., Pentz, C. A., and Wood, W. G. (1979) WAIS performance for different age groups of hypertensive and control subjects during administration of a diuretic. *Journal of Gerontology* 34(2):246–253.

Siegler, I. C. (1975) The terminal drop hypothesis: Fact or artifact? *Experimental Aging Research* 1(1):169–185.

Siegler, I. C., and Botwinick, J. (1979) A long-term longitudinal study of intellectual ability of older adults: The matter of selective subject attrition. *Journal of Gerontology* 34(2):242–245.

Spieth, W. (1964) Cardiovascular health status, age, and psychological performance. *Journal of Gerontology* 19:277–284.

Spieth, W. (1965) Slowness of task performance and cardiovascular disease. Pp. 366–400 in A. T. Welford and J. E. Birren, eds., *Behavior, Aging and the Nervous System*. Springfield, Ill.: Charles C. Thomas.

Steuer, J., La Rue, A., Blum, J., and Jarvik, L. F. (1981) "Critical loss" in the eighth and ninth decades. *Journal of Gerontology* 36(2):211–213.

Terman, L. M. (1916) *The Measurement of Intelligence*. Boston: Houghton Mifflin.

Terman, L. M., and Oden, M. H. (1947) *The Gifted Child Grows Up: Vol. IV. Genetic Studies of Genius*. Stanford, Calif.: Stanford University Press.

Wang, H. S., and Busse, E. W. (1974) Heart disease and brain impairment among aged persons. Pp. 160–167 in E. Palmore, ed., *Aging II. Reports from the Duke Longitudinal Studies, 1970–1973*. Durham, N.C.: Duke University Press.

Wechsler, D. (1944) *The Measurement of Adult Intelligence*. Baltimore, Md.: Williams and Williams.

Wechsler, D. (1958) *The Measurement and Appraisal of Adult Intelligence*. 4th ed. Baltimore, Md.: Williams and Williams.

Wilkie, F., and Eisdorfer, C. (1974) Intelligence and blood pressure. Pp. 87–94 in E. Palmore, ed., *Normal Aging II. Reports from the Duke Longitudinal Studies, 1970–1973*. Durham, N.C.: Duke University Press.

Wilkie, F. L., Eisdorfer, C., and Nowlin, J. B. (1976) Memory and blood pressure in the aged. *Experimental Aging Research* 2(1):3–16.

chapter **11**

Old Age:
An Artifact?[1]

ELLEN J. LANGER

Over the past decade, numerous investigators have assiduously and successfully explored the importance of perceived control to human functioning. This personal belief of response/outcome dependence and its converse, response/outcome independence, have been found to be related to stress (e.g., Glass and Singer 1972); reactive depression (e.g., Seligman 1975); general coping ability (e.g., Langer *et al.* 1975, Lefcourt 1966); academic performance (e.g., Dweck 1975, Dweck and Goetz 1976, Weiner 1974; and Monty *et al.* 1973); reactions to crowding (Baum *et al.* 1978, Langer and Saegart 1977, Rodin 1976); reactions to crime (Bard and Sangrey 1979, Miransky and Langer 1978); and neurosis (Mineka and Kihlstrom 1978), to name only a sample of the areas investigated. Research has shown that it is not the exercise of control that is important, but rather the belief, be it veridical or not, that if one wanted to, one could exercise control in a given situation. Nevertheless, the two are not likely to be unrelated. If a person is used to exercising control, and either environmental constraints or physical limitations deny this opportunity, in the majority of cases that person will in a short time come to perceive the loss.

[1] Preparation of this chapter was facilitated by a grant from the National Institute of Mental Health (1 R01 MH32946–01) to the author.

AGING
Biology and Behavior

Perceived control apparently is so basic to psychological and physical health that even in situations that are completely chance-determined, like lotteries or coin flipping, people behave as if they can control the outcome (Ayeroff and Abelson 1976, Langer 1975, Langer 1978a, Langer and Roth 1975, Wortman 1975).

If the perception of control is a primary motivation (see De Charms 1968, Lefcourt 1973, Heider 1958, Kelley 1967, Langer 1975), as researchers have suggested, it would indeed seem important to investigate populations who characteristically have been denied the opportunity to exercise control. The elderly are clearly one such population.

This chapter explores the degree to which behavioral, cognitive, and physiological deficits that descriptively characterize old age might be experientially determined, and the degree to which they might be experientially reversed or retarded. Since the literature on perceived control has shown that the perceived loss of control results in each of these kinds of deficits, it is an appropriate starting place.

THE ELDERLY AND PERCEIVED CONTROL

It is only fairly recently that the study of perceived control has been applied toward an understanding of the problems facing the elderly; however, the research that has been undertaken thus far yields striking findings.

In one of these experiments (Langer and Rodin 1976), institutionalized elderly adults were given a control-enhancement treatment in order to determine whether physical, behavioral, and psychological deficits, which are often taken as a biologically necessary consequence of aging, might be environmentally determined and, thus, possibly reversible. One group of nursing home residents was brought together in the lounge on their floor of the home to hear a communication delivered by the nursing home director. These residents were told that they were capable of making and should be making all the decisions that they used to make for themselves. They were then given decisions to make and were also given a plant to take care of—something for which they would be responsible. Another group of residents of that home, also gathered together in their lounge, received a different kind of communication from the director. For this group, emphasis was placed on the staff's eagerness to take care of them and help them. They, too, were given plants, but were told that the nurses would water and care for them. Both groups were virtually identical with respect to socioeconomic variables and pretreatment measures of physical and psychological health. However, post-treatment measures taken 3 weeks later revealed a very different picture. The responsibility-encouraged group showed significant improvement over the comparison group on measures of alertness, happiness, active participation, and a general sense of well-being. A follow-up to that study was undertaken (Rodin and Langer 1977) 18 months later to determine whether there were continued positive effects of that intervention. At that time, it was found that approximately half as many people in the experimental group, compared with the comparison group, had died (7 of 47 versus 13 of 44). In addition, of the survivors, those in the re-sponsibility-encouraged group were significantly superior to the comparison group on measures of physical and psychological health. In a somewhat similar study, Schulz (1976) found that increasing control by providing institutionalized elderly adults with the opportunity to decide when they would be visited also resulted in improvement on psycho-logical and physical health measures. These findings are consistent both with earlier laboratory investigations of perceived control and obser-vation studies of such phenomena as concentration camp death or sur-vival and voodoo deaths.

In another investigation concerned explicitly with the relationship between perceived control and cognitive functioning in the elderly (Langer et al. 1979), the experimenters manipulated the cognitive demands made by the environment. It was believed that, unless the environment made it necessary to engage one's memory processes, memory deficits typically found in the elderly would be evident. Since the elderly are believed to be incompetent, younger people characteristically control their environments and refrain from placing demands on them. Thus, outcomes often are effortlessly obtained by the elderly. However, if control over these outcomes required active cognitive processing, it was reasoned that such deficits could be reduced, if not entirely reversed. That is, it was hypothesized that cognitive processes could be restim-ulated. In two experiments, we increased the cognitive demands of the nursing home environment and varied the extent to which residents became involved in attending to and remembering these environmental events. Measures revealed improvement on standard tests of short-term and long-term memory for these experimental groups relative to low-involvement and no-treatment comparison groups.

It appears abundantly clear that the perception of a loss of control may disrupt normal functioning and, when reinstated, this perception may restore normal functioning. For this reason, it is important to ask what determines the perception of control to begin with. One answer to this question has been found in research on learned helplessness (Benson and Kennelly 1976, Seligman 1975, Seligman and Maier 1976). In these studies, subjects typically are exposed to a pretreatment phase in which their attempts to avoid some negative outcomes are repeatedly met with failure. Their situation is uncontrollable. When these subjects are placed in the test phase of the experiment, where the outcome is in fact controllable, they typically give up and remain passive. They do not exert the control that is available to them, control that is readily exercised by those subjects who did not receive the pretreatment. Thus, these studies basically show that the perception of response/outcome independence may result from prior experience with repeated uncontrollable negative outcomes. Individuals generalize from these uncontrollable situations to situations that are, in fact, controllable. While prior repeated experience with uncontrollable outcomes may lead to an erroneous perception of incompetence, this is not the only way, nor necessarily the most pervasive way in which such a perception is induced. Recently it has been found that this illusion of incompetence (see Langer 1978b) may result from an erroneous inference drawn from interpersonal contextual factors that may be orthogonal to outcome. In fact, the unnecessary performance decrement that follows, called self-induced dependence, may occur even in the face of prior success on the very task in question (Langer and Benevento 1978).

In the self-induced dependence studies, pairs of subjects in Phase 1 successfully perform a task individually. In Phase 2, they jointly perform a different task in the role of assistant, boss, or without reference to relative status. (While only the assignment of labels was tested in this study, any interpersonal event that would make one question one's competence may be substituted here.) In Phase 3, subjects individually perform the original task. It has been found that the intervening event may render the individual less able to perform this task. Subjects who were in the dependent (assistant) condition performed only half as well as they did originally.

Langer and Benevento (1978) suggest that various interpersonal contextual factors—if made salient to individuals—may render those people incompetent. Examples of such factors are the following: engaging in a consensually defined demeaning task, no longer engaging in a task that is now engaged in by another, and simply allowing someone else to help one. They suggest that the elderly, as a group, are particularly vulnerable to self-induced dependence. There is a stigma in our society attached to being labeled old; the elderly are most often retired from their previous professions; and the elderly constitute a group for whom people are typically doing things. Beliefs of incompetence held by others are believed to translate into self-perceptions of incompetence, which, in turn, serve to reinforce the original misconceptions.

How might this happen? What process can explain this heightened vulnerability to external circumstances, a situation in which individuals, whose most recent efforts were successful, now perform incompetently? Can we depend on "natural" consequences of aging to explain the debilitation? Obviously not; even though the elderly should be the most susceptible group to self-induced dependence, the subjects in these experiments were younger adults.

Recent research suggests that the explanation for self-induced dependence may lie instead in an understanding of the consequences that result from a reduced level of cognitive activity. When cognitive activity is habitually and automatically reduced, a state of "mindlessness" (cf. Langer 1978c, Langer, in press, Langer *et al.* 1978, Langer and Newman 1979) results that can have severe negative repercussions. In the remainder of this chapter I shall try to elucidate some of these more extreme negative consequences, particularly as they pertain to elderly populations, and explore possible treatments that might reverse these debilitating effects.

MINDLESSNESS

"Mindless" information processing is a reduced level of cognitive activity that may arise either after many repetitions of a particular experience or, in certain instances, after a single exposure. In the former case, reduced cognitive activity occurs because of a change from controlled to automatic information processing (cf. Schneider and Shiffrin 1977, Shiffrin and Schneider 1977). The model proposed by these researchers suggests that as an individual's experience with certain situations accumulates, a cognitive structure of the situation is formed; this cognitive structure represents its underlying "semantics." The appearance of similar cues on subsequent occasions then triggers a (mindless) sequence of behaviors, wherein it appears as if the underlying semantics are no longer available for conscious cognitive work. In the latter case, the single exposure, reduced cognitive activity does not result from reliance on cognitive structures accumulated through repeated experience. It occurs because the individual does not sufficiently scrutinize the information available and, therefore, does not comprehend the circumstances that produce (or fail to produce) a particular situation. Thus, in the latter case, reduced cognitive activity occurs because the person finds nothing about which to think. The object or event is accepted at face value and other interpretations are therefore excluded from consciousness.

It is believed that mindlessness brought about in either way results in heightened vulnerability to external circumstances. If the circumstances are negative ones, then prolonged mindlessness can be severely incapacitating and may even result in premature death (Langer 1978c). Before elaborating on the research in which some of these assumptions (which may appear a bit extreme to the reader at this point) have been tested, a discussion of background information seems in order.

The study of consciousness has only recently come back into vogue. In the past, psychology was largely dominated by learning theories that either ignored the issue completely (e.g., Watson's behaviorism) or assumed that thoughts followed the same reinforcement rules as did overt behavior (e.g., Skinner's reinforcement theory). In contrast to investigators of animal learning who have always studied mindless behavior, most social psychologists (e.g., proponents of attribution theory, consistency theories, social comparison theory, and equity theory) have taken as a given that people move through their environments thinking continually. Even when not consciously processing information, the individual is assumed to be behaving as if he or she were.

More recently, this extreme dichotomy has been breaking down. Attention has been given by experimental psychologists to both automatic and conscious information processing. (For example, in cognitive psychology, see Craik and Lockhart 1972, Mandler 1975, Schneider and Shiffrin 1977, and Shiffrin and Schneider 1977; in developmental psychology see Piaget 1976 and Shatz 1978; in social psychology see Nisbett and Wilson 1977, and Langer 1978c.) In contrast to active, conscious information processing, automatic processing may be characterized in the following ways: it is relatively free from motivational feedback constraints (Kimble and Perlmuter 1970); it results from the repeated practice of voluntary behavior (Kimble and Perlmuter 1970); it does not tax processing capacity (Neisser 1967, Posner and Boies 1971, Schneider and Shiffrin 1977, Shiffrin and Schneider 1977); and attention to it is disruptive (Kimble and Perlmuter 1970, Neisser 1967). While the authors just cited refer to reduced cognitive activity as automatic, involuntary, or preattentive, I prefer to designate it as mindless in order to highlight several potentially important considerations. First, mindlessness may come about without repeated exposure; second, information processed mindlessly may be unavailable for the kind of conscious cognitive activity necessary for survival. Third, the term *mindlessness* suggests a different, more molar, unit of analysis than has been used by previous investigators.

Finally, until now, researchers have concerned themselves primarily with the adaptive function, served by automatic processing, of freeing conscious attention so that it may be paid elsewhere. However, this medium of engagement with the environment may also be quite maladaptive, especially when it is one's primary way of negotiating the environment.

While people have probably always recognized that they have limits, this idea was studied formally as early as the 1890s (Bryan and Harter 1897, Solomons and Stein 1896) and became a popular research topic after information theory (Shannon and Weaver 1949) and the theory of selective attention (Broadbent 1958) were proposed. Since that time, a large and growing body of research has shown that people's limited capacities are best served by the hierarchical chunking of smaller units of information into larger ones (see Fodor *et al.* 1970, and Johnson 1970 for reviews of the use of semantic and syntactic principles as chunking devices) in order to more efficiently perform higher-order tasks.

To say that individuals can conduct complex interactions automatically relies on the understanding that large units of varied social behavior also can be chunked together, forming fewer coherent cognitive units that are capable, in turn, of being overlearned. These units, the abstracted essences of social events, have been called many things, including scripts (Abelson 1976, Berne 1964, Bower *et al.* 1978, Langer and Abelson 1972), frames (Goffman 1974), episodes (Harre and Secord 1973), plans (Miller *et al.* 1960), and caricatures (Thorngate, 1976). Evidence that social behavior is chunked into manageable units comes from work done by Newtson *et al.* (1977). These investigators found that subjects viewing a continuous videotape of people in action displayed very little variance in how the action was broken down into discrete units. However, while the idea of chunking has been demonstrated for molar behavior, there have been very few direct attempts to empirically validate the notion that these larger units of behavior may actually be enacted mindlessly. Some recent work provides some indirect support for this notion, and therefore will be considered in some detail.

In research that Robert Abelson and I conducted (Langer and Abelson 1972), we were interested in seeing whether compliance would vary as a function of the opening words of a request. Groups of subjects in two studies were presented with requests for help in which only the order of the words spoken was varied. For example, "My knee is killing me. I think I sprained it. Would you do something for me? Please do me a favor and call my husband (employer) and ask him to pick me up," versus "Would you do something for me? Please do me a favor and call my husband (employer) and ask him to pick me up. My knee is killing me, I think I sprained it." These messages were designed to evoke either a victim or a target orientation in the listener. If subjects processed the full request, rather than using the first few words to cue them into some familiar scenario, no difference between the groups would be expected, since the content of both messages was identical. Nevertheless, depending on the legitimacy of the request (operationalized, in this case, in the husband/employer distinction), the appeals predictably differed in their effectiveness in eliciting compliance. A victim-oriented appeal, which we suggested would instigate an empathy script, was more effective when the request was legitimate; on the other hand, a target-oriented appeal, which instigates a social obligation script, was more effective when it was not legitimate. In the appropriate situation, reliance on such scripts obviates the necessity for detailed cognitive work. These results have been replicated in the United Kingdom (Innes 1974), in Australia (Innes and Gilroy 1978), and in Germany (Mikula 1977).

Additional evidence comes from a series of studies designed originally to elucidate a phenomenon referred to as the *illusion of control* (Langer 1975, Langer 1978a, Langer and Roth 1975). These studies showed that, with little provocation, people participating in chance events behaved as if they were engaged in a skill situation and attempted to exert influence over the outcome. The theory asserts that by encouraging or allowing participants in a chance event to engage in behavior that they typically engage in when participating in a skill event, the person is initially led into perceiving that it is a skill situation. Continued behavior that connotes a skill orientation demonstrates a reliance on the ''skill'' cues and reduces the cognitive processing of that incoming information that would reveal the ''chance'' quality of the situation. Skill-relevant behaviors that induce this illusion of control include making choices, thinking about the possible strategies that may be employed, exerting effort while actively engaged in the task, familiarizing oneself with the materials to be used and the responses to be made, and competing with other people as a way to assess one's skill. By introducing any of these aspects of a skill situation (choice, passive and active involvement, stimulus and response familiarity, competition) into a chance situation (in which they do not objectively influence the outcome), one induces an illusion of control. When the illusion is operative, people are more likely to take risks. However, when there is an intrusion of reality such that the focus of attention is shifted to the chance elements in the situation and away from the skill characteristics that were predominating, the illusion will dissipate.

Several experiments were conducted to test these propositions. In each study, one or more of these skill-related factors was introduced into a chance setting (e.g., choice of a lottery ticket) and was found to occasion behavior more appropriate to a skill than to a chance activity. Wortman (1975) and Ayeroff and Abelson (1976), employing different methodologies, found virtually the same results. It appears that the presence of the skill-relevant variable cued a familiar sequence of behavior, which subjects then mindlessly enacted. Had subjects been processing all the information in the situation, rather than just relying on a few cues, there probably would have been no difference between conditions in which those "skill" cues were present and in which they were absent, since their presence was objectively irrelevant to the outcome. If people were made to think about the event while engaging in it, the illusion of a skill situation as well as the resulting illusion of control no doubt would dissipate. Because they would be processing more of the information in the situation, people would behave in a way that "thinking" others would view as rational. When the illusion is present, people are not behaving irrationally, but simply mindlessly.

Some indirect evidence that people do not spend much time engaged in thoughtful action is provided by a study that is quite different from those reported thus far (Miransky and Langer 1978). In this study, we compared the thoughtful responses that would seem to accompany a burglary with behavioral responses to the same experience. A pilot study had revealed, to our surprise, that past victimization did not result in an increase in the use of precautionary measures by subjects (e.g., locking doors), when they were either present or absent from home. While 66% of the total sample of burglarized and nonburglarized subjects reported that they believed burglary could be prevented, 65% of these subjects used fewer locks on their doors than they had available even though this was the clearest measure for preventing the crime. With these results in mind, a study was conducted to assess the reason for the lack of differences between burglarized and nonburglarized groups of people. To do this, we tried to push the two groups apart by making burglarized individuals think about their past burglary. Both behavioral and attitudinal measures of reactions to the crime were obtained after the burglary experience was made differentially vivid through a communication. The behavioral measures consisted of the difference between the number of locks subjects had on their doors and the number they used, and the number of people who called the police to make use of a free security service we had advertized in the communication. The attitudinal questions dealt with recalled and anticipated reactions to burglary, such as feelings of helplessness.

Findings revealed that prior to the experimental treatment, the large majority of subjects used fewer locks than they had on their doors (84%), even though 88% of them reported that burglary could be prevented.

Once again, there were no differences on these measures between burglarized and nonburglarized people. Group differences did emerge as a
function of the experimental treatments in regard to questionnaire responses. Subjects who had been burglarized reported greater feelings of
helplessness than subjects who had never been burglarized. However,
both burglarized and nonburglarized subjects were equally unlikely to
take preventive measures against burglary after our intervention as before
it. This is, of course, reminiscent of the attitude–behavior discrepancy
long acknowledged by social psychologists studying attitude change
(Wicker 1969). To expect people who report their beliefs and opinions
under conditions in which they are made to think about issues to later
behave in a manner consistent with those beliefs and opinions is to
assume that they are thinking while they are behaving. However, the
behavioral equivalence of the two groups in this study, despite their
expressed attitudinal differences, suggests that the behavior may be adequately described as mindless.

In another investigation (Langer *et al.* 1978), a series of studies was
conducted to test somewhat more directly the hypothesized mindlessness
of ostensibly thoughtful action. We conducted three field experiments
to test the idea of mindlessness in the domain of spoken and written
communication. It was hypothesized that thoughtful behavior will only
occur when mindlessness is inadequate for the occasion. This will be
the case when either of two considerations are met: (*a*) when the message
transmitted is structurally (rather than semantically) novel or (*b*) when
the interaction between the participants requires an "effortful" response.
Mindlessness is relied on by the individual to reduce the cognitive work
necessary to engage in interactional activity. The recurrence of certain
typical activities in a person's life provides the possibility for, and encourages the perception of, a typical structure to this everyday activity.
As the person is repeatedly exposed to the activity, a structure emerges.
With repeated exposure and emerging structure, the person pays less
and less attention to the semantics of the activity. Rather, he or she cues
into that structure of the activity that signifies that the typical activity
is as it was before. So long as the structures are overlearned, the person
takes it for granted that the unexamined semantics of the (repeated)
activity are similar to the semantics of his or her earliest encounters with
the activity. At that earlier time, when the structure was first emerging,
he or she had fully examined the semantics of the particulars of the
situation.

If the phenomenon just described is a feature of recurring, typical
activities in people's lives, then the more people engage in particular
activities, the more they rely on these cues in order to get these activities

done. As mentioned earlier, the most potent advantage of this feature is that it allows the person to engage in less "mental activity" and effort, because those interactions that he or she has learned are invariably repeated in the person's life. Thus, there is no longer any necessity to repeatedly and laboriously reexamine the semantics of a typical interaction. This mindless approach to activities will not be used by the individual under two circumstances. First, if the structure of the situation is novel, the indications are that the activity does not appear to be representative of earlier experiences. The novel structure indicates novel semantics. Second, if the response required by this activity is an effortful one, then the cues have failed in their purpose of reducing effort. The features of novelty or effort indicate a need to reexamine the semantics of the situation (i.e., thoughtfully process as much of the incoming information that seems relevant as possible). Under "normal" circumstances, however, minimal information (that which invokes a typical activity) will be processed and there will be a reduced level of mental activity. It was hypothesized that the essence of this overlearned sequence of social behavior may at times lie not in recurring semantics, but rather in more general paralinguistic features of the message.

These ideas were tested in the context of a compliance paradigm in which, depending on the study, either a meaningless reason was offered for compliance with a request or the request itself was meaningless. These communications were either structurally congruent with subjects' past experience or not. Generally, we found that when the structure of a communication (either oral or written, either semantically sound or semantically senseless) is congruent with subjects' experience, it occasions behavior that appears mindful, but which in fact may be mindless.

The studies are simple in design but nevertheless may be quite revealing. In the first study, people about to use a copying machine in the library at the Graduate Center of the City University of New York were approached and asked in one of several ways to let another person use it first. Either a request alone, a request plus redundant information, or a request plus real information was made for compliance with a favor that was either fairly large or small (i.e., which required either a large or small amount of effort). Thus, the study was a 3×2 factorial design. The specific request made by the experimenter to use the machine was one of the following:

1. *Request Only:* Excuse me, I have 5 (20) pages. May I use the Xerox machine?

2. *Redundant Information:* Excuse me, I have 5 (20) pages. May I use the Xerox machine because I have to make copies?

3. *Real Information:* Excuse me, I have 5 (20) pages. May I use the Xerox machine because I'm in a rush?

Condition 2 is called "placebic" information because the reason offered is entirely redundant with the request. What else would one do with a copying machine except make copies of something? Thus, if the subjects were processing the sense of the information communicated by the experimenter, the rate of compliance for subjects in the request-only condition and in the redundant information condition should be the same, since the same information is conveyed; furthermore, both conditions should differ from Condition 3, in which additional information is given. If, on the other hand, people are only processing a minimal amount of information and are responding to a structure that is something like "favor X + reason $Y \rightarrow$ comply," then the rate of compliance should be the same for the redundant and real information conditions and different from the request-only group. If the latter case obtained, then the redundant information would be redundant only in an information theory sense (Shannon and Weaver 1949), and not in a mindlessness sense. While we maintained that people proceed mindlessly as long as structural requirements are met (in this case, when request + reason are given), it is also the case that a potentially very effortful response would be sufficient to shift attention from the simple physical characteristics of the message to its semantic content. As long as it is easier to ignore what is being said than to process it, ignoring will be the case. However, when ignoring leads to effortful responses, it pays to think; in that case, thoughtful action will ensue. We predicted that when the favor asked was effortful (determined by the number of pages both subject and experimenter had to copy), subjects would process the experimenter's communication, and a similar rate of compliance for the request-only group and the redundant information group would result; on the other hand, a similar rate for the redundant and real information groups was predicted to obtain when little effort was involved. A look at Table 11.1 shows that this is just what we found. There was a main effect for small–big favor, as one would expect, but note that in the small favor condition, the redundant information group looks like the real information group, while in the big favor condition, the redundant group looks like the no-information (request-only) group.

One would probably have assumed that an interaction between two strangers, where one was making a request of the other, would proceed mindfully. This would seem especially likely when the people involved were spending their time in as thought-provoking an atmosphere as a library. Nevertheless, this appears not to have been the case. Even in

TABLE 11.1
Proportion of Subjects Who Agreed to Let the Experimenter Use the Copying Machine[a]

| | Reason | | |
Favor	No information	Placebic information	Sufficient information
Small	.60	.93	.94
N	15	15	16
Big	.24	.24	.42
N	25	25	24

[a] From Langer, Blank, and Chanowitz (1978), The mindlessness of ostensibly thoughtful actions: The role of placebic information in interpersonal interaction. *Journal of Personality and Social Psychology* 36:635–642. Copyright 1978 by the American Psychological Association. Reprinted by permission.

this situation, when minimal requirements were met, people may have proceeded mindlessly.

Another study in this series was devised to determine whether the processing of minimal information would also be the rule for responding to written communication, another ostensibly thoughtful action. In this study, subjects were randomly selected from the New York City telephone directory and sent a written communication that varied in its adherence to structural requirements for mail. A meaningless 5-item questionnaire was mailed with a cover letter that either demanded or requested the return of the questionnaire and was either signed or unsigned at the bottom of the letter. We assumed that signed requests and unsigned demands were more congruent with the structure of written communications than unsigned requests or signed demands. "Thoughtful" processing of the cover letter would not reveal any rational reason for returning the questionnaire (in a stamped envelope provided addressed to a post office box number). We expected greater compliance for the structurally congruent communications, signed requests and unsigned demands, than for unsigned requests and signed demands. The subjects of the study comprised a high status group made up of physicians and a random-status group.

It was predicted that, because of their experience with greater volumes of mail, high status subjects would return more questionnaires than low status subjects, and that this would be more the case of congruently phrased communications than for those that were structurally incongruent. There were an equal number of returns for the high and random status groups. However, while congruency did not seem to affect returns for the random status group, there were significantly more (mindless) responses to congruent communications than to incongruent communications by the high status group. Rather than assume that only physicians were mindless, we instead assumed that we had not determined the appropriate structure for the random status group. Therefore, we conducted another experiment to test more rigorously the potential mindlessness of responding to written communications.

Memoranda were collected from the trash baskets of secretaries of various departments at the Graduate Center of the City University of New York so that the structure of a communication could be tailor-made to the experience of our next group of subjects. While varying in content, most of the memos we found requested, rather than demanded, that the secretary do something. None of them was signed at the bottom. Thus, incongruent (and thereby thought-provoking) communications for these subjects would be memoranda that contained a signed request or a signed or unsigned demand. We sent secretaries either structurally congruent or structurally incongruent memoranda that asked them to return the memo by interoffice mail to a room that, in fact, did not exist in the building. The workers in the mailroom collected the memos for us. Determined to make our point most convincingly, the memos contained nothing else; the *only* thing that each memo asked was that the memo be returned—"This paper is to be returned immediately to Room 238 through interoffice mail," or "I would appreciate it if you return this paper immediately to Room 238 through interoffice mail." The memo was either signed, "Sincerely, John Lewis" or unsigned. Any thoughtful processing of the communication was expected to result in the secretary's *not* returning the memo. Why return it? If the sender wanted the piece of paper, he or she should not have sent it in the first place! Nevertheless, 68 % of the subjects did, in fact, comply with the request. One could argue that these subjects mindfully, rather than mindlessly, complied with the request in order to avoid potential negative repercussions from someone with greater authority. However, this alternative becomes less viable in light of the fact that there was significantly greater compliance when the memo was structurally congruent with subjects' past experience than when it was not.

These studies support the idea that much of the behavior we assume to be performed mindfully may instead be enacted rather mindlessly; unless the situation is novel or an effortful response is required, people may process only a minimal amount of information to get them through their day. These studies, while suggestive, obviously do not provide unambiguous evidence that people enact molar behavior mindlessly. But there is rather clear support for the idea that people can package a good deal of this complex social information into structures (schemas) that can be evoked by simple cues (see Markus 1977, regarding self schemas; Cantor and Mischel 1977, regarding personality schemas; Tessor 1978, regarding attitudinal schemas). Since research has shown that chunking takes place, it is reasonable to assume that these coherent units may become overlearned. Since other researchers (e.g., Schank and Abelson 1977, Rumelhart and Ortony 1977) are concerned with developing a taxonomy of scripts, schemas, or mindless behaviors, it is sufficient for them to make only a quantitative distinction between scripted and nonscripted behavior, for example, with respect to the degree of mental activity required. However, if one focuses on the clinical implications of mindlessness, as is my concern, one must examine the character and consequences of this medium of engagement with the environment. This focus should reveal that mindlessness is especially consequential for the elderly since, by virtue of their restricted mobility and their age, they have had more opportunity for repeated experiences. Thus, the elderly should experience more mindlessness than their younger counterparts.

NEGATIVE CONSEQUENCES FOR THE ELDERLY

There are basically two ways in which mindlessness may be especially disadvantageous for the elderly. First, as mentioned earlier, mindlessness may lead to increased vulnerability to interpersonal external influences that would lead one to question one's competence. While the consequences of such questioning should be basically the same for all people, the extant stereotypes of the elderly should result in a greater number of these external influences which, in turn, would bring competence into question. Second, it is conceivable that at least a threshold level of active conscious information processing is necessary for survival. That level may be easily reached by younger adults, but not attained, due to extremely routinized environments, by many of the elderly. Not only do the elderly, by virtue of their age and the way environments have been structured, experience much routinization, but also their experience with routinization probably facilitates the ease of further routinization (as in learning to learn). This would further decrease the likelihood that there is very much ongoing active information processing for this group as a whole.

There may be evidence for this relationship between survival and mindfulness in the Langer and Rodin study (1976) discussed earlier. It will be remembered that the responsibility-encouraged group, the group that was encouraged to make decisions, given decisions to make, and given something for which to be responsible, lived longer than the comparison group. An equally plausible explanation for these rather dramatic findings, however, was that the conditions of the study increased thinking for the experimental group. For most people, most of the time, the complex environment in which they find themselves presents too much to think about. Repeated interaction with that environment, however, renders it manageable, and one's limited information processing capacity may be reserved for dealing with novel situations. Thus, in normal environments, mindlessness is often adaptive. However there are environments, like nursing homes, that may be pathologically redundant, and therefore do not necessitate or allow for conscious, active, cognitive work. Because of their restricted mobility, this environmental redundancy may also be experienced profoundly by the noninstitutionalized elderly as well. Just as all people eat and sleep, so too do they consciously process information. Although the physiological mechanisms involved may be very different, when the environment prevents this activity, just as with eating and sleeping, premature death may ensue. Research that my students and I are currently conducting is aimed specifically at teasing apart the mindlessness and loss of perceived control explanations of the mortality findings of the Langer and Rodin (1976) study.

It should be noted that this mindlessness explanation and the original loss of perceived control explanation are not entirely independent. If a person believes he or she has control over his or her environment, there is certainly more to think about than if one perceives no control. Other studies that have been examined in terms of perceived control, for example, those dealing with the death of concentration camp victims, also may be reinterpreted in this light. (That is, it may have been the "concentration" that kept many of the survivors alive—concentration motivated by a belief in control.)

A reasonable question that one may ask is, "If thinking is adaptive for these elderly adults and the nursing home provides no food for thought, why don't they just return to their memories?" There are two answers to this. First, if it is true that when people are younger most of their environment is ignored and mindlessness is the rule rather than the exception, then a rich internal life is almost precluded by definition. Second, those thoughts that are repeatedly thought may come to be qualitatively different from other thoughts. Evidence for this supposition comes from the work cited earlier. That work shows that behaviors and cognitions that are overlearned, as opposed to nonoverlearned, do not tax capacity, are relatively free from motivational and feedback constraints, and can cause disruption when renewed attention is paid to them. Additional evidence for this is presented below.

While overlearning may be especially problematic for the institutionalized elderly, there are also ways in which it may present problems for
younger people as well. When one first approaches a task, one is necessarily attentive to the particulars of the task. Expertise is attained by
successively ignoring more and more of the particulars of the task in
question. With repeated experience the components of the task drop out
(or, stated differently, the components of the task coalesce further and
further to form a whole coherent unit). The result of complete mastery,
then, is that the individual may often be in the position of knowing that
he or she can perform the task without knowing the steps required to
accomplish its performance. When circumstances lead these people to
question their ability to successfully perform that task (e.g., being assigned a label that connotes inferiority), they may be unsure of that
ability because they cannot supply as evidence the steps that are necessary for performing the task. Thus for those tasks about which people
should feel most confident, they may be unconfident. This explanation
may account for the extreme vulnerability to situational factors, like
labels, that was found in the research (Langer and Benevento 1978)
described earlier. It may be recalled that in those studies we tried to
show that, in contrast to the learned helplessness paradigm, individuals
may erroneously infer incompetence from interpersonal situational factors that may be as important or more important than failure; and these
contextual factors might lead people to give up even in the face of prior
success. The tasks used in those studies were all familiar tasks to subjects
(i.e., ones that may have been performed mindlessly). If this mindlessness
explanation is correct, it would suggest a curvilinear relationship between
practice and vulnerability to external circumstance. One would be more
vulnerable to influences like negative labels for a novel task and an
overlearned task than for tasks with which one has only moderate
experience.

This hypothesis was tested explicitly in two studies by Langer and
Imber (1979). Of the several interpersonal contextual factors that could
be varied, the one that was selected for investigation in both studies was
the assignment of labels connoting inferiority. In the first study, using
the self-induced dependence paradigm described earlier, practice (no
practice, moderate practice, overpractice) and label assignment (no label,
"assistant," "boss") were varied factorially. It was predicted that performance decrements would occur for subjects in the dependent groups
in both the no practice and overpractice conditions, but that this would
not be the case for the moderate practice groups. This prediction, again,
was based on the assumption that automaticity leads to inaccessibility.
Therefore, when external factors (e.g., the label "assistant") led subjects

to question their competence, only the moderate practice groups should have been able to summon the evidence (call up the steps necessary to perform the task) that they could, in fact, perform the task. This hypothesis received very strong support. The heightened vulnerability experienced by subjects in the earlier studies seemed to be a function of subjects' losing sight of the components of the task through the very process used to improve performance (i.e., practice). Subjects who were labelled "assistants" performed poorly in both the overlearned condition and in the no practice condition, while moderate practice groups did not show the self-induced dependence effect. With this in mind, a second study was undertaken to see if self-induced dependence could be reversed by making the components of the task salient once again for the overpracticed subjects. The three phases of the self-induced dependence paradigm and label assignment were used again. However, this time, before half of the subjects began the overlearned task in Phase 1, the components of the task were made salient. The salience manipulation was successful in preventing the debilitation. In contrast, the self-induced dependence effect was found once again for the group for whom the components were not made salient. The components salient group remained at their pre-label performance level.

In addition to explaining many performance deficits found for the elderly, this formulation suggests another consideration that may be worthy of further investigation. Because of certain behavioral similarities between the elderly and children, some researchers have suggested that in old age one naturally regresses to childhood status. This research suggests that the observed similarities may be environmentally determined and not a necessary consequence of aging. The elderly may be seen as analogous to the overpracticed group and the children to the no practice group. However the elderly, by this formulation, can perform these tasks. Since people do not realize that overlearned complex behavior may be qualitatively different from nonoverlearned behavior, their thoughtful attempts to try these tasks will only provide evidence of illusory incompetence. That is, it may not occur to people that it would be more effective to perform these tasks mindlessly, rather than mindfully. Nonelderly adults, while susceptible to the same process with respect to overlearned tasks, have many more opportunities to thoughtfully perform nonoverlearned tasks, which then can serve as a means for restoring their self-esteem.

In general, it may be a worthwhile strategy to first seek other explanations for child/elderly similarities—perhaps with respect to cognitive or social deficits—before assuming anything about the natural aging process. For example, both children and the elderly may be seen as impatient in certain situations. Young children may not have yet learned the socially appropriate response in this situation, while the elderly simply may no longer care to enact it. In a sense, children may be uninhibited while the elderly, because of the social changes in their lives (e.g., loss of peer group through death and retirement) from early adulthood to late adulthood, may be disinhibited.

IMPLICATIONS OF MINDLESSNESS FOR THE ELDERLY

If overlearned thoughts are qualitatively different from nonoverlearned thoughts and the latter serve some biologically useful function, this may suggest a very different view of senility than the one most people presently hold. Consider, for example, that a new thought may be arrived at by the recombination of old thoughts. This thought, while not bearing an isomorphic relationship with a particular external event, may provide the opportunity for active conscious information processing. Since these events never occurred in reality, the speaker of such thoughts, if elderly, surely would be labeled senile. Similarly, if one rethought thoughts in some order of importance to oneself, one might expect the elderly to have a greater concern with minutiae, since these thoughts, for a time, would be more novel than more important overlearned thoughts. Thus, if one entered a pathologically redundant environment, like most nursing homes, and found an individual who characteristically thought unreal thoughts and was overly concerned with trivia, the individual would surely seem worse off than a psychologically healthy elderly adult in this environment whose thoughts, while "sane," were few. However, in such environments, senility may actually be biologically adaptive. This hypothesis is now being explored in nursing home populations.

The vulnerability of a person participating mindlessly in an interaction does not rely on any particular method used to acquire the structured cues of that type of interaction. Heretofore I have discussed the consequences of mindless interaction that relied on a sequence of cues acquired over repeated exposure to typical versions of a situation. However, there may be conditions surrounding initial exposure that encourage the person to code that information mindlessly in terms of the presented set of sequenced cues. This would preclude the opportunity for future modification of the sequence of cues, an opportunity that allows for more flexible use of the information under varying conditions. And these circumstances would leave the person equally (and perhaps chronically) vulnerable if the sequence dictated a pattern of behavior that restricted the exercise of the person's full behavioral capacity.

One condition accompanying initial exposure to information that might encourage mindless processing is the fact that the information concerns a situation that will never happen to the person. The information, therefore, is irrelevant. Under that circumstance, the person will most likely uncritically accept and process the information, in an attempt to devote as little effort as necessary. In that process, however, the person commits himself or herself to the set of cues used for structuring the presented information and its unconditional applicability if the information is ever needed as a basis for generating informed behavior. One is precluded from seeing that there are other ways of formulating the information when using it as the basis of behavior for other sets of conditions. Consequently, when the person is confronted with a situation that he or she had initially considered unlikely and irrelevant, the person is forced to rely on the information as it was initially formulated. That is the only way it is available for use in light of the person's earlier premature cognitive commitment to the sequence of cues used in the formulation of the initially presented information. This account also may explain what looks like senility in non-brain-damaged elderly adults.

While most people assume that they will grow old, their own late adulthood has no psychological reality for them. Thus, for all intents and purposes, people act as if they believe others may get old, but they, themselves, will not. Therefore, if these people are led to believe, for example, that senility (and therefore forgetfulness) accompanies old age, there is little reason for them to defend against this conclusion. That is, since it does not have any psychological reality for them, there is little justification to spend time thinking about external circumstances that may result in what looks like senility. For example, since the elderly are often ignored for many reasons, they may not be given as many reminders of things as their younger counterparts; or they may overlook the fact that young nonsenile people also are often forgetful. When this younger person then becomes old, and either sees himself or herself forget things or is told by someone else that he or she is forgetful, the person may very well erroneously assume that he or she is becoming or is senile. The person may then display whatever other symptoms he or she was led to believe were indicative of senility. By not considering the conditional quality of information when first processing it, people do not later have access to other uses to which the information may be put. If circumstances change so that one or more of those other uses would work to the individual's advantage, he or she is necessarily at a disadvantage. This disadvantage may be extreme. A test of the negative consequences of this form of mindlessness with respect to senility could not be conducted for ethical reasons. However, a somewhat analogous experiment was conducted (Chanowitz and Langer in press).

In this experiment, subjects were given information about two hypothetical perceptual deficits. To show how one could be affected by the deficits without being aware of it, an analogy was drawn to dyslexia and color blindness for which an appeal to one's own senses would not reveal either disease's pervasive effect. Information about these hypothetical deficits was codified in one of two ways. Subjects were told that the deficits were either rare or widespread (10% versus 80% in the population). It was expected that subjects would treat information regarding the symptoms of the disorders as irrelevant (10%) or relevant (80%) to themselves, and consequently would process the information with the least amount of effort on the basis of its structural earmarks or would process the information conditionally.

Subjects who believed that they were likely to have the disorder might have expended cognitive work, upon initial exposure, in trying to cope with the information (cf. Meichenbaum and Novaco 1978). To test whether initial coping with the negative information could prevent behavioral deficits, two other conditions were added to the design. Half of each group of subjects, those who were initially led to believe they were likely and unlikely to have the disorder, were instructed to find ways to cope with the disorder if he or she had it. The remaining half were not given the coping instructions. All subjects then were led to discover that they had the disorder. It was hypothesized that only the group that originally thought it was unlikely that they would have the disorder, and was not instructed to cope with the possibility of having it would display subsequent deficits (the "10%–no coping" group). These deficits would be a reflection of the distinctive (i.e., structural) ways in which they had originally processed the information in light of its presumed irrelevance. Subsequent performance tests that required the use of abilities that subjects in fact possessed, but that one who had the disorder would not possess, revealed strong support for the hypothesis. The way subjects initially thought about the information they were given as a function of the relevance of the information for the subject (either as a function of the likelihood of having the disorder or as a function of instructions to find ways of coping with the disorder), resulted in gross behavioral differences. Relative to the other groups who performed equally well, the group for whom the information was initially irrelevant showed a severe decrement in performance. As was the case in the studies in which mindlessness was a result of repeated exposure, these subjects performed only half as well as the comparison groups.

There is much information that people are given when they are young that, while more or less irrelevant to them at that point in their lives, becomes relevant for them later on when they become old. Consider, for example, a myth that may be perpetrated among working people, that people who are not working are worthless. One can only begin to imagine the potential consequences of prematurely accepting this information on people who will eventually be retired from their work. The same may be said for many physical disorders. The first exposure many people have to serious illnesses usually comes at a time when they are in good health. How many of the symptoms that are displayed by the infirm elderly are a consequence of the illnesses (as diagnosed) per se, and how many are a consequence of having uncritically, prematurely accepted information about the illnesses when they were younger? To make the process clearer, let's consider a specific illness—cancer. When people first learn about cancer, they usually hear that cancer is a killer. If a person first learns of the illness because he or she or a significant other has been diagnosed as having the disease, the person may not accept the assumption that cancer is a killer and may, for example, research what is known about the disease to support a more optimistic view. This view may allow the disease to take its natural course, a course that is as yet unknown because most people do first hear that cancer is a killer before the disease becomes personally relevant. When the information is initially irrelevant, pursuing a better understanding about what is and is not known about the disease would take the individual away from concerns that are initially more relevant. Assume, however, that this person later finds out that he or she has cancer. The previous assumption of irrelevance to oneself had implied an acceptance of relevance, validity, and consequences for others. Therefore it may not now occur to the individual to question the prematurely accepted information that cancer is a killer. It does not seem unreasonable to postulate that the individual who previously accepted the information that cancer is a killer now will give up. Would the death that ensued be a necessary consequence of the cancer or an unnecessary consequence of premature cognitive commitment? The work described earlier on the extreme consequences of the loss of perceived control and mindlessness suggests that it may be the latter.

CONCLUSIONS

The consequences described above with respect to the self-fulfilling prophecies initiated by the loss of perceived control, self-induced dependence, and mindlessness are only a few of the many ways in which social conditions may foster what may erroneously appear to be necessary consequences of aging. The experiments that have been discussed, which may have increased our understanding of these processes, have built into them clear ways that one may restructure the environment to prevent the consequent debilitations. Unfortunately, however, many of these ways may be so at odds with current beliefs about how the elderly should be treated that it is not clear that the implications of this work will not be met with great resistance. To increase the control available to one group of people may mean to limit the control available to another group. This will be important for the elderly as long as age is a salient characteristic in society. To change external influences so that they do not lead the elderly to question their competence and do not produce incompetence is difficult in the face of observed incompetence. And to believe that the elderly will necessarily be incompetent certainly works against deroutinizing their environments to minimize the negative consequences of mindlessness. For example, considering together the consequences of the perceived loss of control, self-induced dependence, and mindlessness, one might deduce that it is better to change the physical environment for the elderly so that it is challenging, while still manageable. Present conceptions of the elderly's abilities would lead those who are concerned about the elderly to a very different conclusion. They would probably opt for oversimplifying their physical environment. Such environments, however, would detract from necessary feelings of mastery, which then would help maintain self-induced dependence, and finally would limit the potential stimulation for active conscious information processing. Whether or not such processing is necessary for survival is still an open question. However, its importance for normal cognitive functioning has already been determined (e.g., Langer *et al.* 1979).

The views expressed in this chapter have alternately been optimistic and pessimistic: optimistic, in that many of the consequences of old age may be environmentally determined and thereby potentially reversed through manipulations of the environment; and pessimistic, in that many long-held beliefs about old age may prevent the changes that would provide the most convincing evidence that change is possible. However, there is reason to bring this full circle. While researchers like myself are slowly uncovering social determinants of incompetence that may be characteristically displayed by the elderly, the age population is shifting. As we become basically an old rather than a young society, many of the presumed biologically determined consequences of aging should be reversed by processes initiated by this change alone. Past research on groups like the physically handicapped (e.g., Langer *et al.* 1977) suggests that statistical deviance (i.e., being a member of a minority group) may account for many of the problems of stigmatized groups, problems that then lead to psychological deviance.

While it may be too strong a statement to say that death itself is an artifact, the foregoing analyses suggest that old age, at least as we know it, certainly may be.

REFERENCES

Abelson, R. P. (1976) A script theory of understanding, attitude and behavior. In J. Carroll and T. Payne, eds., *Cognition and Social Behavior.* Hillsdale, N.J.: Lawrence Erlbaum.

Ayeroff, F., and Abelson, R. P. (1976) E.S.P. and E.S.B.: Belief in personal success at mental telepathy. *Journal of Personality and Social Psychology* 34:240–247.

Bard, M., and Sangrey, D. (1979) *The Crime Victim Book.* New York: Basic Books.

Baum, A., Aiello, J., and Caleswick, L. (1978) Crowding and personal control: Social density and the development of learned helplessness. *Journal of Personality and Social Psychology* 36:1000–1011.

Benson, J. S., and Kennelly, K. J. (1976) Learned helplessness: The result of uncontrollable reinforcements on uncontrollable aversive stimuli. *Journal of Personality and Social Psychology* 34:138–145.

Berne, E. (1964) *Games People Play.* New York: Grove Press.

Bower, G., Black, J., and Turner, T. (1978) Scripts in Text Comprehension and Memory. Unpublished manuscript, Stanford University.

Broadbent, D. (1958) *Perception and Communication.* New York: Pergamon Press.

Byron, W., and Harter, N. (1897) Studies in the physiology and psychology of the telegraphic language. *Psychological Review* 4:27–53.

Cantor, N., and Mischel, W. (1977) Traits as prototypes: Effects on recognition memory. *Journal of Personality and Social Psychology* 35:38–48.

Chanowitz, B., and Langer, E. J. (1979) Premature cognitive commitments: Causes and consequences. *Journal of Personality and Social Psychology* (in press).

Craik, F. I. M., and Lockhart, R. S. (1972) Levels of processing: A framework for memory research. *Journal of Verbal Learning and Verbal Behavior* 11:671–684.

De Charms, R. (1968) *Personal Causation.* New York: Academic Press.

Dweck, C. S. (1975) The role of expectations and attributions in the alleviation of learned helplessness. *Journal of Personality and Social Psychology* 31:674–685.

Dweck, C. S., and Goetz, T. (1978) Attributions and learned helplessness. In J. Harvey, W. Ickes, and R. Kidd, eds., *New Directions in Attribution Research,* Vol. 2. Hillsdale, N.J.: Lawrence Erlbaum.

Fodor, J. A., Bever, T. G., and Garrett, M. F. (1974) *The Psychology of Language: An Introduction to Psycholinguistics and Generative Grammar.* New York: McGraw-Hill.

Glass, D., and Singer, J. (1972) *Urban Stress.* New York: Academic Press.

Goffman, E. (1974) *Frame Analysis: An Essay on the Organization of Experience.* New York: Harper & Row.

Harré, H., and Secord, P. F. (1973) *The Explanation of Social Behavior*. Totowa, N.J.: Littlefield, Adams, and Co.

Heider, F. (1958) *The Psychology of Interpersonal Relations*. New York: John Wiley.

Innes, J. M. (1974) The semantics of asking a favor: An attempt to replicate cross-culturally. *International Journal of Psychology* 9:57–61.

Innes, J. M., and Gilroy, S. (1978) The Semantics of Asking a Favor: Cross-Cultural Comparisons. Prepublication manuscript, University of Adelaide.

Johnson, N. (1970) The role of chunking and organization in the process of recall. In G. Bower, ed., *The Psychology of Learning and Motivation*, Vol. 4. New York: Academic Press.

Kelley, H. H. (1967) Attribution theory in social psychology. In D. Levine, ed., *Nebraska Symposium of Motivation*. Lincoln: University of Nebraska Press.

Kimble, G., and Perlmuter, L. (1970) The problem of volition. *Psychological Review* 77:361–384.

Langer, E. J. (1975) The illusion of control. *Journal of Personality and Social Psychology* 32:311–328.

Langer, E. J. (1978a) The psychology of chance. *Journal for the Theory of Social Behavior* 7:185–207.

Langer, E. J. (1978b) The illusion of incompetence. In L. Perlmuter and R. Monty, eds., *Choice and Perceived Control*. Hillsdale, N.J.: Lawrence Erlbaum.

Langer, E. J. (1978c) Rethinking the role of thought in social interaction. In J. Harvey, W. Ickes, and R. Kidd, eds., *New Directions in Attribution Research*, Vol. 2. Hillsdale, N.J.: Lawrence Erlbaum.

Langer, E. J. (in press) Playing the middle against both ends: The usefulness of adult cognitive activity as a model for cognitive activity in childhood and old age. In S. Yussen, ed., *The Development of Reflection*. New York: Academic Press.

Langer, E. J., and Abelson, R. P. (1972) The semantics of asking a favor: How to succeed in getting help without really trying. *Journal of Personality and Social Psychology* 24:26–32.

Langer, E. J., and Benevento, A. (1978) Self-induced dependence. *Journal of Personality and Social Psychology* 36:886–893.

Langer, E. J., Blank, A., and Chanowitz, B. (1978) The mindlessness of ostensibly thoughtful actions: The role of placebic information in interpersonal interaction. *Journal of Personality and Social Psychology* 36:635–642.

Langer, E. J., and Imber, L. (1979) When practice makes perfect: Debilitating effects of overlearning. *Journal of Personality and Social Psychology* 37:2014–2025.

Langer, E. J., Janis, I., and Wolfer, J. (1975) Effects of a cognitive coping device and preparatory information on psychological stress in surgical patients. *Journal of Experimental Social Psychology* 11:155–165.

Langer, E. J., and Newman, H. M. (1979) The role of mindlessness in a typical social psychological experiment. *Personality and Social Psychology Bulletin* 5:295–298.

Langer, E. J., and Rodin, J. (1976) The effects of choice and enhanced personal responsibility for the aged. *Journal of Personality and Social Psychology* 34:191–198.

Langer, E. J., Rodin, J., Beck, P., Weinman, C., and Spitzer, L. (1979) Environmental determinants of memory improvement in late adulthood. *Journal of Personality and Social Psychology* 37:2003–2013.

Langer, E. J., and Roth, J. (1975) Heads I win, tails it's chance: The illusion of control as a function of the sequence of outcomes in a purely chance task. *Journal of Personality and Social Psychology* 32:951–955.

Langer, E. J., and Saegart, S. (1977) Crowding and cognitive control. *Journal of Personality and Social Psychology* 35:175–182.

Langer, E. J., Taylor, S., Fiske, S., and Chanowitz, B. (1976) Stigma, staring, and discomfort: A novel–stimulus hypothesis. *Journal of Experimental Social Psychology* 12:451–463.

Lefcourt, H. (1966) Belief in personal control: A goal for psychotherapy. *Journal of Individual Psychology* 22:185–195.

Mandler, G. (1975) Consciousness: Respectable, useful, and probably necessary. In R. Solso, ed., *Information Processing and Cognition*. Hillsdale, N.J.: Lawrence Erlbaum.

Markus, H. (1977) Self-schemata and processing information about the self. *Journal of Personality and Social Psychology* 36:63–78.

Meichenbaum, P., and Novaco, R. (1978) Stress inoculation: A preventive approach. In C. Spielberger and I. Sarson, eds., *Stress and Anxiety*, Vol. 5. New York: Halsted Press.

Mikula, G. (1977) Bitteformulierung und Hilfeleistungsverhalten. Berichte aus dem Institut für Psychologic der Universität Graz.

Miller, G., Gallanter, E. H., and Pribram, K. (1960) *Plans and the Structure of Behavior*. New York: Holt.

Mineka, S., and Kihlstrom, J. (1978) Unpredictable and uncontrollable events: A new perspective on experimental neurosis. *Journal of Abnormal Psychology* 87:256–271.

Miransky, J., and Langer, E. J. (1978) Burglary (non)prevention: An instance of relinquishing control. *Personality and Social Psychology Bulletin* 4:399–405.

Monty, R. A., Rosenberger, M. M., and Perlmuter, L. C. (1973) Amount and locus of choice as sources of motivation in paired-associate learning. *Journal of Experimental Psychology* 97:16–28.

Neisser, U. (1967) *Cognitive Psychology*. New York: Appleton-Century-Crofts.

Newtson, D., Engquis, G., and Bois, J. (1977) The objective basis of behavior units. *Journal of Personality and Social Psychology* 35:847–862.

Nisbett, R., and Wilson, T. (1977) Telling more than we can know: Level of reports on mental processes. *Psychological Review* 84:231–259.

Piaget, J. (1976) *The Grasp of Consciousness: Action and Concept in the Young Child*. Cambridge, Mass.: Harvard University Press.

Posner, M., and Boies, S. (1971) Components of attention. *Psychological Review* 78:391–408.

Rodin, J. (1976) Crowding, perceived choice and response to controllable and uncontrollable outcomes. *Journal of Experimental Social Psychology* 12:564–578.

Rodin, J., and Langer, E. J. (1977) Long-term effects of a control-relevant intervention with the institutionalized aged. *Journal of Personality and Social Psychology* 35:897–902.

Rumelhart, P. E., and Ortony, A. (1977) The representation of knowledge in memory. In R. C. Anderson, R. J. Spiro, and W. E. Montague, eds., *Schooling and the Acquisition of Knowledge*. Hillsdale, N.J.: Lawrence Erlbaum.

Schank, R. C., and Abelson, R. P. (1977) *Scripts, Plans, Goals and Understanding*. Hillsdale, N.J.: Lawrence Erlbaum.

Schneider, W., and Shiffrin, R. M. (1977) Controlled and automatic human information processing: I. Detection, search, and attention. *Psychological Review* 84:1–66.

Schultz, R. (1976) Effects of control and predictability on the psychological well-being of the institutionalized aged. *Journal of Personality and Social Psychology* 33:563–573.

Seligman, M. E. P. (1975) *Helplessness*. San Francisco: Freeman.

Seligman, M. E. P., and Maier, S. F. (1976) Learned helplessness: Theory and evidence. *Journal of Experimental Psychology: General* 103:3–46.

Shannon, C., and Weaver, W. (1949) *The Mathematical Theory of Communication*. Urbana, Ill.: Illinois University Press.

Shatz, M. R. (1978) The relationship between cognitive processes and the development of communication skills. In B. Keasey, ed., *Nebraska Symposium on Motivation*. Lincoln: University of Nebraska Press.

Shiffrin, R. M., and Schneider, W. (1977) Controlled and automatic human information processing: II. Perceptual learning, automatic attending and a general theory. *Psychological Review* 84:127–190.

Solomons, L. M., and Stein, G. (1896) Normal motor automism. *Psychological Review* 3:492–512.

Tesser, A. (1978) Toward a theory of self-generated attitude change. In L. Berkowitz, ed., *Advances in Experimental Social Psychology*, Vol. 2. New York: Academic Press.

Thorngate, W. (1976) Must we always think before we act? *Personality and Social Psychology Bulletin* 2:31–35.

Weiner, E. (1974) Achievement protestation as conceptualized by an attribution theorist. In B. Weiner, ed., *Attribution Theory, Achievement Motivation*. New York: General Learning Press.

Wicker, A. W. (1969) Attitudes versus actions: The relationship of verbal and overt behavioral responses to attitude objects. *Journal of Social Issues* 25:41–78.

Wortman, C. (1975) Some determinants of perceived control. *Journal of Personality and Social Psychology* 31:282–294.

chapter 12

The Function of Denial
in Stress, Coping, and Aging[1]

RICHARD S. LAZARUS
GLORIA Y. GOLDEN

Does denial have positive implications for psychological and physical health? Although a number of researchers have studied denial processes, particularly in the last two decades (cf. Goldstein 1973, Janis and Mann 1977, Kübler-Ross 1969, Offer and Freedman 1972), there is still no adequate resolution of this issue. The function of denial in coping with stress and adapting to aging is one of the key questions addressed by the Stress and Coping in Aging research project currently under way at the University of California, Berkeley; directed by the first author of this chapter, this research has provided the impetus for our discussion here of the process of denial and its relevance to aging.

Several features of aging provoked curiosity about the function of denial in the later years. Since decreasing physical capacity is a prominent aspect of aging, some researchers have inquired whether denial of physical incapacity could have positive implications for adjustment to old age (Clark and Anderson 1967, Tobin and Lieberman 1976). Furthermore, grief at the loss of loved ones is an increasingly frequent accompaniment

---

[1] This is a substantially modified version of a paper by the first author entitled "The Costs and Benefits of Denial," to appear in S. Breznitz (Ed.), *Denial of Stress* (New York: International Universities Press, in press).

AGING
Biology and Behavior

of aging, and some researchers of death and dying have postulated that denial promotes psychological healing in certain phases of the grief process (Kübler-Ross 1969, 1974). Finally, a progressive loss of social roles frequently characterizes the transition from middle age to old age, and some sociologists of aging have focused on denial as a struggle to cope with status and role losses (Blau 1956, Rosow 1967).

In this four-part chapter, we interweave our conceptual exploration of denial with thoughts and data on its relevance to aging. In the first section, we present a discussion of the importance of illusion to the human psyche. One premise of this paper is that throughout human development the use of illusion represents a major contribution to human coping. As Becker (1973) wrote: "The defenses that form a person's character support a grand illusion, and when we grasp this we can understand the full drivenness of man [p. 56]."

Because denial is often confused with closely related concepts, including illusion, we devote the second section to a discussion of the differences between denying and related forms of coping, such as repressing, avoiding, and not knowing; we also cover distinctions between well-consolidated and tentative denying, and between denying and using illusions. In part three, we selectively review studies in which denial has been shown to be beneficial and those in which it has been shown to be damaging. This review treats first the general psychological literature, then studies specific to aging. In the final section, we briefly summarize salient points regarding denial as an adaptive process.

THE SUSTAINING FUNCTION OF ILLUSIONS

About 30 years ago, nearly everyone involved in clinical work believed that self-deception was tantamount to mental disorder. While the reality-oriented definition of mental health was at its height and the positive mental health movement was in vogue (cf. Erikson 1950, 1963, Jahoda 1958, Maslow 1954, etc.), there also existed an unsettling discrepancy between the way most mental health professionals viewed the matter and the perspective of writers of fiction and poetry, who believed that life was intolerable without illusion. This latter message is the core theme of Eugene O'Neill's *The Iceman Cometh*. The chief protagonist, Hickey, becomes *persona non grata* and destroys one man by insisting that he face the unpleasant reality of his life; satisfaction does not return until reality-testing is abandoned in favor of illusion.

The same theme is found in Ibsen's play *The Wild Duck*. Ibsen has Gregers, a neurotic moralist, press his own destructive truths on another man whose illusions about the past and present are thereby shattered, with the resulting tragic suicide of his 14-year-old daughter and the destruction of his family's happiness. Here, too, it is affirmed that illusions must be preserved to sustain the value of life.

In the musical *Man of La Mancha*, based on Cervantes's *Don Quixote*, author Wasserman comments that instead of writing a cynical commentary on the remarkable human capacity for self-deception, his adaptation of the Cervantes novel is a plea for illusion as a sustaining human force. We are urged to "dream the impossible dream," "fight the unbeatable foe." "Facts," says Don Quixote, "are the enemy of truth."

In *The Illusionless Man*, psychoanalyst and writer Alan Wheelis describes "a man who had no illusions about anything." Wheelis proposes that without illusions our lives would be empty; illusions are pivotal parts of human belief systems at every stage of life.

> Once upon a time there was a man who had no illusions about anything. While still in the crib he had learned that his mother was not always kind; at two he had given up fairies; witches and hobgoblins disappeared from his world at three; at four he knew that rabbits at Easter lay no eggs; and at five on a cold night in December, with a bitter little smile, he said good-bye to Santa Claus. At six when he started school illusions flew from his life like feathers in a windstorm. . . . At eight he could read, and the printed word was a sorcerer at exorcising illusions—only he knew there were no sorcerers. The abyss of hell disappeared into the even larger abyss into which a clear vision was sweeping his beliefs. Happiness was of course a myth; love a fleeting attachment, a dream of enduring selflessness glued onto the instinct of a rabbit. At twelve he dispatched into the night sky his last unheard prayer. As a young man he realized that the most generous act is self-serving, the most disinterested inquiry serves interest. . . . Of all those people who lose illusions he lost more than anyone else, taboo and prescription alike; and as everything became permitted nothing was left worth while [1966, pp. 13–14].

Certainly some of the beliefs that Wheelis's illusionless man had to forego had little or no basis in reality, despite the fixity with which they are commonly held. Yet, as becomes clear later in Wheelis's story, if we are stripped of beliefs in which we are heavily invested, regardless of their validity, we may become deeply threatened, alienated, and perhaps even seriously disrupted in our capacity for involvement and satisfaction. We pilot our lives by virtue of illusions that give meaning and substance to living.

Rather than equating the use of illusion with pathology, a stronger and more appropriate conclusion, one consistent with Otto Rank's views, would be that without some self-deception, psychopathology would be more likely. Rank (1936), too, asserted that life cannot be lived without illusion; the problem of the neurotic person is that he or she senses the truth and struggles to deal with it.

> To be able to live one needs illusions, not only outer illusions such as art, religion, philosophy, science and love afford, but inner illusions which first condition the outer (i.e., a secure sense of one's active powers and of being able to count on the powers of others). The more a man can take reality as truth, appearance as essence, the sounder, the better adjusted, the happier will he be. . . . [T]his constantly effective process of self-deceiving, pretending and blundering, is no psychopathological mechanism [pp. 251–252].

Still, we must face the seeming paradox that illusion or self-deception is both adaptationally sound and capable of eliciting a heavy price. We propose that a new question must be confronted: What kinds and degrees of self-deception are constructive or damaging to adaptation, and under what conditions? Or, as Becker (1973) put it: "On what level of illusion does one live [p. 189]?"

In *House of the Sleeping Beauties,* Japanese novelist Yasinari Kawabata pushes the limits of illusion. An old man, Eguchi, finds comfort in a secret house where he lies on occasional nights beside a young and beautiful sleeping girl. In accordance with the rules of this house, the girl is oblivious to him due to drug-induced sleep, thus allowing Eguchi to indulge in the fantasy that he can still command the sexual company of a very young girl. In this elusive contact with youth and beauty, Eguchi finds relief from the tortured inner dialogues with which he daily condemns himself for having grown old. "But it seemed a pity to go to sleep tonight when he felt none of the gloom and the loneliness of old age [p. 69]."

Similarly, at the close of Wheelis's story, when the illusionless man, Henry, and his wife, Lorabelle, are old, Wheelis tells us that illusion is the only workable way of life.

> [H]e could see himself striving toward a condition of beauty or truth or goodness or love that did not exist, but whereas earlier in his life he had always said, "It's an illusion," and turned away, now he said, "There isn't anything else," and stayed with it [p. 44].

There are, indeed, indications that the use of illusion as well as forms of denial have importance as one approaches old age, a matter we examine later in this chapter.

DENIAL, ILLUSION, AND OTHER RELATED PROCESSES

There are a number of denial-like processes, and we must make distinctions among them before we can address the issue of their adaptational consequences. We must also recognize that the costs and benefits of denial and denial-like processes depend on the contexts in which they occur, for example, the demands a person faces, the constraints on action, the resources at a person's disposal for coping in alternative ways.

Too often the processes of coping are treated as static states of mind, fixed cognitive achievements (or traits) by which a person has arrived at a stable interpretation (or defense). A more useful way of thinking is that, except for relatively rare instances of consolidated defenses, people are constantly seeking ways to comprehend what is happening to them. This ongoing process of construing reality is a constantly changing one, depending on both experiences within a person and events outside. Thus, denial or other kinds of self-deception implies flux; we must always be aware of the slippery nature of what we are trying to understand.

Denial means the "disavowal" (Freud 1966) or negation of something in thought or act or, more properly, both, since thoughts and actions are apt to be conjoined in any defense process. Logically, the negation can be either of an impulse, feeling, or thought, or of an external demand or reality—although Freud, and later Anna Freud (1946), distinguished denial from repression by conceiving of denial as focused on external rather than on internal conditions. In our usage here, however, denial can refer either to environmental realities or to intrapsychic forces. Thus, examples of denial statements could include: I do not love you; I am not seriously ill or dying; he doesn't mean any harm; she is not a competitor, etc.

It is not possible here to undertake a thorough exposition of the concept of denial in theoretical terms. Such a task would take us back to Freud, following his shifting conceptions of defense in general (Freud 1966) and proceeding to subsequent psychoanalytic writers. Such an account is available in a book by Sjöbäck (1973), who gives considerable space to the history of thought about denial. Currently, denial is commonly used both colloquially and in psychoanalytic and other research to indicate a repudiation of reality, be it internal or external in origin (e.g., Hackett and Cassem 1975, Jacobson 1957).

Anna Freud stated that "*Repression* gets rid of instinctual derivatives, just as external stimuli are abolished by *denial* [p. 174]." Sjöbäck's elucidation of Anna Freud's conceptual distinction is worth noting briefly, since it helps us move toward an understanding of how denial and repression are related. For Anna Freud, denial occurs only in a situation in which a danger is actually present. "Inhibitions of behaviours due to repressions, by contrast, are generalized. In no situation does the behaviour defended against appear [p. 104]." Actually, Anna Freud also asserted what has generally become accepted today—namely, that the

288RICHARD S. LAZARUS AND GLORIA Y. GOLDEN

defensive processes aimed at internal and external threats often work in close conjunction. Fenichel (1955) made this point emphatically; he also explained that behind every repression there were once acts of denial.

> The defensive attitudes which are directed against the external world and those which are directed against the instincts can by no means be sharply separated. Repression, which does not come into being until relatively later, is not sharply distinguished from the various forms of denial: external impressions are forgotten or left unnoticed, because they constitute a situation of temptation for the proscribed drive, and the drive is defended against from fear of a punitive intervention by the external world [p. 43].

Thus, that which is now internally repressed was originally linked to external stimuli that were denied. However, not all that was once denied becomes repressed.

A close reading of Anna Freud's *The Ego and the Mechanisms of Defence* (1946) shows that although current usage of the term denial departs from her precise meaning, the current rendering nevertheless captures her central intent—namely, that most defenses are an attempt to repudiate reality. Interestingly enough, Weisman (1972) proposed that Freud's book might have been titled "The Ego and the Mechanisms of Denial." However, although it is bothersome to try to disentangle denial from other defenses, such as displacement or projection, it is also important to maintain these distinctions in order to obtain accurate measurement of denial processes.

We must recognize that, historically, denial has been regarded by some theorists as largely pathogenic and by others as a basically normal psychic function. Anna Freud emphasized the healthy ability of a child's ego to move easily in and out of denial and yet not lose its reality-testing facility. She assumed that as the child matures, denial is replaced by avoidance, and that in the adult, persistent denial is likely to signal rigidity and neurosis. Fenichel (1945) linked excessive denial to a variety of pathological disturbances, including schizophrenia and anxiety attacks. Lewin (1950) discussed denial in relation to elation in manic-depressive illness and anxiety attacks. As we shall see later in this paper, current clinical and research opinion is divided in its views of the constructive and destructive function of the denial processes in normal adults.

There clearly remains general uncertainty about definition and measurement, including which variants to include under the general rubric (see also Janis 1958, Lipowski 1970). The concept of denial is frequently used with considerable ambiguity as to the nature of the process being described. As noted earlier, among the prominent sources of ambiguity are failures to distinguish between denial and avoidance, denial and not knowing, well-consolidated and tentative denial, and denial and illusion.

The equation of denial with avoidance is one of the most common problems. Since the behavioral indications of both denial and avoidance consist of not paying attention to or speaking of threatening content, it is often difficult to establish the distinction without further inquiry. For example, it may seem logical to conclude that if a patient does not verbally acknowledge having terminal cancer even when there is provocation to talk about it, he or she is therefore denying the imminence of death. Yet, this conclusion may be inaccurate. A patient may know full well that death is near but may prefer not to think about it. This behavior is avoidance rather than denial, and there is a world of difference between the two.

There are some indications in the research on aging that avoidance of disturbing thoughts may well be a coping strategy frequently employed by elderly persons. In their study of mentally ill and well elderly San Franciscans, Clark and Anderson (1967) noted avoidance, as opposed to denial, in some responses to the prospect of death. One participant reported: "I can't help but think about it [death] sometimes. But I certainly don't worry about it. . . . What good does it do? I go bake a cake instead."[2]

There is also considerable difference among having no information, shading things a bit in the face of ambiguous input, and engaging in full-fledged denial. Once again, the behavioral indications—acting naively or claiming to be uninformed—may be misleading. The distinction between denying and not knowing becomes especially relevant to aging when one considers illness behavior. Regarding myocardial infarction, an affliction whose incidence climbs dramatically after age 50, ignorance, uncertainty about, or denial of the meaning of initial pain costs lives (Goldstein and Moss 1972). Von Kugelgen (1975) has reviewed studies analyzing the factors affecting treatment delay. Most of the studies offered little insight into the relative contributions of lack of information, misinformation, and denial to the critical delay period between onset of pain and diagnosis and treatment. Von Kugelgen's own exploratory study, however, points

---

[2] In this connection it is instructive that a scale to measure denial published by Hackett and Cassem (1974) for use with post-coronary patients is based on the view of Anna Freud that denial is a psychological goal that can be achieved by a great many diverse cognitive and behavioral tactics. Their scale includes items involving explicit verbal denial and implicit denial in which "the patient avoids talking about the disability." From our standpoint, this risks confusion between denial and avoidance, and may muddy the definition and measurement of the denial process. At the very least, we should aim at distinguishing such processes in our measurement efforts.

strongly to the possibility that ignorance, rather than denial, of the meaning of remitting pain leads to dangerous delay. For example, patients with acute, unremitting pain were far less likely to delay.

Still another problematic definitional issue is the extent to which the process of denial is tentative or well-entrenched, or as clinicians used to say, well-consolidated. A well-consolidated denial is presumably unshakeable. Most denials are probably fluctuating constructions, responsive to this or that bit of information, mood, or whatever. Those who interact with the dying recognize that many patients who seem not to "know" really do know at some level of awareness, perhaps only dimly. This idea is expressed in Weisman's (1972) concept of "middle knowledge." As Oken (1961) has put it, "A patient who is sick enough to die knows it without being told," although he or she must often "play along" with the reassuring, denial-focused statements of physicians, friends, and relatives (Hackett and Weisman 1964). What is called denial in such cases may be, at best, only a partial denial process that depends on social circumstances to sustain it. It is not a full-fledged self-deception but only a tentative "suspension of belief."

In his analysis of denial in terminal cancer patients, Weisman (1972) asks the question, "What is being denied?" The answers lead him to distinguish three "orders" of denial that operate in analogous ways in terminal illness and in the gradual movement toward death in old age. First-order denial is a denial of superficial facts, for example, that one has cancer, or that one's strength is rapidly failing due to illness accompanying old age. In illness, such denial is usually short-term, since in a progressive or life-threatening disease the facts ultimately make the first-order denial untenable. In second-order denial, the potentially damaging or threatening primary facts have been accepted, but the implications are being denied. After all, the ultimate meaning of the facts for one's well-being constitutes the threat. Third-order denial refers to the refusal to accept one's future extinction or personal death. The numerous cases with which Weisman illustrates these denial processes convey the strong impression that for some persons these orders of denial zealously protect the patient from being psychologically immobilized by too rapid a confrontation with reality.

Although they do not use the word *denial,* Feifel and Branscomb (1973) conceptualize another sort of continuum, which suggests relationships between tentative and well-consolidated denying and aging and dying. In their study of 371 individuals, ranging in age from 10 to 89, they found that while both terminally ill and healthy subjects repudiated death verbally on a conscious level, they responded to it ambivalently on a fantasy or imagery level and were clearly negative about it "below-the-level-of-awareness," to use Feifel and Branscomb's term. The data contained curious age differences. While all persons manifested an un-conscious anxiety about death, persons 50 to 79 saw death in a fairly positive light on the fantasy and conscious levels. Related findings have been reported in other research (Kalish 1976). Their results led Feifel and Branscomb to speculate on the impact of the life-cycle on acceptance and denial of death. Nearness to death may not be in itself "sufficient condition to predict a benign and accepting outlook of death [p. 287]." Rather, it is possible that a sense of having fulfilled the potential of one's life makes it much easier to achieve a partial acceptance of death.

The distinction between illusion and denying is elusive, yet critical. An illusion is something that "deceives and misleads intellectually," according to Webster (*Webster's Seventh New Collegiate*), and is a perception involving "a false belief," according to Oxford (*The Concise Oxford, Fourth Edition*). To deny is to declare something untrue or nonexistent. To hold an illusion is to be wrong or mistaken in a belief or an assumption (but often unwittingly so). Broadly, there are two classes of illusions: (1) those that we truly believe to be reality—these are illusions we might abandon if shown convincing proof they are in-accurate, and (2) those that we believe despite conscious or unconscious knowledge to the contrary.

In *Something Happened,* Joseph Heller's hero tried unsuccessfully to convert avoidance into illusion. But, alas, he knew that he knew. Repelled by the infirmities of age, this less than admirable middle-aged, middle-level manager could not face his mother's decline after her stroke.

> I was silent also with my mother when she had the first of her brain strokes, and am silent also with everyone else I know in whom I begin to perceive the first signs of irreversible physical decay and approaching infirmity and death. (I write these people off rapidly. They become dead records in my filing system long before they are even gone . . .). . . . I pretended by not speaking of it, for my sake as well as for hers (for my sake *more* than for hers) that she was not seriously ill in a nursing home she hated and that she was not crippled and growing older and more crippled daily. I did not want her to know, as she did know (and I knew she knew) . . . [pp. 95 and 97].[3]

Among the situations in which illusion can take hold are those in which facts are not known or are partially known; there may only be implications from which a whole range of conclusions could be drawn. With this in mind, we can now link illusion to some of the definitional distinctions made earlier in this section. We would suggest, for example, that a person with an as yet undiagnosed myocardial infarction may not be denying the meaning of pain that has temporarily abated. It is probably not only kinder but more accurate to say that he or she may have chosen

---

[3] Reprinted by permission of Alfred A. Knopf, Inc.

among various implications, and in the sudden absence of pain, pursued the more consoling possibility, thinking perhaps that the subsiding pain was indigestion (which it could be) or that something as serious as a heart attack "could not be happening to me." Both possibilities may or not prove to be illusions. (In fact, Von Kugelgen [1975] counsels that since there is no way to clearly self-diagnose the symptoms of myocardial infarction, the only implication that should be allowed to reign is one that precludes illusion—namely, that one must quickly get to a hospital and find out what the pain means.)

Weisman (1972) applies his concept of second-order denial to aging and nearness to death as well as to serious illness. Since he is referring to a rejection of the implications or "extensions" of aging, we suspect that periods of transition from being middle-aged to young–old and to old–old are ripe for illusions. That is, illusion, more than denial, may be the appropriate concept for describing some of the ways people distort age identity or react to physical decline. Bultena and Powers' (1978) research on changes over a 10-year period in the age identities of persons over age 70 provides indirect support for this hunch, although what we would term illusion, they call denial. A third of Bultena and Powers's 235 respondents continued to think of themselves as middle-aged in the 10-year follow-up; those who now referred to themselves as old and elderly mentioned a decline in their physical health and in their ability to be independent. With these declines, they were no longer able to compare themselves favorably with a middle-aged reference group. The implication fostered by positive comparison with middle-aged groups had formerly permitted the illusive attribution of a younger age identity. When these implications were replaced by evidence of decline in health and autonomy, illusion was no longer tenable.

RESEARCH ON DENIAL-LIKE PROCESSES

The definitional and conceptual confusion that surrounds denial, as it does most other defensive processes, makes the evaluation of outcomes even more difficult. Thus, although there are a substantial number of research studies of denial, it is difficult to compare them because of variations in the way the defensive process is understood and measured. Nevertheless, it is worth trying to wade into some of this research in an effort to extract whatever hypothetical principles we can, recognizing that they must be tentative at best. To undertake this we have chosen to examine two types of studies within psychological research, those in which denial seems to have damaging adaptational consequences and those in which denial seems to have positive adaptational consequences. We have also performed a similar examination of studies of denial in human development and aging research. No attempt has been made to provide a thorough review of all research. We have also had to overlook some of the definitional and measurement problems, an oversight that is partially redressed along the way as particular studies are examined. (In fact, we have used the term *denial-like processes* rather than denial, since various processes are involved in these studies.)

Studies in Which Denial Is Linked to Negative Outcomes

One line of thought about denial has come down from the work of Lindemann (1944) on grieving, which has some of its roots in the psychoanalytic tradition (cf. Bowlby 1961) and some in direct clinical observation of the bereaved. Studying those who mourned the victims of the Coconut Grove fire in Boston, Lindemann found denial of pain and distress a common feature of the grief process. Other observers have suggested a similar pattern for incapacitating loss, as in spinal cord injury (cf. Dembo *et al.* 1956, McDaniel and Sexton 1970, Rogal 1969, Wright 1960). Implicit in Lindemann's concept of *grief work*, however, was the presumption that if the bereaved person was prevented from fully engaging in the process by defense mechanisms such as denial, there was a greater likelihood that he or she would fail to negotiate the bereavement crisis normally or healthily, since successful resolution requires emancipation from the emotional bondage to the deceased and the formation of new relationships.

The same basic theme was also developed later by Janis (1958, 1974) in the concept of the *work of worrying*. Janis's research with surgical patients, in which low fear prior to surgery was associated with high distress and behavioral difficulties during the recovery period, seemed consistent with the view that denial of fear (or of being threatened) prevented the patient from anticipating realistically the postsurgical difficulties and discomforts. Although the findings on which this concept was based have not been replicated, despite a number of tries, the concept has had good staying power because of its ring of truth and the existence of supporting findings from other types of investigations. In more recent writings about decision making (Janis and Mann 1977), vigilance is viewed as desirable because it potentiates a search for information and the weighing of alternative coping strategies in the face of threat.

Research by Horowitz (1975) makes use of an idea similar to the work of worrying, namely, the tendency for unresolved threats (in the form of thoughts and images) to enter into awareness as unwanted intrusions. Intrusive thoughts represent one type of stress response while denial represents another. Breger's (1967) treatment of dreams as efforts to cope with unresolved conflicts clearly falls within the same conceptual tradition. Anything that deflects this process is damaging to a person.

Another direct descendent of this line of thought is the series of studies generated and reviewed by Goldstein (1973), using a sentence completion test measure of vigilance (or sensitization) and avoidance (repression) as the extremes of a continuum. Vigilants are those who accept and elaborate fully on the threatening meaning conveyed by the incomplete sentence stem (e.g., to the stem *I hate,* they write, "my parents," "nosy people," "anyone who is smarter than me," etc.); avoiders seem to evade or deny the threatening content (e.g., to the stem *I hate,* they write, "to be caught in the rain without an umbrella," or "no one"). Nonspecific defenders fall into neither extreme category and are assumed to adapt their form of coping flexibly to the circumstances. To oversimplify a bit, in general this research (cf. Andrew 1970, Delong 1970) has suggested that avoiders do not do well in anticipatory threat situations or when they are exposed to repeated threats (e.g., when they are shown a stressful movie more than once). The assumption is that their characteristic mode of coping prevents coming to terms with the threat. Avoiders and vigilants seem also to be differentially benefited by diverse interventions in anticipatory stress situations, avoiders doing better when left alone and vigilants responding best to extensive preparation. Although, as is usually the case, the data are more complicated and less clear than one would wish, they seem consistent with the concepts of grief work and the work of worrying, and point to avoidance and denial as processes that can interfere with successful mastery by preventing appropriate cognitive coping prior to a stressful confrontation.

A recent study of asthmatic patients (Staudenmayer *et al.* 1979) further supports the notion that avoidance and denial are disruptive of mastery. Asthmatics were divided into those who respond to symptoms with vigilance and those who disregard them. When the slightest sign of a developing attack is noticed, the former grow fearful and vigilant; the latter evade or deny the seriousness of the symptom and wait out the situation, expecting or hoping that the attack will not materialize and the symptoms will disappear. Staudenmayer *et al.* found that the high-fear, vigilant patients were far less likely to be rehospitalized over a 6-month period than the low-fear, denial-oriented patients. The vigilants tended to take action quickly when breathing difficulties ensued, while the avoiders tended to disregard these difficulties, and hence allowed the attack to progress too far to treat short of hospitalization. Here, too, we are shown the value of vigilance and the high cost of denial–avoidance in a medical outcome; in such cases, the coping process leads to the failure to act in one's own best interest.

An even clearer demonstration of the view that denial may interfere with actions necessary for survival may be found in the research of Katz *et al.* (1970) concerning women who discovered a breast lump. Denial, mixed with rationalization, appears to have been the most prevalent form of coping, being used by 11 of 30 subjects. Katz *et al.* found that there was often considerable delay in getting medical attention, which, in the event the lump were malignant, would have added greatly to the danger of metastasis and reduced the chances for surgical care. Denial-based delays in seeking medical help for a heart attack have also been reported (Von Kugelgen 1975), and Hackett and Cassem (1975) cite cases of men who, while undergoing such an attack, did vigorous pushups or climbed flights of stairs to convince themselves that what they were experiencing was not a heart attack.

Studies in Which Denial Is Linked to Positive Outcomes

Clinical thought has, in recent years, shifted considerably from an emphasis on intrapsychic conflict to environmental forces, such as catastrophic illness, as factors in adaptational crises in ordinary people. In all likelihood, this shift reflects in part, the positive mental health movement and a retreat from a preoccupation with pathology. One series of studies influenced by the research and theorizing of Roy Grinker, Sr. (cf. Offer and Freedman 1972) has been particularly influential in the growing agreement that denial-like processes can have positive as well as negative adaptational consequences, and that defensive processes are not the exclusive property of "sick" minds but an integral feature of healthy coping as well.

This series includes research on the victims of severe and incapacitating burns (Hamburg *et al.* 1953) and of paralytic polio (Visotsky *et al.* 1961), summarized analytically by Hamburg and Adams (1967). A major thesis was that self-deception by denial was often a valuable initial form of coping, occurring at a time when a person is confused and weakened and therefore unable to act directly and constructively. In a severe and sudden crisis, "time for 'preparation' is likely to be bought by temporary self-deception, in such a way as to make recognition of threatening elements gradual and manageable [Hamburg and Adams 1967,

p. 283]." Davis (1963), too, has observed that denial of the gravity of an illness (polio) and its implications for the sick child and its family permits the parents to have a more extended time perspective about the child's recovery, and to be able to accept as milestones comparatively small steps toward recovery, such as being fitted with leg braces. In writing about the atomic holocaust at Hiroshima, Lifton (1964) suggested that early denial might facilitate ultimate adjustment by allowing the survivors to engage in a "psychic closing off" in order to provide protection from "the threat [of psychosis] posed by the overwhelming evidence of actual physical death [p. 208]." All of the above examples, then, offer a stage-related concept of denial in which the "disavowal" of reality is temporary and helps the person to get through the devastating early period of loss and threat, setting the stage for later acknowledgement and the mobilization of more realistic coping efforts.

Other research reports also suggest that there is a high incidence of denial-like coping processes in severe, incapacitating illness, and that these coping activities can have positive adaptational consequences. Denial has been reported as prevalent in patients with cancer (Cobb et al. 1954), having been identified through retrospective depth interviews in 90 % of a sample of 840 patients. In patients with spinal cord injuries, Dinardo (1971) used the Byrne questionnaire scale of repression–sensitization, a dimension akin theoretically to Goldstein's (1973) sentence completion measure, and found that repressers displayed greater self-esteem than sensitizers but were, however, significantly less happy. In considering such evidence we must, of course, be wary of the measure itself (see also Lefcourt 1966). First, the Byrne scale is a trait rather than process measure. Second, there appears to be no correlation among three diverse trait measures of presumably the same process (Lazarus et al. 1974).

Stern et al. (1976) assessed the coping process through interview techniques following acute myocardial infarction. Deniers (representing 25% of the sample) were more generally optimistic and did very well in returning to work and sexual functioning, and they suffered less from postcoronary depression and anxiety. This finding is consistent with the impression of Hackett et al. (1968) that denial is associated with decreased mortality in the coronary care unit.

Cohen and Lazarus (1973) have reported a study of vigilance and avoidance of relevant information by patients the night before surgery. Patients who avoided such information showed a more rapid postsurgical recovery, fewer minor complications, and less distress than vigilant patients, a finding opposite to that of Janis. The process measure did not correlate at all with a trait measure of repression–sensitization (similar to Byrne's), which in turn failed to correlate with outcome. The authors offer two interpretations. It is possible that an environmental context (the hospital) that encourages passivity and conformity may make vigilance a useless coping strategy, since what one does may have little or no impact on one's actual fate. Physicians may also have been guided in their decision to send a patient home by the patient's manifest attitude: "pollyanna" avoider–deniers would seem better candidates for early dismissal by the physician than worried, complaining vigilants. This use of avoidance–denial would ill serve the needs of patients such as those with diabetes or kidney disorder, who must closely control their diet in relation to their activity and obtain medication or dialysis when conditions warrant it. In contrast with postsurgical patients, considerable vigilance will pay off as a mode of coping for the patient with diabetes or renal failure.

More equivocal evidence concerning the outcome of denial is found in the research of Wolff *et al.* (1964) on the parents of children dying of leukemia. This well-known study found that parents who were "well-defended," largely through denial-like forms of cognitive coping, showed lower levels of corticosteroid secretion during the child's illness than those who were poorly defended. Thus, to the extent that lowered stress levels can be considered a positive consequence, denial-like coping had positive adaptational value. On the other hand, a follow-up study with the same parents (Hofer *et al.* 1972) obtained data suggestive of a later reversal: Those who had high secretion levels prior to the child's death showed lower levels many months later; and those who had low prior levels had higher ones later.

If this finding is solid and does not merely represent regression to the mean, it also points up the idea that one must be time-oriented in evaluating adaptational outcomes of coping. One might say, for example, that the well-defended parents were benefited during the illness but more vulnerable after as a result of the child's death because they failed to do grief work; in contrast, those who continued consciously to struggle with the impending tragedy were better off later because of their anticipatory coping. To complicate matters further, a later study by Townes *et al.* (1974) suggests that fathers did the work of grieving prior to the child's death while mothers did not, so that subsequent mourning was sustained and more intense for the latter. Although data such as these are suggestive (the difference did not reach statistical significance in the study by Townes *et al.*), none of the studies cited in this research arena is capable of clearly settling the issue of denial and the passage of time. We are still left with the possibility that denial may be helpful only in a limited time frame, and may exact a price later on.

Recent observations by Levine and Zigler (1975) on denial in stroke victims may also be considered here, although the issue of positive or negative outcome in this study is equivocal. Denial was measured idiosyncratically through an examination of real- versus ideal-self disparity. Stroke victims were found to have the greatest use of denial—that is, they showed a larger discrepancy between actual mental condition and how it was appraised—when compared with victims of lung cancer and heart disease. Denial appeared to produce a state of comparative emotional equanimity in the stroke patients, despite the fact that they actually suffered the greatest damage to functioning among the three disorders. We are inclined to believe that a more realistic self-assessment by the stroke victims would have had little value, adaptationally, since even with a more realistic appraisal they could not have done more than they were doing about their deficits. Perhaps it could be said that ignorance is more functional than the bitter truth at such times.

Before leaving studies in which denial has proved constructive, it is worth noting a recent neurohumoral discovery that, with a small leap of the imagination, seems to be relevant. Biochemists (cf. Guillemin *et al.* 1977) have discovered that, simultaneous with the secretion under stress of ACTH by the pituitary gland, another hormone called endorphin-B is also secreted. ACTH stimulates secretion of corticosteroids by the adrenals; endorphin-B seems to affect morphine-sensitive brain tissue, presumably acting like an analgesic and psychedelic. A severely wounded animal, or a badly frightened or enraged one, might well be expected to produce not only corticosteroids (Selye's GAS stage of resistance) but also this morphine-like substance. This may help explain why Beecher (1956–1957) and others have observed a remarkable absence of pain in wounded soldiers, or why in battle men sometimes throw themselves into combat seemingly oblivious of the consequences. It may not be altogether fanciful to suggest that chemicals such as endorphin-B could be the neurohumoral analogue of denial and other comforting cognitions (Mechanic 1962, 1978) or, as we have elsewhere referred to them, palliative forms of coping.

Research on Positive and Negative Aspects of Denial in Aging

Although research on denial-like forms of coping in aging is not extensive, it does show both constructive and destructive consequences. Rosow (1967) devotes considerable attention to explaining the link between the socially devalued status of old persons and the widely reported finding that old persons persistently push their age identities back in time. In Rosow's study of Cleveland apartment dwellers over age 65, only 37% of the respondents thought that persons over 65 were still productive, yet 83% felt that they themselves were still useful. Most of the respondents agreed with a statement ridiculing older persons who still regard themselves as middle-aged, yet nearly half the sample thought that they were not old. Reflecting the differential loss experienced by the social classes, middle-class persons in this sample were more likely to deny age-linked loss of prestige than working-class persons. According to Rosow, denial is one of the few defenses available to persons in a society that relentlessly erodes the roles and statuses of the old and provides no new role prescriptions or rewards. "Age is denied as long as the illusion can be maintained [p. 33]"; writes Rosow: "Even though they may finally admit they are old after incurring the most extreme losses of health, roles and associations (especially after the age of seventy-five), this very concession is often the symptom of demoralization [p. 255]." Rosow's case can also be related to sociological and anthropological evidence that analogous coping processes are used by disadvantaged and maligned classes, castes, or social categories across societies (e.g., Berreman 1960). Rosow, of course, is not claiming that denial is intrinsically negative; it is, in his view, an adaptation to a harsh and deflating social reality.

Tobin and Lieberman (1976) have stated that a "central task of aging is to transcend bodily decline and the imminence of death [p. 165]." They propose that rather than being pathological, a certain level of denial may be absolutely vital to the attainment of this transcendence for the very old:

> [When] denial or counterphobic maneuvers . . . appear in extreme forms in younger persons, we tend to think of such mechanisms as indices of psychopathology. But for elderly persons such mechanisms are clearly less psychopathological because they facilitate the maintenance of functioning. Giving in to the underlying deficits may quickly lead to decompensation and death [pp. 34–35].

In their study of elderly persons awaiting admission to a home for the aged, Tobin and Lieberman observed that the mechanisms we have discussed here as variants of denial were used by many of the elderly persons in their samples. For example, there was a sharp disparity between the actual high incidence of disease in the 35 community participants and their hopeful emotional tone and "minimal anxiety and depression." It appeared that some respondents ignored their disabilities and others denied them. However, still others met their difficulties head on as challenges to be overcome. This latter approach was certainly true of the heavily medicated woman who had a weak heart but nevertheless negotiated three flights of stairs several times a day, and humorously chided the out-of-breath interviewer for not being in better shape.

It is difficult to assess directly from Tobin and Lieberman's account the extent to which illusion as opposed to out-and-out denial operates in coping with the losses of very old age. It is remarkable, however, that despite severe physical deficits and despite the fact that 40% of the sample had lost a significant other in the last 3 years, the community sample was not only hopeful and functioning well, they were also "not focused on losses." Sixty percent did not bring up loss themes; only three persons introduced interpersonal loss themes, eight noted injury, and none initiated talk about death. If very old age is a time of enormous "event uncertainty," as Tobin and Lieberman assert, then such findings beg for further investigation into the psychic processes at work.

What, after all, does it mean to say that these persons were not focused on loss? Heyman and Jeffers (1965) reported that 50% of their elderly sample experienced no concern about the future. Tobin and Lieberman suggest that one explanation for this is that older persons "fear talking about an uncertain future that may include a long period of debilitation and dependency before death [p. 51]." How illusory, then, is the dominant sense of hopefulness of the very old in Tobin and Lieberman's sample?

Denial and avoidance were important coping mechanisms for those in Tobin and Lieberman's sample who were awaiting entry into a home for the aged. A sentence completion and self-sort test and a special version of the Thematic Apperception Test (TAT) were used to assess denial and avoidance. The results turned up a very high incidence of both processes. In response to the sentence completion measure, 70% did not discuss the home or did so only once (there were 12 opportunities); with the TAT, half of the sample showed "extreme to complete denial and only eight % showed no denial [p. 115]." According to Tobin and Lieberman, "The unavoidable implication of these analyses was that denial was central to coping with the impending event [p. 115]." Thus, despite their dread of admission to the home, their sense of abandonment, and their abhorrence of loss of privacy, many of these respondents chose to deny their negative cognitions and affects and to emphasize the positive.

Denial, specifically denial in solving interpersonal conflicts, was not a viable coping mechanism when considered as a predictor of survival in the first year following admission to the home. This predictor variable operated independent of actual institutional effects. Persons who deteriorated severely or died soon after admission had poor functional capacity (cognitive and self-care), less hope, and were said to use denial in solving interpersonal conflicts. Overall, then, denial had both adaptive and maladaptive implications for the stresses of institutionalization.

Within the realm of urban anthropology, Clark and Anderson (1967) used the evidence from intensive interviews of elderly San Franciscans to study the adaptational tasks of aging. What these researchers called denial emerged as one of the prominent factors distinguishing hospitalized mentally ill persons from mentally well community residents. The hospitalized respondents expressed horror of aging by using immensely varied techniques of refutation of the evidence of their own aging, and were particularly terrified of seeing themselves in the mirror. These elderly deniers were of two types—those who expressly refused to admit that they were old or that any of their problems were aging-connected, and those who displaced their denial onto physical ailments, refusing to admit that aging was a problem in and of itself.

Reflecting on findings similar to those of Rosow on denial of age identity, Clark and Anderson make an enlightening observation: They suggest that whereas mentally well young-old persons generally cling to middle-age identity as long as possible, mentally well old-old persons "may be able to accept change in themselves with more resignation and better grace [p. 89]." In view of this, the tenacious denials of the mentally ill old-old persons in their San Francisco sample are all the more striking.

The denial described by Clark and Anderson was not limited to verbal statements of youthfulness. The denial-prone respondents, both hospitalized and nonhospitalized, also tended to live in isolation in order to protect themselves from proof of age decline, which could come in a number of threatening forms. They might be visited by other old persons who were similarly incapacitated or, worse yet, by those who were physically and psychologically stronger. Or they might be compelled by social contact to expose serious needs for physical and/or emotional sustenance. Such needs would be sure indications that they no longer fulfilled the uncompromising American criteria of sturdy adulthood—unwavering self-reliance and autonomy. True, the mentally ill elderly might well have had shaky self-esteem, unrelated to their age decline. But the blows dealt by a youth-oriented, autonomy-obsessed culture might have proved intolerable to egos already low in resilience. In such person–environment transactions, the degree to which denial and withdrawal are adaptive or maladaptive becomes a relative matter that must be evaluated in light of both cultural demands and individual vulnerability. Thus, according to Clark and Anderson (1967):

> What in one case might seem to be a dangerous withdrawal from all social interchange into a hermitage might, in fact, be a valid attempt to preserve self-esteem in the face of acknowledged decrements in physical and mental

functioning. If such decrements are not yet so severe as to merit professional or institutional care, we are obliged to acknowledge such withdrawal as reasonably functional to the individual's culturally-sanctioned need for autonomy and self-reliance. However, in other cases—those where withdrawal from others represents a pathological denial of physical and mental illness—then greater circumspection is required in assessing the disengagement as functional or malfunctional [p. 380].

The foregoing consideration of the concept of denial in research on aging was not intended as a comprehensive treatment. There is, after all, comparatively little research to be cited on denial and aging. We have tried to indicate that in this research, as in the more general body of studies, denial-like processes have both beneficial and harmful consequences. The dynamics and outcomes must be understood in relation to the aging-relevant context. From the literature, one gets a clear sense that denial-like processes have substantial significance for adaptation to the stresses of both gradual and sudden, dramatic changes involved in growing old.

SUMMARY OF THE ADAPTATIONAL COSTS AND BENEFITS OF DENIAL-LIKE PROCESSES

In accordance with our analyses and the research we have cited, we will summarize very briefly the adaptational consequences of denial, with these four points:

1. The first is a version of an old scientific and wise person's truth, namely, that circumstances alter cases. Forms of denial can have positive value under certain conditions and negative value under others—a point illustrated in Tobin and Lieberman's study (1976) by the positive effect of denial on coping with the anticipation of institutionalization and by the negative implications of denial of interpersonal conflict on survival after admission to the institution. Generally, if direct action to change the damaging or threatening person–environment transaction is adaptationally critical or useful, denial will be destructive. On the other hand, when direct action is irrelevant to the adaptational outcome, then denial has no necessarily damaging consequences and could even be of value in reducing distress.

This point allows us to extrapolate to other circumstances where the amount and focus of denial may have crucial import for survival. Illnesses such as kidney failure and diabetes provide examples. Control of these illnesses depends on vigilant attention to behavioral and bodily signs that signal the need for dialysis or insulin. To the extent that denial pushes the person to overlook such signs and therefore to evade suitable actions, denial is counterproductive and could even be fatal. However, depression is also an enemy of efforts to stay alive and functioning well. Relatively good morale and the feeling of hope are required if one is to mobilize the necessary vigilance over a long time. Thus, some denial in the face of such severe hardship might also prove of value.

The distinction implied here relates to what we have called problem-focused coping and emotion-focused coping, and which was spoken of in an earlier paper as direct action and palliation (Lazarus and Launier 1978). They represent two of the most important functions of coping, namely, that of changing a damaging or threatening relationship between person and environment (problem-focused) and regulating the emotional distress produced by that relationship (emotion-focused). Denial-like processes clearly fall within the emotion-focused function; and, when denial is partial, tentative, or minimal in scope, it does not necessarily preclude the simultaneous use of problem-focused forms of coping, if these are relevant to the person's plight. In current research, Folkman (1979) has found that in every complex stressful encounter people use a mixture of both kinds of coping. Moreover, when an encounter is appraised as permitting little or nothing to be done, there is a pull toward emotion-focused coping, and when it is appraised as permitting constructive actions, the shift is to problem-focused modes.

2. The timing of denial may have crucial implications for whether it functions as a positive adaptive strategy. Denial can have value at an early stage of coping when the person's resources are insufficient to cope in a more problem-focused way; however, the costs may be great if denial is not abandoned at later stages when problem-solving coping is needed. Severely injured patients gain from denial at an early stage when their lives hang in the balance, when they are too weak or shocked to act constructively and need to be supported by others. Thus, the paraplegic is helped for a while by believing that some bodily function that has been lost will return, or that the incapacitation is not as severe as it seems. Only later will the person be strong enough to come to terms with the reality of the condition and ultimately struggle to cope in a practical, problem-focused way. The timing of denial is also relevant to life-span issues. Denial of actual age identity may have positive motivational value for relatively healthy young-old persons but may be seriously maladaptive for physically disabled mentally ill elderly persons.

3. It is generally more dangerous to deny what is clear and unambiguous than to deny what cannot be known for certain, as in the dif-

ference between the denial of fact and the denial of implication. For example, in the immediate present, one is likely to incur greater risk by denying the fact of illness than by denying the implication that illness may lead to death.

We speculate that some persons tolerate the problems of old age partly by denying or avoiding its implications. But we also take note of Feifel and Branscomb's (1973) finding: It was easier for older persons to accept the implications of death than it was for younger persons; this acceptance may have been made easier by older persons' sense of having fulfilled their life goals.

4. When denial is partial, tentative, or minimal in scope, it tends to be far less pernicious, and often useful, permitting a mixture of denial, illusion, and reality-testing. We started by noting some of the illusions we live by and how important they are for mental health. It is useful to remember that these "self-deceptions" are not usually challenged by evidence, nor do we normally even try to test them by the methods of science. They are closer to the sense of "as if," or to illusion in the literary sense. They are working fictions within which we can live comfortably, keeping our realization of relentless decline and eventual death within manageable proportions.

REFERENCES

Andrew, J. M. (1970) Recovery from surgery with and without preparatory instruction for three coping styles. *Journal of Personality and Social Psychology* 151:223–226.

Becker, E. (1973) *The Denial of Death.* New York: The Free Press.

Beecher, H. K. (1956–1957) The measurement of pain, prototype for the quantitative study of subjective responses. *Pharmacological Review* 8–9:60–209.

Berreman, G. (1960) Caste in India and the United States. *American Journal of Sociology* 66:120–127.

Blau, Z. (1956) Changes in status and age identification. *American Sociological Review* 21:198–203.

Bowlby, J. (1961) Process of mourning. *International Journal of Psychoanalysis* 42:317–340.

Breger, L. (1967) Functions of dreams. *Journal of Abnormal Psychology Monographs* 72(No. 5, Whole No. 641).

Bultena, G. L., and Powers, E. A. (1978) Denial of aging: Age identification and reference group orientations. *Journal of Gerontology* 33:748–754.

Clark, M., and Anderson, B. G. (1967) *Culture and Aging: An Anthropological Study of Older Americans.* Springfield, Ill.: Charles C. Thomas.

Cobb, B., Clark, R. L., McGuire, C., and Howe, C. D. (1954) Patient-responsible delay of treatment in cancer. *Cancer* 7:920–926.

Cohen, F., and Lazarus, R. S. (1973) Active coping processes, coping dispositions, and recovery from surgery. *Psychosomatic Medicine* 35:357–389.

Davis, F. (1963) *Passage Through Crisis: Polio Victims and Their Families.* Indianapolis, Ind.: Bobbs-Merrill.

Delong, D. R. (1970) *Individual differences in patterns of anxiety arousal, stress-relevant information and recovery from surgery.* Unpublished doctoral dissertation, University of California, Los Angeles.

Dembo, T., Leviton, G. L., and Wright, B. A. (1956) Adjustment to misfortune—a problem of social psychological rehabilitation. *Artificial Limbs* 3:4–62.

Dinardo, Q. E. (1971) *Psychological adjustment to spinal cord injury.* Unpublished doctoral dissertation, University of Houston, Texas.

Erikson, E. H. (1950, 1963) *Childhood and Society.* New York: W. W. Norton.

Feifel, H., and Branscomb, A. (1973) Who's afraid of death? *Journal of Abnormal Psychology* 81:282–288.

Fenichel, O. (1945) *The Psychoanalytic Theory of Neurosis.* London: Routledge & Kegan Paul.

Fenichel, O. (1955) *The Collected Papers. Second Series.* New York: W. W. Norton.

Folkman, S. (1979) *Analysis of coping in an adequately functioning middle-aged population.* Unpublished doctoral dissertation, University of California, Berkeley.

Freud, A. (1946, revised edition 1966) The Ego and the Mechanisms of Defence. In *The Writings of Anna Freud,* Vol. II. New York: International Universities Press.

Freud, S. (1966) *The Standard Edition of the Complete Psychological Works.* London: Hogarth.

Goldstein, M. J. (1973) Individual differences in response to stress. *American Journal of Community Psychology* 1:113–137.

Goldstein, S., and Moss, A. (1972) Symposium on the pre-hospital phase of acute myocardial infarction. *Archives of Internal Medicine* 129:720–724.

Guillemin, R., Vargo, T., Rossier, J., Minick, S., Ling, N., Rivier, C., Vale, W., and Bloom, F. (1977) B-endorphin and adrenocorticotropin are secreted concomitantly by the pituitary gland. *Science* 197:1367–1369.

Hackett, T. P., and Cassem, N. H. (1974) Development of a quantitative rating scale to assess denial. *Journal of Psychosomatic Research* 18:93–100.

Hackett, T. P., and Cassem, N. H. (1975) Psychological management of the myocardial infarction patient. *Journal of Human Stress* 1:25–38.

Hackett, T. P., Cassem, N. H., and Wishnie, H. A. (1968) The coronary-care unit: An appraisal of its psychologic hazards. *New England Journal of Medicine* 279:1365–1370.

Hackett, T. P., and Weisman, A. D. (1964) Reactions to the imminence of death. Pp. 300–311 in G. H. Grosser, H. Wechsler, and M. Greenblatt, eds., *The Threat of Impending Disaster.* Cambridge, Mass.: The MIT Press.

Hamburg, D. A., and Adams, J. E. (1967) A perspective on coping behavior: Seeking and utilizing information in major transitions. *Archives of General Psychiatry* 17:277–284.

Hamburg, D. A., Hamburg, B., and deGoza, S. (1953) Adaptive problems and mechanisms in severely burned patients. *Psychiatry* 16:1–20.

Heller, J. (1975) *Something Happened.* New York: Ballantine.

Heyman, D., and Jeffers, T. (1965) Observations on the extent of concern and planning by the aged for possible chronic illness. *Journal of the American Geriatrics Society* 13:152–159.

Hofer, M. A., Wolff, E. T., Friedman, S. B., and Mason, J. W. (1972) A psychoendocrine study of bereavement, parts I and II. *Psychosomatic Medicine* 34:481–504.

Horowitz, M. (1975) Intrusive and repetitive thoughts after experimental stress. *Archives of General Psychiatry* 32:1457–1463.

Jacobson, E. (1957) Denial and repression. *Journal of the American Psychoanalytic Association* 5:61–92.

Jahoda, M. (1958) *Current Conceptions of Positive Mental Health.* New York: Basic Books.

Janis, I. L. (1958) *Psychological Stress.* New York: Wiley.

Janis, I. L. (1974) Vigilance and decision-making in personal crises. Pp. 139–175 in G. V. Coelho, D. A. Hamburg, and J. E. Adams, eds., *Coping and Adaptation.* New York: Basic Books.

Janis, I. L., and Mann, L. (1977) *Decision Making.* New York: The Free Press.

Kalish, R. (1976) Death in a social context. Pp. 483–507 in R. H. Binstock and E. Shanas, eds., *Handbook of Aging and the Social Sciences.* New York: Van Nostrand Reinhold.

Katz, J. L., Weiner, H., Gallagher, T. G., and Hellman, L. (1970) Stress, distress, and ego defenses. *Archives of General Psychiatry* 23:131–142.

Kawabata, Y. (1965) *House of the Sleeping Beauties.* New York: Knopf.

Kübler-Ross, E. (1969) *On Death and Dying.* New York: Macmillan.

Kübler-Ross, E. (1974) *Questions and Answers on Death and Dying.* New York: Macmillan.

Lazarus, R. S., Averill, J. R., and Opton, E. M., Jr. (1974) The psychology of coping: Issues of research and assessment. Pp. 249–315 in G. V. Coelho, D. A. Hamburg, and J. E. Adams, eds., *Coping and Adaptation.* New York: Basic Books.

Lazarus, R. S., and Launier, R. (1978) Stress-related transactions between person and environment. Pp. 287–327 in L. A. Pervin and M. Lewis, eds., *Perspectives in Interactional Psychology.* New York: Plenum.

Lefcourt, H. M. (1966) Repression–sensitization: A measure of the evaluation of emotional expression. *Journal of Consulting and Clinical Psychology* 30:444–449.

Levine, J., and Zigler, E. (1975) Denial and self-image in stroke, lung cancer, and heart disease patients. *Journal of Consulting and Clinical Psychology* 43:751–757.

Lewin, G. D. (1950) *The Psychoanalysis of Elation.* New York: W. W. Norton.

Lifton, R. J. (1964) On death and death symbolism: The Hiroshima disaster. *Psychiatry* 27:191–210.

Lindemann, E. (1944) Symptomatology and management of acute grief. *American Journal of Psychiatry* 101:141–148.

Lipowski, Z. J. (1970) Physical illness, the individual and the coping process. *International Journal of Psychiatry in Medicine* 1:91–102.

Maslow, A. H. (1954) *Motivation and Personality.* New York: Harper & Row.

McDaniel, J. W., and Sexton, A. W. (1970) Psychoendocrine studies of patients with spinal cord lesion. *Journal of Abnormal Psychology* 76:117–122.

Mechanic, D. (1962, 1978) *Students Under Stress.* Madison, Wis.: University of Wisconsin Press.

Offer, D., and Freedman, D. X. (1972) *Modern Psychiatry and Clinical Research: Essays in Honor of Roy R. Grinker, Sr.* New York: Basic Books.

Oken, D. (1961) What to tell cancer patients: Study of medical attitudes. *Journal of the American Medical Association* 175:1120–1128.

Rank, O. (1936) *Will Therapy and Truth and Reality.* New York: Knopf.

Rogal, R. A. (1969) Psychological treatment of spinal cord injured patients. Pp. 141–151 in E. S. Stauffer, N. W. Wilcox, V. L. Nickel, and E. R. Erickson, eds., *Interdisciplinary Clinical, Education, and Research Aspects of a Regional Center for the Rehabilitation of Spinal Cord Injured Persons.*

Rosow, I. (1967) *Social Integration of the Aged.* New York: The Free Press.

Sjöbäck, H. (1973) *The Psychoanalytic Theory of Defensive Processes.* New York: Wiley.

Staudenmayer, H., Kinsman, R. A., Dirks, J. F., Spector, S. L., and Wangaard, C. (1979) Medical outcome in asthmatic patients: Effects of airways hyperactivity and symptom-focused anxiety. *Psychosomatic Medicine* 41:109–118.

Stern, M. J., Pascale, L., and McLoone, J. B. (1976) Psychosocial adaptation following an acute myocardial infarction. *Journal of Chronic Diseases* 29:513–526.

Tobin, S., and Lieberman, M. (1976) *Last Home for the Aged.* San Francisco: Jossey-Bass.

Townes, B. D., Wold, D. A., and Holmes, T. H. (1974) Parental adjustment to childhood leukemia. *Journal of Psychosomatic Research* 18:9–14.

Visotsky, H. M., Hamburg, D. A., Goss, M. E., and Lebovits, B. Z. (1961) Coping behavior under extreme stress. *Archives of General Psychiatry* 5:423–448.

Von Kugelgen, E. (1975) *Psychological determinants of the delay in decision to seek aid in cases of myocardial infarction.* Unpublished doctoral dissertation, University of California, Berkeley.

Weisman, A. D. (1972) *On Dying and Denying.* New York: Behavioral Publications.

Wheelis, A. (1966) *The Illusionless Man: Fantasies and Meditations.* New York: Norton.

Wolff, C. T., Friedman, S. B., Hofer, M. A., and Mason, J. W. (1964) Relationship between psychological defenses and mean urinary 17-hydroxycorticosteroid excretion rates, parts I and II. *Psychosomatic Medicine* 26:576–609.

Wright, B. A. (1960) *Physical Disability: A Psychological Approach.* New York: Harper.

PART IV

HEALTH

chapter 13

Life Changes and Disease in Elderly Populations: Coping with Change

WILLIAM A. SATARIANO
S. LEONARD SYME

Old age is identified as a leading risk factor for most chronic diseases. It is reported that approximately 86% of people over 65 have one or more chronic health problems (Shanas and Maddox 1976, Harris 1978). Despite this relation between aging and disease, there are elderly people who are in remarkably good health. This fact raises two important research questions: Why do some elderly people become ill while others do not? And of those who become ill, why are some physically impaired and others not?

There are many reasons why some elderly are in poor health and others are not. It is unlikely, however, that even well-established risk factors such as cigarette smoking and high blood pressure will provide a full explanation for the differences in disease rates. Consider the case of coronary heart disease, the leading cause of death among the elderly. In studies of people in the general population, the recognized risk factors for coronary heart disease do not explain all the disease that occurs. Data from the pooled findings for the six main prospective studies in the United States show that of men with two or more risk factors, only about 10% develop coronary heart disease over a 10-year period, while 90% do not. Viewed differently, 42% of these cases that developed in the 10-year period occurred among men with two or more of these risk factors

AGING
Biology and Behavior

(Inter-Society Commission for Heart Disease Resources 1970). Without denying the importance of such risk factors as serum cholesterol, cigarette smoking, and blood pressure, it is clear that other, as yet undiscovered, risk factors are also important. In light of these findings, it has been suggested that researchers investigate behavioral and psychosocial factors in order to develop new information on what causes disease (Cassel 1974, Syme 1974). This proposal is based on numerous studies showing associations between social and psychological variables and health status (Antonovsky 1979, Moss 1973). Of all the research in this area, studies on life changes and disease have been particularly suggestive.

It has been shown that the risk of coronary heart disease increases with major changes in place of residence, major changes in occupation, and discrepancies between culture of upbringing and current social situation (Cassel and Tyroler 1961, Syme et al. 1964, Tyroler and Cassel 1964). In all cases, the findings of increased risk are independent of the effects of such recognized risk factors as age, sex, serum cholesterol, cigarette smoking, and blood pressure. While these studies were based on samples of the general population and did not focus specifically on the elderly, the findings suggest research strategies for investigating disease patterns in elderly populations. We know, for example, that major life changes, such as the death of a spouse and retirement, are more likely to occur among the elderly. It may be, therefore, that life changes associated with aging contribute to different rates of disease among the elderly. Indeed, several commentators have described aging as a process of life changes (Rosow 1976).

In this chapter, we review and evaluate the available evidence regarding the relation between life change and disease in elderly populations. We will suggest that the effects of life changes on health can be best understood in terms of a mediating factor—namely, the person's network of social contacts with others. Finally, we propose a new research strategy for investigating disease patterns among the elderly.

LIFE CHANGES AND DISEASE

Most of the research on age-related life changes has focused on bereavement and retirement. There are two basic findings in this area. First, people undergoing a particular life change such as bereavement are at greater risk of death than people not undergoing that change (Jacobs and Ostfeld 1977, Maddison and Viola 1968, Parkes 1964, Rees and Lutkins 1967). In their review of the bereavement literature, Jacobs and Ostfeld (1977) report that the attributable risk of death for people losing a spouse may be as high as 50%. However, the evidence for a relation between bereavement and morbidity is mixed. In a prospective study of bereaved elderly, Clayton (1974) reports that while the bereaved were more likely to report psychological and physical depressive symptoms than controls, there was no difference between the groups in the number of visits to physicians, hospitalizations, and the use of tranquilizers during the first year of bereavement. Second, bereavement is clearly more important than retirement for predicting subsequent health status. The general consensus among researchers is that occupational retirement *per se* affects neither mortality rates nor morbidity rates (Eisdorfer and Wilkie 1976, Haynes *et al.* 1978, Sheppard 1976). In fact, Haynes *et al.* (1978) report that prior health status is the only significant predictor of 5-year mortality rates among early retirees. There is some evidence, however, that the anticipation of retirement may lead to health-related absences (Riley *et al.* 1968).

In reviewing the work on age-related life changes, it is still unclear why bereavement is strongly related to subsequent health status while retirement is not. This is an important question. By understanding why bereavement is more important than retirement, it may be possible to obtain a better understanding of why life change itself affects health. Cassel (1976) offers a useful approach to this question.

In his review of social epidemiology, Cassel (1976) hypothesized that a life change reduces a person's resistance to disease by disrupting the person's "meaningful" social contact with others. In Cassel's view, the key is social contact. The life change itself may represent a disrupted or broken social contact such as with the death of a spouse. A broken social contact, in turn, may strain or disrupt other social relationships such as with friends and relatives and lead to the person's relative social isolation. It is possible to hypothesize, therefore, that bereavement is more serious than retirement for a person's health; the death of a spouse is more likely than retirement to disrupt an important social relation and lead to the disruption of other social relationships. Following this reasoning, life changes should be measured in terms of the number and types of disrupted social relationships.

It is also possible to hypothesize from Cassel's position why some people survive bereavement and others do not. If life changes disrupt social contacts, then the number and type of social contacts a person maintains should determine whether the person can avoid isolation and cope with the changes. Are there other people available to fill the void left by the loss? In general, Cassel's position suggests that, all other things being equal, the people who do not survive are those people with fewer social contacts, or those people whose contacts are more seriously damaged by the change.

Cassel's position suggests a more parsimonious research strategy than those employed previously. Rather than assessing the effects of different life changes such as bereavement and retirement, it is possible to focus on "social contact" as the basic unit of analysis. Not only is it possible to examine the social contacts that are disrupted by one or more age-related life changes, but also those social contacts that are maintained. A measure of severity of the life change can be obtained by comparing the number and types of social contacts that are disrupted with those contacts that are preserved. This measure of severity, in turn, can be compared with measures of health status. While Cassel's ideas are provocative, a number of important questions remain to be answered. What are "meaningful" social contacts? Most importantly, why are "meaningful" social contacts related to health? To answer these questions, it is necessary to review and evaluate the research on social relationships and health.

SOCIAL RELATIONSHIPS AND HEALTH

To our knowledge, the independent and joint relations between life changes, social relationships, and health status have not been examined in elderly populations. Though researchers have used data on social contacts to investigate the elderly's sense of well-being and their management of existing health problems (Cutler 1976, Lowenthal and Robinson 1976, Larson 1978, Markides and Martin 1979, Shanas 1979), these data have not been used to investigate the incidence of illness among the aged. The most notable exception is Lowenthal's and Haven's (1968) research showing that an important confidant seems to help people avoid psychiatric symptoms.

While not concerned with the elderly in particular, there are a number of studies showing that social relationships play a protective role in health maintenance (Moss 1973). The general assumption is that they provide social support that, in turn, protects against morbidity and mortality (Cassel 1976, Cobb 1976, Dean and Lin 1977, Lin et al. 1979, Moss 1973). It is possible to assume that Cassel's "meaningful" social relationships are those that provide social support. It is still unclear, however, why some are "supportive" while others are not. More important, how does social support affect health? One position is that social relationships are supportive by encouraging and enforcing proper preventive health behavior (e.g., a proper diet, medical checkups, and avoidance of known risk factors). Another position is that relationships are supportive by providing resources for coping with life problems, which, in turn, facilitate a person's resistance to disease (Cassel 1976). We will present and evaluate the evidence for both positions.

Social Support and Health Behavior: The Evidence

Even though there is modest evidence that social contacts with others influence a person's preventive health behavior (Langlie 1977), there is no evidence that health behavior accounts for the relationship between the number of social relationships and longevity (Berkman and Syme 1979).

In the Berkman and Syme (1979) study, the relationship between social and community contacts was assessed using the Human Population Laboratory survey of a random sample of 6928 adults in Alameda County, California. Social and community relationships included four types of reported contact: marriage, contacts with close friends and relatives, church membership, and informal and formal group associations.

There was a clear relationship shown between social relationships and longevity. People without social and community contacts were more likely to die in the 9-year follow-up period than those with the most developed social contacts. Each measure of social contact predicted mortality. The age-adjusted relative risks for those most isolated when compared with those with most social contacts were 2.3 for men and 2.8 for women. Surprisingly, the relation between social contacts and mortality could not be explained in terms of such preventive health factors as health practices, obesity, physical activity, and reported alcohol and smoking consumption. The relation between social contacts and longevity is clear, but it cannot be accounted for in terms of preventive health practices.

Despite this finding, it may be premature to disregard preventive health behavior as a source of social support. The hypothesis states that social relationships are related to health, because they encourage and enforce proper preventive health behavior. In most cases, however, not enough information is obtained to test the hypothesis directly. While respondents are asked about their preventive health behavior, they are not asked whether their friends and associates encourage and enforce that behavior. That missing information is crucial for testing whether preventive health practices are obtained directly from social contacts. For example, do family members encourage respondents to moderate their smoking? Are friends likely to remind respondents to go for a health checkup if they forget? We feel that the role of preventive health behavior as a form of social support is still unclear, and that more work in this area is needed.

Social Support and Coping: The Evidence

It is also hypothesized that social relationships are supportive by providing resources for coping (Cobb 1976, Dean and Lin 1977). However, there is only indirect evidence supporting this hypothesis. For example, Nuckolls *et al.* (1972) studied a sample of 170 pregnant women who completed questionnaires measuring the degree of life change and their psychosocial assets. Social support items were included in the general index of psychosocial assets. Support was measured specifically in terms of the emotional and economic support their extended family could be expected to provide. It also was measured in terms of the respondents' perceptions of support offered by their friends. Life changes were measured by a modified Holmes and Rahe (1967) life-events scale, designed to assess the number of major and minor recent stressful events. Life change and psychosocial assets were compared with the degree of subsequent pregnancy complications. Ninety-one percent of women having complications were those who exhibited both stressful life changes and low psychosocial assets earlier during their pregnancies.

In a more recent study, Gore (1978) examined the protective effects of social support for unemployed men. The health effects of unemployment (job loss due to a plant closing) were examined in 110 men. Men were examined at five points: after the closing was announced but before the actual termination, at the time of the closing, during the period of adaptation following the closing, 1 year after the closing, and 2 years after the closing. Information obtained from the men included degree of social support, perceived economic deprivation, depression, self-blame, illness symptoms, and recorded level of serum cholesterol. Social support was measured in terms of the person's perception of whether wife, friends, and relatives were supportive and the perceived opportunity for engaging in social activities. Gore (1978) found that men with higher levels of social support were less likely to exhibit psychological and physiological problems.

Lin *et al.* (1979) examined the independent and joint effect of social support and stressful life events on self-reported psychiatric symptoms. The sample consisted of 170 Chinese Americans. Stressful life events were measured with a modified Holmes and Rahe (1967) scale. Social support was measured in terms of the respondents' frequency of contacts with friends, neighbors, "people nearby," and Chinese cultural organizations. It also was measured in terms of respondents' feelings toward particular social contacts. The self-reported psychiatric symptoms covered 24 possible symptoms occurring in the last 6 months. They found that an increase in the number of reported symptoms was associated with both an increase in the number of life events and a decrease in the degree of social support. They also discovered that social support was more strongly associated with reported symptoms than were recent life events. However, there was only a weak relationship between life events and social support. They concluded, therefore, that while social support was associated with fewer reported symptoms, the relationship could not be explained in terms of support acting as a buffer against the stress of recent life events.

In each of the three studies, access to social support is clearly shown to be related to fewer reported health problems. It is unclear, however, what kind of support was available, and whether it was, in fact, related to coping. The importance of coping resources was implied but never tested directly. It is also unclear from these studies why social support was related to health. One interesting possibility is that social relations provide supportive resources for coping that, over time, lead to a general sense of control (Antonovsky 1979). Characteristics of a sense of control such as feelings of confidence and responsibility to others may contribute in some way to health and well-being.

Social Support and a Sense of Control

There is a growing number of studies relating a sense of control to health. Seligman's (1974, 1975) work in this area points to a relation between learned helplessness and depression. Seligman argues that if people learn that attempts to deal with particular problems are futile, they not only retreat from those problems but also from other problems that can be controlled. In short, people learn to be helpless, withdrawn and apathetic, behavior characteristic of the clinically depressed. In contrast, people who have learned to expect mastery and control seem to be resistant to depression. Seligman (1974) writes:

> The life histories of those individuals who are particularly resistant to depression or resilient to depression may have been filled with mastery. These people may have had extensive experience controlling and manipulating the sources of reinforcement in their lives and may therefore perceive the future optimistically. These people who are particularly susceptible to depression may have had lives relatively devoid of mastery [p. 106].[1]

Seligman speculates that learned helplessness may lead to a variety of other health problems besides depression. He cites the work of Engel

[1]Reprinted by permission of Hemisphere Publishing Corporation.

to support this hypothesis. Engel and Schmale (1972) report that a variety of acute and chronic conditions follow a person giving up or passively withdrawing in the face of an environmental stress, such as the loss of a valued object. Along these lines, Cole and Lejuene (1972) find that people who express feelings of failure to fulfill role expectations also are more likely to report illness.

Langer's work (Chapter 11 in this volume) offers even more convincing evidence for Seligman's point. Langer contends that a sense of control and learned helplessness may be related to "mindless" behavior (behavior not requiring cognitive awareness). More importantly, she suggests that both a sense of control and mindful behavior may be necessary for well-being: "Just as all people eat and sleep, so too do they consciously process information. Although the physiological mechanism may be very different, when the environment prevents this activity, just as with eating and sleeping, premature death may ensue."

Langer (Chapter 11 in this volume) further suggests that "environmental factors" can either enhance or erode a sense of control. In an experiment with a group of institutionalized elderly, Langer and Rodin (1976) examined the effects of a "control enhancement treatment" on physical, behavioral, and psychological well being. Nursing home residents were assigned to two groups, both groups being alike on socioeconomic factors and physical and psychological health status. The nursing home director told the residents in the first group they were competent people and should be making many of their own decisions. Following the talk, the residents were each given a plant and told they were responsible for its care. In contrast to the "responsibility-enhanced" group, the residents in the second group were told that they were in the nursing home to be served, and the staff was anxious to help and care for them. They also were given a plant, but told that the staff would be responsible for its care. After 3 weeks, Langer and Rodin (1976) found a noticeable difference between the groups. The responsibility-enhanced group demonstrated greater improvement than the other group on several measures of well-being and activity. They found even more convincing evidence in a follow-up study conducted 18 months later (Rodin and Langer 1977). While there was no difference in health status between the groups before the experiment, members of the responsibility-enhanced group now showed a lower mortality rate. As Langer (in this volume) writes, "At that time, it was found that approximately half as many people in the experimental group (7 of 47) had died as in the comparison group (13 of 44)." From these findings, Langer suggests that many "aging problems" may result from an environmentally induced loss of control.

It may be that social relationships and support contribute to a sense of control. Social relations with others may provide the resources, encouragement, and opportunities for feeling that one is in control or not. For example, social relations may affect the number and types of decisions people are expected to make, a measure of control. Social relationships also may provide the opportunity to help and care for others, another measure of control. Along these lines, Langer's work underscores the point that the type of social relations and support must be investigated. If social relations make people dependent or "mindless," it may dissipate their sense of control and be detrimental to their health and well-being.

Finally, both Seligman and Langer note that general societal factors threaten the elderly's sense of control. By examining the social support available to the elderly through their social relationships, we may learn why some elderly maintain their control and others lose it, and why some become ill and others do not.

Unfortunately, current measures of support do not specify clearly what types of support are provided, nor how they are related to coping with particular problems or "stressors" (Nuckolls *et al.* 1972, Gore 1978, Lin *et al.* 1979). The measures of support also are sometimes defined in terms of both the number of social contacts and the feelings people have toward those contacts (Lin *et al.* 1979). These measures make it impossible to distinguish between social contacts and social support. Furthermore, they make it impossible to identify what kinds of social contacts are supportive and what kinds are not.

We recommend that measures of support refer specifically to the type and source of support provided. We also recommend that social support not be measured in terms of the number of social contacts. If we are interested in testing whether the number and the type of coping resources explain the relation between social relationships and health, we must determine specifically if and how social relationships provide those resources. The important task is to learn what types of social relationships determine what kinds of support, in what ways, and under what circumstances.

Social Demographic Factors, Social Relationships, and Support

Most researchers studying social relationships and health neglect to consider the antecedent effects of social demographic factors, such as age, sex, social class, and ethnicity. This neglect limits our understanding of health patterns. If we only focus on social relationships and health and neglect age, sex, class, and ethnicity, we are failing to consider a major set of factors that affects both social relationships and health status. As Fisher *et al.* (1977) note, each social and demographic factor has an independent and joint effect on the options people have for establishing, maintaining, and modifying social relationships. Aging has a dramatic effect on family and friendship patterns (Fisher *et al.* 1977). Indeed, Fisher *et al.* (1977) argue that of the social demographic factors, age has perhaps the most profound effect. Unlike the other social variables, aging implies life-cycle development and, in turn, the establishment and termination of social relationships. Ethnicity and social class also affect social relationships and health. Using social class as an example, it is clear that people with low income and education have higher rates of ill health, perhaps due to inadequate diet, housing, and medical care. Low income also may affect health more indirectly. People with low income and education may find it more difficult to establish and maintain supportive relationships, a fact that may help us understand why ethnic minorities and people in lower socioeconomic positions show a higher incidence and prevalence of disease (Antonovsky 1967, Nesser *et al.* 1971, Syme and Berkman 1976).

The decision to focus on social demographic variables, social relationships, or even psychological variables depends ultimately on the particular research question. Nevertheless, an appreciation of how these sets of variables are interrelated should help us answer our own specific question, regardless of particular focus.

CONCLUSIONS AND RECOMMENDATIONS

We have based our examination on two questions: Why are some elderly people more likely than others to become ill? And, why are some elderly people impaired by their illness while others are not? Based on epidemiological evidence showing a relation between life changes and health problems, we focused on the age-related life changes of bereavement and retirement. Our brief review of these life changes raised two additional questions: Why is bereavement more likely than retirement to be related to subsequent health status? And, of those people who are bereaved, why do some become ill while others do not? Following Cassel's review, we hypothesized that the health effects of age-related life changes could be best understood in terms of a mediating factor, namely, the person's network of social relationships. Specifically, if a life change disrupts "meaningful" social relationships, it is more likely to reduce the person's resistance to disease. Furthermore, the fewer the number of social relationships disrupted by the life change, the more likely the person will cope with the change and escape its negative effects. While these hypotheses are suggestive, they have not been tested systematically in elderly populations.

In studies of the general population, there are studies showing a relation between the number and type of social relationships and health status. Although the reasons for the relation are still unclear, it is generally assumed that "supportive" relationships are somehow related to healthful well-being. One hypothesis is that social relationships are supportive by encouraging and enforcing proper preventive health behavior, such as proper diet and reasonable exercise. Another hypothesis is that social relationships are supportive by providing resources for coping with particular problems. While methodological problems thus far have prevented acceptable tests of these hypotheses, we feel that it is possible to identify and measure the independent and joint associations between life changes, social relationships, and health patterns among elderly populations.

Based on our review of the literature, we feel new survey research strategies should be developed along the following lines:

1. Research should focus on a socially heterogeneous, noninstitutionalized or free-living elderly population. Unlike an institutionalized population, a free-living population is more socially and culturally representative of the general population. With a free-living population, it is possible to conduct a better test of the effects of factors such as social class, ethnicity, sex, and age on both social relationships and health. Finally, by focusing on a free-living population, it is possible to assess the effects of housing and community services on social relationships and health (Cantor 1975, Carp 1976, Lopata 1975).

2. Research should focus on measures of general health status and all-cause mortality. Given that the elderly are at risk for such a variety of health problems, this seems to be the most realistic strategy. The health index should include a broad list of health problems, including symptoms and acute and chronic conditions. This information could be obtained through interviews or self-administered questionnaires. There are several existing health measures that can be adapted for studies of elderly populations (Belloc and Breslow 1972, Breslow 1972).

3. Research should focus on general measures of impairment and disability. In addition to assessing general health status, it is important to determine whether the elderly are impaired or disabled by their conditions. This is important. Two people may list the same health problem but differ dramatically in whether they see the problem as impairing their

activities. Impairment and disability can be assessed in various ways. One technique is to assess the degree of impairment associated with each particular health problem. If respondents note that they currently have a particular problem, they can be asked if the problem has limited their activities, how it has limited their activities, and for how long. Another technique is to focus on particular physiological functions without regard to particular diseases. For example, respondents could be asked about their relative ease in seeing, hearing, and walking. Of course, both techniques could be incorporated into the same interview or questionnaire instrument. There are several existing impairment measures that can be adapted for this purpose (Breslow 1972, Katz and Akpom 1976).

4. Research should examine the independent and joint effects of different life changes on social relationships and health. While bereavement is the most predictive of subsequent health status, other life changes should be identified. For example, respondents could be asked whether in the past they have experienced life changes such as marriage, death, or illness of close friends and spouse, retirement, financial difficulty, or changing residence. The timing of life changes is also considered important (Holmes and Rahe 1967, Neugarten 1970). Holmes and Rahe (1967) recommend asking about life changes or events that have occurred in the previous 6 months. Neugarten (1970) suggests that it is important to determine whether the life change was expected or anticipated. Factors such as the type of change, the timing of the change, and the expectations associated with the change can be easily incorporated into the same research instrument.

5. Research should focus on the entire network of social relationships. Information should be obtained on the number and type of social relationships the elderly maintain. A measure of social relationships should include questions dealing with "intimate or personal" relationships (e.g., with family, friends, and relatives). It also should include questions on the number and types of groups and organizations such as clubs, voluntary organizations, senior centers, and church functions. It is also important to determine how frequently the elderly see or hear from their friends, relatives, and family; and how often they participate in organizational activities. A useful measure of social relationships can be found in the Berkman and Syme (1979) study of social relationships and health. In addition to identifying the number, type, and frequency of contact, it is important to assess the elderly's feelings of "commitment" to various social relationships (Fisher et al. 1977). How "important" is it for the person to maintain contact with the friend or organization? Obtaining a complete picture of the social network is very important. In addition to being able to assess the independent and joint

associations between different types of social relations on health, a complete network analysis enables us to identify how the network changes over time. For example, what factors are related to changes in social relationships with others following the death of a spouse (Petrowsky 1976, Treas and Vanhilst 1976). A complete picture of the network is also necessary for comparing the number and type of social relationships that are disrupted by one or more life changes with the number and type of relationships that are maintained. As we indicated previously, this comparison should provide a useful measure of the severity of the life change. Finally, a complete picture of the network is necessary for identifying which social relationships are supportive and which are not. The ultimate objective is to determine if particular combinations of social relationships and social support are related to health and disability status in the elderly.

    6.   Research should examine preventive health behavior as one form of social support. With regard to health behavior, questions should address dietary patterns, smoking and alcohol consumption, frequency and type of physical exercise, and sleep patterns (Belloc 1973, McGlone and Kick 1978). In addition, questions also should address the frequency and type of physical health examinations and general utilization of medical care. To test the hypothesis of the relation between social relationships and health behavior, it is necessary to inquire whether preventive health behavior is encouraged and enforced by the person's various social relationships.

    7.   Research should examine coping resources as a second type of social support. This is perhaps the most difficult measurement problem in this area of research. The inability to measure supportive resources well has been the major shortcoming with the research in this area. To develop better measurement procedures, it is worthwhile to consult Pinneau's (1975) detailed examination of social support and coping. Pinneau (1975) contends that social support consists of three parts: tangible support, informational support, and emotional support. Tangible support refers to the instrumental resources (e.g., money) designed to help achieve a particular goal. Informational support refers to the advice and instruction necessary to learn the appropriate coping strategies. It also can refer to the standard by which people judge whether they are using the strategy appropriately. This can be achieved by people comparing their own performances with the performances of their fellow group members. Finally, emotional support refers to affective support, which would seem to be particularly important for coping with failure. Questions could be developed to tap each one of those dimensions. It is also necessary to identify from whom the support is obtained. For example,

questions could deal with the presumed opportunities to obtain financial assistance from friends in a crisis. In addition to hypothetical situations, respondents could be asked about their current situation. For example, questions could be developed dealing with major problems currently facing the respondents and their plans for dealing with those problems. In addition to identifying major "stressors," answers to those questions could help us understand more about coping strategies used by the elderly and, more importantly, the supportive resources available to those elderly. A related series of questions also could deal with a sense of control. It is possible to measure control by identifying the number and types of decisions the elderly make which affect themselves and others. This is important. Following from Langer's review (in this volume), it is clear that losing responsibility for making personal decisions is one of the major problems facing the elderly. Questions could be developed to deal with different types of decisional issues facing the elderly (e.g., questions on financial affairs and medical care). Another useful measure of control is the extent to which elderly people are confident about their decisions. The ultimate objective is to measure the independent and joint associations between particular supportive resources, a sense of control, and health status.

8. Research in this area should be longitudinal or prospective. Despite the required time and expense, longitudinal studies represent the only way to clarify the temporal associations between psychosocial factors and health.

In conclusion, the study of life change, social relationships, and social support may help us to understand the relation between aging and susceptibility to disease. With this information, we can work to design more effective preventive health strategies for the elderly. Although it is impossible to protect the elderly from life changes, it may be possible to encourage the development of supportive relationships to help them moderate the negative effects of change.

REFERENCES

Antonovsky, A. (1967) Social class, life expectancy and overall mortality. *Milbank Memorial Fund Quarterly* 45(2):31–73.

Antonovsky, A. (1979) *Health, Stress, and Coping.* San Francisco: Jossey-Bass Publishing Co.

Belloc, N. (1973) Relationship of health practices and mortality. *Preventive Medicine* 2(1):67–81.

Belloc, N., and Breslow, L. (1972) Relationship of physical health status and health practices. *Preventive Medicine* 1(3):409–421.

Berkman, L. F., and Syme, S. L. (1979) Social networks, host resistance, and mortality: A nine-year follow-up study of Alameda County residents. *American Journal of Epidemiology* 109(2):186–204.

Breslow, L. (1972) A quantitative approach to the World Health Organization definition of health: Physical, mental and social well-being. *International Journal of Epidemiology* 1(4):347–355.

Cantor, M. H. (1975) Life space and the social support system of the inner city elderly of New York. *The Gerontologist* 15(1):23–26.

Carp, F. M. (1976) Housing and living environments of older people. Pp. 244–271 in R. H. Binstock and E. Shanas, eds., *Handbook of Aging and the Social Sciences*. New York: Van Nostrand Reinhold Company.

Cassel, J. (1974) An epidemiological perspective of psychosocial factors in disease etiology. *American Journal of Public Health* 64(11):1040–1043.

Cassel, J. (1976) The contribution of the social environment to host resistance. *American Journal of Epidemiology* 104(2):107–123.

Cassel, J., and Tyroler, H. A. (1961) Epidemiological studies of cultural change: I. Health status and recency of industrialization. *Archives of Environmental Health* 3(1):25–33.

Clayton, P. J. (1974) Mortality and morbidity in the first year of widowhood. *Archives of General Psychiatry* 30(6):747–750.

Cobb, S. (1976) Social support as a moderator of life stress. *Psychosomatic Medicine* 38(5):300–313.

Cole, S., and Lejeune, R. (1972) Illness and the legitimation of failure. *American Sociological Review* 37(June):347–356.

Cutler, S. J. (1976) Membership in different types of voluntary associations and psychological well-being. *The Gerontologist* 16(4):335–339.

Dean, A., and Lin, N. (1977) The stress-buffering role of social support. *The Journal of Nervous and Mental Disease* 165(6):335–339.

Eisdorfer, C., and Wilkie, F. (1976) Stress, disease, aging and behavior. Pp. 251–275 in J. E. Birren and K. W. Schaie, eds., *Handbook of the Psychology of Aging*. New York: Van Nostrand Reinhold Co.

Engel, G. L., and Schmale, A. H. (1972) Conservation-withdrawal: A primary regulatory process for organismic homeostasis. Pp. 57–85 in Ciba Foundation, Symposium 8. *Physiology, Emotion, and Psychosomatic Illness*. Amsterdam: Elsevier.

Fisher, C. S., Jackson, R. M., Stueve, C. A., Gerson, K., Jones, L. M., and Baldassare, M. (1977) *Networks and Places: Social Relations in the Urban Setting*. New York: Free Press.

Gore S. (1978) The effect of social support in moderating the health consequences of unemployment. *Journal of Health and Social Behavior* 19(June):157–165.

Harris, C. S. (1978) *Fact Book on Aging: A Profile of America's Older Population*. Washington, D.C.: National Council on Aging.

Haynes, S. G., McMichael, A. J., and Tyroler, H. A. (1978) Survival after early and normal retirement. *Journal of Gerontology* 33(2):269–273.

Holmes, T. H., and Rahe, R. H. (1967) The social readjustment rating scale. *Journal of Psychosomatic Research* 11(2):213–218.

Inter-Society Commission for Heart Disease Resources: Primary Prevention of the Atherosclerotic Diseases. (1970) *Circulation* 42(December):A-55, A-95.

Jacobs, S., and Ostfeld, A. (1977) An epidemiological review of the mortality of bereavement. *Psychosomatic Medicine* 39(5):344–357.

Katz, S., and Akpom, C. A. (1976) A measure of primary sociobiological functions. *International Journal of Health Services* 6(3):493–507.

Langer, E. J., and Rodin, J. (1976) The effects of choice and enhanced personal responsibility for the aged: A field experiment in an institutional setting. *Journal of Personality and Social Psychology* 34(2):191–198.

Langlie, J. K. (1977) Social networks, health beliefs and preventive behavior. *Journal of Health and Social Behavior* 18(September):244–260.

Larson, R. (1978) Thirty years of research on the subjective well-being of older Americans. *Journal of Gerontology* 33(1):109–125.

Lin, N., Simeone, R. S., Ensel, W. M., and Kuo, W. (1979) Social support, stressful life events, and illness: A model and an empirical test. *Journal of Health and Social Behavior* 20(June):108–119.

Lopata, H. Z. (1975) Support systems of elderly urbanites: Chicago of the 1970s. *The Gerontologist* 15(1):35–41.

Lowenthal, M. F., and Haven, C. (1968) Interaction and adaptation: Intimacy as a critical variable. *American Sociological Review* 33(1):20–30.

Lowenthal, M. F., and Robinson, B. (1976) Social networks and isolation. Pp. 432–456 in R. H. Binstock and E. Shanas, eds., *Handbook of Aging and the Social Sciences*. New York: Van Nostrand Reinhold Company.

Maddison, D., and Viola, A. (1968) The health of widows in the year following bereavement. *Journal of Psychosomatic Research* 12(4):297–306.

Markides, K. S., and Martin, H. W. (1979) A causal model of life satisfaction among the elderly. *Journal of Gerontology* 34(1):86–93.

Marris, R. (1958) *Widows and Their Families*. London: Routledge Kegan Paul.

McGlone, F. B., and Kick, E. (1978) Health habits in relation to aging. *Journal of the American Geriatrics Society* 26(11):481–488.

Moss, G. E. (1973) *Illness, Immunity and Social Interaction*. New York: Wiley-Interscience.

Nesser, W. B., Tyroler, H. A., and Cassel, J. C. (1971) Social disorganization and stroke mortality in the black populations of North Carolina. *American Journal of Epidemiology* 93(3):166–175.

Neugarten, B. (1970) Adaptation and the life cycle. *Journal of Geriatric Psychiatry* 4(1):71–100.

Nuckolls, K. B., Cassel, J., and Kaplan, B. H. (1972) Psychosocial assets, life crises and the prognosis of pregnancy. *American Journal of Epidemiology* 95(5):431–441.

Parkes, C. M. (1964) The effects of bereavement on physical and mental health: A study of the medical records of widows. *British Medical Journal* 4(October):13–16.

Petrowsky, M. (1976) Marital status, sex, and the social networks of the elderly. *Journal of Marriage and the Family* 38(November):749–756.

Pinneau, S. R. (1975) *Effects of social support on psychological and physiological status*. Unpublished Ph.D. dissertation, University of Michigan.

Rees, W. D., and Lutkins, S. G. (1967) Mortality of bereavement. *British Medical Journal* 4(October 7):13–16.

Riley, M. W., Foner, A., Hess, B., Roth, B. K. (1968) *Aging and Society: Vol. 1, An Inventory of Research Findings*. New York: Russell Sage Foundation.

Rodin, J., and Langer, E. J. (1977) Long-term effects of a control-relevant intervention with the institutionalized aged. *Journal of Personality and Social Psychology* 35(12):897–902.

Rosow, I. (1976) Status and role change through the life span. Pp. 457–480 in R. H. Binstock and E. Shanas, eds., *Handbook of Aging and the Social Sciences*. New York: Van Nostrand Reinhold Co.

Seligman, M. E. P. (1974) Depression and learned helplessness. Pp. 83–113 in R. J. Friedman and M. M. Katz, eds., *The Psychology of Depression*. New York: John Wiley.

Seligman, M. E. P. (1975) *Helplessness: On Depression, Development, and Death.* San Francisco: W. H. Freeman and Co.

Shanas, E. (1979) The family as a social support system in old age. *The Gerontologist* 19(2):169–174.

Shanas, E., and Maddox, G. L. (1976) Aging, health, and the organization of health resources. Pp. 592–618 in R. H. Binstock and E. Shanas, eds., *Handbook of Aging and the Social Sciences.* New York: Van Nostrand Reinhold Company.

Sheppard, H. L. (1976) Work and retirement. Pp. 286–309 in R. H. Binstock and E. Shanas, eds., *Handbook of Aging and the Social Sciences.* New York: Van Nostrand Reinhold Co.

Syme, S. L. (1974) Behavioral factors associated with the etiology of physical disease: A social epidemiological approach. *American Journal of Public Health* 64(11):1043–1045.

Syme, S. L., and Berkman, L. F. (1976) Social class, susceptibility and sickness. *American Journal of Epidemiology* 104(1):1–8.

Syme, S. L., Hyman, M. M., Enterline, P. E. (1964) Some social and cultural factors associated with the occurrence of coronary heart disease. *Journal of Chronic Disease* 17(March):277–289.

Treas, J., and Vanhilst, A. (1976) Marriage and remarriage rates among older Americans. *The Gerontologist* 16(2):132–136.

Tyroler, H. A., and Cassel, J. (1964) Health consequences of cultural change: II. The effect of urbanization on coronary heart mortality among rural residents. *Journal of Chronic Disease* 17(February):167–177.

chapter 14

Social Stress and Mental Disorders in the Elderly[1]

DAN G. BLAZER

Many years ago Thomas Rennie, a pioneer in social psychiatry, defined social psychiatry as that branch of psychiatry that "seeks to determine significant facts in family and society which affect adaptation (or which can be clearly defined as of etiologic importance) as revealed through studies of individual groups functioning in their natural setting [1955]." The growth of social psychiatry and psychiatric epidemiology during the late 1950s and early 1960s was founded on the premise that the social environment contributes to the etiology of mental disorders. Even though it was recognized that many mental disorders were multidetermined, one factor could be identified and studied, such as the social environment, without denying the existence of other contributing factors.

The hypothesis that social stress is in some way causative of mental illness in late life is certainly not new. Unlike the biologically based sciences, in which the generation and the testing of new hypotheses of relationships, associations, pathways, etc. lead to interesting and productive work, those epidemiologic studies in psychiatry that have been most valuable have not been based on the brilliance of stated hypotheses

[1] Paper supported in part by Dr. Blazer's Research Career Development Award Grant #5 K01 MH00115-02 from the National Institute of Mental Health.

329

AGING
Biology and Behavior

but on the methodology used in testing these hypotheses. Over the years, there have been a number of epidemiologic studies that have shown a relationship between social stress and mental disorder (Langner and Michael 1963, Leighton *et al.* 1963, Hollingshead and Redlich 1958). The particular interest in social stress as a contributing factor in the mental disorders of late life stems from a number of findings concerning the elderly. First, most mental disorders in later life are first-time events. Such findings discourage the assumption that genetic factors play a major role in the development of these disorders. Second, it is intuitively recognized and experimentally shown that the elderly are placed under social and economic pressures following transition into late life, such as prejudice, declining incomes, and possible declining physical health (Palmore 1969). Yet the researcher must remember that a number of biological changes are occurring in the elderly that definitely contribute to the development of mental illness, such as the almost universal decline in catecholamine levels.

This chapter centers around the testing of the following hypothesis. Life stress is a causative factor in mental illness:

Social Stress		Mental Disorder
(independent variable)	$\longrightarrow$	(dependent or outcome variable)

Actually, our understanding of the development of mental illness at any stage of the life-cycle must include a number of etiologic factors. Figure 14.1 demonstrates the genetic, historical, developmental, and environmental factors that contribute to the behavior of an individual at a given point in time within a developmental model. Therefore, as the hypothesis stated above is tested, the basic question is not "Does life stress as it is defined in a particular case cause a given mental illness?" but rather "How much of the variance in behavior can be explained on the basis of social stress?" A first step toward testing the above hypothesis is a review of the literature with particular attention paid to defining social stress and mental disorders. Following this review, attention will be centered on study design and potential pitfalls in study design that may lead to bias in the results of such a study. Finally, the issues of transduction and prevention will be discussed.

DEFINING THE DEPENDENT VARIABLE

A review of the literature can be valuable for at least two reasons. First, it presents the investigator with an overview of the types of studies

PHYSICAL ENVIRONMENT

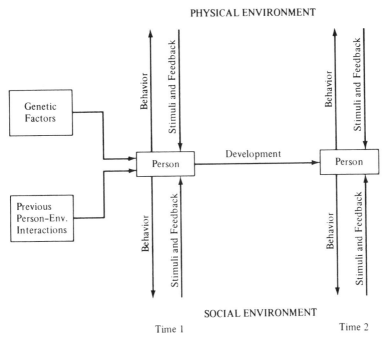

SOCIAL ENVIRONMENT

Time 1   Time 2

Figure 14.1. Some components in the ideology of mental disorders in late life. (From *Handbook of Geriatric Psychiatry,* edited by Ewald W. Busse and Dan G. Blazer. © 1980 by Litton Educational Publishing, Inc. Reprinted by permission of Van Nostrand Reinhold Company.)

completed to date, indicating areas that have been well established and gaps in current knowledge. Second, a review of the mechanisms of defining the dependent and independent variables that have been used to test the overall hypothesis that life stress leading to mental disorders can be instructive in designing future studies. If a study of mental disorder in the elderly is to be generalized to other populations, criteria for the diagnosis of mental disorders should be clearly understandable and reproducible. Regardless of the age group, there are two basic difficulties in identifying individuals with mental disorders. First, there are many and varied concepts of the meaning of "mental illness" in general and specific mental disorders. For example, anxiety disorder (anxiety neurosis) is a psychological construct (Nunnally 1967) and does not exist as an isolated observable dimension of behavior, such as blood pressure or reaction time. Instead, the construct of anxiety disorder represents a hypothesis that a variety of behaviors correlate with one another, and studies of individuals with these behaviors will have a similar etiology outcome and/or will be similarly affected by treatment. The larger the domain of observed behaviors related to a construct such as anxiety disorder, the more difficult it is to define which behaviors do and do not belong within the construct. Unfortunately, a large domain of possible behaviors is associated with the prevalent constructs of anxiety disorder, as with most other specific psychiatric abnormalities.

Of more immediate importance, however, is the variety of criteria suggested for the diagnosis of the different mental disorders. Differences can be found in diagnostic criteria in almost every major textbook of psychiatry. Though most of these differences are minimal, some are extreme. For example, the St. Louis group has defined a series of psychiatric disorders strictly on the basis of a set of observable symptoms (Feighner *et al.* 1972). More dynamically inclined psychiatrists, on the other hand, have defined most psychiatric disorders on the basis of formulations of particular conflicts underlying a given symptom pattern (Nemiah 1961).

The diagnosis of mental disorders in the elderly becomes even more complicated. It has been suggested that the elderly mask many of their psychiatric disorders with somatic complaints, for example, depression may be masked (Goldfarb 1974). The symptoms of depression have been demonstrated to be highest in the age group 65 and older (Blumenthal 1975, Zung 1973), yet the diagnosis of mild depression peaks before the age of 40, and severe depression peaks between the ages of 40 and 65 (Kramer *et al.* 1968). These depressive symptoms are coupled with many somatic complaints, and a diagnosis of hypochondriasis or even a physical diagnosis such as arthritis may mask the presence of a depressive disorder.

An important step forward in the diagnosis of psychiatric disorders for epidemiologic studies is the development of operational criteria for psychiatric diagnosis, as emphasized in the third edition of the *Diagnostic and Statistical Manual* (American Psychiatric Association 1980). Operational means that something pertains to an operation or procedure; compositions, concepts, constructs, and theories are given their meaning by the methods of observation or investigation used to arrive at them, not by assumptions concerning etiology. In other words, constructs have no other meaning than that which is yielded by the procedures or operations by which they are determined (Freeman 1962). The criteria are the output of clinicians who hypothesize the construct of a psychiatric disorder and then select associated behaviors from all behaviors of psychiatric interest (Leighton 1967). The proof of the validity of operational criteria in defining a construct, such as a depressive disorder, anxiety disorder, or affective disorder, depends on the ability of these criteria to categorize individuals into distinct reproducible groups that demonstrate a unique prognosis (Woodruff *et al.* 1974).

Regardless of the criteria that are used to diagnose and identify a "case" of mental illness, varied methods may be used to identify these conditions in community surveys. The most common diagnostic procedure in psychiatry is the unstructured interview. Psychiatric interviews have also been used to identify mental disorders in community populations, but they may contribute significant bias on the bases of the uniqueness of interview techniques, the location of the interview, etc. Studies have demonstrated that psychiatric interviews are quite unreliable when one interviewer's findings are compared with another—though each may contain significant and valid information (Beck *et al.* 1962, Ward *et al.* 1962). When psychiatrists were asked for the reasons for inconsistencies in diagnostic agreement, the most common complaint was inadequacy in the nosologic system. These problems have led to the use of other methods for psychiatric diagnosis.

A very common method to be used is the symptom checklist (Zung 1973, Overall and Gorham 1962). Those symptom checklists that are useful with other age groups may prove to be of less value with the elderly (Gallagher *et al.* 1978). In addition, symptom checklists are generally scored on the basis of the total number of positive responses to a series of symptoms. Dohrenwend (Dohrenwend and Crandell 1970) has pointed out that, though the total score from such checklists may be equivalent for certain groups of community, clinic, and hospital patients, specific items may separate these groups. For example, symptoms such as severe guilt, suicidal ideation, etc. would be more frequent in the hospital population than in the community.

Another method that has been recently used in psychiatric epidemiologic surveys is the structured interview (Wing *et al.* 1974, Spitzer 1970). Such interviews have been extended to a computerized form (Wing *et al.* 1974). These interviews have been criticized by clinicians, because they restrict unique individual techniques gained through years of training and practice for obtaining significant symptomatic data, yet they may be among the most useful instruments for epidemiologists.

In conclusion, many and varied techniques are available to the researcher for defining the dependent variable—mental disorder. Yet there are advantages and disadvantages in each of these techniques. The researcher must clearly think through the cost effectiveness of using specific interview and/or questionnaires, the ability to generalize data to a population, and the specific bias that each of these techniques may have when administered to an elderly population.

DEFINING THE INDEPENDENT VARIABLE

Defining and measuring social stress can be even more problematic than defining and measuring a mental disorder. For purposes of this chapter, studies that have considered the social environment will be divided into (*a*) those with a structured orientation and (*b*) those with a transactional orientation. The social environment, however, can be considered from many other perspectives. For example, the overall ecology of a given environment can be contrasted with those factors within the environment that directly affect a particular individual or macro-social network of interaction; for example, the federal government can be contrasted with much smaller networks, such as the family. Social structure may be defined as "the multidimensional space of social positions among which a population is distributed and which reflect and affect people's role relations and social associations [Blau 1977]." Social structure, for the most part, can be directly observed and measured and includes such concepts as status, role, stratification, and differentiation. Social transactions may be defined as the interactions between the social environment and the individual as well as the interactions between organizations within the social environment. Social transactions are less easily measured but can be assessed in terms of durability, intensity, frequency, flexibility, etc. The quality of social transactions can be assessed in terms of the feedback and support available to an individual via these interactions (Blazer 1978). This conceptualization assumes that people vary their behavior extensively in different social and physical environments and that individuals relate to social environments differentially. The human organism negotiates life by a continual series of interchanges with the social environment. The social environment of a given individual may be stressful on the basis of (*a*) structure—for example, lack of opportunity secondary to social stratification, (*b*) transactions—for example, a lack of meaningful feedback from the environment to the individual, or (*c*) the occurrence of significant events or changes in the social environment that adversely affect the individual.

Many of the original classical studies of social stress and mental disorders were structured in orientation. Faris and Dunham found that individuals with a diagnosis of schizophrenia who were admitted to hospitals in Detroit tended to live in the inner city (a stressful environment) (Faris and Dunham 1939). Later analysis of these data has raised questions as to the validity of these original considerations (Dunham 1976). Hollingshead and Redlich have considered socioeconomic status as the independent variable that predicts the utilization of psychiatric services in New Haven (Hollingshead and Redlich 1958). Sheldon and Moore have considered a series of social indicators, including family size, education, economic status, etc., as predictors of mental illness (Sheldon and Moore 1968). Dowd and Brooks have looked at the relative status of the elderly within society as it relates to feelings of anomia—a cause of suicide, according to Durkheim, many years ago (Dowd and Brooks 1978, Durkheim 1951).

A number of researchers have considered social stress and mental disorder from a combined structural and transactional viewpoint. Langner and Michael defined social stress as a function of socioeconomic status, a negative family background, marital worries, work difficulties, etc. (Langner and Michael 1963). Barker studied the "behavior settings" (standing patterns of behavior occurring in specific locations) by direct observation and concluded that the territorial range (the percentage of behavioral settings occupied) and the extent of active participation of both the young and the old might have significant association with the behavior of these individuals (Barker 1968). More recently, Rudolph Moos has considered social ecology along the dimensions of (a) ecology—including geographical, meterological, and architectural and physical design variables, (b) behavior settings, (c) organizational structure, (d) the collective personal and/or behavioral characteristics of the milieu inhabitants, (e) psychosocial characteristics in organizational climates, and (f) the function or reinforcement of environments (Moos 1974).

Other researchers have considered social stress from an almost totally transactional viewpoint. Leighton and Leighton, in testing the hypothesis that social disintegration is a causative factor in the development of mental disorders, defined disintegration in terms of the malfunctioning of families, the lack of meaningful association, the quality of leadership, patterns of recreation, frequency of hostility, crime and delinquency, and weakened and fragmented networks of communications. Bott has considered family and social networks (Leighton 1959).

Much work has been done recently to better conceptualize and measure the particular social functions of family and social support. Cobb, Cassel, Kaplan, and others have suggested that social support is a significant factor in predicting both physical and mental health outcomes (Cobb 1976, Cassel 1976, Kaplan *et al.* 1977, Berkman and Syme 1979). The Duke–OARS survey conceptualized social support in terms of the availability and use of a series of generic tangible services, the degree of social interaction, and the perception of a caretaker in the social environment for an indefinite period of time if severe impairment developed (Duke–OARS 1978).

An additional significant development in the study of social stress and mental illness has been the conceptualization of a measurement of major life changes. Holmes and Rahe, working from the original conceptualizations of Adolph Meyer, have developed a schedule of life changes that have been very popular in recent social and epidemiologic surveys that have considered both mental illness and physical illness as an outcome variable (Holmes and Rahe 1967). Earlier studies have considered the relationship of certain life events, such as widowhood (Parkes and Murray 1965, Lopata 1973), to future health outcome. Dohrenwend and Dohrenwend have looked at the difficult issue of measuring life support and have considered and worked on the important distinction between actual changes within the environment and perceived changes by individuals (Dohrenwend and Dohrenwend 1974).

This brief overview of approaches previously used in the study of social stress as the independent variable highlights many of the varied techniques used to define social stress. There has been a significant movement in the literature over the past few years toward measuring the social environment as it more closely relates to the individual—for example, life changes, family networks, social support, etc. as opposed to the more structured measures of the past. However, sociologists such as Blau would criticize our ability to measure society meaningfully in "transactional" terms and insist that more work needs to be done in testing hypotheses that can be directly derived from theorems concerning social structure (Blau 1977).

STUDY DESIGN

In testing the hypothesis, "social stress contributes to the etiology of mental disorders," study design is very important. The definition of the dependent and independent variables in a study, as described above, will contribute significantly to the selection of a particular study design. For example, if an inclusive definition of the dependent variable, such as *depressive symptomatology,* is selected, and the expected prevalence of this symptomatology is greater than 10% in a community population, a cross-sectional or an incidence study would be feasible. However, a true random sample of the community is costly, regardless of the size of the sample and should be used only as a last step in identifying an association. However, if a more exclusive definition, such as *depressive disorder* (as defined in the *Diagnostic and Statistical Manual* [see American Psychiatric Association 1980]) is chosen, with an expected prevalence of 1% to 2% and a small incidence rate, a case control study may be more cost effective. There are potential difficulties with both methods. In the cross-sectional or incidence study, the researcher must be concerned with potential misclassification bias with respect to the dependent variable. Such misclassification is usually evaluated in terms of sensitivity—the extent to which a subject who truly has a disorder is so classified, and specifically, the extent to which subjects without the disorder are correctly classified. Most survey instruments used in the past have been highly sensitive (such as symptom checklists) but not specific. This is a valuable characteristic of a test or instrument used for screening populations, such as the Pap smear for cervical and uterine carcinoma. Unfortunately, when hypothesis testing is the goal of a study, specificity, not sensitivity, is the critical issue. The case control or retrospective approach suffers from the difficulty of bias being introduced by the perceptions of the individual concerning their previous social environment, that is, the independent variable. For example, if life changes are used to measure social stress, then the memory of an individual for these events over a period of time will be an important consideration in testing the validity of a particular study (Jenkins *et al.* 1979). In summary, the researcher must make a decision between the relative cost of a particular research design and the effectiveness of that design to allow one to generalize from the study population to a larger population.

A second consideration in designing a study to test the hypothesis, "social stress contributes to the etiology of mental disorders," is that of confounding. A confounder is any known or hypothesized risk factor for the dependent or outcome variable that, if not "controlled for" in the analysis, will result in bias. If you consider the following model:

Social Stress ⟶ Mental Disorder

a confounder would change this model in the following way:

⟶ Mental Disorder
Confounder
⟵ Social Stress

Physical health, previous mental illness, age, sex, race, personality factors, genetic factors, etc. are all potential confounders in a study of our hypothesis. Unfortunately, most methods that allow one to control for confounding also require a larger study population in order to achieve significant results. Confounders can be controlled for through stratification and by various regression or logistic techniques. The researcher must also determine whether the confounder is in fact an intervening variable. For example, if social stress led to mental disorder directly through a change in the diet of an individual, and one wished to control for changes in diet, a true relationship would be lost in the analysis.

Social Stress ⟶ Dietary Change ⟶ Mental Disorder

If social stress is positively predictive of change in diet, which in turn is positively predictive of mental illness, then the control of change in diet can seriously reduce or eliminate any manifestation in the data of a truly strong association between social stress and mental disorder.

Another potential consideration in study design is whether the dependent variable may actually be leading to the independent variable.

Social Stress ⟵ Mental Disorder

Brown has recently demonstrated that, within the hospital setting, depressive patients are observed to display significantly lower degrees of positive affect than they subjectively report (Brown et al. 1978). This suggests that the behavior of an individual with a mental disorder can lead to certain responses of the environment that might possibly be considered stressful. For example, a withdrawn, dysphoric individual may be avoided by others because of his or her behavior, yet report the experience of social isolation. The researcher can reject this possibility if it can be demonstrated that, temporally, mental disorder follows social stress. Incidence studies are of most value in determining the temporal relationship of the independent and dependent variables. Studies of the development of mental as well as physical disorders following a move of a long-term care facility are examples of methods by which association between a social stress and a mental disorder can be strengthened, given the temporal design of the study.

Despite the difficulties mentioned above, there appears to be rather consistent evidence that certain types of social stress do contribute to the etiology of mental disorders in older people. Further studies of better design and with more rigorous definitions of independent and dependent variables can contribute to our understanding of the exact nature of the association. However, association of these variables does not necessarily imply causation.

TRANSDUCTION

Once the researcher is confident of a temporal association between social stress and mental disorder, another question must be answered. How is a social experience such as social stress translated by the central nervous system into a physiological event or organized pattern of behavior recognizable as a mental disorder? (Weiner 1972). An external event can both give rise to a mental experience and produce a concomitant neural and bodily process (Moore *et al.* 1967, Hofer and Weiner 1971). Therefore, one cannot assume that social stress alters mental function solely by its initial impact on the "mind." In fact, there is considerable evidence that stressful conditions can lead to neurophysiological changes that may directly contribute to emotional disorders. For example, both physical and sociological stress stimulate the pituitary adrenal axis in human beings and animals (Mason 1974). Most of these studies indicate no difference in plasma levels of cortisone in human beings and little change in the size of the adrenal cortex with age. Cortisone, however, is disposed of at a slower rate with increasing age (West *et al.* 1961). A particular stressful social event may lead to an increase in cortisone levels, which in turn may diminish at a slower rate in the elderly than in other stages of the life-cycle. Increased cortisone levels have been associated with mental disorders, such as depression (Sachar 1973).

In addition to the neurobiological adaptation of the organism to stressful conditions, there is also a psychosocial adaptation. Psychosocial adaptation has often been labeled "coping" and has been defined as the means by which individuals or groups are effective in meeting the requirements or utilizing the opportunities of the specific environment they encounter (Hamburg *et al.* 1976). Though many life changes may be traumatic, only a small portion of those exposed to such events are subject to the development of mental disorders. An elderly person who has lost a spouse and who has difficulty in coping may demonstrate maladaptation by: (*a*) taking responsibility for the loss (i.e., the loss is punishment), (*b*) separating self from family and friends, (*c*) denying the loss and continuing in an inappropriate fashion to live as if the spouse were alive, or (*d*) demonstrating outbursts of inappropriate anger or attempts to manipulate others. Again, the researcher is faced with the issue of defining mental disorder. Some typically define mental disorder in terms of maladaptive behavior (Pfeiffer 1968), while others would argue that such definitions reflect only prejudicial attitudes of society (Szasz 1961).

Experimental evidence suggests that older persons, because of a handicap in memory load, are less able to carry out complex operations (Clay 1954). In fact, a literature has arisen that demonstrates certain specific types of decreased problem-solving ability in the elderly. Verwoerdt points out that personality patterns relying on coping styles requiring little energy may be relatively better equipped to deal with social stress, such as the passive dependent personality. On the other hand, the obsessive compulsive or aggressive personality may have more difficulty in dealing with the inevitable changes of aging (Verwoerdt 1976).

Neugarten warns that it is not the occurrence of a social or life event itself that precipitates an adaptational crisis, for most such events are anticipated and rehearsed and the transition is accomplished without shattering the sense of continuity of the life-cycle. When such events occur "off time," however, such as a major illness or an unexpected death, a crisis may occur (Neugarten 1970). Lowenthal further suggests that adaptation in younger years is the best predictor of successful adaptation in late life (Lowenthal 1965).

PREVENTION

If transduction of social stress into a mental disorder can be demonstrated and/or theorized at either a neurophysiological or psychosocial level, the next step toward the verification of causation would be to set up intervention studies. Elimination of social stress should lead to a decrease in mental disorders. If a preventive study is developed that would decrease or eliminate a particular form of social stress experienced by older persons and could be compared with a similar situation in which the form of stress is present, the researcher can compare the rates of mental disorder in the two populations. Unfortunately, when dealing with such a broad concept as social stress, developing an experimental design that would relieve such stress is next to impossible. However, it is possible to utilize a quasi-experimental design, that is, a natural experiment, and compare individuals who experience different social environments. For example, a community may be moved because of the building of a new expressway. If a group of elderly individuals within that community is compared with individuals in a community in which the stress of moving is not present, then the hypothesis is strengthened if real differences can be shown in the rate of development of mental disorders.

A second preventive approach is to undertake a modification of the individual in order to decrease the impact of social stress. An example of this type of intervention would be the implementation of a peer counseling service in a retirement community that would enable individuals to develop better adaptive techniques for coping with social stress. The researcher could compare the relative benefit of such an attempt to modify the individual's response to stress, and this would further lend credence to the causal association between social stress and mental disorders.

CONCLUSION

The researcher who wishes to test the hypothesis that social stress contributes to the etiology of mental disorders must conceptualize a hierarchy of experiments. Initial experiments should demonstrate an association between the independent and dependent variables. If such an association can be demonstrated, the hypothesis is further strengthened by demonstrating a temporal association through incidence or cohort studies. Further studies should be directed toward identifying and defining those mechanisms by which social stress is transduced into a mental disorder. Both neurophysiological and psychosocial adaptation must be considered. Finally, preventive studies, which are directed toward either the elimination of the independent variable or modification of the individual so that the impact of the independent variable on the dependent variable is decreased or eliminated, provide assurance that the association is causative if the relationships and findings make biologic and epidemiologic sense.

REFERENCES

American Psychiatric Association (1980) *Diagnostic and Statistical Manual of Mental Disorders,* 3rd edition. Washington, D.C.: American Psychiatric Association.

Barker, R. G. (1968) *Ecological Psychology.* Stanford, Calif.: Stanford University Press.

Beck, A. T., Ward, C. H., Mendelson, M., Mock, J. E., and Erbaugh, J. K. (1962) Reliability of psychiatric diagnosis: II. A study of consistency of clinical judgments in ratings. *American Journal of Psychiatry* 119:351–357.

Berkman, L. F., and Syme, S. L. (1979) Social networks, host resistance and mortality: A nine-year follow-up study of Alameda County residents. *American Journal of Epidemiology* 109(2):186–204.

Blau, P. (1977) *Inequality and Heterogeneity.* New York: Free Press.

Blazer, D. G. (1978) Social Support: Toward a Unified Theory. Unpublished paper. Center for the Study of Aging and Human Development, Duke University Medical Center, Durham, N. C.

Blumenthal, M. D. (1975) Measuring depressive symptomatology in a general population. *Archives of General Psychiatry* 32:971–978.

Brown, S., Schwartz, G. E., and Sweeney, D. R. (1978) Dissociation of self-reported and observed pleasure in depression. *Psychosomatic Medicine* 15:536–548.

Busse, E. W., and Blazer, D. G., eds. (1980) *Handbook of Geriatric Psychiatry.* New York: Van Nostrand Reinhold Company.

Cassel, J. (1976) The contribution of the social environment to host resistance. *American Journal of Epidemiology* 104:107.

Clay, H. M. (1954) Changes of performance with age on similar tasks of varying complexity. *British Journal of Psychology* 45:7–13.

Cobb, S. (1976) Social support as a moderator of life stress. *Psychosomatic Medicine* 38:300.

Dohrenwend, B. P., and Crandell, D. L. (1970) Psychiatric symptoms in community, clinic and mental hospital groups. *American Journal of Psychiatry* 126:1611–1621.

Dohrenwend, B. S., and Dohrenwend, B. P. (1974) *Stressful Life Events.* New York: John Wiley & Sons.

Dowd, J. J., and Brooks, F. P. (1978) Anomia and Aging: Normlessness or Class Consciousness. Paper presented at the Scientific Meeting of the Gerontological Society, Dallas, Texas.

Duke-OARS (1978) *Multidimensional Functional Assessment: The OARS Methodology.* Durham, N. C.: Duke University Center for the Study of Aging and Human Development.

Dunham, H. W. (1976) Society, culture and mental disorder. *Archives of General Psychiatry* 33:147–156.

Durkheim, E. (1951) *Suicide: A Study in Sociology.* New York: Free Press.

Faris, R., and Dunham, H. W. (1939) *Mental Disorders in Urban Areas.* Chicago: University of Chicago Press.

Feighner, J. P., Robins, E., Guze, S. B., Woodruff, R. A., Vinokur, G., and Munoz, R. (1972) Diagnostic criteria for use in psychiatric research. *Archives of General Psychiatry* 26:57–63.

Freeman, F. S. (1962) *Theory and Practice of Psychological Testing,* 3rd Ed. New York: Holt, Rinehart and Winston.

Gallagher, D., McGarvey, W., Zelinski, E., and Thompson, L. W. (1978) Age and Factor Structures of the Zung Depressive Scale. Paper presented at the Scientific Meeting of the Gerontological Society, Dallas, Texas.

Goldfarb, A. I. (1974) Masked depression in the elderly. Pp. 236–249 in S. Lesse, ed., *Masked Depression.* New York: Jason Aronson.

Hamburg, D. A., Adams, J. E., and Brodie, H. K. H. (1976) Coping behavior in stressful circumstances: Some implications for social psychiatry. In B. H. Kaplan, R. N. Wilson, and A. H. Leighton, eds., *Further Explorations in Social Psychiatry.* New York: Basic Books.

Hofer, M. A., and Weiner, H. (1971) Physiological and behavioral regulation by nutritional intake during early development of the laboratory rat. *Psychosomatic Medicine* 33:468.

Hollingshead, A. B., and Redlich, F. C. (1958) *Social Class and Mental Illness.* New York: Wiley.

Holmes, T. H., and Rahe, R. H. (1967) The social readjustment rating scale. *Journal of Psychosomatic Research* 11:213–218.

Jenkins, C. D., Hurst, M. W., and Rose, R. M. (1979) Life changes: Do people really remember? *Archives of General Psychiatry* 36:379–384.

Kaplan, B. H., Cassel, J. C., and Gore, S. (1977) Social support and health. *Medical Care* 15:47–58.

Kramer, M., Taube, C., and Starr, S. (1968) Patterns of use of psychiatric facilities by the aged: Current status, trends and implications. In A. Simon and L. Epstein, eds., *Aging in Modern Society.* Psychiatric Research Report #23. Washington, D.C.: American Psychiatric Association.

Langner, T. S., and Michael, S. T. (1963) *Life Stress and Mental Disorder.* London, England: The Free Press of Glencoe.

Leighton, A. H. (1959) *My Name is Legion.* New York: Basic Books.

Leighton, A. H. (1967) Is social environment a cause of psychiatric disorders? Pp. 337–345 in R. Monroe, G. Klee, and E. Brody, eds., *Psychiatric Epidemiology and Mental Health Planning.* Psychiatric Research Report #22. Washington, D.C.: American Psychiatric Association.

Leighton, D. C., Harding, J. S., Macklin, D. B., MacMillan, A. N., and Leighton, A. H. (1963) *The Character of Danger.* New York: Basic Books.

Lopata, H. Z. (1973) *Widowhood in an American City.* Cambridge, Mass.: Schenkman.

Lowenthal, M. F. (1965) Antecedents of isolation and mental illness in old age. *Archives of General Psychiatry* 12:245–254.

Mason, J. (1974) Specificity in the organization of neuroendocrine response profiles. Pp. 68–80 in P. Seeman and G. Brown, eds., *Frontiers in Neurology and Neuroscience Research.* Toronto, Canada: Toronto Press.

Moore, R. Y., Heller, A., Wurtman, R. J., and Axelrod, J. (1967) Visual pathway mediating pineal response to environmental light. *Science* 155:220–223.

Moos, R. (1974) Systems for the assessment and classification of human environments: An overview. Pp. 5–28 in R. Moos, ed., *Issues in Social Ecology.* Palo Alto, Calif.: National Press.

Nemiah, J. C. (1961) *Causes of Mental Disorders: A Review of Epidemiologic Knowledge.* New York: Milbank Memorial Fund.

Neugarten, B. L. (1970) Adaptation and the life cycle. *Journal of Geriatric Psychology* 4(1):71–87.

Nunnally, J. C. (1967) *Psychometric Theory.* New York: McGraw-Hill.

Overall, J. E., and Gorham, D. R. (1962) The brief psychiatric rating scale. *Psychological Reports* 10:799.

Palmore, E. (1969) Sociological aspects of aging. Pp. 33–69 in E. W. Busse, and E. Pfeiffer, eds., *Behavior and Adaptation in Late Life.* Boston: Little, Brown and Company.

Parkes, C. M., and Murray, C. (1965) Bereavement and mental illness: A clinical study. *British Journal of Medical Psychology* 28:1–26.

Pfeiffer, E. (1968) *Disordered Behavior.* New York: Oxford University Press.

Rennie, T. A. C. (1955) Social psychiatry—a definition. *International Journal of Social Psychiatry* 1(1):11–12.

Sachar, E. J. (1973) Endocrine factors in psychopathological states. Pp. 175–197 in J. Mendels, ed., *Biological Psychiatry.* New York: John Wiley & Sons.

Sheldon, E. B., and Moore, W. E. (1968) *Indicators of Social Change: Concepts and Measurements.* New York: Russel Sage Foundation.

Spitzer, R. L., Endicott, J., Fleiss, J. L., and Cohen, J. (1970) The psychiatric status schedule: A technique for evaluating psychopathology and impairment in role functioning. *Archives of General Psychiatry* 32:41.

Szasz, T. S. (1961) *The Myth of Mental Illness.* New York: Dell.

Verwoerdt, A. (1976) *Clinical Geropsychiatry.* Baltimore, Md.: Williams and Wilkins.

Ward, C. H., Beck, A. T., Mendelson, M., Mock, J. E., and Erbaugh, J. K. (1962) The psychiatric nomenclature: Reasons for diagnostic disagreement. *Archives of General Psychiatry* 7:198–205.

Weiner, H. (1972) Some comments on the transduction of experience by the brain: Implication for our understanding of the relationships of mind and body. *Psychosomatic Medicine* 34(4):355–379.

West, C. D., Brown, H., Simons, E. L., Carter, D. B., Kumagai, L. F., and Englert, E. (1961) Adrenocortical function and cortical metabolism in old age. *Journal of Clinical Endocrinology* 10:1197–1207.

Wing, J. K., Cooper, J. E., and Saratorius, N. (1974) *Measurement and Classification of Psychiatric Symptoms.* Cambridge, Mass.: Cambridge University Press.

Woodruff, R. A., Goodwin, D. W., and Guze, S. B. (1974) *Psychiatric Diagnosis.* New York: Oxford University Press.

Zung, W. W. K. (1973) From art to science: The diagnosis and treatment of depression. *Archives of General Psychiatry* 29:328–337.

chapter 15

Some Psychosocial Influences on the Health Status of the Elderly: The Perspective of Social Epidemiology

STANISLAV V. KASL
LISA F. BERKMAN

Even though the boundaries and orientation of social epidemiology are somewhat nebulous (Kasl 1977, Syme 1974), in general we may recognize within this segment of social science and medicine collaboration a primary concern with the psychosocial determinants of: illness or disease onset (incidence of new events), the course of illness or disease (exacerbations, repeat events), and the outcome of disease process and/or degree of recovery. There is also a concern with indirect psychosocial influences operating via medical care utilization and the whole gamut of contacts with health professionals and health services (health behavior, illness behavior, and the sick role behavior spectrum) and behaviors and practices with health implications (life-style, health habits).

Within an (idealized) infectious disease model, the role of psychosocial influences on health status can be schematically represented (Kasl et al. 1979) as those that affect: (a) initial immunity–susceptibility status, (b) exposure to infection among susceptibles, (c) development of inapparent versus clinical illness among the exposed, (d) medical care seeking among those with clinical illness, and (e) response to treatment and/or natural cause of illness.

Overall, then, psychosocial factors can influence human health in many different ways and through many different pathways—exposure

345

AGING
Biology and Behavior

to risk factors, exposure to medical care system, differential susceptibility, social relationships, social change, habits and customs (Hinkle *et
al.* 1976)—and none can be a priori rejected as irrelevant to social
epidemiology.

This chapter deals specifically with the health of the elderly. It is a
frequent and fully appropriate goal of descriptive epidemiology to zero
in on one particular population subgroup and to describe its morbidity
and mortality experience and its medical care needs. Many objectives
and issues of public health planning and policy can make such a focused
look at one subgroup intrinsically useful. However, if our orientation is
etiological, and we are trying to understand the causal influences on
variations in health status (analytical epidemiology), then the targeting
of a particular population subgroup for scrutiny becomes a much more
troublesome enterprise. The fundamental problem is that we create a
presumption of uniqueness—that the processes under observation are
special to the targeted population subgroup—and we collect evidence
that grows and accumulates in splendid isolation from similar data on
the rest of the population. Such intellectual and conceptual isolation at
best leads to duplication of effort; at worst, it leads to misinterpretation
of data and to adoption of distorted or misleading theoretical positions.
It is our belief that such theoretical disasters as the disengagement hypothesis are due to intellectual straining after the uniqueness of the
elderly, which would in turn justify why we study them separately.

The objective of this chapter is to sidestep the vast descriptive literature dealing with the association between age and the many indicators
of health status and biological functioning, and to zero in on some of
the psychosocial influences on the health status of the elderly. In view
of the above comments, this task poses somewhat of a dilemma: to keep
the elderly in focus without losing sight of the fact that the evidence and
the etiological picture may or may not be unique to this population
subgroup. One way out of this dilemma is to ignore it, as is done all too
frequently in handbook chapters on the elderly; an author typically either
reviews only the studies in which the elderly are the subjects and ignores
the picture for the other population subgroups, or reviews the studies
irrespective of the age range of the subjects (hence not dealing primarily
with the elderly) and lets the reader assume that evidence relevant for
the elderly is being examined. In this chapter we intend to put up more
of a struggle with this dilemma. Essentially, we propose to concentrate
on two types of evidence: First, studies that suggest that the association
between a psychosocial risk factor and a health status indicator is notably
altered or conditioned by age and second, studies that deal with psychosocial influences that are particularly relevant to the elderly, either

because they represent experiences found predominantly among the elderly (e.g., retirement, bereavement) or because such experiences have different social meaning for the elderly (e.g., residential moves). In addition, we will also briefly consider the issue of age in relation to health maintenance behavior and medical care seeking.

One of the most persistent and seductive notions in gerontology is the concept of biological aging as an intrinsic, *sui generis* process that can be separated from the accumulation of environmental influences and insults that the aging organism also experiences. For example, Busse (1969) distinguishes between "biological aging," those genetic processes that are time-related and independent of stress, trauma, or disease, and "secondary aging," which consists of disability resulting from trauma and chronic illness. If biological and secondary aging were cleanly separable conceptually and operationally, then it would be a primary task of social epidemiology of the elderly to study the interactions of social–environmental influences and the biological aging process as they affect health status. However, it seems to us that despite a great accumulation of normative data on age and biological functioning (e.g., Finch and Hayflick 1977), there is little evidence to support the notion that biological aging processes, independent of stress, trauma, and disease, exist and have been identified. We are not convinced that the numerous biological theories of aging (Shock 1977) can, at the moment, do much more than point us toward those age-dependent changes in biological functioning that are particularly uniform or particularly variable across diverse population groups.

CHOOSING INDICATORS OF HEALTH STATUS

It is useful to confront, however briefly, the issue of indicators of health status. This problem area has been examined many times (e.g., Balinsky and Berger 1975, Belloc *et al.* 1971, Berg 1973). The difficulty is not in the assessment of specific diseases; certainly, a large number of diagnostic criteria have been adequately operationalized. Rather, the problems arise when we aim for global or composite indices of health status; health-related social functioning and/or disability; subjective components of health status; or a clean separation of illness from illness behavior. It goes without saying that many additional problems arise when we are dependent exclusively on self-report interview methodology.

The range of typical health status indicators available to an epidemiologist include: general and specific mortality rates; expectations of life at a specific age; rates of specific morbidity; levels of impairment (e.g., hearing, sight, paralysis of extremities); indices of disability (e.g., disability days, restricted activity days, bed days, hospital days, work loss days); contacts with the health care system (e.g., doctor visits, clinic visits). These indicators are obviously not interchangeable; moreover, they have unique problems: They never quite measure all of a phenomenon of interest, and they always measure, in addition, part of something that is not of interest.

Since the interests of social epidemiology and social gerontology are more etiological than descriptive, and since they concern more complex independent variables, the more common, straightforward indices of health status are generally found to be less useful and more opaque. For example, mortality data alone do not tell us which end of the disease spectrum is most influenced by the psychosocial variable in question: levels of risk factors, onset of clinical disease, gap between onset and diagnosis and/or treatment, case fatality, and so on. This is a serious limitation, since the mechanisms by which psychosocial variables influence health status are poorly understood; for example, the health consequences of some behaviors may become manifest 20 or 30 years after the individual engages in the behavior, whereas other behaviors appear to have much more immediate effects. Similarly, the cumulative effect of lifelong practices is rarely explored in most studies, and dose-response or length-of-exposure relationships have generally not been identified.

The self-evident "validity" of mortality as an end point makes this a seductive indicator. In contrast to prospective studies of new disease (morbidity), for which we need a cohort initially free of that disease, many psychosocial cohort studies of mortality establish at inception only that the subjects are alive. Since so many psychosocial variables are influenced by poor health status—which will obviously relate to subsequent mortality— we have a serious problem of confounding that we cannot directly assess.

Two examples illustrate this problem. The first concerns the often cited finding that work satisfaction can be a strong predictor of longevity, especially among men (Palmore 1971). Unfortunately, close inspection reveals that four of the six items reflect ability to carry out work rather than satisfaction. It is virtually certain that the index is sensitive to physical functioning and thus confounded with health status. The second example concerns the finding that aged individuals being institutionalized voluntarily had lower subsequent mortality rates than those who had no other alternative (Ferrari 1963). Since the concept of control (or internal–external orientation) is rapidly becoming a hot topic in health research (e.g., Krantz and Schulz in press, Strickland in press), we shall keep hearing about this finding. Yet there is no question that seriously deteriorated health status is a major determinant of involuntary institutionalization among the elderly.

In an article provocatively entitled "The Failure of Success," Gruenberg (1977) reminds us that the life-saving technology of the past several decades has outstripped our health-preserving technology, with the net effect of worsening people's health, especially among the elderly survivors. The implication is that health status indicators such as mortality rates or life expectancy paint an incomplete or misleading picture, and that we need to be concerned also with indices that reflect disease, disability, social functioning, and "quality of life." One such useful index is presented by Sullivan (1971), who computed expectations for people 65 years old of years free of disability and free of bed disability, broken down by sex and race.

THE CHANGING RISK FACTOR PICTURE WITH AGE

Biological and psychosocial risk factors for a particular disease, or for adverse health status changes in general, may change in their potency as one goes from younger and middle-aged study samples to older subjects. The general issue here is the extent to which older age changes vulnerability to disease for a given level of risk factors.

The report of the Pooling Project Research Group (1978) on incidence of major coronary events in men reveals that the risk ratio goes up with age for blood pressure (and electrocardiogram abnormality), but goes down for serum cholesterol, cigarettes, and relative weight. Ostfeld *et al.* (1974) in their prospective study of stroke in an elderly population receiving welfare, found that, among those elderly free of preexisting cardiac and vascular disease, none of the following predicted stroke: blood pressure, ponderal index, cigarette smoking, serum cholesterol, and plasma glucose. Among those with preexisting disease, only blood pressure and ponderal index were significant risk factors for stroke.

Such findings as these suggest that, among the elderly, only high blood pressure remains as the risk factor of concern in the development of stroke and coronary heart disease. Conversely, the results indicate caution in initiating interventions regarding such life-style habits as smoking and diet in the elderly. Of course, no picture is as simple as this. For example, the data from Hagerstown (Abraham *et al.* 1971) revealed the highest prevalence of hypertensive vascular disease and cardiovascular renal disease among obese adults who were not obese as children; those obese in both childhood and adulthood had lower rates. This might suggest that obesity among the elderly does continue as a risk factor for those diseases, but only among those who obesity is of more recent origin.

Broad sociodemographic factors may also change as risk factors with advancing age. Kitagawa and Hauser (1973) analyzed mortality data on United States' residents in relation to age and education. Among white men, standardized mortality ratios (SMR) for all causes revealed a negative gradient in relation to years of education only among those age 25 to 64; white men 65 and older showed no gradient whatever. Among white women, a somewhat stronger negative gradient was observed in the 25–64 age group than in the 65 and older group, but the latter still revealed a definite negative association between SMR and education. Analyses by cause revealed that the disappearance of the gradient among men 65 and older held for all major causes except two: For influenza and pneumonia and for accidents, the higher levels of education conferred an advantage even in those men older than 65. These data, overall, suggest a simple interaction between SMR, education level, and age, and a more complex interaction involving sex.

Analyses by socioeconomic level of city tracts and age (Antonovsky 1967) reveal the expected negative gradient in SMRs and its weakening in the older age groups. However, unlike the data on education, the gradient never quite disappears even in the oldest group (75 and older) and is about the same for both sexes. Computations of SMRs for men 20 to 64 by age and occupation (Antonovsky 1967, National Vital Statistics Division 1962) reveal that nonfarm laborers, the one group with a notable excess mortality, have an SMR of more than 170 in the 25–44 age group, but it drops to a little more than 120 in the 55–64 age group.

Race remains an ambiguous social indicator in health studies and presumably reflects many sociocultural variables in addition to average social class differences. Consequently, the race-dependent differences in various health status indicators that are also modified by age are difficult to interpret. For example, age-specific death rates are higher for nonwhites only until age 74; the situation then reverses (National Center for Health Statistics 1979). However, these do not appear to be additional years free of disability; days of restricted activity and days of bed disability continue to be higher among nonwhites even in the 75 and older age bracket (National Center for Health Statisitics 1972). Other studies also suggest changing race differentials for specific diseases with change in age. For example, the strong increase in rheumatoid arthritis with age holds only for whites; blacks have higher rates until age 64, while whites have higher rates in the 65 and older age group (Cobb 1971). Prevalence rates of diabetes, determined in a mobile multiphasic screening program, are much higher among blacks than whites, but over age 65, the rates are virtually identical (Adler *et al.* 1966).

Analyses of 1959–1961 mortality by marital status (National Center for Health Statistics 1972) clearly document the well-known excess mortality associated with the three marital status categories of single, widowed, and divorced (compared with married). Moreover, in 11 of the 12 sex-by-race by status groups, the elevated SMR goes down in the older age groups: Only among divorced nonwhite women does the SMR show no change with age, remaining in the vicinity of 135. Additional analyses of similar mortality data from 1940 and 1949–1951 reveal one interesting secular trend: Among divorced women of both races the SMRs went up with older age groups for the 1940 and the 1949–1951 years. In other words, in 1940 divorced older women had much higher SMR than divorced younger women; by 1959–1961, this trend was reversed for white women and wiped out for black women. Additional analyses of the 1959–1961 mortality data by cause (e.g., arteriosclerotic heart disease, ICD [International Classification of Diseases] 420; vascular lesions affecting the central nervous system, ICD 330–334; malignant neoplasm of digestive organs and peritoneum, ICD 150–159) repeatedly confirm the decline in SMR for single, widowed, and divorced people in older age groups.

Data from the Human Population Laboratory (HPL) survey of almost 7000 adults in Alameda County have been examined for the relationship between health habits and mortality. Preliminary analyses (Belloc 1973) suggested that only the benefits of physical activity persist into old age. More recent analyses with a refined health practices index (smoking, alcohol consumption, physical activity, sleep, and relative weight), however, reveal that even among subjects 70 and older, a low score on positive health practices is associated with significantly greater mortality. These data are summarized in Table 15.1. It is also worth noting that there is not much of an association between age and health practices for either men or women.

The changing risk factor picture with advancing age becomes most complex—and most fascinating—when some factors become less potent while others emerge as more potent. Haynes *et al.* (1978), in their report on the relationship of selected psychosocial factors to coronary heart disease (CHD) in the Framingham study, showed that the Type A personality dimension was significantly associated with CHD among both men and women, but only in the younger age group (45–64); among older (65 and older) men and women, this association did not hold. On the other hand, marital dissatisfaction and/or marital disagreement were

TABLE 15.1
Mortality Rates from All Causes (per 100) by Health Practices Index, Age, and Sex, Alameda County, California 1965–1974

Health Practices Index (number of positive practices)	30–49		50–59		60–69		70+	
	Percentage	Number	Percentage	Number	Percentage	Number	Percentage	Number
Men								
0,1,2 positive health practices	9.3	(323)	19.7	(122)	30.9	(81)	77.6	(58)
3 positive health practices	3.1	(485)	16.3	(190)	34.8	(132)	66.3	(86)
4,5 positive health practices	1.2	(594)	6.9	(189)	17.7	(113)	50.7	(75)
Women								
0,1,2 positive health practices	5.7	(318)	10.3	(136)	30.4	(92)	55.1	(69)
3 positive health practices	3.4	(555)	8.8	(205)	16.6	(157)	42.2	(147)
4,5 positive health practices	1.7	(662)	5.6	(233)	9.4	(138)	43.4	(129)

associated with CHD among men and women, but only in the older age group. Interestingly, an index called "aging worries" showed an association with CHD among younger men and women only. Equally fascinating results are to be found in the study of acculturation and CHD among Japanese men living in California (Marmot and Syme 1976). The basic finding was one of low CHD prevalence among the more traditional Japanese–Americans, a result that could not be accounted for by differences in the major coronary risk factors. How did this picture change for different age groups? On one index, "culture of upbringing," the benefits of being traditional weakened considerably in the oldest of three age groups (55 and older). On another index, "cultural assimilation" (degree of retention of Japanese cultural forms), it was the oldest group that showed the biggest differences in CHD prevalence due to degree of assimilation.

In summary, then, the selected findings discussed in this section were primarily intended to alert the readers to a particularly interesting issue: the changing risk factor picture with age, and what that may say about the vulnerability of older people. We cannot make any claims that these findings are easy to interpret or that they form a coherent whole. Certainly it is possible that, in part, we are simply observing the selective survival of the fittest. Similarly, calculations intended to reveal the strength of the impact of a particular variable on health status, such as standardized morality ratio or relative risk, are ratio calculations that encounter a ceiling effect when the outcome variable is quite common in the total group under observation (e.g., morality among the very old). Calculations based on linear differences (e.g., difference in percentage between two groups) might lead to somewhat different statements regarding the changing risk factor picture. However, neither of these explanations is particularly compelling when one finds subgroup differences, such as the difference between men and women in the impact of education on mortality among younger and older persons, or when new risk factors emerge as others weaken among the progressively older age groups in the study sample.

The results from the Pooling Project Research Group (1978) and the stroke study (Ostfeld et al. 1974), on one hand, and from the analysis of the health habits among older Alameda County residents (Berkman 1977), on the other, reveal some troubling differences in the significance of smoking, obesity, and excercise among the elderly. It is not yet clear, for example, to what extent exercising among the elderly may be a more sensitive index of health status than self-reports of disability, chronic conditions, and symptoms. Thus, adjusting for level of health, based on the later indicators, may not remove all of the variation in prior health status, and amount of exercise among elderly would remain somewhat contaminated as a predictor of mortality.

In the long run, however, we need a substantive rather than methodological interpretation of the findings on the changing risk factor picture. This will call for a broad life-cycle perspective and for an understanding of the adaptation processes of different age groups. For example, the impact of social status variables may differ because life-style adaptations and aspirations change with age and because, in retirement, the effects of some components of social status may be considerably blunted. Ultimately, in order to understand the changes in biosocial vulnerability of people as they age, we will need to know more about the intrinsic, *sui generis* process of biological aging (if it exists), the cumulative impact of environmental conditions and experiences, and the changes in the meaning and dynamics of the psychosocial risk factors under scrutiny.

THE IMPACT OF SELECTED SOCIAL EXPERIENCES ON THE HEALTH OF THE ELDERLY

In this section, we propose to look at the impact of three types of psychosocial experiences or changing conditions: social networks and relationships, residential environments, and retirement. While these three topics represent an illustrative rather than a comprehensive coverage of the stress and disease literature (e.g., Dohrenwend and Dohrenwend 1974, Eisdorfer and Wilkie 1977, Henry and Stephens 1977, Hill 1976, Kasl and Reichsman 1977, Lazarus and Cohen 1976, Levi 1971, Lipowski *et al.* 1977), it is also true that they are three types of situations that are highly salient to the elderly and for which the accumulated research literature is quite plentiful. In contrast, the general literature on stressful life events, in which the combined impact of many possible events is studied, seldom deals specifically with elderly subjects and includes many events of limited relevance or applicability for the elderly. Nevertheless, it is interesting to note that the elderly tend to report fewer events and score the list of events lower on severity or seriousness (Masuda and Holmes 1978).

Social Networks

The importance of maintaining social connections for the physical and mental well-being of an individual has been recognized for some time

(Durkheim 1951, Freud 1926, Bowlby 1958). Recently, investigators have hypothesized that social and community ties may alter host resistance and consequently play a role in the etiology of a wide range of diseases (Cassel 1976, Kaplan *et al*. 1977, Cobb 1976, Antonovsky 1972). Social isolation has also been proposed as a critical aspect of the aging process itself (Lowenthal 1964, Cumming and Henry 1961). It is commonly expressed that the elderly are an isolated group with widowhood, retirement, and grown children leaving home bringing about an irreversible loss of social attachments and community ties. Thus, if the relationship between social isolation and poor health is a causally strong one, we would expect this to have profound effects among the elderly for whom such losses are common. In fact, while there is some evidence to suggest that social networks play a role in disease etiology, there is less convincing evidence regarding increasing social isolation as an age-linked phenomenon, and even less evidence supporting the notion that the relationship between social networks and health status may be unique to, or different for, the elderly.

In the following pages, we will briefly review the research relating social and community ties to health status among people of all ages. We will then discuss the prevalence of such ties among the elderly and review some evidence indicating the potential of some factors to modify the impact of social losses and isolation on health status in this group. Finally, investigations will be presented in which the relationships between social networks and health among the elderly are explored.

MARITAL STATUS

It has been repeatedly observed that those who are married have lower mortality rates than those who are single, widowed, or divorced (Ortmeyer 1974, Durkheim 1951, Price *et al*. 1971). This mortality risk does not appear to be as great for women as for men and seems to decline with age. Some evidence also suggests that the relationship between marital status and health is independent of many "traditional" physiological risk factors. In a random sample of 6672 men and women between the ages of 18 and 79, Weiss (1973) examined the relationship between marital status, coronary heart disease (CHD) and serum cholesterol, systolic and diastolic blood pressure, and a ponderal index. Although Weiss found increased CHD mortality rates present among the nonmarried to some extent at all ages above 25, his results revealed that no differences in any risk factor explained the married/nonmarried CHD mortality differential. In fact, there were no consistent differences in any of the risk factor levels between married and nonmarried men and women at any age levels. The excess risk in CHD found among the nonmarried is, thus, not due to any increases in any of the more obvious CHD physiological risk factors.

The association between widowhood and increased morbidity and mortality is particularly striking. Maddison and Viola (1968), Marris (1958), and early studies by Parkes (1964) indicate that widows, especially in the first year following bereavement, report many more complaints about their health, both mental and physical, and believe they have sustained a lasting deterioration to their health. The relationship between widowhood and increased mortality risk from a wide variety of diseases has been reported both in studies using vital statistics (Kraus and Lillienfeld 1959; Young et al 1963, Cox and Ford 1964, McNeil 1973) and in cohort studies (Rees and Lutkins 1967; Clayton 1974, Gerber et al. 1975, Ward 1976).

In one of the more conclusive studies, Parkes, Benjamin, and Fitzgerald (1969) report that of 4486 widowers 55 and older, 213 died during the first 6 months following bereavement. This is 40% above the expected rate for married men the same age. After 6 months, the rates gradually fell back to those of married men and remained at that level. Through an analysis of husbands' and wives' concordance rates for cause of death, the authors concluded that neither the sharing of similar pathogenic environment nor the tendency toward the selection of the unfit to marry the unfit (homogamy) was likely to explain more than a part of the increased 6-month mortality rate.

The existence of a supportive marriage has been shown to mediate between stressful life events and poor health outcomes. In one study of the mental and physical health consequences of job loss due to a factory shutdown, Gore (1978) reports that those men who had "the emotional support of their wives while unemployed for several weeks had few illness symptoms, low cholesterol levels, and did not blame themselves for loss of job." In general, men who were both unemployed for a longer time and unsupported tended to have the worse health outcomes (Cobb and Kasl 1977). In another study of psychiatric disturbance among women, Brown et al. (1975) found that having a husband or boy friend who was a confidant served as a powerful mediator between a severe event or major difficulty and onset of psychiatric disorder. In this sample of women aged 18 to 65, 38% of those who had a stressful event and no husband or boy friend as confidant had onset of disturbance. (For those without such a confidant or without severe event, the percentage of psychiatric disturbance was under 4%.) When the confidant named was a sister, mother, or friend seen weekly, the relationship was not observed to mediate between life events and psychiatric disturbance.

These data suggest that there is something protective about a supportive spouse or partner that is capable of shielding an individual against the otherwise deleterious effects of some objective life circumstances. The morbidity and mortality findings also indicate that the loss of a spouse, a major enduring tie to another person, may be at least a precipitating factor in the increased death rates found among widowers. The relationship appears to be at least to some extent independent of the traditional CHD physiological risk factors, homogamy, and equal exposure to pathogenic environments.

The elderly, particularly elderly women, are increasingly likely to lose a spouse with advancing years. Jacobs and Ostfeld (1977), in a comprehensive review on the mortality of bereavement, estimate that 2–3% of married Americans over the age of 50 will become widowed each year. Between the ages of 65 and 74, 10% of men and 43% of women are widowed. For those 75 years and older the respective percentages are 29.5 and 70.2 (Siegal 1975). Clearly, this is an extremely frequent event among the elderly. However, there is also some evidence to suggest that the nature of bereavement is in some ways modified for the elderly. Several investigators (Stern and Williams 1951, Gramlich 1968, Gerber *et al.* 1975, and Heyman and Gianturco 1973) indicate that grief among the elderly is not the same as grief at younger ages. Jacobs and Douglas (1979) have summarized this work, reporting that among the elderly a loss is faced with more cognitive acceptance and is associated with less numbness, denial, and guilt. However, hallucinations and illusions and psychosomatic symptoms may occur with greater frequency. Jacobs and Douglas (1979) suggest that these differential characteristics of grief among the elderly may be the result of the process of anticipation of death, which is probably associated with older age. This ability to anticipate and accept widowhood may also play some role in the decreased relative risks associated with bereavement at older ages reported by researchers (Kraus and Lilienfeld 1959, McNeil 1973). This finding also supports Neugarten's (1970) viewpoint that what makes events traumatic is their being "off time" and unanticipated. "Major stresses," she emphasizes, "are caused by events that upset the sequence and rhythm of the life cycle . . . when the empty nest, grandparenthood, widowhood, or retirement occur *off time* [pp. 86–87]." It may also be that the experience of becoming a widow or widower at a time when one's peers are also becoming single provides a structural support that buffers against some of the stressful circumstances encountered by younger widows and widowers. We discuss this topic in greater detail in the next section.

OTHER SOCIAL TIES

Apart from spouses, other social ties are relied on by most people to fulfill a variety of emotional and pragmatic needs. Some of these ties are characterized by enduring and emotionally important relationships, while other contacts are characterized primarily by their task orientation. Some people in these links may fulfill a variety of needs; others may have one specific need for which they are relied on. Taken as a whole, these relationships and informal associations form a web or a social network in which most people spend a significant part of their lives. Although network configurations have been described in detail by many social scientists, relatively little is known about the impact that various network configurations have on health status. We will briefly review some of the evidence relating social networks to health status and then focus on situations of special interest to the elderly. For more extensive reviews on the topic of health and social networks the reader is referred to two recent papers (Kaplan *et al.* 1977, Cobb 1976).

Most health and network investigations have focused on mental health, in terms of either psychiatric disturbance, morale, or symptomatology. Phillips (1967), in a study of 600 adults, finds that people who have frequent contacts with friends, neighbors, and organizational associates (taken together or separately) report higher rates of "being happy" and are less likely to score in the "impaired" category on Langner's 22-item scale. Henderson *et al.* (1978a), in a study of a random sample of 142 adults in Canberra, have also reported a strong inverse relationship between social bonds and the presence of neurotic symptoms. In a larger sample, Henderson (1978b) confirmed these findings and found that when controlling for level of adversity, as measured by life events, there was a statistically significant decline in symptoms with increasing level of social bonds. An indirect test of the importance of extended ties is provided by a study by Wechsler and Pugh (1967) of approximately 25,000 first admissions to Massachusetts mental hospitals. The investigators hypothesized that the difference between an individual's characteristics and those of others in his community would represent the degree to which there was an easily available peer group to promote the formation of interpersonal relationships. In the study, people who did not "fit" in terms of age, marital status, occupation, or place of birth were found to have higher than expected rates of hospital admissions.

Social support systems have also been presumed to play a crucial role in problems with pregnancy, differential efficacy of treatment, and the process of recovery and survival. For example, in a study of primiparae army wives, women with many life changes and many psychosocial resources had one-third the pregnancy complication rate of women who also had many life changes but few psychosocial resources (Nuckolls *et al.* 1972). In another study of social factors and postpartum emotional problems (Gordon and Gordon 1967) the absence of supportive family and friends was an important predictor of postpartum depression. An example of social support influencing treatment effects is the study of steroid requirements for chronic asthma patients (DeAraujo *et al.* 1973): the Berle Index, a composite measure of psychosocial resources including family and interpersonal relationships, was found to be negatively associated with steroid requirements. Greater use of health services in general appears to be associated with the feeling of not having enough friends (Segal *et al.* 1967) and with poorer integration into a new society (Shuval *et al.* 1970). Cobb (1976) in his review suggests that withdrawal from alcohol and compliance with medical regimes are all tied to social support and affiliation. Haynes and Sackett (1974), in a review of 22 articles concerning compliance and social support, report that for 15 of the studies, evidence shows that variables relevant to social support are associated with compliance to therapeutic regimes. One article reported negative evidence, and six showed no difference. And there are many studies that have examined the positive role of social support in such crises as bereavement and severe illness, and in the process of recovery and rehabilitation (e.g., Croog *et al.* 1972, Doehrman 1977, Hyman 1972, Litman 1966, Walker *et al.* 1977).

The research results discussed so far tend to focus on the importance of what we naturally think of as strong ties (e.g., ties with friends and family, characterized generally by emotional intensity, intimacy, and reciprocity). However, another aspect of network analysis stresses the importance and cohesive power of what are usually defined as "weak ties" (Granovetter 1973). Such ties are characterized by lack of intimacy and by the limited time spent in the relationship. Granovetter argues that these ties may be of critical importance in the diffusion of influence and information, mobility opportunity, and political and community organization. Walker *et al.* (1977)suggest that such weak ties aid the adjustment of the bereaved at a time when they need new information and new contacts. Other studies also indicate that people who have more differentiated networks or more varied types of sources of contact may have better access to medical care resources (e.g., Lee 1969, McKinlay 1973) and to have spouses with more successful recoveries from heart attacks (Finlayson 1976). It would appear that closed networks, although closely knit and capable of providing strong social support, may also exert a limiting influence by reducing access to information and resources; when the dominant in-group values and beliefs are incompatible with appropriate preventive behavior or medical care seeking, the social support from closed networks may be associated with poorer health status (e.g., Suchman's [1966] analysis of this issue).

The relationship between nonintimate "weak" ties and health status has not been well investigated. Most research in this area has been limited to the study of group affiliations, organizational membership, and social participation instead of more direct measures of extended ties. Palmore and Luikart (1972), in an analysis from the Duke adaptation study of 502 people aged 45 to 69, report that while self-rated health was the strongest variable associated with life satisfaction, organizational activity was found to be second. Similarly, in a study of alienation and social structure in a small city (Mizruchi 1960), formal social participation was found to be negatively associated with alienation, even when controlling for social class position. These results agree with Srole's (1956) original findings.

Church attendance has long been thought to be positively associated with mental and physical health. It is unclear whether this is the result of religious belief, associated favorable health behaviors, associated sociodemographic factors, or support provided by a group of people. Compared with people who attend church infrequently, churchgoers have been found to respond more favorably to cervical cancer screening programs (Naguib et al. 1968), have a lower incidence of tuberculosis (Comstock et al. 1970), and have decreased risk of arteriosclerotic heart disease, pulmonary emphysema, suicide, cirrhosis of the liver (Comstock and Partridge 1972), and high blood pressure (Graham et al. 1978). The comparatively good health status of certain religious groups, for example, Seventh Day Adventists and Mormons, has also been noted; the most plausible explanation of this difference is presumably in terms of their favorable health behaviors. An Israeli study (Medalie et al. 1973) has reported a lower incidence of myocardial infarction among the more religious subjects. However, in contrast to the above evidence that religion may play a role in mortality and new morbidity, response to serious illness seems to be little influenced by different dimensions of religious identity (Croog and Levine 1972).

A more precise understanding of the above data on religion and health status is of more than academic interest. Since frequency of church attendance appears to decline with age among the elderly, even as their religious feelings and attitudes grow stronger (e.g., Moberg 1968), it is important to know whether the influence on health status involves the social interaction associated with attendance or certain feelings and beliefs that require no particular social setting to be effective.

Studies dealing with the association between social isolation and health are a natural extension of our concern with strong and weak social ties. However, there is a cause and effect issue concerning these data that is even more difficult to disentangle than for the studies already discussed. Since few of the isolation studies are prospective or longitudinal, it is impossible to know whether social isolation predisposes people to low morale, depression, or other health consequences or whether it is the result of such conditions. Furthermore, it is likely that some of the observed relationships are confounded by the presence of other variables, such as marital status and socioeconomic status, which are themselves predictors of many of the outcomes measured in these studies.

In what ways does this evidence have any bearing on our understanding of health problems of the elderly? First, it is frequently assumed that with increasing age comes increasing social isolation. The increasing disabilities and functional limitations that come with age make it more important to have social relationships and environments that will help the elderly maintain themselves. In terms of the most obvious of social contacts—those which result from living arrangements—it is interesting to note that the majority of men and women older than 65 (79% of men and 59% of women) live with other family members, including spouses (Sussman 1976). Among the widowed this situation is different and appears to have changed substantially over the last 30 years. Chevan and Korson (1972), in an analysis of United States census data, report that 50.4% of widows and 47.0% of widowers in 1970 reported living alone. These percentages are double what they were in 1940. In this analysis, black widows and widowers were less likely to live alone than white widows and widowers; and those with more children and less income and education lived alone more than people with fewer children and in higher status groups. Among blacks but not whites, women were less likely to live alone than men.

While living with others protects one from the most severe forms of social isolation, living alone should not be automatically equated with social isolation. Much research indicates that older single people prefer to live alone but close to their children (Troll 1971, Rosenmayr and Köckers 1966). Shanas (1967) has presented international data suggesting that among older people with living children, for more than three-fourths the nearest child was either in the household or within an hour or less distance from him or her. The growing literature on parents and grown children (Adams 1968, Sussman 1953, Townsend 1957, Marris 1958) also indicates an effective, modified extended family structure in the United States and other modern European countries.

Data from the Human Population Laboratory (HPL) Survey of almost 7000 adults in Alameda County, California, in 1965 reveal few decreases in social contacts with age, with a few important exceptions. Table 15.2 reveals that only group membership shows a consistent inverse relationship with age. Other investigators have reported somewhat weaker inverse relationships for men but no association with age for women

TABLE 15.2

Percentage of Men and Women without Social Contact by Marital Status and Age and Source of Contact, Alameda County, California, 1965[a,b]

	30–49		50–59		60–69		70+	
	Percentage	Number	Percentage	Number	Percentage	Number	Percentage	Number
Men								
None or few contacts with friends and relatives								
Married	16.4	(1209)	12.0	(446)	15.3	(268)	18.2	(143)
Nonmarried	21.8	(175)	16.4	(55)	34.5	(58)	23.9	(71)
No group membership								
Married	22.4	(1227)	19.7	(446)	28.7	(268)	42.7	(143)
Nonmarried	34.9	(175)	34.5	(55)	44.8	(58)	52.3	(76)
No church membership								
Married	71.1	(1227)	65.9	(446)	70.5	(268)	68.5	(143)
Nonmarried	78.9	(175)	70.9	(55)	80.7	(58)	75.0	(76)
Women								
None or few contacts with friends and relatives								
Married	15.4	(1249)	10.0	(401)	9.4	(202)	12.8	(86)
Nonmarried	16.1	(286)	10.2	(167)	12.9	(179)	13.3	(241)
No group membership								
Married	32.7	(1249)	37.3	(407)	55.8	(208)	56.2	(89)
Nonmarried	42.3	(286)	44.9	(167)	54.7	(179)	62.1	(256)
No church membership								
Married	66.7	(1249)	60.9	(407)	58.7	(208)	57.3	(89)
Nonmarried	76.9	(286)	65.2	(167)	63.1	(179)	54.3	(256)

[a] From Human Population Laboratory.
[b] Lower totals in age cells are due to missing data.

(Booth 1972) or a weak relationship without controlling for sex (Harvey and Bahr 1974). Among women, church membership increases with age. Contacts with friends and relatives do not vary greatly by age except among nonmarried men aged 60 to 69 who show a sharp decrease in contacts. The finding that single men in this age group are more than twice as likely as their married counterparts to report few contacts agrees with earlier findings (e.g., Blau 1973). The older single man is likely to be in a particularly deviant position since few men aged 60 to 69 are single. Having possibly lost old sources of friendship, originally established through work contacts, marriage, and other social affairs, he is now likely to be an odd person at social gatherings with friends and family. The older woman, in contrast, is likely to know more people in her similar situation (since there are more) and is likely to have an easier time making social contacts. Blau (1973) also notes that, incidentally, this situation disappears for people over 70 when the incidence of widowhood increases dramatically. This diminished difference is also evident in the HPL data. The greater ability of women, compared with men, to maintain intimate friendships with both family and friends has been reported at several other life stages besides the elderly (Arth 1962, Lowenthal et al. 1975, Booth 1972, Powers and Bultena 1976).

To summarize the association of social and community ties with age, we might say that the elderly are less likely than younger men and women to maintain extensive contacts from many sources; however, in most cases these differences are not large. There are important exceptions to this pattern. People who are in structurally deviant positions appear to have a more difficult time maintaining contacts, that is, widowers aged 60 to 69. Furthermore, although space does not permit us to review this evidence, both socioeconomic status and health status exert a powerful influence on the elderly person's abilities to see other people.

The health consequences, both mental and physical, of social isolation do not appear to be very different for elderly people than for people at other ages, but the data are very limited and fragmentary in this area. Studies of people 60 and older in San Francisco suggest that neither lifelong isolates, those who have a voluntary reduction in social activity, nor elderly people who face age-linked trauma such as widowhood or retirement appear to be more prone to hospitalization for mental disorder than others; however, those who have tried and failed to establish relationships may be more vulnerable to mental disorders (Lowenthal 1964, 1965, and Lowenthal and Boler 1965). These data are cross-sectional and the results must be interpreted with great caution since the direction of causation is unknown.

Analysis of mortality data from the Human Population Laboratory suggests that older people who lack social connections are at increased risk of dying in a 9-year follow-up period (Berkman and Syme 1979). Table 15.3 shows age and sex-specific mortality rates by levels of a social network index. The index contains, in addition to marital status, information on contacts with friends and relatives, church membership, and formal and informal group associations. The general finding is one of increased mortality among those with fewer social ties; this holds for both men and women and persists when one adjusts for social class, initial health status, and health practices. Calculations of relative risk for different age and sex groups reveal only a slightly lower relative risk in older age groups and the diminution in relative risk by age not very regular. Calculations done on the 70 and older group, in which a little more than 50% died during the follow-up period, still reveal the predictive power of the social network index. It thus appears that social isolation does not particularly diminish in its potency as a risk factor for mortality in higher age groups. Since the national mortality data by marital status, discussed earlier, revealed a reliable diminution of standardized mortality ratios by age, this difference in results may suggest that the other items in the social network index are particularly notable predictors of mortality in the older population.

Residential Environments and Residential Moves

In this section, we wish to consider briefly selected aspects of the large literature on residential environments of the elderly. Because of limitations of space, we will provide only highlights of this literature, rather than a fully referenced and detailed review; the reader is referred to several recent comprehensive reviews (Carp 1976, Kasl and Rosenfield 1980, Lawton 1977, Lawton and Nahemow 1973) for a more detailed overview.

The great majority of studies deal with one of four topics: (1) the impact of new housing environments, such as planned housing for the elderly; (2) the impact of institutionalization and of institutional environments, (3) the impact of residential moves or relocation as stressful experiences, and (4) the impact of special residential settings, particularly retirement communities. There is wide consensus that the effects of the residential environment (that is, defined in physical terms and encompassing housing and neighborhood conditions, including services and facilities) cannot be understood in isolation, but must be seen in complex interaction with the characteristics of the individual and the nature of his or her social environment. Such a viewpoint leads to the suggestion that this section be best viewed as an elaboration and extension of the previous one on social networks, except that now the interactive effects

TABLE 15.3
Mortality Rates from All Causes (per 100) by Social Network Index Age, Sex-Specific Rates, Alameda County, California, 1965–1974

Social Network Index	30–49		50–59		60–69		70+	
	Percentage	Number	Percentage	Number	Percentage	Number	Percentage	Number
Men								
I (Most connections)	2.4	(457)	9.6	(197)	21.8	(110)	50.0	(54)
II	3.1	(450)	12.1	(157)	26.3	(95)	59.5	(42)
III	5.3	(396)	18.2	(121)	33.0	(88)	65.2	(89)
IV (Least connections)	6.1	(99)	30.8	(26)	39.4	(33)	88.2	(34)
Women								
I (Most connections)	1.5	(460)	7.3	(205)	9.7	(93)	30.4	(56)
II	2.0	(402)	4.9	(122)	16.7	(78)	46.3	(41)
III	4.3	(514)	8.0	(188)	17.7	(158)	44.2	(156)
IV (Least connections)	6.9	(159)	15.3	(59)	29.4	(58)	55.4	(92)

of social and residential environments are being discussed. Thus, for example, rehousing studies reflect both the impact of improved physical conditions of the dwelling unit as well as the effects of the disruption of social networks that frequently accompanies rehousing. Similarly, dimensions of residential distance and crowding exert variable effects, depending on various social characteristics of the residents and the degree of social homogeneity of the neighborhood.

Studies of voluntary residential moves to better housing point to relatively modest benefits (e.g., Lawton and Cohen 1974, Lawton *et al.* 1978): These are strongest on indices of well-being that deal specifically with residential conditions, intermediate on indices of social activity and general evaluations of one's current life circumstances, and weakest on the more traditional indicators of mental health and physical health status. Possibly, elderly movers will experience more changes in health status (for better and for worse) than nonmovers, but no average benefit (Lawton and Yaffe 1970). In these and similar studies, it is unlikely that the modest results can be fully accounted for by the interpretation that the adverse effects of the social uprooting wipe out the benefits of the better housing. Only the Victoria Plaza study (Carp 1966) found impressive benefits due to rehousing; moreover, these benefits appear to persist through 8 years of follow-up (e.g., Carp 1977a). Unfortunately, the results of this study are atypical and the reasons for this a matter of some controversy (Kasl and Rosenfield 1980).

Cross-sectional studies of housing environments and health of the elderly do not contradict the conclusion of—at best—a weak impact on health. Many of the studies are actually more concerned with social dimensions of the residential environments (particularly age composition) and tend to focus on social activities and social interaction (e.g., Rosow 1967). These studies are in reasonable agreement about the results that link amount of social interaction to physical proximity and sociodemographic homogeneity. However, in spite of numerous other studies that have demonstrated an association between social interaction and some indicator of physical or mental health status (most frequently life satisfaction), it has been exceedingly difficult to make the full linkage from residential environment to social interaction to health status and then attach a large undirection causal arrow next to it.

The factors of interest to studies of the housing of elderly have traditionally centered on neighborhood facilities and services. More recently, however, a good deal of interest has switched to issues of transportation and crime (e.g., Cantilli and Shmelzer 1971, Goldsmith and Goldsmith 1976). The latter topic is a good illustration of the complexity of the issues involved: Simple cross-sectional surveys have not yet pinpointed the health costs of crime for the elderly, but any talk that such costs have been exaggerated would be premature, since such study designs are inadequately probing. For example, while the elderly are less likely to be victims of crime, certain types of crimes (e.g., larceny with personal contact) and certain locations (e.g., inside the dwelling, especially involving age-integrated housing) are relatively overrepresented among the elderly. Moreover, older people are more vulnerable to the impact of crime and their fear of crime can be at the same time greater and less closely tied to the actual "objective" crime rates in their neighborhood. Thus actual and potential (subjectively appraised) exposure to crime must be considered, especially since the latter is, in part, influenced by a sense of integration into informal helping networks. Defensive maneuvers that lower victimization rates but severely restrict the mobility and life space of the elderly, thus affecting their quality of life, have yet to be assessed for their impact on mental health. Specific targeted longitudinal studies of elderly crime victims also are still to be undertaken.

Involuntary residential changes of the elderly include relocation within the community, institutionalizations, and institutional transfer. It is generally agreed (e.g., Carp 1976, Lawton 1977) that elderly people as a group are less likely to make residential moves, less likely to desire such moves, and are less successful in anticipating their mobility behavior. Attachment to people in the community and to a place is the primary reason for the older person's unwillingness to make a residential move. Thus, there is every indication that such unplanned or unintended moves should have adverse health impact on the elderly.

Unfortunately, there is a dearth of longitudinal and fully prospective studies that could most securely assess the health impact. This is particularly disturbing in the case of the institutionalization literature, in which the phenomenon is so complex and the potential for confounding influences quite great (Kasl and Rosenfield 1980). Because of this, the frequently observed elevated mortality rates during the year after institutionalization essentially remain uninterpretable, and self-selection factors are the most plausible single explanation. Studies of aged individuals transferred from one institutional setting to another represent a better natural experiment then institutionalization in looking at the impact of environmental change. The impression is that earlier studies found such a transfer to be associated with increased mortality (Kasl 1972), whereas the more recent studies have consistently failed to do so (Kasl and Rosenfield 1980). Variations in the way the transfer process was handled may account for a good deal of this discrepancy, though differences in the quality of the new institutional environments and comparability problems between transferred and nontransferred subjects are plausible additional explanations. It is also interesting to note that in several studies an anticipation effect was observed, that is, elevated mortality rates for a period prior to the move.

The work of Lieberman and his collaborators (e.g., Lieberman 1974, Tobin and Lieberman 1976) represents a prominent part of the institutionalization literature of the last 15 years. It is instructive to note that over the years this team appears to have become more skeptical of their ability to document the impact of institutionalization and tended to move toward the goal of understanding the predictors of adjustment and health outcomes, particularly in reference to institutional characteristics and personality variables related to successful adaptation. Thus, we remain unsure about the impact of institutionalization on the health of the elderly, but have become considerably more knowledgeable about the difficulties of studying this issue convincingly.

In the study of involuntary moves within the community, Fried's (1963) work on urban renewal remains an idealized paradigm: Residents in an old intact neighborhood, in which they had lived for many years and where rich and strong social ties exist, were forced out because of urban renewal or highway construction. They received no help with the move, they were scattered throughout the city, and they "grieve for their lost home." The early studies of relocation specifically dealing with the elderly have been mostly summarized by Niebanck (1968) and there would seem to be little doubt that some psychological distress was one of the consequences: depression, sadness, loneliness, insecurity. The impact on physical health was not documented and seldom studied.

Our recently completed prospective study of forced relocation (Kasl et al. in press) reflects the more current phenomenon: Elderly residents, living not in urban villages but in changing and deteriorating neighborhoods, are assisted to move into federally subsidized housing, which represents a residential improvement (structurally and socially) at a relatively favorable price. It may be an involuntary move, but in many ways it is also sought and desired. The overall results suggested that there were clear-cut benefits in the residential domain (e.g., perceptions of the dwelling and of the neighborhood) and that social interaction was not greatly affected, with any disruptions in social networks relatively easily repaired in the new setting. However, on indices of physical health status, those who were relocated did have more adverse outcomes than controls: more hospitalization events and nursing home admissions, greater incidence of stroke and angina pectoris, and poorer self-assessed health. Among those whose anticipatory perceptions of the relocation were more negative, the adverse health outcomes were more striking.

We have dealt selectively with some of the issues and studies of the residential environment and health of the elderly. The greatest need is for adequately prospective studies in which self-selection factors are minimized and subjects are followed through the several (probably) stages of adaptation and impact. Adaptation processes themselves need to be studied more intensively and from a broad "person–environment fit" perspective. The study of residential changes in conjunction with other stressful life changes taking place would be also desirable. And the study of the impact of lack of residential mobility, in a setting of a changing and deteriorating residential situation, has been also neglected.

The Impact of Retirement on Health

The retirement and health literature poses a peculiar dilemma for the researcher. Unlike the usual situation, in which many studies dealing with a particular broad social influence on health are inconsistent and inconclusive, the health studies of retirement (and the researchers) are in remarkable agreement: The transition from work to retirement is not accompanied by an adverse impact (on the average) on physical or mental health status of the retiree (e.g., Atchley 1976, Friedman and Orbach 1974, Kasl 1980, MacBride 1976, Rowland 1977, Streib and Schneider 1971). The problem is that there is much in the scientific and political Zeitgeist that argues otherwise. Most notably, the whole stressful life events orientation ineluctably forces the "deduction" that retirement will have an adverse impact; see, for example, Carp's (1977b) recent review: "The sheer scope and pervasiveness of *changes* [in retirement] must forecast physical illness, according to the Holmes and Rahe paradigm [p. 149]." Similarly, "experts" dealing with the impact of work environments retain negative values and beliefs about retirement and cite unusual case histories of the devastating consequences following onset of retirement (e.g., Margolis and Kroes 1974). There is also the current political climate and recent legislation that seem to derive from an unquestioned social value that people should not be forced to retire and that it is beneficial for them to continue to work (protecting the financial integrity of the social security system may be an unspoken additional consideration).

Setting aside the issue of the cultural lag represented by the discrepancy between the Zeitgeist and the actual empirical evidence, in this section we wish to address three interrelated issues: How far can we push the conclusion that retirement has no (average) negative impact? How can this finding be best understood? What types of studies are needed to explore the limitations of this conclusion?

The general conclusion about the absence of a negative impact on health is based on results from a variety of studies using different designs and assessing mortality, morbidity, and self-reported health status. The findings are consistent even if no study by itself is immune from methodological criticism. Some studies suggest an improvement in health status after retirement, but they are all based on self-assessed health. Since the "improvement" was observed in physically demanding occupations and among workers whose health appeared to decline during their last work years, it is very likely that only the evaluation of health status improved after retirement, but not health measured by more objective criteria—if such had been also available.

Studies concerned with mental health and well-being have similarly failed to show an average adverse impact. Differences between the employed and the retired tend to wash out when one adjusts for age, health status, income, and functional disability. If adverse impact exists, it is probably in narrow domains, such as reduced perceived usefulness (Back and Guptill 1966).

Understanding variations in postretirement outcomes is the obvious next concern, if the net, average effect of retirement appears to be nil. Here again, the transition from work to retirement appears to be rather unimportant. This is primarily because these variations in outcome are most convincingly seen as reflecting continuities of preretirement status, particularly in the areas of physical health, social and leisure activities, and general well-being and satisfaction. For example, George and Maddox (1977) found a very high temporal stability ($r = .79$) over a 6-year period on the Kutner morale scale.

Among the predictors of variations in postretirement outcomes, prior attitudes toward the process of retirement and expectations about postretirement outcomes have always looked promising. However, it appears that they make their contribution primarily via their association with underlying variables, such as prior health status and financial aspects of retirement. Thus they do not indicate the differential impact of retirement but rather reflect the continuities of powerful preretirement status variables.

Even variables reflecting aspects of the work role (such as job satisfaction and work commitment) do not appear to be strong and consistent predictors of variations in postretirement outcome. However, this is not yet a well-documented conclusion and in view of its counterintuitive nature, we should perhaps reserve judgment. The whole area of the occupational specificity of postretirement outcomes is not yet well studied and is a promising area of future explorations. For example, measuring degrees of work commitment among assembly line workers may be a considerably inferior approach, compared with contrasting occupational groups that vary greatly in work commitment. Blue-collar and white-collar workers appear to go through different stages of adaptation to postretirement status, and this also appears a promising area for further investigations.

Financial considerations, in contrast to work role dimensions, appear to play a major role in the decision process and planning for retirement, in expectations about retirement, and in postretirement adjustment and well-being. Similarly, retired men who say they want a job or that they should have kept on working do so, to a large extent, for financial reasons (Kasl 1980). And the recent increase in the frequency of unfavorable feelings about retirement (Barfield and Morgan 1978) appears to be primarily due to the increased concern over inflation.

The notion that involuntary retirement among healthy employed individuals who wish to continue working may have adverse health consequences remains a viable hypothesis, in spite of the general negative evidence previously mentioned. This is because it has not yet been tested in a proper and adequately probing study design. Studying the effects of "mandatory" retirement among blue-collar workers who overwhelmingly wish to retire before the mandatory age (provided the financial benefits are adequate) fails to examine the hypothesis. Studying retired workers who wish to return to work primarily for financial reasons is at best studying the impact of inadequate financial circumstances, not of deprivation of the work role. And contrasting a cross-section of retirees who label themselves "voluntary" versus "involuntary" tends to load into the latter grouping those who are in poor health, who have had a more irregular work history (including recent layoffs or job loss), and who are in poorer financial circumstances. Once these powerful confounding influences are controlled for, there is little room for detecting the impact of the voluntary–involuntary dimension. Finally, we must recognize that even if the phenomenon of wishing to continue to work and not being able to because of forced retirement were quite uncommon (say, 1%) and strong adverse health effects among them not very frequent (say, 10%), we would still be dealing with a significant public health problem, since retirement is a near-universal experience for those in the labor force.

Given the ethical and practical limitations on social experimentation as well as the powerful self-selection factors that normally contribute to continuing to work beyond the usual retirement age, perhaps the best one can do is to take healthy individuals who experienced mandatory retirement at 65 and who miss work and would want to continue working, at least on a part-time basis. If the demand for such part-time jobs exceeds the supply, such individuals could be randomly assigned to work versus no work conditions. Then the benefits of continuing to work beyond 65 could be evaluated fairly rigorously, particularly if the financial benefits were equalized for the two groups.

Social gerontologists have reminded us that retirement is not simply an event, but also a process (e.g., Atchley 1976, Carp 1977b). But when does the process begin and when does it end? Elsewhere (Kasl 1979) we have argued that perhaps for the majority of blue-collar workers in routine, uninteresting jobs, the significant adaptation process is not to retirement but to the particular work environment in which they find themselves. Moreover, this crucial adaptation (or failure to adapt) may take place decades before actual retirement, perhaps at the time when the worker comes to terms with the dull, monotonous job and gives up any expectation that work will be a meaningful human activity (Chinoy 1955, Kornhauser 1965). Under such circumstances, retirement (as the event of transition) should not be expected to have much of an impact.

There is another side to the argument, which also leads to an expectation of only an attenuated impact of retirement. Essentially, both on theoretical and intuitive grounds, the impact of the loss of the work role via retirement should be the greatest among those with strong job involvement, that is, high psychological importance of work to a person's total identity. Who are the people with strong job involvement? They have a stimulating job (high on autonomy, variety, task identity, and feedback), they participate in decisions affecting them, and they have a history of job success (Rabinowitz and Hall 1977). But they are also likely to be in jobs with greater power and prestige and to be themselves more privileged, socially and psychologically, with more resources to adapt to the transition, and in better physical and mental health. In short, the self-selection factors associated with strong job involvement, and thus a potentially greater retirement impact, are also factors that give the individual a greater capacity to withstand such an impact.

In view of the notable increase during the last 30 years in labor force participation of women, primarily white women (Sheppard 1976), it is useful to end this section with a brief comment on retirement studies of women. Even though the relevant evidence is much more limited compared with studies of men (Kasl 1980), there is no evidence to support the notion that for women who have worked, the work role has less significance than for men and that the impact of retirement is thus lessened. In fact, among the studies showing some sex differences, there was a hint that retired women were more likely to report difficulty adjusting to retirement than were retired men. However, the range of occupations used in these studies remains limited.

MEDICAL CARE BEHAVIOR OF THE ELDERLY

In this section, we wish to examine selected aspects of the broad research literature that deal with the determinants of contacts with the medical care system. The emphasis is on the elderly and on identifying meaningful age-related differences in the dynamics of such behavior. Of course, the experience of symptoms and self-appraisals of health status and disability are powerful partial determinants of medical care behavior, which are also age-related. However, our interest here is in the determinants that operate above and beyond the influence of differential health status. For this purpose, then, the usual data on age differences in doctor's visits or hospitalizations or medications are by themselves too ambiguous and will not be discussed.

The theoretical formulations that have been developed to formalize our understanding of this area are well outlined in Mechanic's (1978) chapter on "illness behavior." However, none of them deals explicitly with age, and the work that needs to be done is to collect systematic data on how age, as a nontheoretical variable, is to be linked to the various theoretical variables that are part of one or another of the formulations. A hypothesis regarding the effect of age that seems to have had a good deal of acceptance (e.g., Eisdorfer and Wilkie 1977) is the idea that serious illness is developmentally "on time" (in terms of the life-cycle) for an older person, thus mitigating its impact and the person's interpretation of it. However, it is not clear whether one can "deduce" from this that elderly subjects should respond with less denial and more readiness for appropriate medical care, or if they should show more apparent denial ("this isn't illness, but is part of getting old") and less readiness for medical care. The kind of finding showing that among the elderly there is an increasing discrepancy between physician evaluations and self-evaluations of health status with increasing age, thereby creating greater numbers of "health optimists" (Heyman and Jeffers 1963, Van Zonneveld 1969), is similarly ambiguous, suggesting either more denial or greater acceptance of illness because of a changing normative standard for self-evaluation. Comparing frequency of doctor's visits, which increase only slightly with age, with percentage with limitation in major activity due to chronic conditions, which increases very sharply with age (National Center for Health Statistics 1978), would seem to suggest inadequate medical care for such conditions among the elderly. However, this is only a crude interpretation, lacking any estimates of appropriate frequency of physician contacts for disabling chronic conditions and not discounting for the fact that acute conditions decline with higher age.

It is also interesting to note that in spite of the usual modest increase in doctor's visits with age (steeper for men), studies of very low users of free or prepaid medical services (Densen *et al.* 1959, Kessel and Shepherd 1965) reveal that older subjects (particularly older men) are overrepresented. This would seem to suggest that among older people (especially men) the above-average utilization rates hide two separate subgroups, those with increasingly frequent visits and those who continue their minimal contacts with the medical care system.

Given this theoretical and empirical complexity, it is difficult to pre-judge the issue regarding the role of age in medical care contacts. Let us then look at some selected studies to see what picture emerges. We shall begin with treatment for high blood pressure because of its high relevance for the elderly.

In a recent review of studies dealing with community control of high blood pressure (Kasl 1978), the following picture emerges: The elderly are more likely to participate in blood pressure (BP) screening activities, particularly so in those that have normally a low yield, such as a letter inviting a visit to the clinic; the prevalence of previously "unknown" high blood pressure is lower among the elderly; the likelihood of being in current treatment among those with "known" high blood pressure is greater for the elderly; the likelihood of having blood pressure controlled for those in treatment is greater among the elderly; the success of referral from screening to a physician, among those who need such referral, is greater among older subjects. Overall, this is an impressive, consistent picture showing the elderly are more successful in the different phases of high blood pressure detection and control. Interestingly, these findings cannot be easily generalized to other areas of medical care.

Drawing on other reviews of the relevant literature (Becker 1974, Blackwell 1972, Kasl 1975, Marston 1970, Sackett and Haynes 1976, Wilson 1973), the following mixed picture emerges: Participation in free multiphasic health examinations is lower among elderly subjects and their attitudes toward such examinations are the most negative; com-pliance with medical care regimen and other recommendations does not bear a predictable or strong relationship to age—it is possible that the age group 45 to 65 has somewhat lower average compliance than other groups. However, a good deal of specificity of findings is in evidence: Premature termination from treatment for tuberculosis is more likely among older men and younger women; failure to keep appointments is not age-related; compliance with recommendations following executive health examinations is lower among older subjects; older subjects may have better compliance in severe disease situations such as classical rheumatoid arthritis (Oakes *et al.* 1970) and chronic hemodialysis (Hartman and Becker 1978); weight reduction studies suggest elderly may remain longer as participants but have less success than the intermediate age categories; older age is not related (prospectively) to smoking cessation, even though older populations yield (cross-sectionally) more ex-smokers. Medication errors are seldom higher among older subjects and complexity of medication is the more important, underlying variable (e.g., Hulka *et al.* 1976). Attitudes toward physicians and medical services may be somewhat more negative among older subjects, especially black patients (Hulka *et al.* 1975). Anxiety about illness is not necessarily lower among the elderly; the elderly rather fear less the diseases of the young and the young fear less the diseases of the old (Levine 1962). Cancer is feared equally by the different age groups, but the elderly may show greater delay in diagnosis and treatment for cancer (Kutner *et al.* 1958). Older subjects have lower expectations of control over health matters (Kirscht 1972).

This is, indeed, a hodgepodge of findings! The intent is to illustrate the variety of findings regarding the influence of age on medical care behavior and to suggest that any crystallization of theoretical viewpoints regarding the role of age would be premature. For example, in the Health Belief Model (Becker 1974), the three major components that feed into "perceived threat of disease" are the importance of health, perceived susceptibility, and perceived seriousness. Do we understand how age influences these components? It is likely, for example, that age increases average perceived susceptibility, but what about seriousness? The reduced role demands in retirement suggest that one aspect of seriousness, interference with other role demands, may decrease. On the other hand, the perceived disability associated with a new chronic condition may increase with age, and the consequences of increased dependence on others may be more devastating to the elderly. Furthermore, since "threat of disease" may actually be curvilinearly related to readiness for medical care, it is also possible that elderly people function more often at the inflection point of the curve: Small increases in threat first increase and then reduce the readiness for appropriate action.

Overall, the success of high blood pressure control among the elderly remains unexplained by references to the other findings. Perhaps the at-risk role (Baric 1969), with all its ambiguities and indefinite time span, is easier for the elderly person to adopt; moreover, the "labeling" impact of being told of increased risk of disease in the absence of symptoms or distress may be lower among the elderly because of their different normative expectations about disease.

CONCLUSION

A consideration of the psychosocial forces that influence the health of the elderly in modern industrial society cannot escape the presumption of uniqueness of the elderly, which is so much part of our intellectual Zeitgeist. Aside from the presumably universal cultural practice of age-grading, there would seem to be at least three other circumstances that reflect and reinforce this presumption: first, the development of academic/scientific disciplines exclusively concerned with the elderly; second, the development of government programs and services targeted on the elderly; and third, the undeniable greater prevalence of adverse conditions among the elderly, particularly those involving economic factors and health status. Perhaps the most common consequence of these circumstances is the corollary presumption of the greater vulnerability of the elderly.

In this chapter, we have implicitly adopted the view that presumptions of the uniqueness and vulnerability of the elderly may be an obstacle to a dispassionate examination of the evidence. In fact, we would be comfortable with the general conclusion that the impact of psychosocial factors on health status is not dramatically altered by age. And when the evidence suggests that age does act to modify this impact, it is more often seen that the impact is weaker in the elderly than that it is stronger. This is perhaps counterintuitive and surprising, since there is much biological evidence suggesting that the elderly are less resilient to stresses, less physiologically adaptable, have showed homeostatic–regulatory functions, and are less immunologically competent (Finch and Hayflick 1977, Timiras 1972).

However, it is possible to offer a perspective that makes the above conclusion less surprising. This perspective suggests that the health of the elderly person, at any one point, can be seen as a cumulative function of the previous experiences, accumulated over a lifetime. Any new event comes to represent a diminishing fraction of this total accumulation of events and the impact thus diminishes proportionally. Of course, this is only a very global and incomplete statement of a perspective, and additional assumptions would have to be included and elaborated, such as: the process of prior attrition of the more vulnerable; accumulation of past learning facilitating adaptation to the next experience; reduced adaptive demands if societal role expectations become more open-ended; diminishing psychosocial significance of events because of life-cycle changes in aspirations, expectations, and perceptions.

The problem with the above perspective is that it can be reasonably invoked after the fact, if the various results support it, but by itself, it has no compelling theoretical status and it cannot be an a priori guide to interpreting results. An opposite formulation would be equally convincing if the results favored it: namely, that the elderly are more vulnerable to the impact of various events and experiences because they come to draw on a diminishing or depleted reservoir of adaptive, equilibrium—restoring capability (Selye's reservoir of adaptive energy). The subthreshold impact of earlier years cumulates to become the suprathreshold health status change in the elderly.

While the evidence seems to favor the perspective of a diminishing impact of events and experiences on the health of the elderly, it would also seem that many of us are not comfortable with such a perspective. After all, the elderly seem to live in a state in which mounting social losses, physical debilitation, economic deprivation, and loss of (conventionally defined) useful work activities are taking place with great inevitability, but we do not seem to be able to detect the intuitively expected corresponding impact, such as in clinical depression or physical illnesses (Jarvik 1976). It is possible, then, that we have an incomplete grasp of the various positive factors in the lives of the elderly—the resources in their social environment, the adaptive strategies available to them—that serve to diminish the impact of the presumptively stressful experiences. Furthermore, we may not have a good understanding of what is specifically stressful to the elderly. That is, if we accept the approximate definition of stress as "demands that tax the adaptive resources," we may well ask if particular events and experiences represent social and personal demands equally for the elderly as for the younger person.

Overall, then, the biological and social sciences dealing with the elderly have accumulated valuable normative data on age-related changes in physiological functioning, health status, and their social conditions. However, these bodies of data cannot be easily juxtaposed to reveal the influence of psychosocial factors on the health of the elderly. We need in particular broader studies of so-called biological aging and secondary aging, which also include psychosocial factors, so that the role of these factors in aging can be assessed more directly.

REFERENCES

Abraham, S., Collins, G., and Nordsieck, M. (1971) Relationship of childhood weight status to morbidity in adults. *HSMHA Health Reports* 86:273–284.

Adams, B. N. (1968) The middle-class adult and his widowed or still married mother. *Social Problems* 16(1):50–59.

Adler. J. J., Bloss, C. M., and Mosley, K. T. (1966) The Oklahoma State Department of Health mobile multiphasic screening program for chronic disease. Part II. *American Journal of Public Health* 56:2066–2082.

Antonovsky, A. (1967) Social class, life expectancy, and overall mortality. *Milbank Memorial Fund Quarterly* 45(2):31–73.

Antonovsky, A. (1972) Breakdown: A needed fourth step in the conceptual armamentarium of modern medicine. *Social Science and Medicine* 6:537–544.

Arth, M. (1962) American culture and the phenomenon of friendship in the aged. Pp. 529–534 in C. Tibbits and W. Donahue, eds., *Social and Psychological Aspects of Aging.* New York: Columbia University Press.

Atchley, R. C. (1976) *The Sociology of Retirement.* New York: Halstead Press, Wiley.

Back, K. W., and Guptill, C. S. (1966) Retirement and self-ratings. Pp. 120–129 in I. H. Simpson and J. C. McKinley, eds., *Social Aspects of Aging.* Durham, N.C.: Duke University Press.

Balinsky, W., and Berger, R. (1975) A review of the research on general health status indexes. *Medical Care* 13:283–293.

Barfield, R. E., and Morgan, J. N. (1978) Trends in satisfaction with retirement. *The Gerontologist* 18:19–23.

Baric, L. (1969) Recognition of the "at-risk" role: A means to influence health behavior. *International Journal of Health Education* 12:24–34.

Becker, M. H., ed. (1974) The health belief model and personal health behavior. *Health Education Monographs* 2:326–473.

Belloc, N. B. (1973) Relationship of health practices and mortality. *Preventive Medicine* 2:67–81.

Belloc, N. B., Breslow, L., and Hochstim, J. (1971) Measurement of physical health in a general population survey. *American Journal of Epidemiology* 93:328–336.

Berg, R. L., ed. (1973) *Health Status Indices.* Chicago: Hospital Research and Educational Trust.

Berkman, L. F. (1977) *Social networks, host resistance, and mortality: A follow-up study of Alameda County residents.* Unpublished doctoral dissertation, Berkeley, University of California.

Berkman, L. F., and Syme, S. L. (1979) Social networks, host resistance, and mortality: A nine-year follow-up study of Alameda County residents. *American Journal of Epidemiology* 109:186–204.

Blackwell, B. (1972) The drug defaulter. *Clinical pharmacology and Therapeutics* 13:841–848.

Blau, Z. (1973) *Old Age in a Changing Society.* New York: Franklin Watts.

Booth, A. (1972) Sex and social participation. *American Sociological Review* 27:183–193.

Bowlby, J. (1958) The nature of the child's tie to his mother. *International Journal of Psychoanalysis* 39 (September–October):350–373.

Brown, G. W., Bhrolchain, M. N., and Harris, T. (1975) Social class and psychiatric disturbance among women in an urban population. *Sociology* 9:225–254.

Busse, E. W. (1969) Theories of aging. Pp. 11–32 in E. W. Busse and E. Pfeiffer, eds., *Behavior and Adaptation in Late Life.* Boston: Little, Brown.

Cantilli, E. J., and Shmelzer, J. L., eds. (1971) *Transportation and Aging: Selected Issues.* Washington, D.C.: U. S. Government Printing Office.

Carp, F. M. (1966) *A Future for the Aged.* Austin: University of Texas Press.

Carp, F. M. (1976) Housing and living environments of older people. Pp. 244–271 in R. H. Binstock and E. Shanas, eds., *Handbook of Aging and the Social Sciences.* New York: Van Nostrand Reinhold Co.

Carp, F. M. (1977a) Impact of improved living environment on health and life expectancy. *The Gerontologist* 16:102–111.

Carp, F. M. (1977b) Retirement and physical health. Pp. 140–159 in S. V. Kasl and F. Reichsman, eds., *Advances in Psychosomatic Medicine, Vol. 9. Epidemiologic Studies in Psychosomatic Medicine.* Basel: S. Karger.

Cassel, J. (1976) The contribution of the social environment to host resistance. *American Journal of Epidemiology* 104:107–123.

Chevan, A., and Korson, J. H. (1972) The widowed who live alone: An examination of social and demographic factors. *Social Forces* 51:45–53.

Chinoy, E. (1955) *Automobile Workers and the American Dream.* Garden City, N.Y.: Doubleday & Co.

Clayton, P. J. (1974) Mortality and morbidity in the first year of widowhood. *Archives of General Psychiatry* 30:747–750.

Cobb, S. (1971) *The Frequency of Rheumatic Diseases.* Cambridge: Harvard University Press.

Cobb, S. (1976) Social support as a moderator of life stress. *Psychosomatic Medicine* 38:300–314.

Cobb, S., and Kasl, S. V. (1977) *Termination: The Consequences of Job Loss.* (NIOSH) Publication No. 77–224. Cincinnati, Ohio: U.S. Department of Health, Education, and Welfare.

Comstock, G. W., Abbey, H., and Lundin, F. E. (1970) The nonofficial census as a basic tool for epidemiologic observations in Washington County, Maryland. Pp. 73–97 in I. I. Kessler and M. C. Levin, eds., *The Community as an Epidemiologic Laboratory.* Baltimore, Md.: Johns Hopkins University Press.

Comstock, G. W., and Partridge, K. P. (1972) Church attendance and health. *Journal of Chronic Diseases* 25:665–672.

Cox, P. R., and Ford, J. R. (1964) The mortality of widows shortly after widowhood. *Lancet* 1:163.

Croog, S. H., and Levine, S. (1972) Religious identity and response to serious illness: A report on heart patients. *Social Science & Medicine* 6:17–32.

Croog, S. H., Lipson, A., and Levine, S. (1972) Help patterns in severe illness: The roles of kin network, non-family resources, and institutions. *Journal of Marriage and the Family* 34:32–41.

Cumming, E., and Henry, W. (1961) *Growing Old.* New York: Basic Books.

DeAraujo, G., Van Arsdel, P., Holmes, T., and Dudley, D. (1973) Life change, coping ability and chronic intrinsic asthma. *Journal of Psychosomatic Research* 17:359–363.

Densen, P. M., Shapiro, S., and Einhorn, M. (1959) Concerning high and low utilizers of service in a medical care plan, and the persistence of utilization levels over a three-year period. *Milbank Memorial Fund Quarterly* 37:217–250.

Doehrman, S. R. (1977) Psycho-social aspects of recovery from coronary heart disease: A review. *Social Science & Medicine* 11:199–218.

Dohrenwend, B. S., and Dohrenwend, B. P., eds. (1974) *Stressful Life Events: Their Nature and Effect.* New York: Wiley.

Durkheim, E. (1951) *Suicide.* Glencoe, Ill.: The Free Press.

Eisdorfer, C., and Wilkie, F. (1977) Stress, disease, aging, and behavior. Pp. 251–275 in J. E. Birren and K. W. Schaie, eds., *Handbook of the Psychology of Aging.* New York: Van Nostrand Reinhold.

Ferrari, N. (1963) Freedom of choice. *Social Work* 8:105–106.

Finch, C. E., and Hayflick, L., eds. (1977) *Handbook of the Biology of Aging.* New York:

Van Nostrand Reinhold.

Finlayson, A. (1976) Social networks as coping resources. *Social Science and Medicine* 10:97–103.

Freud, S. (1926) *Inhibitions, Symptoms, and Anxiety. Standard Edition of the Complete Psychological Works of Sigmund Freud.* London: Hogarth Press Ltd.

Fried, M. (1963) Grieving for a lost home. Pp. 151–171 in L. J. Duhl, ed., *The Urban Condition.* New York: Basic Books.

Friedmann, E. A., and Orbach, H. L. (1974) Adjustment to retirement. Pp. 609–645 in S. Arieti, ed., *American Handbook of Psychiatry*, Vol. I. New York: Basic Books.

George, L. K., and Maddox, G. L. (1977) Subjective adaptation to loss of the work role: A longitudinal study. *Journal of Gerontology* 32:456–462.

Gerber, I., Rusualem, R., Hannon, N., Battin, D., and Arkin, A. (1975) Anticipatory grief and widowhood. *British Journal of Psychiatry* 122: 47–51.

Goldsmith, J., and Goldsmith, S. S., eds. (1976) *Crime and the Elderly.* Lexington, Mass.: Lexington Books.

Gordon, R., and Gordon, K. (1967) Social Factors in Prevention of Postpartum Emotional Problems. Paper presented at American Orthopsychiatric Association annual meetings, Washington, D.C.

Gore, S. (1978) The effect of social support in moderating the health consequences of unemployment. *Journal of Health and Social Behavior* 19:157–165.

Graham, T. W., Kaplan, B. H., Cornoni-Huntley, J. C., James, S. A., Becker, C., Hames, C. G., and Heyden, S. (1978) Frequency of church attendance and blood pressure elevation. *Journal of Behavioral Medicine* 1(1):37–44.

Gramlich, E. P. (1968) Recognition and management of grief in elderly patients. *Geriatrics* 23:87–92.

Granovetter, M. (1973) The strength of weak ties. *American Journal of Sociology* 78(6):1360–1380.

Gruenberg, E. M. (1977) The failure of success. *Milbank Memorial Fund Quarterly: Health and Society* 55:3–24.

Hartman, P. E., and Becker, M. H. (1978) Non-compliance with prescribed regimen among chronic hemodialysis patients. *Dialysis & Transplantation* 7(10).

Harvey, C., and Bahr, H. (1974) Widowhood, morale, and affiliation. *Journal of Marriage and the Family* 36(1):97–106.

Haynes, R. B., and Sackett, D. L. (1974) A workshop symposium: Compliance with therapeutic regimes—Annotated bibliography. Department of Clinical Epidemiology and Biostatistics, McMaster University Medical Centre, Hamilton, Ontario.

Haynes, S. G., Feinleib, M., Levine, S., Scotch, N., and Kannel, W. B. (1978) The relationship of psychosocial factors to coronary heart disease in the Framingham study. II. Prevalence of coronary heart disease. *American Journal of Epidemiology* 107:384–402.

Henderson, S., Byrne, D. G., Duncan-Jones, P., Adcock, S., Scott, R., and Steele, G. P. (1978a) Social bonds in the epidemiology of neurosis: A preliminary communication. *British Journal of Psychiatry* 132:463–466.

Henderson, S., Duncan-Jones, P., Burne, D. G., Scott, R., and Adcock, S. (1978b) Social Bonds, Adversity, and Neurosis. Presented at the World Psychiatric Association Section Committee on Epidemiology and Community Psychiatry triennial meeting. St. Louis, Missouri.

Henry, J. P., and Stephens, P. M. (1977) *Stress, Health, and the Social Environment.* New York: Springer-Verlag.

Heyman, D. K., and Gianturco, D. T. (1973) Long term adaptation by the elderly to bereavement. *Journal of Gerontology* 28:259–262.

Heyman, D. K., and Jeffers, F. C. (1963) Effect of time lapse on consistency of self-health and medical evaluations of elderly persons. *Journal of Gerontology* 18:160–164.

Hill, O., ed. (1976) *Modern Trends in Psychosomatic Medicine*. Vol. 3. London: Butterworths.

Hinkle, L. E., Jr., Dohrenwend, B. P., Elinson, J., Kasl, S. V., McDowell, A., Mechanic, D., and Syme, S. L. (1976) Social determinants of human health. Pp. 617–674, in *Preventive Medicine USA*. New York: Prodist.

Hulka, B. S., Cassel, J. C., Kupper, L. L., and Burdette, J. A. (1976) Communication, compliance, and concordance between physicians and patients with prescribed medications. *American Journal of Public Health* 66:847–853.

Hulka, B. S., Kupper, L. L., Daly, M. B., Cassel, J. C., and Schoen, F. (1975) Correlates of satisfaction and dissatisfaction with medical care: A community perspective. *Medical Care* 13:648–658.

Hyman, M. D. (1972) Social isolation and performance in rehabilitation. *Journal of Chronic Diseases* 25:85–97.

Jacobs, S., and Douglas, L. (1979) Grief: A mediating process between loss and illness. *Comprehensive Psychiatry* 20(2):165–174.

Jacobs, S., and Ostfeld, A. (1977) An epidemiological review of the mortality of bereavement. *Psychosomatic Medicine* 39(5):344–357.

Jarvik, L. F. (1976) Aging and depression: Some unanswered questions. *Journal of Gerontology* 31(3):324–326.

Kaplan, B. H., Cassel, J. C., and Gore, S. (1977) Social support and health. *Medical Care* (supplement) 15(5):47–58.

Kasl, S. V. (1972) Physical and mental health effects of involuntary relocation and institutionalization on the elderly: A review. *American Journal of Public Health* 62:377–384.

Kasl, S. V. (1975) Social-psychological characteristics associated with behaviors which reduce cardiovascular risk. Pp. 173–190, in A. J. Enelow and J. B. Henderson, eds., *Applying Behavioral Science to Cardiovascular Risk*. New York: American Heart Association.

Kasl, S. V. (1977) Contributions of social epidemiology to study in psychosomatic medicine. Pp. 160–223 in S. V. Kasl and F. Reichsman, eds., *Advances in Psychosomatic Medicine: Epidemiologic Studies in Psychosomatic Medicine*. Basel, Switzerland: S. Karger.

Kasl, S. V. (1978) A social-psychological perspective on successful community control of high blood pressure: A review. *Journal of Behavioral Medicine* 1:347–381.

Kasl, S. V. (1979) Changes in mental health status associated with job loss and retirement. Pp. 179–200 in J. E. Barnett, ed., *Stress and Mental Disorders*. New York: Raven Press.

Kasl, S. V. (1980) The impact of retirement. Pp. 137–186 in C. L. Cooper and R. Payne, eds., *Current Issues in Occupational Stress*. Chichester, England: J. Wiley and Sons, Ltd.

Kasl, S. V., Evans, A. S., and Niederman, J. C. (1979) Psychosocial risk factors in the development of infectious mononucleosis. *Psychosomatic Medicine* 41:445–466.

Kasl, S. V., Ostfeld, A. M., Brody, G. M., Snell, L., and Price, C. A. (1980) Effects of "involuntary" relocation on the health and behavior of the elderly. Pp. 211–232 in S. G. Haynes and M. Feinleib, eds., *Second Conference on the Epidemiology of Aging*. Washington, D.C.: U.S. Department of Health and Human Services, NIH Publication No. 80–969.

Kasl, S. V., and Reichsman, F., eds. (1977) *Advances in Psychosomatic Medicine, Vol. 9. Epidemiologic Studies in Psychosomatic Medicine*. Basel, Switzerland: S. Karger.

Kasl, S. V., and Rosenfield, S. (1980) The residential environment and its impact on the mental health of the aged. In J. E. Birren and R. B. Sloane, eds., *Handbook of Mental Health and Aging*. Englewood Cliffs, N.J.: Prentice Hall, Inc.

Kessel, N., and Shepherd, S. (1965) The health and attitudes of people who seldom consult a physician. *Medical Care* 3:6–10.

Kirscht, J. P. (1972) Perception of control and health beliefs. *Canadian Journal of Behavioral Science* 4:225–237.

Kitagawa, E. M., and Hauser, P. M. (1973) *Differential Mortality in the United States*. Cambridge, Mass.: Harvard University Press.

Kornhauser, A. (1965) *Mental Health of the Industrial Worker*. New York: Wiley.

Krantz, D. S., and Schulz, R. (in press) Life crisis, control, and health outcomes: A model applied to cardiac rehabilitation and relocation of the elderly. In A. Baum and J. E. Singer, eds., *Advances in Environmental Psychology*, Vol. 2. Hillsdale, N.J.: Lawrence Erlbaum Associates.

Kraus, A. S., and Lilienfeld, A. M. (1959) Some epidemiologic aspects of the high mortality rate in the young widowed group. *Journal of Chronic Diseases* 10:207–217.

Kutner, B., Makower, H. B., and Oppenheim, A. (1958) Delay in the diagnosis and treatment of cancer: A critical analysis of the literature. *Journal of Chronic Diseases* 7:95–120.

Lawton, M. P. (1977) The impact of the environment on aging and behavior. Pp. 276–301 in J. E. Birren and K. W. Schaie, eds., *Handbook of the Psychology of Aging*. New York: Van Nostrand Reinhold Co.

Lawton, M. P., Brody, E. M., and Turner-Massey, P. (1978) The relationships of environmental factors to changes in well-being. *The Gerontologist* 18:133–137.

Lawton, M. P., and Cohen, J. (1974) The generality of housing impact on the well-being of older people. *Journal of Gerontology* 29:194–204.

Lawton, M. P., and Nahemow, L. (1973) Ecology and the aging process. Pp. 619–674 in C. Eisdorfer and M. P. Lawton, eds., *The Psychology of Adult Development and Aging*. Washington, D.C.: American Psychological Association.

Lawton, M. P., and Yaffe, S. (1970) Mortality, morbidity and voluntary change of residence by older people. *Journal of the American Geriatrics Society* 18:823–831.

Lazarus, R. S., and Cohen, J. B. (1976) Environmental stress. Pp. 89–127 in I. Altman and J. F. Wohlwill, eds., *Human Behavior and Environment. Advances in Theory and Research*, Vol. 2. New York: Plenum Press.

Lee, N. H. (1969) *The Search for an Abortionist*. Chicago: University of Chicago Press.

Levi, L., ed. (1971) *Society, Stress, and Disease*, Vol. 1. London: Oxford University Press.

Levine, G. (1962) Anxiety about illness: Psychological and social bases. *Journal of Health and Human Behavior* 3:30–34.

Lieberman, M. A. (1974) Relocation research and social policy. Pp. 5–17 in J. F. Gubrium, ed., *Late Life: Communities and Environmental Policy*. Springfield, Ill.: C. C. Thomas.

Lipowski, Z. J., Lipsitt, D. R., and Whybrow, P. C., eds. (1977) *Psychosomatic Medicine: Current Trends and Clinical Applications*. New York: Oxford University Press.

Litman, T. J. (1966) The family and physical rehabilitation. *Journal of Chronic Diseases* 19:211–217.

Lowenthal, M. F. (1964) Social isolation and mental illness in old age. *American Sociological Review* 29(1):54–70.

Lowenthal, M. F. (1965) Antecedents of isolation and mental illness in old age. *Archives of General Psychiatry* 12:245–254.

Lowenthal, M. F., and Boler, D. (1965) Voluntary vs. involuntary social withdrawal. *Journal of Gerontology* 29:363–371.

Lowenthal, M. F., Thurnher, M., Chiriboga, D., and Associates. (1975) *Four Stages of Life*. San Francisco, Calif.: Jossey-Bass.
MacBride, A. (1976) Retirement as a life crisis: Myth or reality? A review. *Canadian Psychiatric Association Journal* 21:547–556.
McKinlay, J. B. (1973) Social networks, lay consultation, and help-seeking behavior. *Social Forces* 51:275–292.
McNeil, D. N. (1973) Mortality among the widowed in Connecticut. M.P.H. essay. Yale University, New Haven, Conn.
Maddison, D., and Viola, A. (1968) The health of widows in the year following bereavement. *Journal of Psychosomatic Resources* 12:297–306.
Margolis, B. L., and Kroes, W. H. (1974) Work and the health of man. Pp. 133–144 in J. O'Toole, ed., *Work and the Quality of Life: Resource Papers for Work in America*. Cambridge, Mass.: The MIT Press.
Marmot, M. G., and Syme, S. L. (1976) Acculturation and coronary heart disease in Japanese-Americans. *American Journal of Epidemiology* 104:225–247.
Marris, R. (1958) *Widows and Their Families*. London: Routledge and Kegan Paul.
Marston, M. V. (1970) Compliance with medical regimen: A review of the literature. *Nursing Research* 19:312–323.
Masuda, M., and Holmes, T. H. (1978) Life events: Perceptions and frequencies. *Psychosomatic Medicine* 40:236–261.
Mechanic, D. (1978) *Medical Sociology*, 2nd ed. New York: The Free Press.
Medalie, J. H., Kahn, H. A., Neufeld, H. N., Riss, E., and Goldbourt, U. (1973) Five-year myocardial infarction incidence–II. Association of single variables to age and birthplace. *Journal of Chronic Diseases* 26:329–349.
Mizruchi, E. H. (1960) Social structure and anomia in a small city. *American Sociological Review* 25(5):645–654.
Moberg, D. D. (1968) Religiosity in old age. Pp. 497–508 in B. L. Neugarten, ed., *Middle Age and Aging*. Chicago: University of Chicago Press.
Naguib, S. M., Geiser, P. B., Comstock, G. W. (1968) Responses to a program of screening for cervical cancer. *Public Health Report* 83:990–998.
National Center for Health Statistics (1972) *Disability Days, U.S., 1968*. Public Health Service Publication No. 1000, Series 10, No. 67. Washington, D.C.: U.S. Government Printing Office.
National Center for Health Statistics (1978) *Current Estimates from the Health Interview Survey: United States—1977*. Public Health Service Publication No. 78-1554, Series 10, No. 126. Washington, D.C.: U.S. Government Printing Office.
National Center for Health Statistics (1979) *Vital Statistics of the United States, 1975. Vol. II., Mortality, Part A*. Public Health Service. Washington, D.C.: U.S. Government Printing Office.
National Vital Statistics Division (1962) *Mortality by Occupation and Industry Among Men 20 to 64 Years of Age, U.S., 1950*. Vital Statistics—Special Reports, Vol. 53, No. 2. Washington, D.C.: U.S. Government Printing Office.
Neugarten, B. (1970) Adaptation and the life cycle. *Journal of Geriatric Psychiatry* 4:71–100.
Niebanck, P. L. (1968) *Relocation in Urban Planning: From Obstacle to Opportunity*. Philadelphia: University of Pennsylvania Press.
Nuckolls, K. B., Cassel, J. C., and Kaplan, B. H. (1972) Psychosocial assets, life crisis, and prognosis of pregnancy. *American Journal of Epidemiology* 95:431–441.
Oakes, T. W., Ward, J. R., Gray, R. M., Klauber, M. R., and Moody, P. M. (1970) Family expectations and arthritis patient compliance to a hand resting splint regimen. *Journal of Chronic Diseases* 22:757–764.

Ortmeyer, C. (1974) Variations in mortality, morbidity, and health care by marital status. Pp. 159–188 in C. F. Erhardt and J. E. Berlin, eds., *Mortality and Morbidity in the United States*. Cambridge, Mass.: Harvard University Press.

Ostfeld, A. M., Shekelle, R. B., Klawans, H., and Tufo, H. M. (1974) Epidemiology of stroke in an elderly welfare population. *American Journal of Public Health* 64:450–458.

Palmore, E. (1971) The relative importance of social factors in predicting longevity. Pp. 237–247 in E. Palmore and F. C. Jeffers, eds., *Prediction of Life Span*. Lexington, Mass.: Heath Lexington Books.

Palmore, F., and Luikart, C. (1972) Health and social factors related to life satisfaction. *Journal of Health and Social Behavior* 13:68–80.

Parkes, C. M. (1964) The effects of bereavement on physical and mental health: A study of the medical records of widows. *British Medical Journal* 2:274–279.

Parkes, C. M., Benjamin, B., and Fitzgerald, R. G. (1969) Broken heart: A statistical study of increased mortality among widowers. *British Medical Journal* 1:740–743.

Phillips, D. L. (1967) Mental health status, social participation, and happiness. *Journal of Health and Social Behavior* 8(4):285–291.

Pooling Project Research Group (1978) Relationship of blood pressure, serum cholesterol, smoking habit, relative weight and ECG abnormalities to incidence of major coronary events: Final report of the pooling project. *Journal of Chronic Diseases* 31:201–306.

Powers, E. A., and Bultena, G. L. (1976) Sex differences in intimate friendships of old age. *Journal of Marriage and Family* 38(4):739–747.

Price, J. S., Slater, E., and Hare, E. H. (1971) Marital status of first admissions to psychiatric beds in England and Wales in 1965 and 1966. *Social Biology* 18:574–594.

Rabinowitz, S., and Hall, D. T. (1977) Organizational research on job involvement. *Psychological Bulletin* 84:265–288.

Rees, W. P., and Lutkins, S. G. (1967) Mortality of bereavement. *British Medical Journal* 4:13–16.

Rosenmayr, L., and Kockeis, E. (1966) Housing conditions and family relations of the elderly. Pp. 29–46 in F. M. Carp and N. M. Burnett, eds., *Patterns of Living and Housing of Middle-Aged and Older People*. Public Health Service Publication No. 1496. Washington, D.C.: U. S. Department of Health, Education and Welfare.

Rosow, I. (1967) *Social Integration of the Aged*. New York: The Free Press.

Rowland, K. F. (1977) Environmental events predicting death for the elderly. *Psychological Bulletin* 84:349–372.

Sackett, D. L., and Haynes, R. B., eds. (1976) *Compliance with Therapeutic Regimen*. Baltimore, Md.: Johns Hopkins Press.

Segal, B., Phillips, D., and Feldmesser, R. (1967) Social integration, emotions, adjustment and illness behavior. *Social Forces* 46:237–246.

Shanas, E. (1967) Family help patterns and social class in three countries. *Journal of Marriage and Family* 29(2):257–266.

Sheppard, H. L. (1976) Work and retirement. Pp. 286–309 in R. H. Binstock and E. Shanas, eds., *Handbook of Aging and the Social Sciences*. New York: Van Nostrand Reinhold.

Shock, N. W. (1977) Biological theories of aging. Pp. 103–115 in J. E. Birren and K. W. Schaie, eds., *Handbook of the Psychology of Aging*. New York: Van Nostrand Reinhold.

Shuval, J. T., Antonovsky, A., and Davies, A. M. (1970) *Social Functions of Medical Practice*. San Francisco, Calif.: Jossey-Bass, Inc.

Siegel, J. S. (1975) Some demographic aspects of aging in the United States. Pp. 17–96 in A. M. Ostfeld and D. C. Gibson, eds., *Epidemiology of Aging*. Publication No. 77-

711. National Institute of Health. Washington, D.C.: U.S. Department of Health, Education, and Welfare.

Srole, L. (1956) Social integration and certain corollaries: An exploratory study. *American Sociological Review* 21:709–716.

Stern, K., and Williams, G. M. (1951) Grief reactions in later life. *American Journal of Psychiatry* 108:289–294.

Streib, G. F., and Schneider, C. J. (1971) *Retirement in American Society: Impact and Process.* Ithaca, N.Y.: Cornell University Press.

Strickland, B. R. (in press) Internal/external expectancies and cardiovascular functioning. In L. C. Perlmuter and R. A. Monty, eds., *Choice and Perceived Control.* Hillsdale, N.J.: Lawrence Erlbaum Associates.

Suchman, E. A. (1966) Health orientation and medical care. *American Journal of Public Health* 56:97–105.

Sullivan, D. F. (1971) A single index of mortality and morbidity. *HSMHA Health Reports* 86:347–354.

Sussman, M. B. (1953) The help pattern in the middle class family. *American Sociological Review* 18:22–28.

Sussman, M. B. (1976) The family life of old people. Pp. 218–239 in R. H. Binstock and E. Shanas, eds., *Handbook of Aging and the Social Sciences.* New York: Van Nostrand Reinhold Co.

Syme, S. L. (1974) Behavioral factors associated with the etiology of physical disease. A social epidemiological approach. *American Journal of Public Health* 64:1043–1045.

Timiras, P. (1972) *Developmental Physiology and Aging.* New York, Macmillan Co.

Tobin, S. S., and Lieberman, M. A. (1976) *Last Home for the Aged.* San Francisco, Calif.: Jossey-Bass.

Townsend, P. (1957) *The Family Life of Old People.* London: Routledge and Kegan Paul.

Troll, L. (1971) The family of later life: A decade review. *Journal of Marriage and Family* 33:263–290.

Van Zonneveld, R. J. (1969) On measuring physical health in the elderly. Pp. 128–133 in M. F. Lowenthal and A. Zilli, eds., *Colloquium on Health and Aging of the Population.* Basel, Switzerland: S. Karger.

Walker, K. N., MacBride, A., and Vachon, M. L. (1977) Social support networks and the crisis of bereavement. *Social Science and Medicine* 11:35–41.

Ward, A. W. (1976) Mortality of bereavement. *British Medical Journal* 1:700–702.

Wechsler, H., and Pugh, T. F. (1967) Fit of individual and community characteristics and rates of psychiatric hospitalization. *American Journal of Sociology* 73:331–338.

Weiss, N. S. (1973) Marital status and risk factors for coronary heart disease. *British Journal of Preventive and Social Medicine* 27:41–43.

Wilson, J. T. (1973) Compliance with instructions in the evaluation of therapeutic efficacy. *Clinical Pediatrics* 12:333–340.

Young, M., Benjamin, B., and Wallis, C. (1963) The mortality of widows. *Lancet* 2:454–457.

Biology and Behavior
of the Elderly
June 22–24, 1979,
Woods Hole, Massachusetts

WORKSHOP PARTICIPANTS

Richard C. Adelman, Temple University
Lisa F. Berkman, Yale University
Dan G. Blazer, Duke University
William Bondareff, Northwestern University
Jacob A. Brody, National Institute on Aging
Robert N. Butler, National Institute on Aging
Richard G. Cutler, Baltimore City Hospital
Leon Festinger, New School for Social Research
George M. Foster, University of California, Berkeley
John P. Fulton, Brown University
Sara Gerling, University of California, Irvine
Paul E. Gold, University of Virginia
Roger A. Gorski, University of California, Los Angeles
William T. Greenough, University of Illinois
James S. Jackson, University of Michigan
Lissy F. Jarvik, University of California, Los Angeles
Robert A. Jensen, University of California, Irvine
Jeanie Kayser-Jones, University of California, San Francisco
Sara B. Kiesler, National Research Council
Laurence J. Kotlikoff, University of California, Los Angeles
Ellen J. Langer, Harvard University
Gary Lynch, University of California, Irvine

AGING
Biology and Behavior

Margaret Mackenzie, University of California, Berkeley
James G. March, Stanford University
James L. McGaugh, University of California, Irvine
Marion Perlmutter, University of Minnesota
David W. Plath, University of Illinois
William A. Satariano, University of California, Berkeley
Joanne Steuer, University of California, Los Angeles
Mervyn W. Susser, Columbia University
S. Leonard Syme, University of California, Berkeley
Roy L. Walford, University of California, Los Angeles
Sherwood L. Washburn, University of California, Berkeley
Steven F. Zornetzer, University of Florida

appendix B

Reviewers

Carolyn Shaw Bell, Wellesley College
Edward L. Bennett, University of California, Berkeley
Paul J. Bohannan, University of California, San Diego
Jacob A. Brody, National Institute of Aging
Roy G. D'Andrade, University of California, San Diego
Marion C. Diamond, University of California, Berkeley
Leon Festinger, New School for Social Research
Caleb Finch, University of Southern California
Ronald W. Hart, Ohio State University
David Holmes, University of Kansas
Frederick King, Emory University
Karen Matthews, University of Pittsburgh
Robert Moore, University of California, San Diego
William D. Neff, Indiana University
Adrian Ostfeld, Yale University
Lynne Reder, Carnegie-Mellon University
Austin H. Riesen, University of California, Riverside
Mark Rosenzweig, University of California, Berkeley
Michael Ross, University of Waterloo
Sandra Scarr, Yale University
Thomas C. Schelling, Harvard University

AGING
Biology and Behavior

Ethel Shanas, University of Illinois, Chicago Circle
Ralph E. Stevens, Ohio State University
Claudewell S. Thomas, College of Medicine and Dentistry of New Jersey
Richard Thompson, University of California, Irvine
Roy L. Walford, University of California, Los Angeles
Mark P. Zanna, University of Waterloo

Author Index

The numbers in italics indicate the pages on which the complete references can be found.

A

Abelson, R. P., 256, 261, 263, 269, *278*
Abraham, S., 349, *377*
Abrahams, J. P., 241, *250*
Acsádi, G., 35, *67*
Adam, J., 234, *250*
Adams, B., 295, 361, *377*
Adelstein, A. M., 83, *94*
Adleman, R. C., 204, *223*
Adler, J., 351, *378*
Akpom, C., 322, *325*
Alberman, E., 91, *94*
Almli, C., 189, *196*
Altman, J., 172, *197*
Anderson, P., 208, *224*, 283, 289, 301
Andres, R., 44, *67*
Andrew, S., 294, *304*
Antonovsky, A., 312, 317, 320, *324*, 350, 355, *378*

B

Bach, F., 59, 61, *70*
Back, K., 370, *378*
Bahr, H., 363, *380*
Balinsky, W., 347, *378*
Baltes, P. B., 233, *250*
Bank, L. I., 243, *250*
Bantle, J. A., 203, *223*
Bar, T., 205, *223*
Bard, M., 255, *278*
Barden, H., 151, *154*

Apffel, C. A., 53, *67*
Appell, F. W., 210, *223*
Arenberg, D., 232, 234, *250*
Asdell, S. A., 19, *28*
Atchley, R. C., 369, 372, *378*
Ayeroff, F., 256, 263, *278*

Subject Index

Memory, 232, 233
  loss of, 257, 274
  long–short term, 258
Mental disorders, diagnosing, 332–336
Metabolic rate, 42, 44
  aging rate and, 52
  decrease in, 47
Metabolism, 38
  cellular, 142, 150
  neuronal, 151
  protein, 151
Monkeys
  Baboons, 14, 18
  brain of, 15
  Cebus, 15
  Chimpanzees, 13
  evolution of, 15
  Macaques, 13, 14, 18
  New World, 15–18
  Old World, 15–18
Morbidity, incidence rate, 79
Mortality, 78, 351
  cohort studies in, 80, 82
  rate of, 80, 233, 242, 243, 246
  smoking and, 81
Multigenerational family, in United
    States, 2

N

National Institute on Aging, 1, 3, 6
National Institute of Mental Health, 5
Natural selection, 11, 13
Neanderthal Man, 11, 24
Nervous system
  dendrites, 162, 166
  development, 165
  synapses, 162–165
Neuroendocrine systems, see Immune
    system
Neuron
  aging brain and, 184
  death, 182
  environment, 148
  function, 153
  loss of, 143, 203
  spinal cord, 151
Nissl substance, 153
Nursing homes, see Institutional
    environments

Nutrition
  antioxidants and, 54
  calories, 41, 57
  fasting, 21, 41
  life-span, 40
  preservatives, 54
  restriction, 59
  Vitamin E, 54

O

Olaf Palme, 78
Organs, aging process of, 26
Oxygen, see also Peroxidation
  hyperbaric therapy, 63
  metabolism, 47, 51

P

Parkinson's disease, 6, 46
Pathology, 185, 295
Pavlovian conditioning, 179
Peroxidation, 52, 57
Personality, 339
Plasticity
  brain, 171, 201
  hippocampus, 216–219
  physiological, 173
Poikilotherms, 43, 44
Population
  growth, 99
  life-span and, 99
Preventative health care, 315–317
  as a form of social support, 323
Primates
  diet, 18
  evolution, 15, 20
  maturity, 13
Protein 42
  abnormal, 49
  in brain, 203
  metabolism, 152
Psychiatric services, 334
Psychomotor speed, 237–239

R

Retirement, 101, 369–373
  age, 107